VOICES

in Today's Magazines

Editor
Pamela Glass Kelly

Contributing Editors
Lou Fisher
Patricia Windsor
Barbara Cole
Meredith DeSousa

Production
Joanna Horvath
Marni McNiff
Cheryl Kauer

Cover Design
Joanna Horvath

Pictured on cover, from top left,
Lou Fisher, Scott William Carter, Patricia Windsor,
Willma Willis Gore, Julia Curcio, Paulette Beete,
Majid Mohiuddin, Shirley Raye Redmond, and Kris Franklin.

Photo of Scott William Carter, copyright 2008, Heidi Carter.
Photo of Julia Curcio provided by *Philadelphia Weekly*.

1-800-443-6078. www.WritersBookstore.com
E-mail: Services@WritersBookstore.com
www.LongRidgeWritersGroup.com

International Standard Book Number 978-1-889715-48-3

Table of Contents

About This Collection — 2

Fiction

Menu	*Lou Fisher*	5
The Puzzle	*Kris Franklin*	8
Toast and Jelly	*Scott Graeff*	12
I've Looked Everywhere	*Susan Jackson Rodgers*	16
Familiar Stranger	*Patricia Windsor*	19
My Turn	*Carolyn Matthews*	23
Kursk	*Maria Elena Suarez*	25
The Girl with the Click Click Eyes	*Patricia Windsor*	27
Paul Newman's House	*Lou Fisher*	36
Wants	*Grace Paley*	41
Mrs. Comfrey Wins	*Patricia Windsor*	43
Trucks	*Amy Bechtel*	46
Tonics	*Jennifer Anthony*	51
One by One	*Ryan Scammell*	57
How to Make Flan	*Amina Lolita Gautier*	59
Cellmates	*Willma Willis Gore*	67
The Story of Patent Leather Shoes	*Robert Cormack*	71
Patience	*Jacqueline Guidry*	76
Killer Shift	*Michael Giorgio*	83
One Life	*Kevin Brown*	86
Stargazers	*David Michael Kaplan*	94
The Lover of Horses	*Tess Gallagher*	104
Love Spells	*Barbara A. Barnett*	113
The Tree	*James M. Bellarosa*	119
Fixing Larx	*Lou Fisher*	122
The Knitting Madonna	*Julia Curcio*	129
Road Gamble	*Scott William Carter*	133
Petri Parousia	*Matthew Hughes*	142
A Box Full of Nothing	*Arthur Sánchez*	149
Blood Lilies	*Robert E. Vardeman*	155
The House Spider	*Kurt Newton*	165
Rumple What?	*Nancy Springer*	169

Nonfiction

TheGreatGreenberg's Gift	*Philip Stein*	179
Home Remedies for the Sick Season	*Kris Franklin*	182
My Mom's Song	*Barbara A. Stoughton*	185
Lake Superior, Winter Dawn	*Gustave Axelson*	187
A Christmas Farewell	*Diana M. Amadeo*	190
Mind the Migraine	*Judy Gruen*	193
The Tortilla Cycle	*Rebecca Allen*	196
Turning Heads	*Sharon Wren*	198
An Out-of-This-World Rescue	*Kristin Grant*	201
The Conspiracy	*Kathleen Thompson*	203
The Man Who Carved Lincoln	*Richard Bauman*	206
No Place Like Home	*Shirley Raye Redmond*	208
Snakes Alive!	*Dean Henson*	210
Sneaker Obsession Is Baffling	*Karen Kaufman-Orloff*	213
Chicken-Necking on the Bay	*Cynthia Rott*	215
Plant a Second Season Salad	*Barbara Pleasant*	217
The Time Machine	*Kim Kunasek*	220
Things We Do for Love	*Laurie Klein*	222
Pickles and Salsa	*Cathy Schneider*	226
Nights at the Round Table	*Matthew Hutson*	229
Peggy Hedman Is Driven to Keep Her Charges Safe	*Tricia Booker*	231
Old Man on Campus	*Ehud Havazelet*	235
When 'Tis(n't) the Season to Ride?	*Aida Elder*	238
Colonial Cuisine and the Road to Revolution	*Paulette Beete*	241
Sharing Memories, Sharing Lives	*Arlene Silverman*	244
Total Recall	*Gary Marcus*	247
Deadlines and Diapers and Dinner	*Heidi Drake*	249
Artist, Scientist, Technician, Historian Dudley Giberson	*John Walters*	253
Tapping for Maple's Sweet Gold	*Jessica Stone*	257
My So-Called Genius	*Laura Fraser*	261
I Have a Bunch of Coins . . .	*Harry L. Rinker*	264
Kitchen Knives	*Ken Haedrich*	267
A Sweet and Gentle Land	*Polly Bannister*	271
How to Be a Great Mom	*Julie Tilsner*	277

The Ugly Wedding Present   *Sasha Aslanian*   281
Plant-Based Tableware Redefines
    the Word Disposable   *Marc Schoder*   283
Completely Lovestruck   *Majid Mohiuddin*   285
Under India's Spell   *Steven Slon*   288
Harry London Chocolate
    Hall of Fame   *Robert Fuller Davis*   291
Where the Creek Turkey Tracks:
    Wild Land and Language   *Tim Homan*   294
Be Sensitive When Moving the Elderly   *Robert B. Mills*   300
In the Clutch: Better Shifting
    for Sport-Touring Riders   *Mark Tuttle Jr.*   303
Let There Be Sleep   *Barbara Stahura*   305
On the Record: Collecting
    Oral Histories   *Elizabeth Kelley Kerstens*   309
Flying into Trouble   *George Monbiot*   315
The Art of Camping   *Catherine Newman*   318
Even Keel   *Jim Freim*   321
Wildlife Volunteering in Thailand   *Erika Wedenoja*   324
"There's Still a Girl in There"   *Karen Hammond*   327

Title Index   333
Author Index   335
Magazine Index   336
Acknowledgments   337

About This Collection

Welcome to *Voices in Today's Magazines*, a collection of stories and articles selected from a variety of contemporary publications. This volume features 81 fiction and nonfiction works by 76 authors as they were originally published in 73 different magazines. We invite you to read these selections for pure enjoyment, in hopes that you'll discover for yourself just what makes a successful mystery, romance, how-to article, profile, or inspirational piece.

How We Created This Collection

In deciding what would be of greatest use to students of writing, we read hundreds of short stories and articles: fiction of all kinds, including contemporary stories, science fiction and fantasy, romance, horror, experimental, literary, and short-shorts; and nonfiction in the realms of travel, food, sports, health, science, the arts, self-help, profiles, history, hobbies, and more.

In the process we learned about all kinds of topics—and you will, too, everything from how to manage migraines to crabbing on the Maryland shore to accepting unusual wedding gifts with grace. You'll be drawn into a horrifying spider fantasy, and one man's shocking quest to contract a deadly disease; you'll also laugh at a playfully modern version of a popular fairy tale and sympathize with a woman who's lost a whole lot more than her cell phone. Contemporary magazines publish so much excellent writing—it was difficult to choose!

After making our selections, we interviewed the writers to find out where they got their ideas, what kinds of research and revision they did, and how they zeroed in on the right market for publishing success. A common theme running through most selections is how the story or article idea often began with the author's personal interests and experiences. You'll read about the challenges the authors faced in writing and revising, and the steps they took to find receptive markets for their manuscripts.

Your Own Journey

Voices in Today's Magazines is presented with one purpose: to give you a stimulating reading experience. As an aspiring writer, you can also use these pieces to your benefit. Study them as first-rate models of successful fiction and nonfiction, and use the authors' comments to further your understanding of how ideas and events are transformed into published articles and stories.

Along the way, imagine yourself as one of these writers, discovering the thrill of publication. We hope the experiences in this book will inspire you to discover your own voice.

Enjoy the journey.

The Editors

Fiction

Menu

by Lou Fisher

Today Steve grabs a pizza slice at the mall, a few steps from the bargain shoe store where he works four afternoons a week. Not that he's supposed to get a lunch break. The shoe manager is already peering out the door.

"Eat at home," the manager says.

"I don't cook anymore," Steve tells him, but not why.

In his kitchen space, the front burner of the stove has been taken over by an ugly brown spider who is so quick and industrious that Steve can't bear to watch it for more than a minute. Even if he would get rid of the spider and set up the little folding table that came with the apartment, he has nothing: not oatmeal, not eggs, not egg noodles, not broccoli ever again, not meat or mustard, not his favorite Progresso black bean soup, not a drop of milk, not bran flakes to keep him from getting cholesterol and constipated, not Oreos or other kinds of cookies, not potato chips in any form or for that matter those snappy toasted sunflower seeds—in fact, not a single bag or jar or box or can of anything.

Well, all right, he does have Robin's un-opened can of tennis balls. Though she claimed to play the game, she must have used the court time (and her cozy sky-blue warmup suit) to find a new boyfriend.

"Who is he?" Steve recalls asking at the very last moment.

"Just somebody," Robin said.

"Do I know him?"

Robin wrinkled her tiny nose. "He's not from the neighborhood."

That night when he couldn't sleep he tossed everything from the cupboards into the cans in the alley. He meant only to throw away her finicky foods, but he couldn't stop there. And he hasn't cooked since.

Now when he's home, before or after work or on his several days off, he might drink a glass of water, being sure to let the noisy pipes run for a while to clear the lead deposits. He leaves the glass on the counter near the sink (but upside down, remembering the spider) in case he wants a refill. He uses his own glass for two days. Then Robin's glass. Then he has to wash both glasses: six times washed since she went out the door. He decided recently, and once again at the sink this morning, that if he ever convinces his feet to traverse the full length of the mall to the discount drugstore he will exchange Robin's can of tennis balls for a package of paper cups that he can use for water.

"Got a receipt?" the lanky clerk wants

Author Bio

Lou Fisher lives with his wife in downstate New York and admits only to cooking their scrambled eggs each morning. He is a recipient of the *New Letters* Literary Award for Fiction as well as a writing fellowship from his county's arts council. His stories, which range from literary and contemporary to science fiction and mystery, have appeared in many journals, magazines, and anthologies. His earlier genre novels were published by Dell and Warner.

to know.

"No. No, I don't." Steve twirls the clear plastic can until he comes to a tiny white sticker. "But here's the price tag."

The clerk looks. "That says Wal-Mart."

"Oh . . . right." Steve puts on a big smile. Shows his teeth. Inside, though, he's giving it some somber thought. Could there have been another can of balls, one that Robin really used? How and when did she get to Wal-Mart? Where exactly is she now?

Still, he won't cook.

He won't shop for groceries . . .

He won't slice, squeeze, mix, thaw . . .

He won't broil, boil, bake, fry . . .

Yet he'll admit, sometimes directly to the spider, that eating out can be chancy. A frequent test of his resolve. For example, the best he can do in the middle of a sleepless night is maybe force a Snickers bar from the Exxon vending machine, if he has the right change and the right smash of a fist.

He dines on chili or spaghetti or a cheese omelet.

Worse yet, in this gray January he has to trudge through snow and slush while the itchy blue stocking cap smashes his hair. Suppose at the diner he meets someone as cute as Robin. Sure, just his luck, with his hair like this, with dirty gloves and a frayed scarf. The wet snow worries him in yet another way. Won't he get hypothermia sitting at the table in sneakers that are soaked through to his socks—and aren't these the days when service seems the absolute slowest?

"I didn't get a check," he says at the register.

"That so?" inquires the old lady in her snide way. "Who's your waitress?"

He glances back. "I don't remember."

"We only have two," she tells him.

Despite eating in these cheap neighbor-hood diners and luncheonettes (Gracie's, Lucky Guys, Split Silver Café, and the one with the plastic cow in front), Steve has to worry about expenses. He dines on chili or spaghetti or a cheese omelet. Add in sales tax, fifty-cent tips . . . He makes so little money part-time at the mall. He thinks that's why Robin left him. That it wasn't really the holes in his socks. Or the way he splashes shampoo on the shower doors. Or even the view out the bedroom window of the boarded-up community center and the trash heap that used to be its parking lot. No, at the end he felt certain, as she left, as she departed, as she exited with a flip of her hip, that she'd found a guy with an ATM card and a microwave.

In desperation he takes the bus to the tennis club.

"She had a good backhand," remembers the guy at the desk.

In further desperation he takes the bus to the chiropractor's office where Robin works.

"Not anymore," says the full-faced woman who's in there now.

She's gone for sure. And if it's up to Steve he'll never cook again. Oh, he'll give in and get some peanut butter, some white bread to slap it on, some milk to drink right out of the carton. He's bound to buy sardines too, with the lid that peels open. For breakfast he'll return to bran flakes and also come to discover fruit tarts. And eventually the shoe store at the mall will promote him to full-time (with HMO insurance and a real lunch break), the weather will turn warm, and Robin will fade to a soft dreamy hunger.

"That's the way it is," he tells the spider still secure on the stove.

Bridge

Author's Comments ━━━━━━━━

Although I tend to start a story with no idea in mind, I do know what category of fiction I'm aiming for. So when in recent years literary journals, as well as other magazines, became eager for submissions of short-shorts, I set out to write one.

Literary fiction gives you leeway for experimentation. Once the story's first line came to me out of the blue, I played around with all the foods that Steve wouldn't cook in his apartment, with every draft revising, enhancing the list. Then I turned to foods that Steve might eat at restaurants. That gave me half a story. I let it cool off, and when I returned weeks later I filled in vital story elements like characterization, situation, problem, struggle, action, dialogue, all centered around the reason Steve wouldn't cook. Finally I discovered a story of 1,000 words—exactly my goal.

The story went around to a few journals before it found a home in a Chicago magazine called *Bridge*, where it fit ever so neatly on a single glossy page with room for a tiny illustration. Because of the story's strong food theme, it was picked up later for an anthology called *Hunger and Thirst*.

Advice to writers: Short-shorts remain in demand, perhaps more than ever. You can have fun with them but you still have to provide the pull of a story.

—Lou Fisher

The Puzzle

by Kris Franklin

*D*o you believe in love? Do you believe in forever?

Maybe I'll try that puzzle again.

I hate jigsaw puzzles, and she knew it when she gave me the thing. But it's snowing outside, and I can't see the peaks today.

Rylie comes padding in to watch. She's getting old, and she can't take the cold like she once could. She sniffs the box, then begins to whine.

"You remember, do you, Mrs?" My eyes start to burn, so I give her a scratch behind the ears. "You're going to have to be quiet. That, or leave."

Her hip, with its old injury, is stiff from the weather. She circles twice and lowers herself gingerly, eyes milky and a little vague at the edges.

There's a date on the box. February 14, 1988. Has that box really been in this house for 20 years?

I hate puzzles. They're nothing but a . . .

1988

" . . . pain, Jenni. Besides, you know I can't tell the colors apart."

Author Bio

Kris Franklin is a former English teacher who has spent the past 20 years as a professional writer. He has authored more than 100 articles and several novels of suspense, including *Silvercat* and *Relentless*. He is an instructor for Long Ridge Writers Group.

"There's a message written on the back."

"What kind of message?"

Her grin was mysterious. "A message for Valentine's Day. What else?"

I emptied the box on the kitchen table, parts of the puzzle tumbling over each other. "C'mon, Jen." I pretended irritation. "This thing has a million pieces."

She wasn't fooled. "Oh, at least." She smothered a giggle, green eyes bright. "Maybe two million."

"You know I can't do colors."

"Try turning the pieces over to use the message. You do read, don't you?"

"I may not ever read this. It'll take me the rest of my life."

"Not that long, I bet." She reached over to ruffle my hair. "Besides, that's the only way you'll ever know what it says."

1993

I see the mountains in your eyes . . .

It just popped into my head when I saw her riding along the ridgeline. The aspen were turning gold and scarlet among the green fir and spruce, and early snow gleamed silver in the sun on the high peaks behind her.

Bob glanced up, then went back to feeding wire off the spool.

She hit the ground at a trot, the sorrel with white feet stopping to crop at meadow grass. "Hi, Daddy," she called in Bob's direction, then was into my arms in a bound. I dropped the wire cutters just in time.

"Did we get any mail?" I eased her to the

ground and Bob reached for the spool again, pretending not to listen.

Her smile faded. "Some." She avoided my eyes. "Just the usual . . ."

"Did I hear anything?"

Bob looked up again. He was short and thin, but his hands were huge, scarred beneath the leather gloves.

"Yes, Jennifer," he said. "Did he hear anything?"

She sagged, almost imperceptibly. "Yes." Her eyes were on mine.

Bob nodded. "Well, that's it, isn't it?" His face relaxed, became gentle. "I'm sorry, but I'm not surprised. You're ranching blood, Daniel. Like your father was, and like me. Not a writer."

I felt her start to turn, but I held her in place with my hand.

"That could be, Bob," I said. "Anyway, it's time for a break, and I'm going to take your daughter over to that aspen grove."

There was amusement in his eyes. "You do that, boy," he said. He sat down on the spool and took out cigarette makings. I heard him whistling "Sweet Betsy from Pike" as we walked into the trees.

"Dan, I'm sorry." She reached up to encircle my neck.

"It's okay." I found a sunny clearing and sat beside her.

"You're not giving up." It was a statement, not a question.

"No. I don't know. Maybe. Maybe your dad's right."

"Not about this, he's not. Listen, do you believe in love?"

"Well . . . sure I do . . ."

"Do you believe in forever?"

"What do you mean, forever? I don't know. Maybe . . ."

"There you go again!" She gave my hair a yank. "Maybe?"

"Ouch! Okay, okay!" I laughed, grabbing her hands. "I do."

"You'd better, Daniel Rankin." Her voice

was fierce. "Because I do. I'll love you and I'll believe in you forever. And you're not giving up."

"Of course not," I said, mock serious. "Did you ever think so?"

1994

I see the mountains in your eyes,
Green and gold and silver.
I feel the sun's warmth in your touch,
I'll hold you here forever.

"Dan, what are you doing?"

I looked up from the sheet of paper toward the bedroom. "Nothing," I said. "Fooling around."

"Well, come to bed. It's past midnight."

I slipped the poem back into a notebook and set it on the shelf by the puzzle box. "Hey, when are you going to tell me the message on the back of this puzzle? It's been six years."

"I'm not. You have to put it together yourself."

"I can't . . ."

"Yes, you can. And someday you will, when you want to badly enough."

I straighten my back and glance out the window, where the storm's letting up some. I have the edges of the puzzle done now. Being poor with colors doesn't hinder me there. The hard part is filling in the middle.

Someday, when you want to badly enough . . .

I begin to match up pieces, using the bright primary colors as a guide.

This is that day.

1998

"Dan! Daniel, it's the phone. It's Boston." She ran through the snow in the yard, the dog ripping along behind her.

When I looked up from the splitting log, Bob's stare held me for a moment. His eyes were china blue, and there was no expression there at all. Then he sank his axe into the stump and walked around the corner of the shed.

I turned back as she reached me. "Now, what was that?" I said, trying to sound casual with my heart pounding in my throat.

"What was that?" Her eyes widened. She slugged me with a tiny fist. "What . . . was . . . that? You horse's butt! Hurry up!"

But I was already running for the house.

"Mr. Rankin? Hello, this is Lois Carey at *New England Monthly*. I like your story. I'd like to run it, as is, in our May issue."

"Okay." I tried to think of something a Writer would say. "Okay."

"I was intrigued by the poem you use to introduce the last section. The 'I see the mountains in your eyes' part. Are you a poet also?"

"No." I looked down at her, holding my hand, her eyes filled with tears of excitement. "No, I'm not. I guess I got inspired just that once."

"Oh? Well, the imagery's interesting. Now Mr. Rankin . . ."

Lois Carey talked on, and I agreed with everything she said. Then I put down the phone and took my wife in my arms.

She died the next day. The jeep was in four by four, but it swapped ends on the ice just below the Divide, and the truck hit it broadside. The dog was with her and survived somehow, though its hip was fractured.

Three months later, my short story appeared in the magazine. She'd never read it—I told her I wanted her to see it the first time in print—so I read it aloud there by her headstone, sitting on a hill of new spring grass with melting snow still underneath the trees. An elderly couple came by while I was reading and stopped a little way off. When I looked up, the woman smiled at me, then they walked on.

The door lets in a blast of cold air when it's opened, and Rylie gets painfully to her feet. She limps over to where Bob is standing.

"Dammit, Bob!" I mutter crossly to conceal my surprise. "Come on in and close the door. Were you raised in a barn?"

I haven't seen him much in the past ten years, but he's hardly changed. A little thinner, and his eyes aren't as blue.

"Daniel," he nods, sitting across the table from me. "How's the new book coming along?"

"Slow," I say. "But I have some hopes for it. Coffee?"

"I'll get it." He goes to the stove. "I never believed you'd make it. You know that, don't you?"

"I know."

"Didn't mean any harm by it. Just trying to help you two see things straight." He sits down and rubs Rylie under the chin. "She believed it, though, didn't she? Jennifer believed it."

"Yeah." I feel my eyes start to burn again. "Oh, yeah."

"What're you doing? Jigsaw puzzle?" He leans over to look. "I did many of them in my time. Try this green one—"

"No!" My voice is harsh, and it surprises us both. It's the first time I've ever raised my voice to him.

He sits back and looks out the window at the diminishing storm. His hands tremble a little. Coffee spills into the saucer.

"Bob . . . look, I'm sorry."

"It's okay."

"No, it's not. It's just that I have to . . . do this by myself. It's kind of hard to explain."

He takes the cup to the sink and rinses it out. "Well," he says, "I better get along. Just stopped by to see how the book's coming. Slow, you said."

"Slow," I nod, standing up. "Listen, Bob,

I'm glad you came by. I mean that. And I . . . well, I wish you'd do it more often."

He looks surprised, and then he smiles. "Okay," he says. "Maybe I will."

After he's gone, I go back to the puzzle. I get the last pieces in and it's done. It shows a mountain meadow with horses grazing in the foreground. One of them is a sorrel with white feet.

I look at it, all together after 20 years in the box, and my heart starts beating faster, almost painfully. Rylie comes over and pushes her head into my hand, whining down in her throat.

"Hush, Mrs," I say. I slide the puzzle onto a place mat and put another on top of it. Carefully I turn it over.

"Okay, girl." I look down at the mat through blurring eyes. "Okay, girl, what do you have to say for yourself?"

I lift the mat.

The handwriting is familiar. FOR DANIEL, it says. FEBRUARY 14, 1988.

Then beneath that . . .

I see the mountains in your eyes,
Green and gold and silver.
I feel the sun's warmth in your touch,
I'll hold you here forever.

Do you believe in love? Do you believe in forever?

The tablecloth's patterns brighten as sunlight suddenly pours through the window, caressing the back of my neck.

"Jenni . . . ?" I say.

Pagosa Springs Sun

Author's Comments

One Valentine's Day, my wife Kathy told me she had a present for me. Instead of something chewable, I found a small box on my office desk. It was a jigsaw puzzle.

"You know I don't do these things," I told her.

"You'll do this one," she said. "It has a message on the back."

"You mean you put the whole thing together and . . ."

"Flipped it over." She nodded. "And wrote the message. I guess we'll see how badly you want to find out what I wrote."

So, a quandary. On the one hand, I really dislike jigsaw puzzles, partly because color is often the key to successful assembly, and I have roughly the color perception of a mole in a gunny sack at midnight, and partly (mostly?) because they require patience and ability to delay gratification.

On the other hand, I've always been a sucker for romance, and this was definitely a romantic gesture—with maybe a tinge of sadism tossed in—on Kathy's part.

And I do love her dearly.

During the lengthy process of assembling the puzzle, a story idea began forming. At this time I'd recently left teaching to pursue a writing career, and was doing features for a small newspaper. I'd never run a fiction story idea past my editor, and I was surprised when the story decided to take itself away from the original humor slant and into something emotionally harder to write. Still, I stayed with first person because it felt more personal. The published version was pretty much the version that appeared partway through, when I realized where it was headed, with only some minor structural edits.

I was with the newspaper for a couple of years. During that time I wrote some other short fiction, aimed at humor in the way the nonfiction pieces were. "The Puzzle" was the only non-humor fiction I wrote during that time, and it remained the story that received the greatest response.

I did complete the puzzle. It was worth the effort.

—Kris Franklin

Toast and Jelly

by Scott Graeff

The big guy was hurting; we all were—my father, my sister and me. At 44, I wasn't prepared for the thing I knew would happen someday. And now that it was here, I wasn't sure which bothered me most: the death of Mom or seeing Dad grieve.

But here we were, my father, my sister and me, nine days after our loss, sitting in a restaurant, trying to get on with our lives, attempting a stab at our new normalcy. The conversation was sparse, boring.

My sister: "What are you having?"

Me: "I don't know."

My sister: "Me either."

The waitress arrived: "Are you ready?"

Dad: "Give us a few more minutes."

The waitress walked away. Our eyes followed her until she went around the corner. Silence. We turned to our menus.

These past few days had been a hubbub of happenings. The visits from aunts, uncles, cousins, friends, my wife by my side, my sister's husband by her side, the remember-that-time-your-mother conversations, the making of arrangements for the memorial, the picking up of Mom's ashes afterwards; all of it had helped us get by.

Today, things were different. Today, for the first time in nine days, there was just the three of us. My wife was at home, my sister's husband at work, and Dad, after 46 years of marriage, was—well—by himself.

The waitress came back. We ordered. She thanked us and gathered up the menus, taking the only thing we had to look at—except for each other—or the restaurant—or the ceiling. More silence.

I listened to the sounds in the restaurant. People laughing, conversing, glasses clashing against silverware clashing against dishes as restaurant staff bussed tables. It sounded no different than any truckstop restaurant I'd ever been in.

As if he could read my mind, Dad broke the silence. "When are you going back to work?"

"Wednesday," I said. "I'll call tomorrow and see what dispatch has going on."

I almost asked him if he wanted to come along, but decided not to. Dad had tried trucking some 20 years ago, back in the early '80s. The first time was with a moving company. He'd traveled to the Midwest for orientation and training but had gotten sick during his classes. After missing too many days they sent him home, telling him to call and reschedule when he was ready. Dad never called back. He never said why.

A year or two later he got the itch again, this time signing on with a flatbed company based right here in Pennsylvania. Dad bought himself a truck and was bobtailing up to

Author Bio

Scott Graeff was a truck driver who now works from the comfort of a small office, helping truckers who are broken down on the road. A former Long Ridge Writers Group student, he lives in the Pacific Northwest on the Olympic Peninsula, where he is currently working on a novel.

Berwick for his very first load when a drunk crossed the median and hit him head on. The drunk walked away from it, Dad wasn't so lucky. He was thrown from the truck (this was in the days before seatbelt laws), where he struck the guardrail and then bounced into the median where he came to rest. Dad physically recovered from this accident, but his desire to drive a truck did not.

Before his very brief love affair with trucking, and all through it, for that matter, Dad had been a self-employed electrician. For years it paid the bills, and it was what he retired from last year. He'd done well for himself, managing to have enough money to be able to buy a fifth-wheel camper and afford his and Mom's first camping trip to Arizona this past winter. They'd loved playing snowbirds.

Now Dad was alone. It broke my heart thinking about it.

Our food came and I was grateful for it. Eating was something to do—and it kept my mind off other things.

"It's not supposed to happen this way," Dad said.

My sister and I looked at him. "No, it's not," she said.

"Why do you eat your toast that way?"

Mom was a month away from her 64th birthday when she died. Young, really, by today's standards. I agreed with them by nodding my head. We turned to our food, eating in silence.

I watched my father. I loved him. I felt for him. I was struck by how frail he seemed. All my life he'd filled the role of a dad. He was as fine a father figure as I could have wished for. But today I saw him for what he was: a human being dealing with the loss of a loved one. He was plenty tough, I had no doubt about that, and I also had no doubt

that he would get through this. Still, it was like seeing him for the first time.

So I sat there, eating, watching my dad. We were very different, he and I. I'd realized that years ago and was reminded of it again today. He was engaged in one of those differences right now.

Dad always scooped his jelly out of its container and plopped it on the side of his plate. Then he took his knife and spread a small amount of jelly on his toast, enough for about two bites worth, ate each bite, along with some egg or hash browns, and then repeated the process until the toast was gone. Me, I saved my toast for last, spreading my jelly on it and eating it all at once.

Granted, it was a small, petty difference, and one I had forgotten about (I'd moved out of his house more than 20 years ago), but it was one of those things my father did that I was curious about. When I thought about it, I'd never seen anyone else eat toast that way.

I asked him straight out: "Why do you eat your toast that way?"

"What way?" he asked.

I explained what I was talking about and by the look on his face I could tell he was more than a little surprised I would notice such a small thing.

"It's the way my dad did it when I was growing up. I imagine I got it from him," he finally said. "Never really thought about it before now."

Habits. Parents pass them on to their children. Yet here was one my father hadn't passed on to me. I wondered why that was. Dad provided the answer.

"You and your sister eat like your mother," he said. "You eat your eggs, then your potatoes, then your toast. You should try mixing your food together. It all goes to the same place."

He was right. One dish at a time, it's how my sister and I ate. And it made sense. When we were little, Dad was up early and arrived home late. He was busy growing his electrician's business. Mom was the one who taught us our day-to-day living habits.

That led me to another realization. Another difference, and this was a big one, between Dad and me was the way we handled our money. He was, and still is, the biggest tightwad I know. I, on the other hand, pretty much see money as easy come, easy go. Much like my mother, I spend money on the things I enjoy. Dad would just as soon stay at home, letting his cash grow in a savings account. It made for some pretty big arguments over the years, particularly when I was a teenager.

There was a more recent conversation, however, that struck me just now. Maybe 10 years ago, when Dad physically started to slow down, when he began to think about how and when he would retire, he offered to apprentice me to take over his electrical business.

"I'll give you the whole shebang," he said. "Tools and all."

It was a sweet deal and one that surprised me. My father is the type of guy that would rather scrap something than let someone have it for nothing. Nevertheless, I turned him down. I had my reasons, and I told him what they were.

At the time, I had just started into the trucking business, and saw the kind of money a truck driver can make. Dad couldn't afford to pay me anywhere close to that kind of figure. We didn't argue over it; we just sort of put the matter on the back burner.

As I knew he would, he approached me again, offering me the exact same deal three years later. My answer was the same, and this time he was a little put out about it.

"I don't see why you want to continue to gallivant around the country in a truck. You're not home that much, and when you are, it seems like you're too busy to come around," he said.

"I visit you," I said. "And you know it."

"That's not what I mean," he said.

"Then what are you trying to say?" I asked.

"I'm telling you that someday you're going to be my age, and when you are, you might find yourself looking back wishing you'd done things differently. It'll be too late then. Can't you see how this trucking thing is robbing you of your home life?"

. . . I also came to understand just how much alike we were.

I didn't see it that way at all. I wasn't even sure of what he was trying to tell me, so I answered in the only way I could think to.

"You might be right, Dad, but I like what I do. I may wake up one day in the future glad for things I've done. How will I know until I get there?"

He dropped the issue. When he retired, so did his electrical business. Months later, when he came to respect my decision, he apologized.

But sitting here in this restaurant, watching him eat his toast and jelly, thinking of our differences, I also came to understand just how much alike we were.

I remembered as a child, when he was first starting out, how he worked his day job, and at night he fixed toasters and irons down in the cellar of our house. Sometimes he went to someone's home to fix a television, or washer, or dryer, or stove. Then one day he quit his day job, deciding to go the self-employed route. He was a good electrician who did quality work. He soon became selective about the jobs he'd take, leaving the toaster ovens to lesser electricians. More power to him.

Growing up, Dad kept food in my belly, clothes on my back, and a roof over my head. We weren't a poor family by any means, but we weren't well off either. I couldn't recall any family vacation that we ever took. We rarely went out to eat, for that matter.

All his life, my father worked hard. He provided well, giving freely of his love, but the one thing I wish I'd had more of was his time. I can't complain, I suppose, but I wonder if he couldn't have done things differently.

He scraped and scrimped and spent as little of his money as possible so that one day he would have a brighter future. That future was now. He finally had the money to do the things he wanted, and now he had the time. The one thing he never planned for was that my mother would not be around to spend it with.

Dad thought trucking was robbing me of my home life. I wondered how I could tell him that he was wrong, that a man does that to himself.

I looked down at my plate. Everything was gone except my toast. Out of habit, I began to spread jelly on it.

Truckers News

I've always been attracted to the broad genre of creative nonfiction because it's about real life. Nevertheless, writing it made me feel limited in the sense that I had to be "honest" to the story if for no other reason than that I was telling the "truth."

"Toast and Jelly" was a breakthrough piece in my development as a writer because, though there are several kernels of real-life events in the story, a very large part of it—about 40 percent—is fictional. I had finally found that fine line between make-believe and real life while still maintaining the level of verisimilitude that I like in a story.

At the time I was a truck driver who regularly read *Truckers News*. I was familiar with the fiction that appeared in it and had previously submitted two very different stories, both of which I thought were sure winners; neither was published. Feeling dejected, yet positive I could tell a trucking story worthy of being published, I decided to give it another try.

On a typical Pacific Northwest Saturday afternoon in October 2005, using the now-lame-sounding working title of "What's This Life For?" I pieced together the elements of a story that had been running through my head for the past year. The story was written that same day with a few minor changes, and one big one—the title—which is pretty much the only revision there was.

I had tried to write this story a few times before and was unsuccessful at keeping it interesting. The major difference this time was that I was more determined than ever to get published. I was convinced this story, if told the way I envisioned it, would be the one that allowed me to achieve that goal. Most importantly, I believed that *Truckers News* was a magazine within my league.

—Scott Graeff

I've Looked Everywhere

by Susan Jackson Rodgers

I lost my cell phone yesterday. This afternoon I heard it ringing faintly from deep inside its hiding place: a totebag, purse, kitchen drawer, pocket? I tried tracking the sound—first it seemed to be coming from the bedroom, then the study—but just as I thought I was getting close, the battery must have lost power, or else the person hung up. I went through the possibilities. Not very many people have the cell phone number. You, my sister, my ex-husband, my massage therapist, my housepainter who is also maybe my boyfriend, though maybe not. I called them all, all except you and the ex-husband, because he'd only call in case of an emergency and he'd try the land line first for that; and the housepainter, because I've called twice this week, and I don't want to appear desperate.

I decided to go to the library, to return the overdue books, but remembered that they are lost too. Three of them, checked out two months ago, and the fines have almost exceeded the value of the books. One was a book of poetry that I used to keep by my bed, because after you left I discovered that reading poetry before I went to sleep produced interesting, poetic dreams. The other was a biogra-phy of a child actor; I love stories about people doing drugs. And the third I can't remember.

I'm losing confidence, but not weight. I'm losing my glasses, my mind, my sense of balance. In yoga class I used to be able to do the Stork and now I can't, I topple over like a badly constructed block tower. Everyone pretends not to notice because they're practicing

I've lost two husbands— one to heart failure, and one to a twenty-year-old.

their serene yoga faces. I'm losing estrogen, instant recall, the ability to spell words I have always known how to spell. The stocks I own are losing money, have lost money, are worthless. The country I live in is losing wars—against drugs, fat, violence, stupidity, invisible forces we can't name, enemies we've only imagined who now rightly despise us. I'm losing faith. Altitude. Ground. I've lost two husbands—one to heart failure, and one to a twenty-year-old—and children—one to her dreaded Peer Group, and the other to a cultish mentality about a particular heavy metal band that shall go unnamed. I lost my name, twice, and now I can't get it back again. I'm losing elasticity, skin and otherwise. Losing perspective. Losing my appetite, but not for food. I've lost my mother's recipe for honey cake. I've lost the receipt to the beige dress I bought for my daughter's high school graduation that she said made me look like a matronly cow so I decided to wear the purple rayon pantsuit

Author Bio

Susan Jackson Rodgers is the author of a collection of stories, *The Trouble With You Is*. She is an associate professor of English and Creative Writing at Oregon State University.

instead. Without the receipt, I'm stuck with the cowsuit, which hangs in my closet with many other articles of clothing my daughter has forbidden me to wear.

I've lost my taste for older men, because really, how much older can I go? I've lost my yen. For transatlantic travel, for driving a stick-shift, for falling snow, loud dinner parties, loud noise of any kind except certain rock bands from an entirely different era, late-night phone calls. I've lost the left shoe from my favorite pair, the black sandals for whom I get regular pedicures in the summer, the sandals that I bought three years ago in Italy—you were with me. Do you remember the sandals? Where in God's name does a single black leather Milanese sandal go? Is it at your house? Under the bed, perhaps, or in your closet, with your shoes?

I've lost my place in the book I'm reading.

Old friends. The desire to be first in line. The need to fit in, to do what I'm told, to accept second best, to fight the good fight, to be quiet. I've lost the remote control—forever this time, my car keys, a pair of $200 sunglasses I promised myself I would never lose, three skin cancers off my back, the directions to your sister's summer house, the children's baby teeth, many important documents that I'm certain I had signed by a notary public but did not, apparently, store in a safe place, a charcoal sketch of my childhood home, and the Maxime Le Forestier album I bought in Quebec in 1975. On the list of lost things also is the list of things I keep meaning to do, and the list of things I'm sorry I did—though when I wake up at four in the morning, there they all are, crowded around my bedside like eager dogs, pawing my hand, begging me to scratch their ears.

I've lost my place in the book I'm

reading, the negative for the picture of us I wanted to enlarge (standing on the stone steps, the lake behind us), the phone number for the acupuncturist my neighbor recommended. Both parents and a brother, six dogs, eight cats, four hamsters, three birds and, I'm not kidding, a pear tree which died of blight. The instructions to the Cuisinart, the breadmaker I got for my second wedding— and you tell me where a breadmaker could possibly be hiding. The extension cord I swore I bought last week, this week's *TV Guide*, my favorite pen.

I've looked everywhere.

Every day there's something else, things dropping away like the careless removal of clothing or make-up after a party, like the diamond earring that slips from my fingers into the bathroom sink and down the drain, disappearing so quickly it seems to have planned its daring escape. We both watch it fall, incredulous, as if this kind of thing never happens. You kindly take apart the pipes underneath the sink (still wearing your handsome evening clothes, crisp white sleeves rolled up to your elbows) but the earring is gone. You straighten, unroll your sleeves, pluck the remaining earring from my palm and drop it into the drain just like that, without looking at me. And I can't read the gesture or the expression on your face; can't decide if what you mean is, See, it doesn't matter, it's just a *thing*; or, Now the two earrings will be together forever; or, Through your terrible carelessness, your inability to watch what you're doing, your consistently wretched sense of timing, you've sealed your fate, and mine.

There! Did you hear that? The phone— it's ringing again. Three rings, four. Now is the moment when I realize I could have just dialed the cell number myself, and tracked down the phone. "Dur," my oldest daughter would say. I stand in the middle of the room—six, seven—the afternoon light fading now, the shadows lengthening across the woven rugs. The rings stop. It must be later than I think, the way the light falls across the floors. The day must have gotten away from me, as it does sometimes. Does that ever happen to you? The day slipping by? Who knows where it goes. But it's late, in any case, it's starting to get dark, it's getting dark a lot earlier now, and in the mornings when I go for my walk, there's a chill, a dampness. Sometimes I wear a sweatshirt, my favorite one, faded blue, extra large, soft from many washings. The one you must assume, by now, that you've lost.

StoryQuarterly

Author's Comments

The story "I've Looked Everywhere" grew out of an exercise in my advanced fiction writing course. We were reading "list" stories—Rick Moody's "Boys," Jamaica Kincaid's "Girl," Leonard Michael's "In the Fifties"—and brainstorming prompts for lists. The prompts included Worst Dates Ever, Superheroes I Want to Be, Things I Ate I Wished I Hadn't, Jobs I've Been Fired From, and Things I Have Lost.

I made a "lost things" list that included typical objects (car keys, sunglasses) and some not-so-typical ones. As the list evolved, I could feel the piece begin to be about someone else, a character whose history I could glean through the concrete and abstract losses she had experienced.

Of course, a list story has to rise above a mere list, and that was the primary challenge with this short-short—to make it mean something beyond the list.

I chose *StoryQuarterly* because I'd had a story published there already, a short-short called "The Rice In Question," and because it's a literary journal I enjoy reading.

Young and emerging writers, in their (understandable) impatience to get published, often submit blindly to journals they've never even read. Find a few journals whose work you love, subscribe to them, and read them, not just to find out what those editors are publishing, but because reading is your best teacher.

—Susan Jackson Rodgers

Familiar Stranger

by Patricia Windsor

She first saw him in the pub and, although she was with Graham, she stared shamelessly, willing him to look back. It didn't work. Without a glance her way, he disappeared into the smoke and din.

Later on when she'd almost forgotten, she saw him again, standing between two girls, turning his face to one and then the other, as if giving them equal time. She wanted to get closer to hear the sound of his voice . . . then she had to laugh at herself.

"Private joke?" asked Graham.

The trouble with Graham was that he was boring. She knew that now.

But this other man, the one who wouldn't look her way, he was different. She knew his face—maybe from another life?—and his face was right. Again, as she muttered in monosyllables to Graham, she willed the stranger: *Look at me!* If only he would, she was sure he'd feel something too. But he went on talking to his two girls.

"What are you staring at?" Graham asked, glancing around the pub.

"That man over there," she said.

Sighing but always anxious to please,

Author Bio

Patricia Windsor's fiction for young people and adults has appeared in *Mademoiselle*, *Seventeen*, and other magazines. Her novels and short stories have been published in Great Britain, Scandinavia, Germany, Israel, Japan, Australia, New Zealand, and South Africa.

Graham looked across the room. "Which one?"

"That one, with the black hair and black eyes. I wish I knew him."

"Why not go up and introduce yourself then?"

"Don't be silly," she answered, surprised that he sounded almost irritated.

She'd never have had the nerve to go right up to someone like that. It was easier to believe in the force of will, predestination, the power of her vibes sent madly across a crowded room.

That night, she dreamt of him, his perfect face, how right it would be with him.

"Miranda, are you staying in bed all day?" Jane, her flatmate, asked. The blinds were up. Sun streaming in. Morning.

The fantasies of the night still warming her, she went to the office, his face sharply etched in her memory. It wouldn't fade.

How long can you go on pretending? Very long. Office, home, sleep, wake. Some evenings the pub with Graham. Some evenings the washing. One evening the cinema. With Graham.

"Who is it?" Miranda heard herself asking, stupidly hopeful, irrationally jubilant whenever the telephone rang and Jane said it was for her.

"It's Graham," Jane said, as if it couldn't possibly be anyone else. And that was the truth. Dark eyes, dark hair didn't know she existed.

She almost forgot. And then, there he was again: on the bus this time. She stayed in her seat, stealing glances at him. She had to get off at the next stop. Or she could stay for one more and walk back. And then, miraculously, he stood up and they got off the bus together. Being as close to him as that, it took her breath away.

"Don't I know you?" she asked, because she managed to catch his eye at last.

"Do you?" he asked back, faintly amused, maybe pleased?

"Yes," she said and started to tell him about the pub, wanting to turn it into a witty story but people came between them and he was swept away by the crowd, because, obviously, he really didn't care.

She watched the back of his disappearing head. Dark hair curled over the collar of his blue jacket.

I love him, she thought suddenly.

She didn't see him for two weeks and gave up hope. She should never have expected anything. All her life it had been the same. Any boy she'd wanted was sure not to care. The ones she wasn't interested in wouldn't leave her alone. The icier she was, the harder they tried. It was the secret of life: you only get what you don't want.

That's why it was a miracle that she met him again—in the same pub. She was with Graham, of course.

He came in and she turned around, trying to pretend it was nothing, sick with joy and regret. I won't look, she thought. But she eyed his reflection in the glass behind the bar.

"Don't I know you?" his reflection said into her ear.

"Do you?"

"Are you cold, Miranda?" Graham asked. Funny that he would even notice.

"Yes, I do," the man said. "Miranda."

Graham interrupted: "Have we met before?"

The man shrugged and put out his hand. "James Sidwell."

"James," she sighed before she could stop herself. He looked at her and said, "Jim."

But she would call him James, even after he told her that only his family called him James and that he didn't really like it.

After awhile, Graham went to get cigarettes.

James whispered: "Can I steal you away?"

Her knees weak, she managed to do the right thing (for once) by saying no.

There was no time to exchange numbers. He simply said, "I'm in the book," before Graham came back.

"Your voice is beautiful."

So it seemed quite reasonable that she would ring him. All he knew was her first name and anyway she wasn't listed; it was Jane's phone. So she looked him up and phoned him and he remembered who she was.

His voice was beautiful. She could hear the beauty in it now that she wasn't looking at him at the same time. She hoped and did not hope; the sensible side of her told her she was being ridiculous.

He'd asked her to come over to his place because he didn't have a car. Neither did she but never mind. Her feet measured out his directions, her heart fluttered. She rang the bell anxiously and not until he actually called down the stairs "Hello?" did she stop feeling it was going to turn into a joke.

He was doing his washing up. It was very cozy and domestic and somehow much better than in her dreams.

He made her a pot of tea and they sat across from each other. He looked at her. She looked at him. He smiled.

"Thank you," he said, "for coming over." Maybe he was teasing her but the way he smiled, she didn't care. She wanted to keep the moment.

"Your voice is beautiful," she said.

"Oh yes," he said, sadly. "They call me the poor man's Richard Burton."

He was an actor but currently out of work, he told her. Then he told her more about himself. His hopes . . .

My love, she thought. James.

He told her about his family. She pictured herself meeting them. They would like her. He told her funny things and she laughed. She wanted to listen to him forever.

Perfection.

There was a moment of quiet. She could hear her own breath. He got up and went to a cupboard. Then he came to her and knelt . . . kneeling at her feet, looking up at her, his arm resting lightly on her knee! Her knee trembled.

"Let me have your hand," he said.

Even before she looked she felt the cool metal circle moving down her finger—her ring finger, marriage finger. It's coming true! She felt afraid. This had to be a dream.

"Do you like it?"

She looked at the twisted silver, the polished stone. Unable to speak, she nodded. What did it mean? She couldn't believe it was actually happening.

"It suits you," he said but there didn't seem to be the right emotion in his voice. Quickly he slipped the ring off, tossed it from palm to palm, staring up at her from his haunches.

"I have others. Would you like to see them? I can let you have one for a very good price. They're all genuine silver—American Indian. I get them from a friend in the States."

He was up again, burrowing into the cupboard, coming out with a box of rings.

"Here, try another one."

She stared into the box. They were beautiful rings. A very good price but high. More than she ever thought of spending on a ring.

But he told her they were worth much much more.

An actor, currently out of work . . . her tea splashed on him as she leapt up, never mind, it wasn't hot, it wouldn't burn.

"I'm sorry. I must go."

"Already? I thought you were staying the night." His black eyes looked at her, puzzled. They had somehow lost their magnetic glow, she thought.

Seeing him clearly now, she knew all he felt was mild disappointment. Evening's entertainment cancelled. A bother now, to find someone else. And he hadn't even sold a ring.

When she got home Jane said, "Graham rang. He said it was urgent."

"Urgent? Huh!"

But she went to the telephone to dial his number. It rang and rang until she thought he wasn't there, surprised that it suddenly worried her.

Then him saying sleepily: "Hullo? Miranda? You were out." Was that jealousy in his voice?

"I'm in now."

"Look, I wanted to know if you want to come . . ." he went on, outlining details of his plans.

She knew she would never be able to tell him his voice was beautiful. Something inside her had been stilled. But she felt warm, at ease. Dear old Graham.

Long afterwards, she often told herself: I did love him. Not the man on his knees with tea-stained trousers but the other one. The one who, constantly and purposely, would remain a familiar stranger forever.

Cleo Magazine (Australia)

Familiar Stranger

Author's Comments ───────

Shortly after I moved into a new neighborhood, my neighbors invited me to a cocktail party. What a nice gesture, I thought, relieved that these people weren't put off by a single woman, someone not always welcome at parties given by married couples in the suburbs. I soon found out that the party was more than a friendly get-together.

After being supplied with drinks, guests were herded into a room where sheet-covered tables and a screen and slide projector were set up. The ensuing presentation was about impoverished Native Americans on a reservation out West. It was moving, but where was it leading? I soon found out.

Cloths on the tables hadn't been hiding yummy hors d'oeuvres but displays of silver and turquoise jewelry for sale. A percentage of sales would go to help the Indians. The group was small enough to discourage non-participation and I felt a bit pressured.

A while later, I met an actor not unlike the character in this story, in a setting somewhat similar. Since I was with a friend, we made a dinner date for the following weekend. I admit I took special care with makeup and clothes, and had butterflies in my stomach. But he drove me to a large garish diner, the kind with a 25-page menu, Naugahyde booths, fluorescent-like lighting and utensils wrapped in paper napkins. I felt a bit out of place in my little black dress and diamond studs. He seemed oblivious.

After dinner, I suggested driving straight home and we bade each other goodnight at the door. I never heard from him again.

Somehow the two disappointments—the unexpected flogging of jewelry and my dashed romantic expectations—melded into a story. Since I'd been living in England and had a British agent, I set the story in London but it sold to magazines in Australia and South Africa.

—Patricia Windsor

My Turn

by Carolyn Matthews

Faster and faster I spun till the dry leaves swirled up around my ankle socks and the skirt of my dress stood out nearly as far as Sylvie's did over her sugar-starched net petticoats. I spun so fast Dad's newly painted picket fence melted into a ribbon of white tied around me, the lawn, the house, the old wood-paneled station wagon sitting in the driveway, and Sylvie, of course.

Then the front door slammed and Mom and Dad came hurrying out. I twirled my way toward the car. "It's my turn to sit up front," I said half to them but mostly to Sylvie.

"You sat up front yesterday," Sylvie countered, "on the way to church."

"I know but that doesn't count. We had to pick up Aunt Billie. She's so fat I'm the only one who fits. And besides, I had to sit in the middle on the hump, with no window."

Sylvie hugged her books and her new red sweater to her chest. She was always holding things against her chest these days, as though she'd spilled soup down her front and didn't want anyone to see.

"You got to sit by Dad," she said. "And on

the way home, too. That's twice in a row. Besides, you helped him paint the fence on Saturday. You got to—"

"Don't start girls," Mom cut in. She tossed us brown paper lunch bags, bologna again, I could smell it. "Hurry up," she said. "Your father is—"

"Late for work." Dad flung his black leather briefcase into the back seat. "I don't know what it is about Mondays. Why can't this family pull together for a change?"

"Henry, you were the one who forgot to set the alarm."

"Why is it always my fault? I'm the major breadwinner. Do I have to tend to all the little details too?"

"You've told me, *never* touch the alarm."

"Get in the car, please. All of you."

I hopped in, front seat of course. Sylvie grabbed at my arm and caught the sleeve of my dress instead. I yanked away. The thin cotton gingham ripped.

"Now look what you've done," Mom said to her.

Dad pointed a finger at Sylvie's chest. "You're in for some punishment, young lady. When I get home from work we'll see to it." Sylvie's face went from red to white.

Mom fumbled in her pocketbook for her keys. "Henry, she'll have to change. She can't go to school in a torn dress."

"Why the hell not? Here, take this." He grabbed Sylvie's sweater and shoved it toward me. "You can wear it over the dress. No one will see."

"But, Dad," Sylvie whined, "that's my

Author Bio

Carolyn Matthews is published in multiple genres, from children's short stories to romance novels to feature newspaper articles. Currently, she writes literary short stories from her home in New Hampshire, freelance edits both fiction and nonfiction, and teaches for Long Ridge Writers Group.

new sweater."

Mom glanced toward heaven and let out one of her signature sighs. "Sylvie, dear, do what your father says. It won't hurt you to be generous with your little sister for a change."

"But she got to paint the fence. Now she gets to sit up front." Mom glanced over the hood of the car at Dad. Stony faced, he stared at the fence.

I put on the sweater. It had buttons that looked like miniature American flags, and it smelled like Tabu. "Mom, Sylvie's been wearing your perfume again," I said as I scooted across to the middle of the seat.

Mom glared at Sylvie. "I do wish you'd stay out of my things."

"It's not true. Remember last week? I was in your room trying on my new sweater while you were getting ready for work. You didn't see me. The spray went everywhere."

"She's probably right," Dad said. "You wear too damn much of the stuff. I like my women *au naturel*. Will the rest of you, please, get in the car. I'm going to count the pickets on that fence. This car will roll when I get through, ready or not."

"*Your* women. Plural of course," Mom muttered through her teeth, the words as pointed as the pickets on the fence. She slid into the front seat beside me and slammed the door. She took out her lipstick and leaned toward the rear view mirror.

Dad bent down, his face in the window, level with hers. He took a breath that seemed to suck all the air out of the car. When he let it out his suit coat hung limp around his shoulders, as though he'd grown smaller. Mom didn't look at him. She just pressed her lips together over and over, spreading the deep red color.

Finally Dad straightened. Sylvie crept into the back seat, alone. Dad got in on his side and started the engine.

"It's not fair," Sylvie whined.

"Life's not fair, Sylvia," Dad said without turning around. "High time you figured that out."

Sylvie pulled Dad's briefcase to her lap and hugged it. The car rolled out of the driveway. The fence faded as we sped down the street. It would be there when we got home, though, all painted and shiny and sturdy, holding things together.

I settled back and buttoned up all the little flags on the sweater. Not a single one was loose. But that didn't matter. In my desk at school, I had scissors.

Thema

Author's Comments

The idea for "My Turn" came about one afternoon when I witnessed a particularly unpleasant example of sibling rivalry at our local playground and (as always) began to weave it into a story. Unique to this scene was a tottering fence, which seemed a symbol of the family's deteriorating relationships.

That afternoon, *Thema* arrived in my mailbox, and as I turned to the last page to read the list of upcoming premises and check the deadlines, "Henry's Fence" jumped out at me. For *Thema*, the premise given must be an integral part of the plot, not necessarily the central theme but not merely incidental, so my story began to take clearer shape. Once again, *Thema* had given me just the push I needed to turn my idea into a literary short story.

In the shrinking world of short story journals, *Thema* stands out because its contributors are often ordinary people from all walks of life who just happen to be writers. I've used *Thema* for years to jump-start my own writing, as a teaching tool in writing workshops, and as a viable market suggestion for my Long Ridge students and for my clients.

—Carolyn Matthews

Kursk

by Maria Elena Suarez

I am watching about submarines when you come out of the shower with your freckles and your solid shoulders. We have talked about everything possible except that our baby died in my body before it was born, and that you are worried about me. In a way though we talk about only that, and when you ask me if I want apples from the store, you are really asking when I will be alright again, what you can bring me to make me alright. You sit very close to me, still in your towel, and together we watch doomed Soviet sailors on television. The narrator tells about the failing of the nuclear submarine, about the utter ruin for the men inside. It sinks slowly and there is no hope of power resurgence just in time, there is no hope of rescue, and it is a slow, ballet drift down to death through universes of cold water. As you leave the room to get dressed, the physical ocean has overwhelmed them, and they will die soon. The water gathers over them, more and more of it all the time, and they watch it collect on top of them. They can hear its weight as it crowds in on them, and they understand completely what it is to be helpless, to be a collection of tissue and blood at the hands of an entire ocean. I apologize to the sailors in a whisper.

The camera pans slowly across a picture of them all together before the accident, in clean uniforms and smiling, back when they had lives and choices, when they could drive away from the ocean or towards it. I tell them I am sorry for not getting them out. If I were strong enough, I whisper, I would have protected you. If my body were strong enough, I would have kept the violence from your bodies. I would have been a guard against everything that pushes in. Back, now, in jeans and sweater, you put your arm around me with a gust of new soap and skin scrubbed clean.

StoryQuarterly

Author Bio

Maria Elena Suarez is completing her MFA in fiction at San Francisco State, where she also teaches. She currently resides with her husband in a small, portable, metal house.

Author's Comments

After watching a television special on the submariners' accident, I found myself thinking for weeks afterward about that particular nature of loss. The nostalgia for other people's youths, the machinery involved, the unarguably physical forces of nature; all of these things seemed very important to me.

When I tried to write about them, I found myself wanting to write about the body specifically, memories of being tossed in the surf of the Atlantic. I imagined someone feeling like me, terrified and helpless when faced with that kind of power, almost in disbelief of it, and I thought of this woman whose own body was exerting the power on her. Then I wrote about her.

Author's Comments (*cont.*) ━━━━━━

I wrote the story straight through in one sitting—then cut a few words and sent it out. This almost never happens to me. Some stories require the weaving together of dozens of Post-it notes, covered with jotted ideas or language. Sometimes I even make very illogical webs and flow charts.

Everyone has a process, or several different ones even, and I can't say for certain when I do what or why. What I can say is that, for me, a story develops on the backs of the people in it. If I can't see the characters, can't imagine how they dance, what clothes they pick out when shopping, then no amount of pseudo-scientific sketching will help make my story realized and important.

—Maria Elena Suarez

The Girl with the Click Click Eyes

by Patricia Windsor

Sonny had a hard life. He didn't always know it; just recently the idea came into his mind. This doesn't seem right, he thought one night. The two of them, the old man and himself, were eating a meal out of a couple of tin cans. They usually ate out of cans: cold ravioli, spaghetti, beans. The old man was sitting there across the table with red sauce dripping down his chin, and something happened. Sonny's appetite was gone. He pushed the half-finished can of beans away.

"What's a matter?" the old man asked. "You're not hungry?"

"Pop," he said. "This can't be right."

The old man shoveled a few more forkfuls into his mouth before he looked up. "What's a matter? Something wrong with the beans?"

"No, I don't mean that. I mean this. Us. Eating like this."

His father looked around the table. He didn't understand. "I don't get you," he said.

"I know."

They looked into each other's eyes for a long moment, then looked away. The old man straightened his bony shoulders, wiped a greasy hand down the front of the already stained shirt. "Open up another can," he said, half-heartedly.

In that moment, Sonny knew he was through with eating from cans. He sat very still, feeling the knowledge inside him. He inched the length of his gaze across the littered table, to the counters crammed with junk. The door of the broken microwave hung open, its interior stuffed with old mail. The floor tiles that had once been white were now a dirty, unmopped gray. He heard his father belch. Then the cans snatched up and thrown across the room to the open garbage can, making a bull's eye, clank, pop. Leaning back in his chair, the old man reached for the refrigerator, pried the door open, swung it back, extracted a can of beer and nudged the door closed again with the side of his hand. It was an easy, flowing, habitual gesture. Next came the pop and hiss as the beer was opened. Then the gurgling of the liquid spilling down the old man's throat.

Sonny knew all these sounds by heart. He was thinking, for some odd reason, about hot mashed potatoes. Butter oozing. When was the last time we had mashed potatoes he almost asked the old man. He shrugged himself back to reality. The old man was already hoisting a second can of beer.

"You got troubles? I got troubles. We all have troubles." The old man waved the can. "So here's to troubles."

In a little while he wouldn't be so philosophical. Aided by beer, the troubles would emerge and be magnified. They'd be debated,

Author Bio

Patricia Windsor's fiction for young people and adults has received many awards, including an Edgar Allan Poe Award for *The Sandman's Eyes*. Her novels and short stories have been published in Great Britain, Scandinavia, Germany, Israel, Japan, Australia, New Zealand, and South Africa.

torn apart, pulverized, then gathered up and glued together again so the whole process could start over. Sonny pushed his chair back and stood up.

"Huh?" the old man said, taken unawares. "Where are you going?"

"I don't know. Out."

The house was really a dump, ramshackle and tar-papered.

"Out?" The old man looked around the kitchen. "Naw," he said. "Put on the TV."

The TV, Sonny thought, was where he'd last seen mashed potatoes. The TV, now that he came to think of it, was where he first started getting ideas.

"I'm going out for a while," he told his father. There were no more protests. The gesture had been made, the ritual of concern was over. The old man was tired. He slumped, blunt fingers curled around the beer can. The hard part was that Sonny knew his father liked to have him home nights. Even if all they did was sit side by side staring at the television, saying almost nothing. His father liked to have him there so he could say, "Look at that," or "Watch that guy," and Sonny would reply, "Yeah," or "Okay." It was, in a way, a sparse sort of sharing. But it got them nowhere. Sonny could see that now. On bigger issues, his father let him down.

He went to the door and immediately the air cheered him up. It was a balmy spring night. It gave him the feeling anything might happen. Just around the corner, things might change. He kicked some old newspaper out from under the gate and pulled it shut behind him. He moved into the dark street, away from the house and the junkyard, feeling easier with every step. The house was really a dump, ramshackle and tar-papered. It

squatted in the middle of the junkyard, surrounded by heaps of twisted metal, ruptured engines, battered cars that sat like empty turtle shells. Tall grass grew up through the rings of abandoned tires. Hubcaps filled with rain, making a bath for birds. Sonny walked away from it. In the distance, a streetlight beckoned. Beyond the streetlight lay the town.

It was funny but he had traveled this way almost every day of his life, first to school and now to the garage and his job. In the daytime the journey was ordinary. At night it always made him feel he was on his way to something different. The funny part was that nothing different ever happened. He'd come into town, walk a few streets east, cross the highway and arrive at the River Park. Inside, the same people would be standing at the bar or sitting on the tops of the few scattered tables. The same boggy smell seeped out of the men's room. The same players clustered around the pool table, lining up their games by stacking coins along the table's edge. There was a sound of muted conversation, the ping of bottle caps, the sharp click of the balls. The jukebox, blatantly lighted in a far corner, was always silent. Cigarette smoke hung heavy in the brown air, one of the bars that let you smoke.

He entered the River Park now, the spring freshness that he had gathered on his walk quickly falling away from him as he became part of the familiar murk. A few smiles, a couple of waves, his usual greeting. The staccato explosion of a game starting, the schrush of the cash register drawer, the gentle thump of change set down on the damp bar, all these familiar things settled on his mind. He watched a nickel of the change roll away from the rest and hover at the bar's edge. Watched as a long blackly painted fingernail tipped the nickel over on its back. The fingernail attached to a long pale finger; other fingers, silver-ringed on a smooth, tapered hand. The arm slender and vulnerable in its bareness. The girl, poised on a bar stool, jet strands of hair hiding her face. She looked at him suddenly. Suddenly everything was different. Her eyes blinked. Doll's eyes. Thick lashes looked too heavy to make blinking easy. Click. Click.

Sonny realized he was standing in the middle of the room, suspended. He moved, coming up close to the girl. Too close. He moved back, searching with his elbow for a place to lean. She was still looking at him. He arranged his features in an awkward smile. In those few seconds it seemed as if everything else had stopped but as he turned towards Billy behind the bar, the spell was broken and the place came alive. He didn't have to tell Billy what he wanted; the bottle was already waiting. He busied himself with it, acutely aware of the girl. He shifted to face the pool table. In a minute he would go over and put down his own pile of coins to reserve a game. He wondered why she was there.

The River Park had its idiosyncrasies. It wasn't for men only but few women ever came. There were some regulars. Some girlfriends. Once in a while two girls would come in together; nobody bothered them. Nobody tried to pick them up. There were other places for that. The River Park was comfortable. He had, all this time, been entertaining the idea of something different happening and now there wasn't anything he was going to do about it.

He went over to the game, carrying his bottle of beer. He was at the end of the line; he had to wait. He watched but he couldn't settle into it. He felt a prickling at his back. He wanted to turn around but he wouldn't. He finished the beer and held onto the empty bottle, sticking his finger down the neck and popping it back out. He felt uneasy and finally annoyed that the girl's presence was keeping him from going back to the bar as usual. The smoke stung his eyes. He felt restless.

"Hey, how're you doing there, Sonny?" somebody said. He was relieved to make conversation; it kept the minutes passing. He thought maybe whoever it was who was with her would be back by her side soon.

But when he turned around, she was alone. The black strands of hair hid her face. He sauntered up. Not too close this time. Even in that short distance of floor, his legs felt conscious of their walking. Billy gave him another bottle, exchanged a few words and moved off.

"I never saw you here before."

"You going to play pool?" The voice was velvety. He had to look at her.

"Who, me?" he asked, not sure.

"Yes, you." Her smile teased him. Click. Click. The doll's eyes penetrated too deep. He was startled. Like a cold wind breaking through the cozy smog.

"Yeah, sure," he said, uncertain what she was after.

"It's interesting," she said.

He almost asked her what, then realized she meant playing pool. Maybe she meant the River Park itself. She seemed aloof. The way she said it, "interesting," was like she came from another world.

He felt self-conscious, talking to her like that. He noticed a couple of his friends looking over. He hoped they wouldn't give him the high sign, start ribbing him for making time. He would have liked to talk to her somewhere else. There wasn't a chance.

"Do you come here often?" She talked like the television.

He parried. "I never saw you here before." He was pleased with saying that.

"Well you see me now." It was a challenge. He didn't know what to do with it.

"Yeah, well I guess I do."

Click. Click.

He swigged at his beer roughly. Somebody called to him. His game. He walked away. Picking up his cuer, setting up his eye; the green table, the balls neat in the rack, all of this soothed him and he was into the game, his body and mind moving rhythmically, automatically, his experienced eye squinting down the stick. He played well and it was only at the very end that he understood why he felt such exhilaration, why every movement around that table had been so exciting. He was performing. For her. But when he went back to the bar, too keyed-up to feel self-conscious this time, he wasn't prepared for what she said. The words were too intimate in those surroundings. The blood raced to his face.

"You are the sweetest roller on the green."

Don't, he wanted to say, afraid she was playing a game. He felt like asking her to come outside. He knew he would never get the words out. She did it for him.

"Are you staying here long?"

"What?"

"I mean, are you going to be leaving soon?"

"Any time. I can leave any time."

"You wouldn't mind giving me a ride home, would you? I mean, I was supposed to meet someone . . ." She glanced down, ran her fingers, blackly painted nails, along the bar toward him. "But I guess it looks like I've been stood up." Her eyes, challenging and mournful.

The one night he didn't bring the car!

She misinterpreted his hesitation. "Look if you don't want to, just say so," but he broke in, his heart beating fast, "It's not that. It's just . . . I have to get my car. If you want to wait, it won't take long."

She wouldn't believe him. He'd come back and she wouldn't be there. He felt something important, something precious, slipping through his hands like quicksilver.

"No," she said, "no, I don't mind."

He told her how long it would take, careful not to cut the time too short. He left quickly not wanting to be delayed with questions from his friends. In other circumstances, it would be a plus mark to get a girl. But now he felt wary. It might all be a joke. When he came back and she wasn't there, they'd laugh. He kicked himself for not having the car. But he felt that somehow it was all happening because of it.

He didn't even know her name.

He ran all the way home. He knew the old man, if he was still partially sober, would be wondering at the sound of the car going out. But he didn't have time to explain. He didn't have time for anything except to get back. To hurry. To hope she would wait. He drove recklessly. Thinking how stupid it was not to have asked for her number. He didn't even know her name.

She was waiting outside, the glow of the neon River Park sign making a halo in her hair. She had on a white sweater that blinked green and red with the lights.

She peered into the car window and the heavy eyelids clicked in recognition. "Oh!" She slid into the seat next to him, bringing the smell of the bar with her, and a sweet perfume he hadn't noticed before.

"I'm glad you came back!"

"Did you think I wouldn't?" He was touched that she should have worried the same as he had done.

She laughed, for the first time. "I didn't know."

"Well, here I am." He laughed too but then there was a silence. He turned onto the highway. "Where to?"

She seemed surprised. "Home, I guess." Disappointed. He felt uneasy again. What did she want?

"Straight ahead?" he asked. "I never saw you before."

"I never saw you before." She had a secretive smile. "I don't usually go to places like that. The River Park, I mean."

There was something in the way she said it. Places like that. She meant something.

She took out a pack of cigarettes, offered him one. He shook his head but punched on the lighter for her. She asked, "Do you live here? Do you work around here?"

He was noncommittal, not wanting to go into details. He was noticing things about her. The way she spoke, the way she held her chin, the look of her hair. Her own lighter snapped smartly to her cigarette just as the dashboard lighter popped out. The gesture reminded him of the television again. The word was sophistication.

"Why did you pick me out to take you home?" he asked.

"You really want to know? You looked different. Not like the rest of them. I don't usually get stood up." She frowned. "Oh well, look what happened anyway. I met you." She put her hand on his arm. "Turn left here," she said. The hand slithered away.

He had mixed feelings. What was so different about him? If she only knew. The old man and the junk yard flashed into his mind, an incongruous vision. He saw the man asleep in the chair with the sagging springs, the armrest torn out. Four or five beer cans would be lying at his feet. The body slumped in front of the TV, stained shirt unbuttoned, dirty trousers unzipped, bedraggled socks with a big hole in the toe. He pushed the vision aside.

"Left again," she said.

They turned up into a wide tree-lined street. He knew this section. The houses were large, set back in gardens, not junk-yards. People here had maids.

"My house is up there but," she moved imperceptibly closer, "why don't you park here?"

Then, as if sensing he might misunderstand, "Otherwise they'll be hanging out the windows, checking up on me."

He decided, in that instant, to enjoy it. Stop worrying about it. If she was Miss High and Mighty slumming for the night, he'd take her for all it was worth. Her hard luck if she didn't like the scene. You can't play with fire without getting burned. He felt like fire. Unless she came into the garage to get her tank filled, he'd never see her again.

He cut the motor and the lights. The street was dark, the trees hung low, closing them in. He reached his arm across the back of the seat, let it slide slowly down around her shoulders. She turned to face him. Click. Click.

"This is nice," she said. "I feel peaceful with you. Isn't that strange?"

He only murmured yes; he was leaning towards her.

"I mean, I don't even know you and yet I have this feeling about you."

His arm was drawing her closer. The other hand moved along the edge of her hair, smoothing it, pushing it back, down along her cheek, behind her ear. He ran his fingers along the back of her neck. She shivered very slightly and sighed. "It's strange," she said. His lips touched hers for a whisper of a second before she turned her head.

"You can kiss my cheek," she said. An undertone of laughter in her voice. "For tonight."

He stifled the groan that threatened to erupt, turned away and put his hands back on the steering wheel.

"Don't be angry," she said softly. Her hand went over his. The nails were truly black now.

He gave a shrugging laugh.

She was fumbling with her purse. Getting out a pen. She handed him a page from a small notebook. "This is my number," she said. "Will you phone me?"

"When?"

"Tomorrow?" Her hair swung forward; her eyes were in shadow. "Don't forget. I'll be very disappointed if you forget."

She was out of the car so quickly that when he reached for her he was only grabbing air.

He expected to feel angry. Instead he felt a sweet sadness that bewildered him.

He thought about it the next day. Saturday. She wouldn't be working but he was. He imagined her in a plush office during the week, a place with polished desks and trees growing out of flowerpots. On Saturday she would be home in her big house. She wouldn't want to see him on such short notice; she'd want appointments in advance. He alternately made up his mind he would, then he wouldn't phone. He looked at the clock a hundred times. He couldn't leave it too late.

He went around back, not wanting to be overheard. His grease-blackened fingers smudged the slip of paper. At the last minute, when the number was ringing, he wondered who he was going to ask for.

No girl had ever asked him a question like that on the phone.

He heard her voice saying, "Hello?"

"Remember me?" He cupped his hand around the phone to block out the passing traffic.

"Oh yes," she said. "I wondered when you would call."

"Did you?"

There was a sound of muffled laughter and he felt a pang of unhappiness. "You know why I'm laughing? It's so funny. I don't know your name."

He should have laughed with her but it wouldn't come out. "I don't know yours," he said.

"It's Lisa. Do you like that name?" The voice in his ear was unexpectedly intimate. No girl had ever asked him a question like that on the phone.

"Yes." His hand was sweating.

"Well?"

"What?"

"Well, what's your name? Or are you going to be mysterious? I think you're a very mysterious person."

"I'm not."

"Really, you are. I like it." The words tingled in his ear. He felt elated and foolish.

"My name's Ron, Ronald. But . . ."

"But what?"

"But people call me Sonny."

"Ronald Sunshine," she said. He thought he heard her giggling.

"So what are you doing?" he asked.

"Me? Oh nothing."

There was a long pause. "I guess you have a lot of things to do," he said to fill the silence.

"Oh sure, you'd be surprised at all the things I have to do. Listen, why don't you meet me somewhere?"

"Tonight?" He didn't believe it.

"Not too early. Can you meet me at nine?"

He said he could. He didn't know what to say about where. He remembered her words: that place, the River Park. Not there.

She told him, a place in the next town. He had never been there. He listened to her directions. She had it organized. He hung up, surprised.

The old man was in the kitchen when he got home. Sonny went straight to the bathroom to wash. When he came out there was a smell of burning fat. He went into the bedroom to change.

"You ready?" the old man asked, appearing in the doorway.

"Ready for what, Pop?"

The old man watched him putting on a

clean shirt. "To eat," he said.

"Not tonight. I'm going out."

"You're not eating first?"

"No," Sonny said evenly. He hoped he wouldn't have to spell it out. He'd made up his mind last night, a necessary change, long overdue, no more cold beans.

"You don't want to eat," the old man said. His shoulders drooped.

Sonny, intent on getting dressed, was hardly aware of the old man's shuffling offer or of the sizzling sound from the kitchen. He was strung out, thinking of Lisa. Do you like that name? He passed by the kitchen on the way out.

He saw the old man lifting the frying pan off the stove. Four hamburgers in the pan. "Hey Pop," he said, "Listen, I'm sorry . . ." but his father was already dumping the pan into the sink.

"Go on, go out," the old man said and turned his back.

He waited until nine thirty-five before he let himself get suspicious. Up until then, he had accepted every excuse that came to mind. At a quarter to ten he was seriously thinking of leaving. The place was just beginning to fill. He nursed his beer, imagining that everyone knew he had been played for a sucker. When he was ready to give up, she came in.

"I'm sorry." Eyes bright, cheeks flushed. "I couldn't get a ride; had to take a taxi."

"I could have picked you up," he said but his sullenness was vanishing.

"Too complicated. I won't even go into it."

"I didn't think how you would get here," he said. "I guess I thought you'd drive."

Her smile was dazzling. She laughed at him. "Silly. How could we be together in separate cars." Click. Click.

It was an expensive place. He fingered the bills in his pocket. He bought her a drink and they just looked at each other. "The band

comes on at eleven," she said, looking towards the dance floor where musicians were setting up. When they started to play the music was deafening. She wanted to dance. They couldn't talk anyway. He was surprised to feel relieved. He didn't know what to talk to her about. She waved to a few people but somehow steered him into corners away from those she seemed to know.

"Let's get out of here," he said suddenly.

"Okay." That secretive smile again.

In the car she lit a cigarette. "Oh," she said, "I'm really glad you waited."

"I was going to leave."

"I felt terrible. I thought I'd lose you forever. Ronald Sunshine. I wouldn't know how to find you."

"I thought you weren't coming."

"But you knew I would."

He kissed her. She responded but didn't let it last long. "I want to talk to you Ronald. I want to know all about you."

"There's nothing to know."

"There is!" But he didn't have to talk. She did. She talked about things he never heard before. Art galleries, dinner parties, painting pictures.

"I want to paint. My parents want me to go to art school, but I want to go off and just do it. You know, I want to live it and feel it and let it come out through my fingers." The blackly painted nails danced on his arm.

"The kind of pictures in museums, is that what you paint?"

"Wonderful," she said, and laughed.

"Can we go someplace?" He wanted to go where it was dark and private.

"Ronald, seriously, do you think you need a degree to be a real painter?"

"I know a place," he said, starting the engine.

"The days of expatriates, in Paris," she was saying, "that's when I should have lived."

He took her to the back of the junkyard. Dark and undisturbed.

"A landscape of sculpture," she said.

He kissed her and she let it go on this time. She felt warm, very soft. Her scent was in his head. His hands moved over her body.

"Ronald, listen, what time is it?"

He came back slowly, as if out of a dream.

"I have to go home."

He brought her back to the wide tree-lined street. She said, "I'll see you again? Call me?"

"Yes." The sweet sadness was painful now. He wondered why he accepted it.

It was always late when they met. He picked her up after things. She had a lot of things to do. She didn't want him to come to the house. If she was somewhere else, she met him out front. He took her to the junkyard.

"We're not kids," he told her. "We can't go on necking like kids."

"Not in a car, Ronald. Let's not spoil something beautiful."

"Think of a place to go."

"You think. Can't we go to your house?"

"I told you, my father is there." He didn't tell her his father was just across the junkyard. He told her his father was an invalid.

He never had trouble with girls before. He never saw them steadily. He liked them for a while and then he stopped liking them. Love had not occurred to him. He wondered if he loved Lisa. Did you love someone you didn't understand? She had put a spell on him. The junkyard was their world.

He decided to take her to a party, wanting to show her off. There would be rooms where the party was held, rooms to which they could go after a while. Privacy and locked doors.

It was like an anniversary, two weeks and one day from the night they first met. He thought she was having a good time. She danced and laughed and talked. And yet she seemed to be watching them all from a pri-

vate place of her own. Her laughter was too shrill. He saw her turn away from someone, her face clouded, upset. The dark heavy lashes went click click. Her eyes, for a moment, were far away.

They were standing in a hall, outside the room filled with music and people. He pulled her close, his lips against her ear. He was going to whisper, "Let's go upstairs."

She pulled back abruptly. "Ron, get me out of here!"

He was too bewildered to react.

"I've had enough of this."

"Enough of what?"

"This whole thing. These people. They don't know who I am. I don't have to put with it."

> "In your world," she tried
> to explain, "I
> have no identity."

He felt cold. "Put up with what?"

"Oh don't be so stupid!" She was going toward the door.

"Lisa!" She was already outside.

"It's no good," she said in the car. "It won't work." Her eyes glistened with tears that were not for him. "I want to go home."

Her house was blazing with light. Every window glittered. The street was lined with expensive cars. As he watched, a couple emerged from one of them, the man in a tuxedo, the woman in a long dress.

"They're having a party," she said. "I was supposed to be here."

He had not been asked to her party. She had not enjoyed his.

"In your world," she tried to explain, "I have no identity."

"I don't get you," he said, aware he was sounding like his father. He felt disgusted, and tired.

"The sweetest roller on the green."

"Don't," he said. The quicksilver was slipping through his hands; it had never been his. Now he knew he didn't want it.

"I don't know," she was saying. "Maybe we can see each other . . . sometimes."

"No. I have things to do." Things were different, there had been a change. But he still had more changing to take care of.

She looked at him. Doll's eyes. Click. Click. Goodbye.

He walked into the room where his father slept in front of the television set. The picture on the screen was rolling crazily. The old man snored. On the floor were the beer cans. On his lap, an opened can of beans.

"Pop," he said. "Pop." Gently waking him. "Time to go to bed."

He went to his own room and stood in the dark, looking out the window at the junkyard. He thought of the suitcases covered with dust under his bed. His eyes blinked click shut and click open. He was already leaving, not knowing where he was going, his mind too busy wondering who he was.

First Love

Author's Comments

This story is a combination of personal experience and a bit of fieldwork.

A friend came to visit from England and wanted to see an American pub. I explained that bars were nothing like pubs, but he didn't believe me. We commenced a statewide search for a pub and unearthed an out-of-the-way little spot very much like the River Park in this story.

When my friend left (disillusioned with American bars) I began thinking about differences between people.

One day soon after, I passed an enormous junkyard and thought how much the junked and burned-out chassis—so many of them old Volkswagen Bugs—looked like abandoned turtle shells.

Sometime later, I went to a party at which I felt like a complete alien. For some reason, it made me angry.

All of this found its way into the story, in various disguises. The plot itself, however, is pure fiction and is not based on any real-life people or situations.

—Patricia Windsor

Paul Newman's House

by Lou Fisher

O'Toole's was empty except for a woman drinking vodka at the bar. Emil took first a deep breath, then the seat next to her. He never would have been in a place like this, let alone daring to move in close, but what good had come from prowling the aisles at Barnes & Noble, from tending the machines at the Laundromat, or even from mingling with the shoppers at the mall after work. There seemed only this left to pursue, the neighborhood bar in his sad new neighborhood.

"I'm Emil," he said.

Her laugh rattled the still air. "C'mon now. What kind of name is Emil?"

"Good enough for my grandfather," he told her.

"Yeah, I suppose." The woman shifted toward him, crossing her legs on the bar stool, forcing the skirt high above one knee. Though the knee caught Emil's attention, he didn't want to dwell on it. So quickly up from there and past the sweater of small breasts he paused at a deep red mark on the bridge of the woman's nose and then came to the mess of brown hair, all heavy and dingy, like a mop wrung out of basement water. She said, "Your grandfather, he wasn't born here."

"Well, no," Emil admitted in a whisper.

He was glad when his scotch arrived. Such jerky kid stuff, being teased about a name—though, yes, it had gone on in medical school too. Now that he thought about it, how about his boss at the clinic, that pinch-nosed crumb, always calling him Emil instead of Doctor. And every time he was the least bit late with Susan's check, she would wail his name over the phone and make it sound like a bird dying.

Why was all that?

Meanwhile, the woman had wet her lips with vodka. In that more focused way she said, "People ought to change their names when they come to America, don't you think?" Then she turned aside, set down the glass, ran her forefinger around and around the rim. Her face, in profile, seemed thinner, the corner of her mouth etched with spidery lines that brought her closer to his age. Her chin was pointy, but not too pointy, and it gave her a determined look. "I'm clear," she added, still toying with the glass.

"Clear about what?" he wanted to know.

"Listen," she said. "*Claire*—not clear." She studied him, a sideways glance. And though a spark seemed to come to her expression, it wasn't enough to brighten the bar or even to compete with the dim Tiffany lamp above their heads. "Do you play tennis?"

"Well, I'd like to, probably." He felt a rush

Author Bio

Lou Fisher lives with his wife in downstate New York where he stays out of bars but enjoys writing, playing tennis, learning to play the piano, and walking the countryside. One of his stories received the *New Letters* Literary Award for Fiction. Others have appeared in a wide range of journals and magazines, and have been selected for several anthologies. His earlier genre novels were published by Dell and Warner.

of breath at the thought of it. To be darting around. Swinging at a ball. With someone. "You do, Claire? You're good at tennis?"

"Helps that I'm left-handed," she said, and Emil saw now that her drink stood next to his, with that closer hand formed into an imaginary grip on a racquet. "Lefties hit the ball with a different spin and it scoots the opposite way," she explained. "You should see." But even as he attempted to picture a ball's bounce, the tint of excitement drained from Claire's face and her chin became an arrowhead aimed at his throat. "You don't play."

"No, not really," he said.

Then he caught her looking at his chest, at the loose silver watch on his wrist, and he knew she'd not give him credit for any sport, and she was right. Last year, though, after Susan left, he took swimming lessons. Now

He hadn't yet told her that he was a podiatrist.

he could float. He could also paddle across the YMCA pool the short ways, in the shallow end, if he pushed off hard with his legs.

He tried to sit up stronger and straighter, but on the stool the tendency was to lean in, for balance. Made him feel even shorter than he was. Through a long, obvious silence he thought of leaving the bar. Mumbling goodnight. Just going.

But wait . . . that would be giving up, yet again, maybe from then on, maybe forever. During his second shave of the day, and right into his own doubtful eyes, Emil had promised himself a full try.

"So where do you work?" he asked the woman.

"I'm sorry," Claire replied in a mumble. "What?"

"I asked you where you worked."

There was again no answer. Instead she

peered over her right shoulder as two gray-haired men whispered by and settled, or huddled, further down the bar, almost to the very end. The lanky bartender stood there too, just beyond them, wearing unframed half-glasses and reading a tabloid. The tables were still empty.

"God," she said finally, coming all the way around to refocus on Emil.

"That bad?"

Her stare went blank.

"Your job," he said.

"Oh, that. Well, sure it's bad. Hey, what job isn't? Listen, every day I take a million shitty numbers and type them into the computer." Claire showed him how, pianoing her fingertips across the bar. Her nails were cut short but slapped with thick red polish. "By afternoon the screen gets to my head," she continued. "Glows in through my eyes, so awful and deep . . . even aspirin doesn't help." She gave him another sample of that rattling laugh. "Hey, what does the company care? They've got so many bookkeepers."

"Quit," Emil said.

"Quit my job?"

"Yes. Right." He hadn't yet told her that he was a podiatrist. In a clinic at the shopping mall. Lower level. He was never sure why people found that so secretly amusing, what they snickered at—was it the feet or the mall? Maybe if his patients would stop taking off their socks in the middle of the glass-walled reception room. Ought to be a sign posted there, he thought. At any rate, fungus toes, dry cracked heels, bunions, corns, deep-rooted regenerative warts . . . distasteful, if anything. How had he ever fallen in love with Susan after smelling her feet? Well, the camphor liniment, that had helped. "You should just quit," he advised the woman at the bar, "and find something you like better."

"As easy as that?"

"Why not? You do it, and it's done."

"Oh, yeah, sure, don't I wish." Claire

licked her lips, spit air, and arranged herself more evenly on the bar stool. So, okay, he thought, the chin was pointy. But aside from that he saw her somewhat better now. And what's more, he found that across the short reachable distance she was returning his look, brushing a few strands of hair from in front of her eyes.

"Would you like another drink?" he asked.

"No."

"But yours is almost gone."

"Forget it." Claire sighed and lowered her eyes.

"Well, I just thought—"

"Look, Emil," she said metallically. "You don't try to buy me drinks and I won't try to keep you here. Is that a fair deal?"

He nodded; but lately nothing seemed fair.

Susan, for example, wanted a new roof on the house she'd taken from him, and much more money by the month. She was considering a return to court. She thought a podiatrist was like a heart surgeon, even though she knew quite well the meager annoying salary at the clinic. She assumed he'd had a raise.

Dammit, he should have had a raise.

His hand felt clammy where it rested on the bar. He leaned over and blew on the bartop, and afterward moved his glass more toward Claire's. Should have picked a better place. With music. With little wooden bowls of pretzels or those mosaic boards under wedges of pink and white cheese. Straightening, he caught himself in a deep and heartfelt sigh. He was here, and he'd better do something about it because how many more nights alone could he endure? Even if it didn't last with Claire, to have someone to talk to, someone to care about . . .

"I install security alarms," he said finally.

"Yeah?" said Claire.

"You know, security alarms."

"Oh."

"Sure. We did Paul Newman's house."

She was looking past his head. Her eyes were resting on something there, maybe the door to the ladies' room. Maybe so. They'd been sitting for almost an hour. Anyway, he couldn't tell if she'd heard.

"Paul Newman's house," he said again.

Now Claire looked at him, directly, and finished her drink. "Big place?"

"Sure. You can imagine."

"Around here?"

"Yes." He nodded a couple of times, emphatically, as if that would make it true. And true it might be. Why not? He was even beginning to feel strength in his jaw, like an iron rod bent exactly to fit. "Yes," he went on, thus boosted, "but out in the country."

His boss didn't like him to roam the mall . . .

She returned a faint smile for only a second before her mouth recovered its familiar thin straight line. Then, as he had expected, she slid from the bar stool and went off to the bathroom.

Waiting, he stared at his fingers.

Though the medical fees in the shopping mall were relatively cheap and often discounted, this afternoon the clinic had been no busier than the bar. And just as quiet. Actually, he couldn't recall any day he'd been burdened with patients; even Susan, still at his expense, rarely showed up. The more he worked there, the more he came to believe that people with foot problems preferred to be treated at fancy professional locations, like that stone-front building over by the lake. So Emil, stuck alone in his cubicle, pegged away at the daily crossword puzzle in between appointments. His boss didn't like him to roam the mall, especially not in the laundered white jacket with the clinic's name on the pocket; and the boss's niece, who was the receptionist, never offered to bring Emil anything, though he'd seen other doctors get coffee, M&Ms, lottery tickets, whatever they wanted. And besides all that, what even now made Emil's jaw go slack and flooded his mouth with saliva, was that someone—he'd like to know who—kept putting his time card way high in the rack.

"That was fast," he said when Claire returned.

She shrugged and settled on the stool. With her left hand she wiggled the last remaining ice cube, or what was left of it, around the bottom of the glass. After several such swirls, she stopped and gripped the glass with both hands. "Why doesn't he live in California?" she asked, head still down.

"Who?"

"Paul Newman," she said.

Emil gulped in silence until she finally turned and met his eyes. Then he just said, "I don't know," and the bar seemed to close in on him.

"Well, it's probably the crime," Claire observed, frowning. "Out there those people keep coming across the border in the middle of the night. Right through the barbed wire, over the desert . . . and with names a million times odder than Emil." She glanced at her empty, lipsticked glass. "So what time is it?"

"When?" he said.

"Now."

"Oh, must be close to eleven." By tilting his watch, Emil managed to bounce a little light off its face. "Look at that, Claire," he said, himself surprised. "It's five after."

"Five after eleven?"

"Yes."

"Well," she said, "maybe one more."

Emil didn't know what to make of it.

Still, he signaled the bartender and ordered himself another scotch, a vodka for Claire, and when the drinks arrived he paid

for them with the folded ten-dollar bill he had set aside for tomorrow's breakfast and lunch. He lifted his glass, rich in aroma, bountifully layered with ice, ambered full to the rim. Left-handed, Claire lifted hers too—the resulting collision threw a wave of scotch onto the padded front edge of the bar. A second later the drippings hit his lap. He tried to think of something to say, and the confession snuck out of him while he was half focused on the sudden dampness of his pants.

"I'm really a podiatrist."

Claire tilted her head.

"I take care of people's feet," he explained. "But you're a tennis player, you've got good feet."

"Oh, no I don't. There are times . . ." What started as a little squint of pain turned into a grimace that made her let go of the glass to clench a fist, an anguished fist that went tap-tap-tap on a dry area of the bar. "God, Emil, what I go through."

Gently he reached over and stilled that hand, uncurled her red-polished fingers one by one, and when he found them each to be smoother, softer than he anticipated, he could only hope that her toes would feel the same. "I can help you," he said.

Mississippi Review

Author's Comments

Initially my writing career was wrapped up in genres like mystery and science fiction, until I ran out of incentive and ideas. That's when I found new excitement in writing contemporary stories, both mainstream and literary.

This story began in my usual way, by putting an interesting character with a desperate need in a difficult situation. I discovered the woman when he did, as well as the images and interactions that evolved. I discovered a backstory too, in which his low self-esteem let me have fun with podiatry and a suddenly imagined career. Still, I had trouble putting it all together for a satisfying finish. I went back to the draft time and again, over the space of several months, rewriting those last few pages until the ending showed up.

The story didn't win the annual contest at *Mississippi Review*, but the editor liked it enough to include it in the Prize Issue. Later, with an eye out for reprint possibilities, I was able to place it in an anthology called *Bar Stories*.

Advice to writers: You won't make effective changes by sitting and thinking about them. Get the draft back up on the screen and start typing, changing, playing, letting it happen.

—Lou Fisher

Wants

by Grace Paley

I saw my ex-husband in the street. I was sitting on the steps of the new library.

Hello, my life, I said. We had once been married for twenty-seven years, so I felt justified.

He said, What? What life? No life of mine.

I said, O.K. I don't argue when there's real disagreement. I got up and went into the library to see how much I owed them.

The librarian said $32 even and you've owed it for eighteen years. I didn't deny anything. Because I don't understand how time passes. I have had those books. I have often thought of them. The library is only two blocks away.

My ex-husband followed me to the Books Returned desk. He interrupted the librarian, who had more to tell. In many ways, he said, as I look back, I attribute the dissolution of our marriage to the fact that you never invited the Bertrams to dinner.

That's possible, I said. But really, if you remember: first, my father was sick that Friday, then the children were born, then I had those Tuesday-night meetings, then the war began. Then we didn't seem to know them

any more. But you're right. I should have had them to dinner.

I gave the librarian a check for $32. Immediately she trusted me, put my past behind her, wiped the record clean, which is just what most other municipal and/or state bureaucracies will *not* do.

I checked out the two Edith Wharton books I had just returned because I'd read them so long ago and they are more apropos now then ever. They were *The House of Mirth* and *The Children*, which is about how life in the United States in New York changed in twenty-seven years fifty years ago.

I wanted a sailboat, he said. But you didn't want anything.

A nice thing I do remember is breakfast, my ex-husband said. I was surprised. All we ever had was coffee. Then I remembered there was a hole in the back of the kitchen closet which opened into the apartment next door. There, they always ate sugar-cured smoked bacon. It gave us a very grand feeling about breakfast, but we never got stuffed and sluggish.

That was when we were poor, I said.

When were we ever rich? he asked.

Oh, as time went on, as our responsibilities increased, we didn't go in need. You took adequate financial care, I reminded him. The children went to camp four weeks a year and in decent ponchos with sleeping bags and boots, just like everyone else. They looked

Author Bio

Award-winning author Grace Paley began her writing life as a poet. Her short stories have been hailed for their distinctive voice, which she said came in part from listening to the stories of her Russian emigrant parents.

very nice. Our place was warm in winter, and we had nice red pillows and things.

I wanted a sailboat, he said. But you didn't want anything.

Don't be bitter, I said. It's never too late.

No, he said with a great deal of bitterness. I may get a sailboat. As a matter of fact I have money down on an eighteen-foot two-rigger. I'm doing well this year and can look forward to better. But as for you, it's too late. You'll always want nothing.

He had a habit throughout the twenty-seven years of making a narrow remark which, like a plumber's snake, could work its way through the ear down the throat, halfway to my heart. He would then disappear, leaving me choking with equipment. What I mean is, I sat down on the library steps and he went away.

I had promised my children to end the war before they grew up.

I looked through *The House of Mirth*, but lost interest. I felt extremely accused. Now, it's true, I'm short of requests and absolute requirements. But I do want *something*.

I want, for instance, to be a different person. I want to be the woman who brings these two books back in two weeks. I want to be the effective citizen who changes the school system and addresses the Board of Estimate on the troubles of this dear urban center.

I *had* promised my children to end the war before they grew up.

I wanted to have been married forever to one person, my ex-husband or my present one. Either has enough character for a whole life, which as it turns out is really not such a long time. You couldn't exhaust either man's qualities or get under the rock of his reasons in one short life.

Just this morning I looked out the window to watch the street for a while and saw that the little sycamores the city had dreamily planted a couple of years before the kids were born had come that day to the prime of their lives.

Well! I decided to bring those two books back to the library. Which proves that when a person or an event comes along to jolt or appraise me I *can* take some appropriate action, although I am better known for my hospitable remarks.

Enormous Changes at the Last Minute

Mrs. Comfrey Wins

by Patricia Windsor

An old thing, they called her. Well, if they didn't actually say it aloud, they thought it. Mrs. Comfrey knew.

She hurried down the street to where Mr. Dove was waiting. She felt a little frazzled as she went through the door of the pub. Had to stop to catch her breath and pat her hair. Escape was exhilarating, but it could wear you out. Mrs. Comfrey put herself in order.

There he was. Prompt as always. Still a handsome man. Elwyn Dove. Her lover.

They wouldn't understand such a thing, of course. They thought she was too prim and proper to know about such things. Mrs. Comfrey laughed. If she was so ignorant how did she manage to bring four children into the world, she'd like to know? It would be interesting to ask them that question. Except it would embarrass them. Her children were easily embarrassed by her questions, she'd noticed. Middle-aged children, so very prim and proper themselves. "Hello, my dear," said Mr. Dove. He always said it. He gave her a kiss on the cheek. Her drink was waiting.

"Cheers," said Mr. Dove. Mrs. Comfrey smiled and raised her glass.

It was Annabel, she told him. Annabel was the worst. Always had been, even as a child. Led all the others up to terrible tricks although she was youngest. Derek was more reasonable, but he would follow Annabel's lead. Poor Margaret wouldn't open her mouth, she'd do whatever Annabel said. And Basil might just as well be forgotten for all the help he could give, off in some jungle or other, saving animals. Might do him some good to come home to save his own mother.

"I'm an endangered species," said Mrs. Comfrey. Mr. Dove liked that. They laughed together.

"Up the lot of them!" he said. Mrs. Comfrey drank to that.

It was late when she crept home. The light was on in the sitting room, which was always a bad sign. Annabel would be waiting up to scold her.

"Mother!" Annabel said, just as soon as Mrs. Comfrey was in the door. "Mother, where were you this time?"

Mrs. Comfrey had sucked a mint on the way. "Oh, just out," she said.

"You simply can't do this," said Annabel.

"Can't see why not," said Mrs. Comfrey. She scampered up the stairs. Annabel followed, more slowly. She lumbered.

"A diet would help," advised Mrs. Comfrey.

Annabel didn't answer; she banged the door of her room and Mrs. Comfrey could hear the rumble of voices inside. Annabel's husband was grumbling. They often grumbled together, like two bears.

Mrs. Comfrey went to her bedroom door and saw that the lock had been forced again.

Author Bio

Patricia Windsor has taught writing at the university level and is the author of more than 17 novels. Several of her novels have won awards, among them *The Summer Before*, *The Sandman's Eyes*, *The Christmas Killer*, and *Nightwood*.

For a moment, a sad tiredness threatened, then it was gone. She'd have it repaired, as she had in the past. They couldn't help but worry when she didn't answer their frantic knocks. Always expecting her to be lying dead inside. But none of it would be necessary if they allowed her to do the things she pleased. She wouldn't have to think of ways to escape then.

Mrs. Comfrey's room was exactly the way she liked it. That's why she kept it locked. Otherwise they came in, rearranging and telling her what to throw in the dustbin. "All this stuff!" Annabel would lament.

"It's mine," Mrs. Comfrey would reply. Annabel would go off, muttering about dependency. "Clinging to all that stuff," she'd tell her husband and they'd have a good grumble about it.

Mrs. Comfrey slipped between her cool sheets and thought of Mr. Dove. She thought of his strong brown arms and funny pink toes. She thought of the afternoons, when

Of all her children, Annabel had been the naughtiest child.

they drew the blinds and sometimes dozed through tea. Mr. Dove, thought Mrs. Comfrey, I suppose I shall have to give in at last.

In the morning, the atmosphere was fierce. Annabel threw eggs at the children. Mrs. Comfrey ducked her head and quietly munched her seven-grain cereal. She and Mr. Dove always purchased it in bulk at the health food shop. Her grandson Edward caught the egg. He winked. Mrs. Comfrey winked back. Annabel roared something unintelligible. Mrs. Comfrey and Edward smothered their laughs and managed to swallow without choking.

There was no time for Mr. Dove that afternoon.

"Come along, Mother," Annabel announced. "We're going out."

"Out?" said Mrs. Comfrey, caught off guard. But she quickly looked alert. Vagueness was always construed as a sign of senility.

"I did tell you," Annabel was saying. "I've made an appointment to see that place."

"Send my regrets, won't you dear?"

Mrs. Comfrey had hoped it would not come up quite so soon, there was so much to do. Oh well, she thought, Mr. Dove would be glad.

They looked all around the place. Then they looked around again.

A sitting parade, thought Mrs. Comfrey, old people lined up in chairs. She wondered if they ever managed to escape.

"Well?" asked Annabel, in the car.

"Well what?" asked Mrs. Comfrey.

"Do you like it? Isn't it nice?"

"I'm not quite sure," said Mrs. Comfrey, busy calculating how many pieces of luggage she owned. She might borrow that large bag of Edward's. He wouldn't mind.

The car screeched around a bend. "I don't know what I'm going to do with you!" Annabel said.

Some words I used myself, Mrs. Comfrey thought, not long ago. Of all her children, Annabel had been the naughtiest child.

There was a lot of talking on the telephone. Mrs. Comfrey had to wait. Edward gave her the signal when it was all clear. Then she slipped down the stairs and dialed Mr. Dove's number. As she knew he would be, Mr. Dove was glad. In fact, he told her he was rushing out that very moment to buy things for a celebration feast.

"My darling dear," Mr. Dove said with

affection, at which Mrs. Comfrey felt her self go quite warm inside.

Later on, Annabel broke the news. "We've all decided," she said. "Margaret agrees and so does Derek."

"Derek has always been reasonable," said Mrs. Comfrey.

"I knew you would understand," Annabel said.

"I'm all ready." Mrs. Comfrey came down with the last of her cases. She enjoyed that moment, watching her daughter's changing expression. The mouth hung open a bit too long. It was distasteful peering into Annabel's throat.

"But," Annabel managed to say. "You can't go right this very moment. I haven't made arrangements yet."

"Not necessary," said Mrs. Comfrey. "My friend is coming to pick me up."

A supercilious look appeared on Annabel's face. "You don't understand do you?" she said, as if talking to a child. "They won't take you, not just like that."

"Pity," said Mrs. Comfrey. "But never mind. I'm not going there anyway."

Annabel made a peculiar sound, like a snort. But Mrs. Comfrey smiled. This last escape must be done with aplomb.

"Send my regrets, won't you, dear?"

Outside, Mr. Dove had arrived in a taxi. Mrs. Comfrey went to the door.

"Mother!" Annabel wailed. "Where are you going?"

"To get married," said Mrs. Comfrey. Mr. Dove took her by the hand.

Family Circle UK

Author's Comments

I got the idea for writing "Mrs. Comfrey Wins" after working for the British Council of Social Services in London. I had been reading a lot of novels that focused on older people victimized by their children; I don't know why—they were just the ones I chose at the local library in Golders Green.

Finally, I felt all of this personally. Whenever I hear someone say, "Oh Mom/Dad would be better off in a home," I think of myself. I never want to be shipped off to a home no matter how eccentric I become.

That's just the point—eccentricity. Sometimes one's ordinary behavior suddenly seems eccentric to the "children," who would rather Mom retired gracefully into a world of inactivity.

I created Mrs. Comfrey—the kind of person I want to be at her age. (What am I talking about? I'm just about her age now, and I'm lucky that my children are used to my "behavior.")

—Patricia Windsor

Trucks

by Amy Bechtel

Fourteen hundred and seventy-six, Joanna thought automatically, watching frozen peas bounce across the kitchen floor. Some of them disappeared under the stove, where they would be virtually impossible to retrieve. Joanna sighed, holding the empty pea bag in her hands. It really wasn't fair for it to split when all she'd done was lift it out of the freezer.

Joanna's six-year-old son Ryan had been watching the peas fall too. "Ryan?" she said hopefully. "How many?"

Ryan looked bewildered. He gazed across the kitchen floor, as overwhelmed as if she'd asked him to memorize the dictionary.

"Never mind, sweetie," Joanna said sadly. Ryan picked up his toy truck and hurried out of range of the peas, and ten-year-old Lauren skipped into the kitchen.

"Ha, ha!" Lauren said. "No peas tonight! No peas for dinner." She scanned the floor quickly and said, "Fourteen hundred and fifty-nine." She was seventeen short, of course, having missed seeing the peas that had rolled under the stove. Joanna studied her face carefully. Eyes crinkled, thirty-seven percent; right side of mouth up seven degrees, left side up eight degrees, wrinkles on the lateral side of each eye. Happy, laughing.

"Why don't you help me pick these up, Lauren?" Joanna said, watching ruefully as the parameters of Lauren's face changed dramatically. A moment of calculation later, Joanna deduced that her daughter was frowning.

"I didn't spill them," Lauren said.

"No, you didn't, but don't you think it would be nice if you helped me anyway?"

A pause, while Lauren studied Joanna's face, obviously trying to decide if this was an order or not. But Lauren wasn't that far along in school yet, and she still had trouble calculating even the most obvious expressions. She lifted her shoulders (sixteen percent left, twelve percent right), raised her eyebrows, and started picking up peas. Resignation, Joanna calculated. But at least Lauren was helping with the peas.

When they'd gathered eight hundred and ninety-two of them, Lauren said, "Mom? Why does Ryan have to go to that special class?"

Joanna closed her eyes. Her own little boy was in special education, completely unable to manage a normal first-grade class. It was a hard thing to bear. She said, "Because he doesn't learn as fast as you do, honey."

"The other kids call him names. They say he's stupid. They say I'm stupid too, because I'm his sister."

"Well, those other kids are just being mean, aren't they? Besides that, they're wrong. You're a very smart girl. And Ryan isn't stupid. He's just slow."

Author Bio

Amy Bechtel began selling her short fiction after participating in a Clarion Writer's Workshop in Michigan. She is a regular contributor to *Analog* magazine, and has twice won the *Analog* reader's award for best short story. In addition to writing, she runs a veterinary clinic in New Mexico.

"Are you sure I'm smart?" Lauren shoveled her last handful of peas into the trash, her expression changing again. Joanna quickly evaluated the new movements and angles of her face. Anxiety.

"Yes, I'm sure."

"Fifth grade is hard, though. We already have lots of homework, and it's only the first week. Can you help me with it?"

"Of course, honey. As soon as I get dinner on."

Lauren's face changed. A smile. "Dinner with no peas!"

Half an hour later Joanna was at the kitchen table by Lauren's side, looking over her homework. Lauren had sailed through her physics and calculus, but she was struggling with her expressions assignment. This workpaper was all faces, some of the expressions much more subtle than Joanna would have expected to find assigned to fifth graders. Lauren was doing well with the calculations, but kept getting lost when it came to the final analysis.

"All right," Joanna said. "Now you have the numbers for the eyebrows, the eyes, and the mouth. What does it all add up to?"

"Um." Lauren opened her textbook, looking hopelessly at the columns of numbers. "I don't know. Why is it so hard?"

"Because you have to memorize what expression goes with what range of numbers, and there's a lot of them to learn. You're doing fine, Lauren. Everybody has trouble with this part."

"Vroom," Ryan said. He rolled a toy truck across Lauren's homework, peered at the problem she was working on, and pointed at the face. "Scared," he said.

Joanna stared at him. The face was scared. How had he guessed?

"Don't be silly, Ryan," Lauren said. "This is fifth grade homework. It's way too hard for you."

Curiously Joanna turned the page and pointed at another face. "What's this one, Ryan?"

"Happy." He scanned the rest of the page, and his lips moved upward, smiling, reflecting the face he had just solved. He pointed to the next face, and the next, and the next. "Sad, angry, sleepy, sad, happy."

Joanna laughed. No one could calculate faces that quickly, certainly not poor little Ryan. But then she started to work on the faces, and she felt her own face changing as she solved each one. Sad. Angry. Sleepy. Sad. Happy. Ryan had correctly named every one.

What was going on in her little boy's mind?

Ryan pointed at her, said, "Surprised," and picked up his toy truck again.

"Ryan, you're bothering me. Go somewhere else and play," Lauren said. "Mom, I can't find it in the book. Mom? I need help."

But Joanna sat very still for a moment longer, her mind racing, unable to believe what she had just seen. No one could do what Ryan had just done, no one but an utter genius. But Ryan couldn't even count, and the school had put him into special education classes. Deep in her heart she didn't believe he belonged there, but even so they were right that he would never be able to manage a normal class. First grade meant elementary algebra and geometry, and even at recess the other kids would be playing with square roots and primes.

But he'd figured out every single face correctly. In a flash, as if he hadn't had to calculate at all. What was going on in her little boy's mind?

That night in bed, Joanna murmured the news to her husband David.

"He did what?" David said.

"He did all of Lauren's expressions

homework. In seconds. He knew what every face meant."

There was a silence while David shifted in bed and adjusted his pillow. "Joanna, honey," he said, "I know you're really upset about Ryan going into special education, but—"

"Yes, I am, but that doesn't have anything to do with this."

David sighed. "Oh, Joanna. He must have been guessing."

"But he couldn't have been. If he was guessing, he wouldn't have been right every time."

David shook his head. "It's impossible, honey," he said gently, and turned over.

"It is not," Joanna whispered, but David was already asleep. Joanna turned away from him, and lay awake for a long time in the dark.

When Joanna picked up the children at school the next day, Lauren's voice was high and strident from the back seat. Excitement, Joanna decided.

"We have to write a paper," Lauren said, "about what we're going to be when we grow up. I'm going to be a spaceship computer, and navigate all the way to Mars."

Joanna felt her face move into a smile. "That's a good ambition, Lauren."

> *Ryan was a genius with expression, not only of faces, but of voices and body positions as well.*

"I know. What about you, Ryan? What do you want to be when you grow up?"

Silence from the back seat. Joanna pulled out into traffic, headed for the grocery store.

"Come on, Ryan," Lauren said. "You must want to be something when you grow up."

"I'm not going to be anything," Ryan muttered. "I'm too stupid."

Moisture filled Joanna's eyes, and they stung. Ryan had never said anything like that before he'd started school. She rubbed her eyes as she drove past a spindly tree that had recently been planted in the median. It only had seven hundred and eighty-three leaves left, and it looked wilted; it probably wasn't going to survive there.

"You are not either stupid," Lauren said. "You're just slow. And you have to be something when you grow up. Why don't you be a spaceship computer, like me?"

"No," Ryan said. "I can't count."

What would Ryan do when he grew up? What happened to special-needs children when they became special-needs adults? Even if she wasn't imagining it, even if he *was* a genius with faces, what good would that do him in the long run?

At the grocery store she had an inspiration. "Ryan," she said. "That man over there by the bananas. What's his expression?"

"I know, I know," Ryan said. "Bored."

"And how about that woman by the bread?"

"That one, in the yellow pants? She's angry."

After several more rounds she was certain of it. Ryan was a genius with expression, not only of faces, but of voices and body positions as well. Somehow he took in the whole person at a glance, and knew the answer without making a single calculation. He could instantly see expressions as easily as a normal person could instantly count the number of peas falling from a split bag.

Joanna was in a daze when she reached the checkout counter, and she agreed without thinking when Lauren and Ryan asked for a candy bar each. The teenage checkout clerk chewed gum as she tallied Joanna's purchases.

". . . two ninety-eight, four ninety-nine, eleven ninety-nine, one twenty-five, one thirty-five, discount two twenty-three, tax six seventy-six, total ninety-eight thirty-two," the checker said all in one breath, and cracked her gum.

Joanna frowned, pulling out her checkbook. The teenager's brows drew together: confusion.

"What's that expression, ma'am?" the teenager asked. "It's one of the bad ones, isn't it?"

"It's disapproval," Joanna said. "It's rude to crack your gum when you're taking care of customers. I'm surprised your manager lets you chew gum at all."

"Oh." The clerk lifted her shoulders. "I forgot I had the gum. And I have, like, trouble reading expressions."

"Maybe you should work a bit harder in school," Joanna suggested.

"I don't like school," the clerk said, her eyes lowered, her mouth turned down. "I'm slow, see."

"Oh," Joanna said, suddenly and acutely reminded of Ryan. "I'm very sorry to hear that."

She pulled up to the bank next, to make a deposit. There were twenty-nine people waiting in the lobby and the lines were long, but the tellers were generally quick. Lauren was still trying to interest Ryan in something to do when he grew up.

"A bank teller," she suggested, pointing to the counter. "A security guard. Look, see? You could have a gun."

"Maybe," Ryan said, looking at the security guard, and Joanna thought she could analyze a trace of interest in his voice. More people joined the lines. Two men moved to stand behind Joanna, shifting from foot to foot. Their expressions were odd; she couldn't quite figure them out. Nervous, but there was something else as well. "Ryan," she whispered, hoping he remembered the game from the grocery store.

Ryan looked at the two men and his own face changed. His eyes widened, his mouth opened; twenty-nine percent, twenty-seven.

Frightened. "Let's go home, Mom," he said.

"In a little bit, Ryan. See? We're almost to the counter."

"I want to go home now."

"Ryan—"

Ryan pulled away from her, made a wide circle around the two men, and headed for the door. "Ryan! You come back here right now!" She ran after the little boy, with Lauren at her heels, and caught up with him at the door.

"Please, Mom, let's go. Those men are scary. Let's go. Please."

She almost dragged him back into line, to teach him a lesson about running off. But he had looked at the men's faces, and he could read people at a glance, and he was more frightened than she had ever seen him. She took his hand and went out the door, and Lauren followed them.

If only he could see the numbers, like everyone else did.

"Mom, what are we doing?" Lauren asked. "We never got up to the teller. Mom?"

"I've changed my mind," Joanna said. "We're going to go home now."

Joanna watched the news that night after the children were in bed. The top story was about an armed robbery at the local bank, in which customers had been terrorized and two men had escaped with a large amount of cash. Joanna recognized them in the blurry picture from the security camera.

She decided not to say anything to David. He wouldn't believe her, and he would learn the truth soon enough just by being around Ryan. What should she do, now, with her little boy? Suddenly she saw all sorts of futures for him. He could be an interpreter for those who could not read expressions well. He could be a security guard who could see potential problems coming. He could be anything, as long as it had to do with people and not numbers.

But if only he could learn something about numbers, oh, how that would help him in the world. If only he could *see* the numbers, like everyone else did. But he couldn't, no more than she could *see* a face. She had to break down expressions into parts, analyze each one, add them together. Was there some way to do that with numbers?

Joanna turned off the television and sighed. You could break numbers down into primes, of course. Most little kids loved doing that, but Ryan had always been bewildered by the game. Or you could break down a total into its parts, like a grocery sum divided into the amounts due for bread, milk, and bananas. But Ryan would never understand that either. He needed something simpler. What was simpler than a grocery sum?

Disconsolately Joanna got up and began to straighten the living room. Lauren had left her essay on the coffee table, and Ryan's toy trucks were scattered all over the carpet. Joanna put the essay by Lauren's backpack, and then went to get the trucks. She picked up one in each hand, then transferred both to one hand so she could pick up another one. Then she froze, staring down at her hand.

"Mom?" Ryan was standing in the door to the hall.

"What are you doing up, Ryan?"

"I forgot my trucks."

"Yes, you did." Joanna held up the two in her hand. "How many, Ryan?"

He stiffened. "I don't know. I can't count. I'm stupid."

And you're never going back to that school, Joanna thought, *if that's all you've learned there.* "You can't count the way other people do," she said, "but I'll bet you can learn another way."

"What other way?" he said warily.

One truck and one truck is two trucks. He could learn that, and he could learn each tiny progression thereafter; she was sure of it. It

was going to be terribly awkward, terribly slow; it would take years for Ryan to learn numbers in this strange and convoluted manner, and he would still never be able to see numbers the way a normal person could.

But it had taken Joanna years to learn expressions, hadn't it? And she would never be able to see expressions the way Ryan did.

She put a truck on the floor in front of Ryan. "One truck," she said.

Analog Science Fiction and Fact

Author's Comments

I had the idea for "Trucks" at 11 P.M. one night, got inspired, and finished the story by dawn. I did almost no revision on the body of the story—but then I got to the last page.

With a short-short story like this, the ending is especially important, and I wrote about 30 very frustrating drafts of the last page. (This took several weeks—so much for overnight success!)

Where did the idea come from? Figgy Duff's "Song for Paul," which was written for an autistic child, described what the world looked like from that child's viewpoint. Oliver Sacks' books about people with neurological gifts and deficits made me wonder what "normal" really meant. What if the world was turned around, and "normal" meant being an autistic savant?

I thought *Analog Science Fiction and Fact* might take a chance on an odd little piece like this. It's hard to imagine where this story would fit into any magazine's official guidelines. So it's worthwhile to try markets that might not seem to be a perfect fit for your story. *Analog* has a reputation for being a "hard" science fiction market, but it's obvious from "Trucks" that they publish stories in a much wider range.

—Amy Bechtel

Tonics

by Jennifer Anthony

RIG

In Pigwell, time is not measured by days or weeks but by the number of eighteen wheelers that drive past my house.

My brother taught me this trick when I was in the first grade. Each night, after Mary left us alone while she man hunted at the local dive bar, Calvin and I would pounce onto his bed and, noses flattened against the window, count the trucks roaring by on the interstate, tires chewing up the road, chrome flashing even in all that inky dark. Six trucks an hour, and as many as seven or eight on the weekends. Thirty or so before we'd hear Mary's four-tired Toyota hiccupping down the frontage road and turning onto our gravel driveway. There she would cut the engine and sit slumped over the steering wheel for a minute or so. Hailing the demons, according to Calvin.

And I would run. A quick kiss on my brother's furrowed forehead, and my bare feet would propel me, slipping and skidding, across the hardwood floor littered with cosmetology books, down the ten-foot stretch of hall, and into my bed. Under the covers, I'd

count: one-two-three, one-two-three, working to control my breathing to make as if I'd been asleep all those hours.

One night, I had tripped and fallen smack against the unforgiving edge of the doorway. Calvin had comforted me the only way he knew how, by dragging a brush through my coarse mane of hair. Tears still squirted, cartoon-like, from the sides of my eyes, when Mary found us and started hollering about how I was still awake. That night, she was wearing the navy blue dress cut with thin white stripes—vertical and slimming—no fattening horizontals for her. When she had left, she was wrinkle-free and hopeful. But early that morning, in the spooky glow of the hall nightlight, both her dress and her face, with its mouth stretched wide to fit the yelling, were crumpled and worn.

There were times when she wobbled straight into her bedroom and cursed words into the pillow. But most nights, she'd headed straight for Calvin's room for counseling, where he would be sitting up in bed, hands crossed like they always were in dealings with Mary.

Her words—never whispered—stuck in my skin like gravel in a wound. "If it weren't for you two," she'd start, "I'd have a man."

Mary—what our mother insisted we call her in her man-hunting days—was never kind at night.

But weekend mornings, we'd awake to the smell of buckwheat pancakes. Or cinnamon French toast. Or, when she was really playing Mom, she'd pull on black slacks and a

Author Bio

Jennifer Anthony has an MFA in writing from Spalding University. Along with *The First Line*, her work has appeared in *Per Contra: The International Journal of the Arts, Literature, and Ideas*. Her travel writing can be found in several webzines, including *Pology* and *Been-Seen*. Her website is: www.jenniferanthony.net.

billowy silk blouse, drag out the Betty Crocker cookbook, and present some sort of fancy egg dish. We knew breakfast was ready when we'd hear her singing her favorite Alabama song, low, soft, and scratchy-voiced.

Calvin and I would sidle up to the kitchen table, all sitcom smiles and rows of white teeth. Then she'd spoon or spatula whatever she'd cooked up onto our plates and ask us how we had slept. Sometimes, if I smiled just right, acted just so, she'd join me in tending to the

"We got to find her a boyfriend so she'll be happy."

little patch of garden out front for a bit. Every fourth week, her pink-lipsticked, chain-smoking friends from the grocery where they all worked would line up at the picnic table on the back patio while Calvin washed, cut, and set their hair. But most weekends, Mary asked us to do her a favor and let her have some alone time. Then she'd hole up in her bedroom with a self-help book from the secondhand store. Mary's favors were flat-out demands, and Calvin and I were on our own on those days.

Sometimes the lack of sleep had Calvin so tired that even his cosmetology books—also bought secondhand—couldn't rouse him. Glassy-eyed as the mounted stag at Truck Stop Trixie's down the road, he'd sit on the wobbly metal chair at the garden's edge and stare out toward the interstate.

"We got to help her, Cara," he'd tell me, without blinking. "We got to find her a boyfriend so she'll be happy."

And, holding an ear of corn or red ripe tomato or handful of leathery string beans, I'd stare at him staring at the road. And cross my fingers, if I had a hand free.

*****

One September night in 1998 when Calvin was fifteen and I was just eleven and

the jasmine scent from Mary's True Love perfume still hung thick in the house, Calvin and I sat counting trucks on his bed.

"Thirteen," he announced, as a red beast roared by. "You think Mary will find someone at TST's tonight?"

Mary preferred that we called it TST's instead of Truck Stop Trixie's. She said it sounded better, not so trashy.

"I'm sure she will," I said. At that hour, we were always still hopeful. "I bet he'll be—"

An explosion loud enough to rattle the window interrupted me. It was followed by a raucous screeching of brakes. A thud. And, finally, an eerie silence.

"Sounds like that truck is a seventeen-wheeler now," Calvin said, pressing his nose against the window, straining to see.

Calvin turned from the window, his hazel eyes dilated. "The driver could be hurt," he said. He hopped off the bed, pulled on his imitation Nikes, and said, "Stay here."

He ran from the room, slammed out the front screen door, and within seconds was sprinting over the yard, down the driveway, out through the gate, and across the frontage road.

Another truck passed. And another. Finally, two shapes emerged from the darkness. My brother's silhouette—tall and lean and long-necked as a Corona bottle. And a second—shorter and squat.

I hustled to the front door in time to see Calvin ushering a man into our house. His stomach looked ready to burst through a flannel shirt, and when he saw me, he reached one gloved hand up to take off his baseball hat, releasing a hat head of orange hair.

"Evening, miss," he said. "Your brother here was kind enough to offer me a little coffee while I'm waiting to get fixed. Trixie's a bit too far of a walk at this hour."

Calvin waved toward our slumping denim couch, motioning for him to sit.

"Awfully kind of you," the man said,

gravely-voiced. When he heaved down, the smell of cigarettes floated over. Unlike Mary's chain-smoking friends, his personal nicotine cloud had a friendly smell. I let it descend on me as I stood staring at his hair, which looked like licks of flame shooting out from his scalp.

"Never seen a redhead, have ya?" the man said. He motioned toward Calvin's bare arms. "But some of us are no strangers to freckles, I see."

"My brother could cut your hair," I blurted.

"Cara!" Calvin said. "My god." He shook his head but looked at the man out of the corner of his eye, waiting.

The man laughed, deep in his big gut, without exposing a single tooth. "You cut hair?"

Calvin's shoulders eased down, and he leaned against the doorframe. "Yeah, I do my sister's hair and my mother's friends."

The man cocked his head and squinted. "You gay?"

"Why?" Calvin said, his voice cool. "Are you?"

The man laughed his deep laugh again. "Ha! Ha ha! Touché. No, sir, I am not." He pulled his gloves off and laid them on the couch beside him. My smile reversed when I saw the gold metal band, thick and gleaming, on his left hand. "Only ask in case my brother runs through here with his wife someday. He's sure she's in love with her hair stylist, and just about every other gay man she meets. My brother's so jealous that he doesn't understand they're just friends." He laughed again, lightly. "Poor guy's been a little insecure since the Army rejected him."

Calvin and I were silent, staring. I wanted him to be our dad.

The man stopped laughing abruptly. "I hope I didn't offend. Ah, jeez. I always babble when I'm shook up. And that—" He pointed out the window in the vague direc-

tion of the rig. "That was no fun."

"No, you didn't offend us," Calvin said softly. "It's just that, out here, everyone assumes I'm gay just because I like doing hair. It's all they talk about, when they should be paying attention to the cut and the style."

"Well, then, son," the man said. Calvin stood straighter. "Let me know your rate, and let's see what you can do."

"Rate?" Calvin asked.

"How much you charge," the man said. He raked his expanse of belly with short, stubby fingers. "Hope it's reasonable!"

Calvin hesitated. No one had ever paid him.

"Twenty," I said.

Calvin glared at me.

The man's eyes glinted. "Fifteen," he countered.

"Deal," I said.

"Quite the negotiator," the man said. He clasped both hands low across his middle like a pregnant woman. "And what do you do around here, while your brother's cutting hair?"

"I grow vegetables," I said. "After the haircut, I can show you the tomatoes I just picked this afternoon. Maybe you'll wanna buy some."

The scissors flashed and caught the light, disappeared under tufts of hair, and reappeared.

"Don't know about vegetables, on the road," the man said.

I let my gaze flicker across his belly. "Veggies are good for you. And you can eat these tomatoes just like an apple, they're so sweet. I mean, they are technically fruit."

"My, my," the man said. "You two are too much. But I will say you're sure as hell more industrious than my kids back home. They play a lot of Nintendo." His eyes misted.

Calvin wiped his hands on his jeans, which meant he had a perfect style in mind. "Come on out back, and I'll switch the lights on. That's where I have to do the haircuts, so I don't make a mess in here."

Chuckling, the man followed him outside and plopped down on the picnic bench while I set about making coffee, stealing occasional glances out the window. My brother's hands moved quickly, effortlessly. The scissors flashed and caught the light, disappeared under tufts of hair, and reappeared. Orange hair fell in clumps onto the dirt. An occasional wisp escaped and circled under the glow of the porch light before floating off into the darkness.

"I've come for a haircut."

"Wow," I said, when Calvin led the man back indoors.

"I cut three inches off the back, shaved the sides, and left the hair on top a little longer to show off the natural wave," Calvin announced. He popped up from behind us with a hand mirror.

"Whoa," the man said, nodding at his reflection. "Now if I could just shave off a few pounds—"

I plucked a basket of tomatoes from the counter and held it out before him. "Twenty dollars for the haircut and these," I said.

The man tore his eyes away from the hand mirror for a millisecond. "Deal," he said. "Guess I'd better get back on out to the truck. Where's my hat? It seems a shame to put it on, now." He eased the hand mirror down onto the counter.

In the front room, Calvin fetched the hat as the man fished two tens from his wallet. "I feel like a new person. You can really let yourself go, spending so much time on the road." He pushed his wallet back into his

pocket, started to speak, looked at me, and paused. "You know. I'm a married man, but not every trucker is. And truth be told, there are those who like to go over to Truck Stop Trixie's to well, consort with the ladies. Some of the guys look a mess, and they get all shy and tongue-tied once they're there. They could use a cut like this—"

"My brother could cut all of their hair!" I said.

Calvin bit his lip. "The thing is, sir, Mary—our mother—well, she's out most nights."

"Mary, is it?" the man said. His eyes swiveled around, surveying the room, and froze on a framed picture of our mother, holding Calvin when he was just a baby. "Of course, Mary wouldn't want any old fool coming in here. I'd just refer my friends. And no one—not a one of them—would hurt a hair on either of your heads. I can assure you of that."

"Sir?" I asked. "Do any of those men want to do more than consort with the women? I mean, do they maybe want a girlfriend? Our mother—"

He blushed. "Yes, miss. There are those who consort, and there are those who're lonely as all hell and would love a girlfriend. But only let 'em in if they mention me—Phillip."

Watching the man stride across the lawn, Calvin and I agreed he was standing a little taller, a little straighter—all because of a haircut.

*****

Phillip kept his word. Three nights later, twenty minutes or so after we heard an eighteen wheeler motor pass, there was a knock on the door.

"Remember," Calvin warned me. "Not a word to Mary, or she'll flip."

"I've come for a haircut," a man said from the other side of the closed door. "Phillip sent me?"

His shaky voice sounded about as nervous as we felt. But as the weeks passed, the haircuts were as routine as Mary's visits to TST's. We waited for the sound of the trucks braking on the side of the road, the scrunch of boots across gravel, and the knock on the door. Calvin bought new cosmetology books to study the latest hairstyles. And I collected the money, sold the produce when I could, and sized up the men to see if they were suitable for our mother, and for us.

But months passed, and we thought we might never meet someone as perfect as Phillip. Until one night, when the scrunch of boots on gravel preceded three loud knocks, steady and self-assured. "Phillip sent me," said a voice, deep as the retired preacher's three houses down, minus the fire and brimstone.

Calvin opened the door to reveal a man who had to duck his head as he walked into the front room. Thick curls of hair sprung up from his scalp, prickling with static as if he'd just taken off a knit cap. Without turning, I knew that my brother was mentally flipping pages in his cosmetology books, conjuring a hairstyle.

My brother strode up to the man and shook his hand. "I'm Calvin," he said. "I'll cut your hair out back."

"Phillip says you do a fine job," the man said. He pointed at his head. "Hope you can do something with this mop. The name's Johnson. Well, that's what my trucker buddies call me. First name's Frank."

"You going to Truck Stop Trixie's tonight?" I asked.

The man paused, then pulled his bare fingers through his hair, demonstrating why it stood up like it did. "I think I'm done consorting with the ladies. I want something a little more—long-term." One side of his mouth curled up in a half-smile.

Within minutes, Calvin had the man seated on the back patio. Dressed only in a white T-shirt and khakis, my brother was too preoccupied with the scissors to notice the bite in the February air. And the man, wearing only a thin long-sleeved shirt and jeans, also sat still without so much as a shiver.

The man was Phillip's opposite in every way. Where Phillip's cheeks had had smile lines carved into it, this man's face was smooth, save for a crease carving up from his brow to the middle of his forehead. And while Phillip hadn't stopped talking since the moment he came through the door, Frank spoke only when we asked him questions, like a classroom in reverse.

Calvin was brushing off the man's neck when we heard the familiar hiccupping sound of a four-tired, four-doored car lurching down the road. A door slammed shut. Footsteps, quick and determined, crunched across the gravel driveway.

"Mary!" Calvin said. "She only left seven trucks ago—a little over an hour. Maybe she found out? Sir, you've gotta leave!"

We knew it was time to stop counting trucks.

Frowning, the man stood and wiped stray hairs off his jeans, then glanced at the house as if he might consider walking toward it.

But the yelling began the moment she slammed through the screen door. "Calvin! Cara! Where the hell are you?"

Knees popping, the man eased back down onto the bench. "I'm not running anywhere now, in case that Mary of yours is packing a rifle and wants some target practice. I think you'd better let her know you're back here." The man started to pull his fingers through his freshly groomed hair but caught himself. "And then you say you're giving me a haircut, that's all."

Calvin and I stared at the stranger who managed to blanket us with calm, even as our mother was shouting herself toward an aneurism.

"Out here, Mary," Calvin cried. "We're all out here."

And even before Mary stormed outside, tomato-red with anger about the haircutting operation she'd heard about at TST's, we knew. We knew even before she stopped bellowing and turned her still fresh-face toward the man seated on the picnic bench, hands folded on his thighs, and said, in her Saturday morning voice, "Well, hello. That your rig out there?"

We knew it was time to stop counting trucks.

The First Line

Author's Comments

A few years ago, I finally got serious about my writing and pursued an MFA in writing for children at Spalding University. Because I'm a firm believer in being experimental and humble, I've explored various publishing opportunities, ranging from e-zines to print journals.

When I found a call for submissions for *The First Line,* I was immediately intrigued by the journal's premise. At the beginning of each year, the editors provide one introductory sentence for each quarterly issue. Writers can create one story using the sentence provided, or try to tie together all four first lines, which have nothing to do with each other, into one cohesive story to be published as a series throughout the year.

The four-part series (only one is published here) was a tempting feat, although one hadn't been published in years. Instead I approached it as a learning experience. Because each first line and ensuing story would be published in its own issue, each had to work as an independent piece, with its own theme and character/plot arcs, but still be a chapter within a larger, cohesive novella.

I tried something new: I began with the last sentence and its accompanying story, and wrote backward to ensure that every detail and every action of all the characters made sense in the collective plot.

Given the mention of the eighteen wheelers, I knew I wanted to base the story around a trucker subculture, so as I wrote each of the series' biennial stories, I listened to songs (beginning with Alabama's "Roll On," about a trucker's family) to establish mood. And then I set out to create a quiet piece about some unusual characters who wanted basic tonics of love and acceptance.

I learned more from writing and revising this piece—and got closer to its characters—than I ever had before. I actually cried (tears of joy!) when it got accepted, and so it was a sort of tonic for me, too.

—Jennifer Anthony

One by One

by Ryan Scammell

Today you ended it. Which means that yesterday will be the last time you will have been called "my girlfriend" aloud. Today is the last time we will use the phrase "our apartment." The couch will become "yours" and the nightstand will become "mine" and the things we bought together will be too hard for either of us to take with us. Like the bookshelf that we bought giggling at the antique store because I said that my grandmother had owned the exact same one. We duct taped it to the roof of my car that night because we didn't have anything else to strap it on with; and though at the time I had convinced myself otherwise, it turned out you were right. It wouldn't fit in the back seat. In the end, we'll sell it to someone online, a girl about 20 who will come to pick it up with her boyfriend. The only thing she'll say is, "Is this it?" You'll nod yes, and she'll say, "Thanks." And then it'll be gone.

We'll pick times to get our stuff from the apartment to avoid running into each other. I'll come by on a Monday afternoon a week from now knowing that you'll be at work. After I've shoved the last of my things into my car, I'll sit on the floor and drink the refrigerator's last beer and look at the leftovers of our life together. The apartment will look stripped. Patches of white where you hadn't completed repainting the walls. Half the place packed into liquor boxes. It will look like a puzzle with half of its pieces. When I leave the apartment, it will be the last time I will ever see the place we lived together. I'll slide my keys under the door and be forever locked out.

Two weeks from now you'll call me at night from our old bed. You'll be lonely and you'll say that the sheets feel empty; that the queen bed we bought to fit the two of us feels enormous, like the big flat of the Midwest, where you were born. I'll come over straight away, and we'll sit on the couch together, with your head in the V of my shoulder, watching old 60s reruns. Nothing will happen between us. After all the talk of the bed, we'll both fall asleep on the couch that night. That night will be the last time you ever call me on the phone. And five years from now, you will erase my number.

We'll have sex together one last time five months from now. We'll randomly end up at the same rooftop New Year's party in New York together, and something between the champagne and starlight and the twinkling bridges, we'll fall in love with each other again for just a moment and make love right there on the roof when the party makes its way

Author Bio

Ryan Scammell is a writer, filmmaker, and audio-producer in New York City. He currently writes and produces a podcast called Phonography: Writing In Sound (www.writinginsound.com), where he layers his writing with sound effects, music, and sometimes imagery. His audio work has appeared on National Public Radio and his film work has appeared in *Ninth Letter*. He is also a contributor to *Storyscape Literary Journal*.

back inside. Afterwards, I'll ask to come back to your place and you'll say to me: "I don't know if that's a good idea."

The last time we'll see each other will be three years from now. We'll bump into each other at random in a totally different part of the country. You'll have come in for a friend's wedding and I'll have moved there for work. You'll look as beautiful as ever and I'll have started wearing my glasses again. It will have been over two years since I was in the city that we shared. You won't even have known that I'd left. We'll say: "It was great to see you" and "Likewise." And then you'll walk away, turning back just once to smile and wave. For the next week, I'll keep thinking I see you. I'll keep hallucinating you in the face of every dark haired girl in Chicago, wondering if at any moment we'll run into each other again. When it doesn't happen, I'll go out of my way, swapping to an El-train in the opposite direction of my house, just to go back to the spot where I saw you. I don't know if a part of me will really believe that you will be there, but I'll feel a little crushed when you don't show, as if I've been stood up. That moment the week before, on the edge of the park, with the sun setting in your hair, and the city rising around us, will be the last time we ever look at each other.

Forty-five years from now will be the first time I forget your name. Fifty years from now will be the last time I speak it aloud to anyone. Sixty years from now I will remember that day we spent in San Francisco, watching the fog rolling in over Sausalito and your arms around me too. It felt like I was in the middle of the everything, the centrifuge of the planet. That will be the last time I ever think of you.

It all starts right now.

Flashquake

Author's Comments

"One by One" is one of those pieces that just happened. My girlfriend of three years and I had, literally, just broken up. I sat in the apartment and started to think about how this was the beginning of the process of her disappearing from my life. I wrote "One by One" right then and there in about 30 minutes. I did minor edits over the next few days, but the piece was largely completed in those first moments after we broke up. I tend to find that my best work comes out of that sense of immediacy.

In terms of my process, I generally start with a theme—what is it about this story that is compelling me to write it? Once I have that theme, every choice I make (every scene, every line) is chosen to support that theme. Because I tend to only write shorter works, I usually write the entire piece in one sitting. Then a few days later, I look back at it from further away, and say "this works," or "this doesn't work." Then I'll go back and rework, step away again, rework again, and so on.

I think of the process as a little like sculpting. As if you've found this boulder, and there's something about the boulder that's compelling you; that's your theme. And from there, you keep chiseling away at the rock, trying to figure out what the statue is that's inside it, and bit by bit, you get closer to what your piece wants itself to be.

—Ryan Scammell

How to Make Flan

by Amina Lolita Gautier

I was settled in for the evening, comfortably watching early evening game shows when my father called. "Come home," he said.

"How're you doing?" I asked, pretending as if hearing from him were not a rare, rare thing. For the last four years, I'd been living in West Philadelphia, in a converted Victorian house on a quiet tree-lined street just blocks away from campus. I had not seen my father in all this time.

"How soon can you come?"

I looked at the books stacked on my coffee table. Most were overdue at the library. A few had been recalled. I had been meaning to start my paper for the last few hours, but had somehow managed to postpone it in favor of dinner and *Jeopardy!* I was only two and a half hours from home, but I thought of my poverty, my debt, and my courses, and made excuses. I reminded my father that this was the fall semester of my last year at Penn, a delicate time. I told him I was in the middle of writing a paper. That I couldn't afford it. That I had enough credit card debt to make a grown man cry. That I had neither the time nor the money to come to Brooklyn right now. I ended with, "It was good of you to call."

"Not so good," he said.

"Is something wrong?"

"Your abuela is in the hospital."

"Why didn't you tell me?"

"I just did. That's why I called. She wants to see you."

"Is she okay? I mean, what's wrong with her?"

He said, "Everything."

The *Final Jeopardy!* subject was "Twentieth Century U.S. Presidents." Alex Trebek asked the contestants to make their wagers. This could be a trick, I thought. Only I couldn't guess why my father would want to see me so badly that he'd resort to this. I would not come back home for him, but I would for Abuela and he knew it. My father moved back in with Abuela once my parents divorced. Had it not been for that, I would have seen more of her. I listened as my father predicted she wouldn't recover. I promised to see them in the morning as Alex asked the contestants to name the only president whose first middle and last name all had the same number of letters. Who is Ronald Wilson Reagan? I silently guessed. I lifted the shade of my window and looked out onto my front porch, idly watching the brittle leaves pile up on the railings.

Author Bio

Amina Gautier is Assistant Professor of English at Saint Joseph's University and a Postdoctoral Fellow at Washington University in St. Louis. More than 45 of her stories have been published in various literary journals. They have also been anthologized in *The Sincerest Form of Flattery: Contemporary Women Writers on Forerunners in Fiction*; *Best African American Fiction*; and more. Her work has been honored with fellowships from Breadloaf Writers' Conference, Ucross Residency, and Sewanee Writers' Conference. "How to Make Flan" was the winner of the 2006 Jack Dyer Fiction Prize.

The wind was swirling them, lifting them, hinting at snow.

Despondent security guards nod as I walk past them. Receptionists don't even lift their heads from the latest magazines. No one asks me for ID or makes me sign in. I find my own way down hallways painted in muted colors and retro designs.

I hear my father's voice as I near Abuela's hospital room. "Mami, try to be reasonable."

"But I don't want a TV. Why do you come here to bother me?"

Abuela is swathed from neck to toe in layers of thick white cotton sheets, topped by a beige blanket. She looks as if she is being prepared for burial. My father sits by her side, looking older than he did when I saw him last.

"Dios mío, who is this?" she asks. "You did this for me. You are my favorite son."

"Mami, I'm your only son," he says.

When she smiles, I see that her face is frozen on one side. The left side of her smile slides downwards into a frown. When she talks, only one side of her face moves. "Nieta," she murmurs, "Ven acá."

Abuela struggles to sit up, stretches out a hand to me. I can't help but think that this woman is not Abuela; that someone has switched her with a bad fake. Abuela chases people with wooden spoons and smacks them hard on their hands. She bangs pots and pans. She is always standing, always on her feet.

Her hospital bed is the old-fashioned kind with a crank at the foot of the bed to raise or lower it. It is closer to the window than it should be. I walk to the head of it and press her hand to my lips, kissing the paper thin skin. "How's my abuelita?" I ask. "How are you feeling?"

"Like a prisoner," she says and then bursts into a fit of coughing. A nurse, stand-ing just outside the door, runs in with water. Soon Abuela settles down. She sits up against her pillows, stronger and more alert.

"Mami, be careful," my father says, hold-ing her arm.

"Are you okay?" I ask.

She tries to shake my father off. "They're just trying to impress you. They won't even give me water when I ask for it, only when they want me to have it. I can't drink when I'm thirsty and when I'm not they try to drown me."

"They have their reasons," my father says.

She curses in Spanish and my father rises from his seat. This is more like her.

"Mami!"

She waves him off. "You can go now. I just want my nieta. Wait outside."

Once he is gone, she says, "I missed you. Why did you stay away so long?"

Before I can answer, she says, "Men and women divorce, not families."

"I'm sorry. I—"

"It's okay," she says. "You're here now. My nieta. You've grown so beautiful." Then she motions me closer. "They won't let me go home. I tell them I'm fine and they say 'let's see.' These doctors are crazy. Do you under-stand that?" she asks.

"Nieta, I want you to make me some flan."

"Maybe they want to make sure you're one hundred percent," I say, not wanting to take sides.

"How can I get better in here? The food they feed me is not fit for a pig." She grabs my hand and tugs me down so I am looking into her eyes. They are cloudy, the irises milky gray; her left eye threatens to close. She searches my face. "I want you to bring me something. Will you?"

"What did the doctors say?"

"Do you think I listen to crazies?" she asks. Although we are the only ones in the room, she pulls me down even closer to her and whispers, "Nieta, I want you to make me some flan."

"I don't think the doctors would want you to have anything they haven't given you," I say.

"Flan is not going to kill anybody," she says.

I shake my head to let her know I mean business, but she doesn't let go of my hand.

"I want some flan," she says. "You remember I used to make it for you when you were sick?"

"I remember."

"You don't want to deny my last wish?"

"Don't talk like that," I say. "Trying to give me a guilt trip won't work."

"No guilt trip," Abuela says. "Blackmail. You owe me." She turns adult now, that I have matured. I resist the urge to twist Ken's plastic head off, and I try to get some sleep.

My father and grandmother are arguing when I get there the next day.

They stop when they see me. "Look who's here," my father says.

I ask, "How are you feeling, Abuelita?"

"Not so good."

"What's wrong?"

"Tengo más hambre que maestra de escuela," she says. Then she looks at me. "You don't understand me?"

I tell her that I stopped taking Spanish after my sophomore year. She rolls her eyes in disgust. "This is your child," she says to my father.

My father explains, "She said she's hungry."

"As hungry as a schoolteacher," Abuela adds. "But I'd be better if your father here would stop trying to make me eat."

The table by her right arm can be wheeled closer or further for her convenience.

On it are a Styrofoam cup of flat ginger ale, a small ramekin of pudding, and a clear container of fruit salad. Chunks of watermelon and pineapple sit in their own juices.

"But Mami, you know what the doctors said. You have to eat. You have to build up your strength," my father says. "You're too weak."

Abuela waves him off. "Ya, mijo. Ya ya. Déjame en paz. I'd have to be a pig to eat the food they give me here. You know that I can't eat that stuff. It makes me go to the bathroom."

"Am I dead yet? I still have ears."

He says, "You'll never get better that way."

Abuela looks at me like a supplicant. "It's so greasy. Who could eat it?"

"Mami, it's not that bad," my father says.

Abuela's hand comes down on her tray. "You like it so much you can eat it!" She knocks over the ginger ale.

My father grabs tissues and kneels to clean up the mess. He apologizes, "She's been like this since she got here. She won't listen."

"Am I dead yet? I still have ears," she says.

"What's wrong with your food?" I ask.

"That fruit is older than I am," she says.

"What about the pudding?"

She looks at it suspiciously.

"Want to try it?"

"Maybe a little bit."

My father throws his hands up. "I just tried to get you to eat that!"

"You're not my nieta," Abuela says, a crafty smile on her face. "Give me the slop. I'll taste it."

She tries to hold her cup with her bad hand, but she cannot steady it. The ramekin wobbles. Each time she dips her good hand with the spoon into the container, the yellowish pudding slides out.

"Here, Abuela, let me," I say as I take the ramekin from her.

I spoon the pudding out for her and feed it to her. She is like a greedy child, gobbling every bit I give her as my father watches, unspeaking.

"How is that?"

"It's slop, but it's better than nothing," she says. She tries to grab my wrist with her weak left hand. "That's enough. Thank you."

"You've got to keep your strength up," I tell her.

"We don't want to lose you," my father says.

She makes a face at him. "I'm not going anywhere."

I go home with him to find her comb and brush. We don't talk about my mother.

In my grandmother's house are many candles, knickknacks, and saints. She has tried to cram a whole island into her overcrowded apartment. Elephants march across the coffee table, trunks up. Coasters bear the faces of parrots and coquis. Large wooden spoons in three different sizes hang from the wall in the kitchen. A green can of soda crackers sits on a counter, and I know it is

Her bedroom is a walking botanical.

filled to the brim with rice, not crackers. A pilón, mortar and pestle, wait above the refrigerator for her to come home and mash cooked green plantains with fresh garlic to make mofongo. A large aluminum pot with its blackened bottom sits on the back burner of the stove, ever ready.

My father takes me to her bedroom and opens her door, leaving me to find the comb

and brush. Everything is just as I remembered it. Over her bedroom door, a palm leaf is twisted into the shape of a cross. It will remain there until next Palm Sunday. A bust of Jesus adorns the end table in her bedroom. Four near-empty bottles of prescription medicine sit on her dresser. Next to them lie her brush and comb, still filled with long strands of her hair. I see Abuela here, vital and alive, dusting off her dresser mirror, allowing me to help brush her hair, showing me which of her medicines thinned her blood, kept her pressure down, or helped her to breathe, and which ones protected her from all the other ones. Her bedroom is a walking botanical. Scientific medicine jostles for space with Santería concoctions. Catholic remedies and vials of holy water and holy oil are lined up next to health food store medicines in clear plastic pouches. These medicines were toys to me when I was younger, things to be suspicious of when I was older and forewarned by my mother and others who didn't believe in that stuff, things to make fun of once I went to college and learned to know better. Now as I look at them, I just see an old woman's attempts to prolong her life as creatively as she could.

"Get out of here! ¡No me molestes!"

The next day she is arguing with my father over the television in her room.

"It's wasting your money, I don't need it."

"But Mami, you might change your mind. You might want to watch some shows."

"I've seen enough Phil Donahue and Jerry Springer to last my whole life."

"How about if I just turn it on so you can see what there is to watch?"

"Do you think I want to be watching things that aren't real?"

"Mami, just look at—"

"Leave it!"

My father moved to turn the TV on. "Just see—"

"Get out of here! ¡No me molestes!"

"But Mami—"

"I don't want to see your face anymore. Go!"

My father walks to the door slowly as if waiting for her to call him back. She pretends he is already gone. She pats the bed and I go to her. "Did you bring me what I asked for?"

"Not exactly."

She makes a face at me. "But I did bring your comb and brush, Abuela."

"Okay," she nods. "But tomorrow, I want flan. Is your father standing outside my door?"

Now he is my father, not her son. I go and check. The hallway is clear. "No. He's gone."

"Good."

"He was just trying to help," I say. Sitting on the edge of her bed with a comb and brush, I work out the snarls and kinks in Abuela's hair.

"Help me put my foot in the grave!"

"Don't you think you're being a little harsh on him?" I ask. "He loves you."

"I know," she says, breathing like it's hurting her. "I love him too. No mother ever loved a son more, but he's killing me." She looks at me, imploring. "I don't want to be here. I don't want to eat that food. I want to go home and be in my own bed. I don't want to die here."

"Don't say that." Something in me trembles. "You're not going to die. Remember what you said? You're not going anywhere?"

Tears slip from her eyes. "Tell that to my son. Every time I look into his eyes, I see death looking back at me."

"Abuela." I take her hand. She doesn't look good. If at all possible, she seems smaller and weaker than a moment ago.

"No more talk about that," she says. Her face brightens momentarily. "Tell me about your school and Philadelphia."

I have been happy and comfortable away in Philadelphia. I tell her about Clark Park and the Farmer's Market. I tell her what it's like to have a porch instead of a stoop. I try to explain the difference between a water ice and an Italian ice.

"I would like to visit you," she says.

"Anytime," I say, glad to talk of getting better. "But I'll have to clean up first."

She laughs and falls into a fit of coughing that lasts too long. Her cough rattles in her chest and leaves her spent. She won't let me call the nurse. I offer her water. I hold her hand. I wish for my father to come back and take over.

"Let me get someone."

The hand that I am holding tightens on mine with surprising strength. Her hands squeeze, but I don't pull away. "No me dejas," she says. *Don't leave me.* It's easy for me to forget how sick she has always been

"My hair is from Spain and my face is from Africa."

when I hear her arguing and yelling. She's been this way for so long that sometimes I take it for granted. Her voice trembles and she squeezes my hand harder and harder. I have never seen her afraid.

"No," I say. I swallow hard. "I won't leave you."

I have no idea how long it takes before her breathing has calmed. Too long. Finally, she looks at me and pats my hand, smiling weakly. "Tell me, nieta, would I like Philadelphia?"

"You would," I tell her. When I say this, I am thinking of the vegetable stands between Chestnut and Locust. The large white trucks the Senegalese men drive, the rickety wooden stalls they erect to sell their fresh vegetables.

The long snaking lines of people crowded onto the curb and spilling out into the street, thumping melons and inspecting yams, arguing over the price of overripe produce. I remember Abuela taking me to market and inspecting mangoes, avocados, guavas and breadfruits, arguing with the vendors and loving every minute of it.

She wants me to continue to brush her hair. I scratch out the tiny white flakes of dandruff that nurses have ignored, pulling her long hair out from behind her and brushing it all the way down to the straggly ends. Each stroke relaxes her a little more, making her sleepy, just like it used to. Yawning, she says, "My hair is from Spain and my face is from Africa. And you, nieta, you look just like me."

"Abuela, what am I?"

I laugh at our old joke. When I was younger, I didn't know who or what I was. I had a black mother and a Puerto Rican father, and I didn't know what that made me. By fourth grade I had learned that in this country, it was neither possible nor desirable to be both. Kids teased me, calling me "elstupido." Girls pulled my hair, wondering if it was a weave. Grown men approached me in Spanish on my way to or from school, angry when I didn't answer because I couldn't understand. There were two sides of me and one of them was always getting in trouble. My mother blamed the Puerto Rican side of me and my father blamed the black side.

I don't remember what caused it, but I came to my grandmother in tears one afternoon, asking, "Abuela, what am I?"

She didn't ask me what happened. She just shook her head at me. "Don't you know who you are?" She laced her fingers through mine. "You are my granddaughter, my nieta. You are everybody's daughter. You are the conquistador, the Indian and the slave, struggling to be one. You are three kings bringing gifts. You are a fortress. You are chains and shackles. You are the ocean. And the sand beneath the waves. You are the pride of the sea. You are the breeze that blows from the shore. You are my granddaughter, my nieta. You are me, nena. You are me."

As my grandmother drifts off to sleep, I pull the comb through her hair and think of how much I still need her. I want to lie down beside her on her hospital bed. I want her to wrap her arms around me. I want her to give me all her answers.

I find my mother and father necking on the couch. One shamefaced, the other daring, they partly detach, long enough for my father to help my mother sit up. Long enough for her to smooth her skirt, blow hair out of her eyes. Long enough for him to drape his arm over her shoulder and leave it there.

"Will I see you tomorrow?" I ask him before either of them can speak.

He shrugs. "What difference does it make? She only wants her nieta," he mocks, sounding like a small child.

Once he has gone, my mother tries to explain. "He told me what happened. He said he didn't know where else to go."

"So he came here?" I can't keep the sarcasm from my voice. "After not stepping foot in this apartment since I was what—twelve—he decides to drop by today?"

"It was the one place he knew he wouldn't have to face you." Suddenly, miraculously, my mother has become an expert on my father. Suddenly, she knows so much.

"Except here I am."

"We kind of lost track of time."

"I see," I say, although I don't.

"He was very hurt. He pouts when he doesn't get his way," she says. "She threw him out, but kept you. He was jealous of you."

"That's ridiculous."

"He's always been like that."

I don't know how he has always been and

I don't want to know now. "So am I supposed to be sorry that—"

"No, no. Of course not. He should have understood. You've always been special to her. She was always willing to take you when you were young and your father and I were so busy with everything." She changes the subject. "Do you think she would mind if I came to see her?"

"No," I say. "You should."

"If I could change the past—" my mother begins. She stops, seeming to stare at something in the corner of the kitchen. "We were so young and stupid then. It's a good thing you spent more time with her than us," she says, the closest she will come to an apology.

As I lay out the ingredients for the flan, I remember one winter when I was eleven and Abuela made flan to cure my strep throat. She said that the flan would be good for my throat, that it would soothe the soreness and that it wouldn't hurt me to swallow it. Her tiny kitchen was just a rectangle of space sectioned off from the large open living room by a tall counter. I remember the comfort of the living room. From the hi-riser, I could see the back of her, her head and back and shoulders bent over a small saucepan, stirring sugar over a low heat until it caramelized. I could close my eyes and listen to the hushed steps she made in the small square of kitchen space, the sound of metal hitting aluminum as she scraped the clinging bits of caramel from the pan, the crack and spill of eggs, the flourish of water running in the sink to set the mold, the creak of wooden cabinet doors on old iron hinges as she opened the cupboards and pulled out her custard cups, the ping of milk in a glass bowl, all the ingredients of my flan, all of the steps she took to let me know that she was with me and she was making my cure. No matter how high my fever or how dry my throat, the pain all seemed lessened by those safe secure sounds of someone seeking my welfare.

After she'd make the flan and I'd eaten it, she'd settle me once more on the hi-riser to sleep. She'd brush back the hair from my forehead and lean down to kiss me, and I'd feel the dry press of her lips against my hot, feverish skin.

At that moment she'd say, "Te quiero, nieta." *I love you.*

Tomorrow, whether or not my father decides to show up, I will go and sit with my grandmother.

Tonight I make the flan.

In my mother's kitchen, I pour sugar and a bit of water into a saucepan, stirring it over a low heat until the caramel forms. I pour the caramel out into my mold and set it to the side. I beat eggs until they are frothy. Then I add condensed milk and vanilla, mixing well. Finally, I pour the custard over the caramel. I place my mold inside a larger pan and fill the larger pan partway with water, putting it in the oven to bake.

Tomorrow, my grandmother will be better and stronger than she was today.

Tonight I take my flan from the oven and invert it on a dish. I leave it in the refrigerator overnight and wait for it to take its shape.

Crab Orchard Review

How to Make Flan

Author's Comments

Grandmothers are tricky characters. Too often have I seen them appear in the fiction of beginning writers merely as foils and types. Loving, kind, and smelling of home-baked goods, they exist in the story only to help the central character sort out his or her own personal drama. Carrying the wisdom of the ages, these elderly women appear like fairy godmothers, drop kernels of wisdom and then conveniently die after serving their purpose. Rarely do they have conflicts or problems of their own. These grandmothers are nothing like the grandmother in Flannery O'Connor's "A Good Man Is Hard to Find," which remains for me the best example of a grandmother in short fiction.

The first line of O'Connor's story begins: "The grandmother did not want to go to Florida." From the outset of the story, the grandmother's desires influence the actions and conflict of the story, ultimately leading to the death of herself and her family. O'Connor's grandmother is sneaky and not particularly kind. I did not go that far in my characterization of Abuela, the grandmother in my story, "How to Make Flan," but O'Connor's story compelled me to make Abuela real enough to walk off the page.

With Abuela, I wanted to create a character with spunk. Her refusal to take her illness lying down and acquiesce to the doctor's advice and her son's coddling introduces the central conflict of the story— her desire is to leave the hospital and return to her home. But if she has to stay she wants to eat something other than "hospital food."

Specifically, she wants to eat flan, a traditional Puerto-Rican dessert, a comfort food that reinforces her cultural identity and also enables her to feel like something other than a patient. She has decided that flan will make her feel better, and she is not above defying the doctor's orders, alienating her son, or blackmailing her granddaughter to get it.

All of the characters in the story are forced to deal with her wants. Finally, it is Abuela's hospitalization that incites the forward movement of the story; i.e., it sets the granddaughter in motion, getting her to leave Philadelphia and return to Brooklyn, forcing her to interact with her divorced parents and her latent resentment.

Although she is lying in a hospital bed, Abuela orchestrates the story—not your typical grandmother.

—Amina Lolita Gautier

Cellmates

by Willma Willis Gore

nother metallic clank, another happy shout. Leah looked up from the pared fruit in her hands to take in the scene beyond her kitchen window. Husband Craig and son, Marty, source of the exuberant sounds, were sorting through the Warhol-esque pile of rusted pipe, lumber and wire as though they were mining a mountain of gold.

In only three days since she cleaned the window glass, a diligent spider had holed up in the corner of the frame, rebuilding its web, remaking its own silken bars to cage her in this country place. She sighed and returned to slicing apricots—half the box still to be done.

Why did we come here? She'd shared Craig's enthusiasm at first for his old home ground in the San Joaquin Valley, but by now the question plagued her daily. Leaning against the sink board, she felt Jokey kick inside her belly, and shifted the bulge. "Jokey" was her private name for the baby, her crowning stupidity in timing. Of course they wanted another child, but she'd been careless in a spontaneous hour of lovemak-

ing, joyous over the prospect of Craig's being home every day with her and Marty.

"Just the three of us in our own country place," Craig had whispered, holding her with the tenderness that drove all logic from her mind.

"Three, going on four at practically that very moment," she muttered. Sure, she had complained about his being home so little in the city. OK, now he was home. Oh, God, was he ever home! In and out all day. Pawing through drawers for pliers and screwdrivers, taking innumerable coffee breaks. Mud on the porch, dust prints on the carpet, engine oil in the lavatory, and work clothes to launder every day. Tears filled her eyes. The knife grazed her chin as she brushed drops from her cheek.

How could she, a city girl and an artist— yes, she could say *artist*. Since the show last year, she was considered a professional. How could she have been conned into thinking she'd like country life? She'd treasured her gift, knowing it was something uniquely her own. Until she actually arrived here, she be-lieved creativity was so much a part of her that she could paint anywhere. She flexed the fingers of her artist hands. *Don't argue*, she told them. *Back to the apricots.*

Setting the pot on the range, she moved quickly to the counter to re-read the recipe. She didn't want to can apricots and didn't want to learn how. But when Craig delivered the grain he'd milled for their neighbor, they sent back a huge box of fruit.

"A whole lug!" Craig had beamed. "Just stew them and put them in jars. That's the way

Author Bio

Willma Willis Gore has published over 200 travel articles and has won a number of nonfiction and fiction awards, including first prize for fiction in the Society of South-western Authors 2007 contest. Her book titles include *Long Distance Grandparenting*; *Just Pencil Me In: Your Guide to Moving and Getting Settled After 60*; *Independence Day*; and *Something's Leaking Upstairs*. She keeps a blog at http://willmagore.com/blog/.

Mom used to do it and I love them that way."

"Me too," said Marty, the carbon copy of his father, a child who didn't know a home-stewed apricot from a stewed fig, having had neither in his seven years.

"You know, Honey, home-grown produce takes me back." Craig's tone held a youthful exuberance she'd never heard when he was climbing the corporate ladder.

"When I was a kid, Mom grew the biggest tomatoes you ever saw, right out there." He'd beckoned her to the window and swept his hand to define a section of brown stubble, and she knew then that his program for redevelopment of the old homestead included a vegetable garden grown by her. If his Mom could do it, he knew his wife could also. She had been too choked with emotion—the bad kind—to speak, and he hurried off to the corral, a kid in a candy store of memories. Ever supportive of her art, he was the one who said, "After we get settled in, you'll have lots of time of paint."

"Mom, come see the scorpion."

She shared his love of the vast expanse of open country, and the beautiful bordering Sierra, but where was the inspiration, the stimulation she'd found daily among her artist friends in the city? And what could compare in efficiency and practicality to vegetables that come in neat rectangular packages, cradled in the hands of the Jolly Green Giant?

Miserable, talking to herself, Leah stared at the page of the canning book without seeing it. *Get back to business,* she ordered. Read.

"Mom, Mom. A jar, please, quick!" She heard Marty at the door. From the back step, he panted. "We need a jar. We found a scorpion."

Jars for apricots, jars for scorpions. What's a scorpion-size jar?

"Quick, Mom, before it gets away."

At the sink, she selected a quart jar, ready for fruit, then rejected it. The scorpion didn't need a newly-sterilized jar. "That one, Mom." Marty pointed from the doorway. She touched a pint mayonnaise jar, still decorated with a scab of label. "Lid too." He stepped inside, disregarding the "no muddy shoes in the house" rule.

"Thanks, Mom."

Her hands were still cupped in the jar shape when he slammed the door leaving a between-the-cleats size chunk of dried mud on the floor. Leah picked up the clod, dropped it into the wastebasket and washed her hands—again.

Now, read the directions. Concentrate. Add the sugar. How much? See chart on page 103. Good God, two pages of charts. Who'd ever can that much fruit? Low fire under apricots.

"Mom, come see the scorpion," Marty called.

Leah turned the cookbook on its face and went to the door. Behind the jar held out to her, Marty's face was a wonder-filled chalice, animating freckles into dancing dots. For a crystal moment, Leah saw him as answer to all questions. She wanted to hold him close, but he pushed the jar toward her. "See!" He shook it.

Inside, what looked to be about three inches of dry grass flicked suddenly to life. Mandibles raised at one end, threatening. A jointed tail curved over the back, the barb at the tip poised, menacing. She gasped and backed away.

"It can't get you, Mom. Dad says punch a hole in the lid so it can breathe." Gingerly, she took the jar, warm from his hands. "What do we do with it?" she asked, mesmerized.

"It's a mommy, like you. It's gonna have babies." The door slammed and he was gone.

The hell, you say! Can apricots, work down the list through zucchini, and midwife scorpions in between. Johnny Cash could have set it to music.

How does Craig know it's pregnant? From beneath the jar she studied the elongated body, slender as the barbed tail. *Maybe the babies are in the tail and she squirts them out?* Along the insect's back was a whitish ash. Leah carried the jar to the window. With the light full on the scorpion, she saw that the white streak was not ash. It was tiny eggs. *OK, biology lesson over. It's almost a mother.*

So what do we do with a mama scorpion? She twisted the lid to make sure it was secure and smelled apricots. Another lid—the one on the pot—was working like a face ready to sneeze. Quickly she set the scorpion jar on the back of the sink board and turned off the fire.

Finally, four quart jars were sealed against the red-letter hazards of ptomaine and botulism. *And one jar of scorpion. Correction: scorpion with child.*

Leah kept her distance from the mayonnaise jar as she cleared the counter. Then, remembering that Marty said to make a hole in the lid, she got the hammer and drove the point of a beer opener through it.

Now where? She decided on the linen shelf inside the pantry. Plenty of room. As she lifted the jar to an empty space, she noticed that the torn label still bore the letters MAYO, the first letters of the mayonnaise label. As good a name as any for a scorpion.

"Looks like we're in this together, Mayo," she whispered and closed the cabinet.

She dropped on the sofa and lifted her feet to the stool as Dr. Webb had advised. Dear Dr. Webb. Before Jokey was due, she would go back to L.A.'s civilization and stay through the delivery. She wasn't sure about these country doctors. She might find herself delivered of a colt or a calf.

She watched the late, soft light of the April sun play on her painting, the only one she had hung here in the Boonies—her big winner. She raised the hand that had held the brushes that painted the tight, clean triangles in shades of blue deepening to black—the coral band weaving a diagonal. Since she'd

become a country wife, her artist's hands had developed amnesia. They had forgotten how to hold a brush and palette. Her brain remembered, but it was like remembering an episode in a novel. Someone else was involved.

The opening of her one-man show, a little over a year ago, had been a grand day. Exciting to be hung in the elegantly-appointed Bowers Gallery for the association's big show. It was the first time they'd featured the works of a single member—all abstracts, at that.

She stretched out her hand and sighted through the "V" angle she formed with her fingers. They neatly bordered two sides of one of the two hundred and three figures this hand had painted in about that many hours. She loved defined shapes—triangles, circles, trapezoids, narrow bands of S curves.

She looked at the hand that had held the brushes. "Why won't you paint?" she asked aloud.

How do you expect to paint ideas in this barren place? Leah dared a prod. "Georgia O'Keeffe painted in the desert."

Go to hell. The hand dropped to her lap.

"Honey," Craig called from the back door. "I'm taking the tractor to Gil now. He'll bring us back. Marty's going with me. I'll put the trout on the barbecue as soon as I get back. You rest."

That night Leah dreamed of the scorpion. She could get nearer the sink in the dream because she and Mayo had traded burdens. Leah had a big egg on her back and Mayo had a bulge on her front and had to walk upright, supported by her tail.

Mayo complained in the dream. She could see through the walls of her maternity ward, but she wanted out.

"Sorry," Leah said. "You're stuck in there."

"So are you," returned Mayo, matching Leah's matter-of-fact statement as though they were comparing recipes for apricot jam. For response, Leah dropped the jar into the trash basket under the sink. The jar tipped over and Mayo crawled through the air hole in the lid.

Leah wakened in fright. The dream was so real she was afraid it was true. She put one foot out of bed and quickly pulled it back. What if Mayo had come down the hall and was waiting, bent on revenge against the monsters that caged her?

Craig still slept. It was nearly light but she turned on the table lamp and searched the rug beside the bed. *Silly. It's just a dream,* she told herself. Mayo was still on the shelf beside the dishtowels.

But she was awake now. She grabbed her robe, tying the sash over the Jokey bulge, and slipped into mules. In the kitchen she opened the cabinet door. The jar was there, Mayo still inside.

She sighed, relieved, and turned to make the coffee. In minutes she was curled on the sofa, cradling the hot cup as she watched the new day's cloud-streaked gold, framed by the east window.

"Hands," she whispered, "will we paint today?"

Nothing doing. The hands replied, warming against the cup. *Unless you want a still life—Scorpion In Mayonnaise Jar, perhaps?*

"No, I won't paint Mayo. I don't want to paint her but I do want her out of the house. I'll have Craig throw the jar away—scorpion, eggs and all." She didn't want to disappoint Marty, but he'd understand if she told him that Mayo gave her nightmares.

With that resolve, she rose and went to the linen closet. As she lifted the jar, wonder engulfed her. A few eggs had hatched. Mayo had babies, whole, miniature Mayos, scampering around the treadmill of the slick glass jar. Mayo sat stoically in the center, raising her lethal tail when Leah moved the jar. Fine white dust, the residue of the first hatched eggs lay in the trough circling the jar bottom.

"You're a miracle, Mayo," she said softly and carried the glass nursery to the window.

Sunlight streamed into the jar. She turned it slowly, breaking the darting arrows of light into rainbow colors. The curl of her fingers against the glass framed half-spheres and whole spheres, graceful shapes in muted shades.

"Yes, a miracle," she whispered, watching Mayo's mandibles lift to the sun.

Holding the jar in both hands, she moved to the back door and hurried out, down the steps and across the yard to the junk pile.

She unscrewed the lid and set the jar on the ground, then tipped it over near a gray weathered board. She jumped back as Mayo and babies ran helter-skelter to disappear homeward beneath the refuse.

Circles and egg-shapes filled her mind and tumbled through prisms of light as she hurried back to the house. Not stopping to dress, she pulled easel and paints from the closet.

MO: Writings from the River

Author's Comments

"Cellmates" derived from a number of personal experiences—living on a mini-ranch; knowing an artist whose lovely paintings were composed of multi-colored triangles; and greeting a young son who found and captured in a jar a scorpion with eggs on her back. These elements were distant from each other in chronology. Unlike the heroine in "Cellmates," I loved country life—but knew women who hated it.

My stories write themselves, with my characters dictating them to me. Once I have a character I like, that character tells the story. I edit over and over—"Cellmates" probably went through about 12 revisions.

I made my first sale, a short nonfiction piece, to *Westways Magazine* when I was 19, and at age 89 I am still writing and selling.

—Willma Willis Gore

The Story of Patent Leather Shoes

by Robert Cormack

I was down in the basement packing when the doorbell rang. It rang two times, stopped and rang again. I listened. I wasn't expecting anybody. I came up to the hall and saw a shadow move across the frosted pane in the door. Then hands formed on the glass near the edges where the beveling was clear. I looked out the living room window. Some guy was standing there on the porch writing on a clipboard. He was wearing a windbreaker covered in racing decals, and out on the street there was an extended pickup with the same decals. A ramp was pulled down at the back. Two kids were riding their bikes around it but the guy didn't look at them. He rang the doorbell again, glanced at his clipboard, then scratched his head.

I went and opened the door just as he was starting down the walk.

He turned and smiled. His teeth looked too white for his face. I put the guy around fifty, tanned, hair combed back like an old pompadour.

"You're there," he said. "I didn't think anyone was home." He came back up the steps and flipped through some order forms. "Gilroy?" he said.

"That's my wife's name," I said. "Mine's Andrews."

"Michael Andrews?"

"That's right."

"It's here, too," he said and held out the clipboard. Down at the bottom was a signature. He tapped it with his pen. "That your wife's writing?"

I looked and nodded. Then I saw my name printed in a box.

He wrote something in the margin and clicked his pen.

"Okay," he said. "We got that out of the way. Your wife around?"

"She's not here," I said.

He looked past me down the hallway.

"I guess I could leave the samples," he said. "Most of the time we like both parties present. It's better if everyone's agreed. Will you two be here this evening?"

"She moved out," I said.

The man frowned and looked down. A sample case of upholstery swatches was at his feet. That's when I noticed he was wearing patent leather dress shoes.

"I'm supposed to show some samples," he said and glanced at his clipboard again. "Appointment for the April fifth. That's today."

He pointed to the order form again.

"See here? April fifth."

"I don't know anything about it," I said. "Samples for what?"

"A couch," he said. "Your wife wants it recovered."

"You'll have to talk to her," I said.

He thought about it for a minute.

"Can I use your phone? I have to call this in to my boss."

I pointed to the phone in the front foyer.

Author Bio

Robert Cormack has been an advertising copywriter for 32 years and is a regular freelance writer for *Rosebud*.

He went over and picked up the receiver. "She leave a forwarding address?" he said.

"Not yet," I said.

He scratched behind his ear.

"Okay," he said. "Let me see what they want me to do."

While he was talking on the phone, I stood in the living room. I heard him read off the order number. "She left," he told his boss.

Out the window I could see the kids out by the truck. One of them made like he was going to ride up the ramp. The other was leaning over trying to look through the tinted glass.

The guy hung up the phone and brought his sample case into the living room. He put it on the coffee table.

Then he took out a pack of gum.

"You want a piece?" he said and shook a stick out. "Go ahead."

I shrugged and took it.

"Best sales tool there is," he said. "They tell us to do that. Anybody gets sore, you offer them a piece of gum. You'd be surprised."

"Surprised at what?"

He looked at me. His eyes were pale blue.

"Calms them down," he said. "They stop being sore."

"I'm not sore," I said. "I just don't know anything about this."

> ## *"I've had four wives. I know where you're coming from."*

"Fair enough," he said. "You're not telling me anything new. They have a saying in my business, Michael. Don't be afraid to do a little social work." He started to open the sample case. "You couldn't spare a drink could you? I've been all over the place today. It's been a hot drive."

"All I've got is water," I said.

"Water's fine. I took the pledge. Have for three years now."

I went out to the kitchen and unwrapped a glass from one of the boxes. Everything else was packed up except a fork, spoon, knife, plate and coffee mug. My wife had already taken most of her stuff. I turned on the tap, let it get cold, then filled the glass. When I came back to the living room, he was looking at the order form again. I handed him the glass of water.

"Much obliged," he said. "I was checking the dates. She must have left in a hurry. See the date here?" he said. "Less than two weeks ago."

"It hasn't been that long," I said.

"You don't get much warning," he said and shook his head. "I've had four wives. I know where you're coming from. One day it's all gravy. The next isn't so good. I'm not telling you anything new."

He saw me glance at the clock on the mantel. "Things to do, eh, Michael? Okay," he said, slapping his knees. "I guess we'd better get to it."

He went around to the side of the couch and knelt down.

"Don't worry, Michael, this isn't a sales job," he said.

He lifted the skirt. I noticed he kept his windbreaker zipped up. Every so often, he pulled the elastic waistband down but it came up again when he bent over. His skin was white underneath. "See this?" he said, and tugged at some tacking. He let it fall on the rug. "You don't upholster a couch right and this is what happens. You're not looking."

"I don't care about the couch," I said.

He sat back on his patent leather shoes and stared at me.

"I'm trying to show you something here, Michael."

He sighed and stood up.

"Let's try this again," he said. "See the truck out there? I used to race stocks. I know you don't care what I did. But I raced every-where, Kentucky, Louisiana, Florida. Last time I came back my fourth wife was gone. Took everything." He opened his arms. "This is all I've got left. So I know what it's like."

He picked up the glass of water and finished it.

"You know what my boss said?" he asked. "He told me to take the couch, any-way. He figures she'll get in touch with us. Women do strange things, Michael. She's been gone less than two weeks. If that, you're saying. Okay. Say she already knew she was going to leave. She gets the couch out of the house by having it reupholstered."

"Why would she do that?" I said.

"Say a husband doesn't want to give his wife the couch," he said. "Maybe she figures he'll make a fuss. My boss sends me and maybe another big guy over. I take the heat. See what I'm saying?"

"We never argued over the couch," I said.

"Okay," he shrugged. "Maybe I'm way off base here. I've been wrong before. You want some water? I could use another one myself."

I told him everything was wrapped up in boxes.

"I'll figure it out," he said and went to the kitchen.

I could hear him unwrapping a glass, then the tap ran, then he was back handing me the water. He sat down and rubbed the arm of the couch.

"That's one side of the coin," he said. "Other side? She hadn't decided she was leaving. She figured she'd fix the place up. She was still hoping. That's why your name's on the invoice, too. Again, just speculation."

"I don't think she was," I said. "Hoping, I mean."

"Two sides of the coin, anyway," he said. "Either way, I told them I'd pick up the couch. That doesn't mean I'm not on your side. Look at this for a second."

He knelt down again and pulled up the skirt of the couch. "See where the material is rubbing against the frame here?" he said. "Humor me, Michael. You might learn some-thing." His voice had a strange edge. "It's right against the wood. It wouldn't have lasted, anyway. You're not giving up anything, Michael. That's what I'm saying."

He took a long pocket knife out of his pocket. He flicked it open. He got down low on the rug. "You were married, what? A few years?" he said. He twisted the knife under-neath the couch and pulled it out again. Tacking and batting fell on the rug.

He picked it up and shook his head.

"I don't know where she is."

"It doesn't matter," he said. "I've seen it happen with new and old ones. Some people are only together a couple of months. You didn't know she was leaving, did you, Michael? Not until she did. She staying with friends? A lover, maybe? Again, doesn't matter either way."

"I don't know where she is," I said. "I told you that."

"You see what I'm saying, though?"

"I don't know what you're saying," I said. "Take the couch if that's what she wants. It doesn't matter to me either way."

I was thinking about my wife's last mes-sage on the machine. She said she was mak-ing arrangements. Maybe this was one of them.

The guy sat back on his heels and then stood up.

"Okay," he said. "I can do that. You want the couch out, no problem. We can take it to the truck right now if that's what you want."

The knife was still in his hand. He put it on the coffee table.

"Or there's another way we could do this, Michael," he said.

He nodded to the knife.

"You could have some fun," he said.

I didn't move.

"Michael," he sighed. "She made a deposit. She's committed. You or a new guy. She's doing it for one of you. My bet is a new guy."

"There's no new guy."

"That a fact?" he said. "You know that for a fact?"

I rubbed my head. I didn't look at him.

"It's okay, Michael," he said finally. "You decide what you want to do. She's not coming back either way. Her kind don't. See what I'm saying?"

One of the kids yelled to the other outside.

The knife was there on the coffee table.

"Think about it, Michael," he said. "You say there isn't someone. Maybe you're right. I'll know next week. She has to come in to the shop. We can't go out again. We're only allowed one courtesy call. One per customer."

He nodded to the knife again.

"Give it some thought," he said. "My bet is she'll come in with the other guy. Just a premonition. I get those sometimes. I'm going out for a smoke."

The screen door barely made a sound when he left. I looked out the window. He was standing there with a cigarette in his mouth. He leaned against the porch rail and crossed his legs at the ankles. The he crossed his arms. He watched the kids ride around his truck.

The knife was there on the coffee table. It was an ugly thing. I picked it up and looked at the blade. Then I looked out the window again. The guy had his sunglasses on now. They shone like aluminum in the light.

One of the kids said something to him. He shrugged and let cigarette smoke trail up from his nose. I realized my wife and I didn't know any of the neighbors. She wasn't interested. I don't want to know them. Do you?

That's when I drove the knife into the arm of the couch. It was nothing with a knife like that. I drove the blade right up to the hilt. Then I was pulling it across the cushions. I worked my way right down to the skirt and across the back. The knife went right through the tacking to the wood.

I was breathing heavily at this point. I had to sit down. Things were dancing around in my eyes. I put my face in my hands.

When I looked up the guy was standing there.

He didn't say anything at first. He picked up his case off the coffee table.

"I'll put this in the truck," he said finally. "We can take the couch out when you're ready. No rush. This is my last call today. You want a water or something?"

I shook my head.

"Okay," he said.

"She'll see this?" I frowned.

"She'll have to, Michael," he said. "I told you. One courtesy call per customer. That's policy. We'll let her know that when she calls."

He adjusted his sunglasses and went outside.

The kids rode off and stopped when he came to the truck. He put the swatch case on the front seat and came back. He stood on the porch.

"We're going to need something to prop this door open," he said.

I looked around the living room.

"Never mind," he said.

He was wedging one of his patent leather shoes in the door when I came into the hall. "This'll do," he said. "Found them in the trash when my last wife left. Guess they didn't fit the new guy."

He motioned me back to the living room.

"Grab an end," he said. "We'll tilt it up at the door."

I lifted one end and he lifted the other.

Then he nodded to his clipboard on the coffee table. "Get that if you can," he said. "Put it on the cushion."

I did that and we went outside, setting the couch down at one point so he could get his shoe out of the door. We put the couch onto the bed of the truck and then the guy picked up the clipboard. He pulled down the bottom of his windbreaker. "Just need your signature," he said. "Policy again. Lets everyone know I didn't walk off with this thing."

He handed me a pen from his inside pocket. I noticed he wasn't wearing a shirt. "That'll do it," he said when I signed. "We're done."

He clicked the pen and went around to the driver's side.

"Pleasure, Michael," he said and got in the truck.

He started the engine and waved. Then he made a salute. I watched him drive off and went back in the house. Tacking and fibers were all over the living room rug. You could see an outline where the couch had been. I got the vacuum cleaner. I ran it back and forth. It didn't do much good. I finally got a clothes brush out of the kitchen drawer and tried that. I got down real low on the rug. I watched each fiber pull away from the nap. I went at it until you couldn't tell a couch was ever there. I went over every inch.

Rosebud

Author's Comments

I've learned that every piece of writing is a problem waiting to be solved. The problem with "The Story of Patent Leather Shoes" was the race car driver. He was an interesting character, a man who lost everything to his wife (wives). But I realized I needed a foil, someone with similar marital problems, someone the race car driver would try to befriend and reveal his story at the same time. That's why I kept the story in the present tense.

I went through 38 drafts on this one. It was hard to get it right, but I think it's an interesting story now. Roderick Clark, the editor at *Rosebud*, accepted it right away (I usually send in three stories at a time and get one accepted). In terms of a batting average, it's not great, but, like anything, you get better with time.

I think the most important thing is developing a relationship with an editor, finding someone who likes your work. Most stories are chosen because they fit a publication. Find that publication and you stand a better chance of getting your stories accepted. I've been with *Rosebud* for eight years now. They always get my stories first.

—Robert Cormack

Patience

by Jacqueline Guidry

He devised an elaborate code. Two flashing lights meant pit stop. One light, look for the next exit. Two lights, space, two more lights—you're following too closely. Too complicated, she argued, teased. But he insisted, always a man of systems.

So now Anita was alone in her car, the only cell phone either of them owned on the passenger seat, following him across the unending flatness of Kansas, trying to remember the rest of the code she'd promised to memorize before they left St. Louis. But they left sooner than she expected, robbing her of the time she needed for this scheme. That's what she should have told Evan, her fiancé, when his nose turned red from swallowing too many angry words because she pulled to the side of the road at his three flashing lights when she was supposed to speed up. There were too many signals in his code, too many ways for her to go wrong, mistake his instructions.

As long as he had his systems, he was fine. But she could not accept reassurances bought with such an easy price—flash, flash, everything is fine—and could not match his enthusiasm about this move to Utah. The job

Author Bio

Jacqueline Guidry's stories have appeared in *Louisiana Literature*, *Rosebud*, *Alembic*, *Yemassee*, and other magazines. In 2007, her novel, *The Year the Colored Sisters Came to Town*, was selected as the community read for Windsor, Connecticut.

offer was too sudden, had not allowed time for adequate adjustments. But he was too excited to hear her protests, too taken with his triumph to bother with her misgivings.

"Do you know how many applications they received? How many people wanted this job I got?" He had leaned across the table at Mama Rosa's, his hand buckling the red checked oilcloth. His pupils dilated, maybe from the wine, maybe from the headiness of so much success come his way.

She thought about the question, tried to formulate a reasonable answer. But he didn't wait for her response, wasn't interested in her guesses, no matter how reasonable. He was the one blessed with truth.

"Seven hundred thirteen." He strung out the number, giving each word its earned emphasis.

Anita wondered whether "thirteen" carried a dose of bad luck, but was wise enough to keep the question to herself.

Evan raised his right hand, fingers splayed as if in an odd Dr. Spock salute, then his left hand, only pointer and middle fingers raised. "Over seven hundred," he said, the raised fingers thrusting towards her.

"You were lucky," she said, thinking thirteen might bring good fortune, not bad, when associated with job applications.

"Luck nothing." He started to lower both hands, then kept the left one raised to motion the waiter for a second bottle of wine. "We can afford it, Babe. We can afford lots of things now," he said as if she'd protested the extravagance of two wines at one dinner. But she hadn't said a word.

After the waiter brought the second bottle and poured into both glasses, though hers was still half full, Evan speared a stray mushroom from her plate. "Not bad. Could use more garlic."

She offered quick agreement on this.

"This is it. The big time now. Me and you, Doll, we're going places." He puffed an imaginary cigar, gave her a wink. "Movers called when you were out. They're arriving at 3:00 next Thursday. Can you believe they're moving our stuff? Not that we have much. But still, paying to have it moved?"

"Imagine that." She forked chicken, mushroom, pasta to her mouth, disguising the sarcasm with an eager assault on food.

"Yeah. Imagine that." He grinned, oblivious as ever to her secret messages, her hidden signals. Between bites of lasagna, glasses of wine, he reminded her the company was also looking out for her, sending her those application packets for nursing positions from every hospital and a lot of clinics within a thirty-mile radius of Salt Lake City.

That was her opening, the time she should've said she didn't know whether she wanted to nurse in Utah, a state filled with Mormons who only a few years ago decided blacks were welcomed into heaven. Picture the stampede through heaven's gates when millions of black souls, waiting all those long years for Mormon permission, entered God's Kingdom. Would they allow hands as dark as hers to nurse them back to health? Had they barred brown people from eternal salvation as they had black ones? Was she now as welcome in heaven as the black brethren? Evan was too white to carry such worries.

At home that night, they made love with the bedroom shades raised. A bilious half moon speared their bodies with yellow light at Evan proceeded with his systematic approach to orgasm which Anita had well memorized but which did not serve her well this night.

After he fell asleep, she padded into the darkened kitchen, fixed a cup of apricot tea sweetened with three dollops of honey, a treat she had not earned but felt she deserved anyway. At the counter, she spread open the map of Utah Evan had been studying. In the dim light of moon glow, she could not make out much. The state was indistinct, a place too amorphous to be real.

In Salina, they stopped at the Prehistoric Indian Burial Grounds Museum. Evan's series of five lights with three-second pauses between flashes had signaled a tourist attraction.

They walked around the small hills covered with grass. "Do you think people are really buried here?" she asked.

"Of course." He held her hand, pulled her to another mound. "Why would they build a museum, then announce this is a burial ground, if it isn't?"

"You have a tendency towards the ghoulish."

"Tourists like us would stop and buy things. I don't know." She freed her hand and stooped to the ground, separated blades of grass at the foot of a mound.

"Always the skeptic," he said.

"Do you think tourists will visit our graves in a thousand years?" She stared up at him from her crouch. "Will they be mesmerized by what we did with our dead?"

"Sure. Why not?"

"Doesn't that give you the creeps? Strangers walking over your grave and making comments. 'Wasn't that interesting' or 'How quaint.' They couldn't know who you were or how you lived or died. They couldn't know anything about you."

"Why should they? I would've been dead centuries. Nobody cares about people dead that long." He looked towards the horizon where the sun was still about an hour from setting. "You have a tendency towards the ghoulish. Did you know?"

She stood, stretched her arms above her head, to her left side, then to her right.

"Tired of driving?"

"Just tired," she said.

"We can stop for the night."

"If you want."

He wasn't in any particular hurry now that he'd beaten out 712 other applicants. He didn't report to work for another ten days. The plan, his plan, was to meander to Salt Lake, arriving at least two days before work started, but, in the meanwhile, stopping when the spirit moved him. "Salina it is then." He turned toward the parking lot.

"Wait. Let me get a picture." She posed him in front of a particularly green mound.

"Must be extra bodies, more fertilizer," he said when she commented about the color.

"Hey, I'm the most respectful guy you know." He grinned as she snapped the camera, preserving forever the image of his happiness against a background of dead people reduced to feeding grass and bearing the weight of strangers.

At the window, she parted the drapes smelling of mildew covered with pine spray.

"You filled out any of those applications yet?" He asked as they stretched on a too soft mattress in Motel 6.

"No yet."

"No rush. I was just wondering." He flipped channels, stopped when he saw a John Wayne war movie. "We don't need the money. Not now." John Wayne's plane was shot and looked as if it might crash. But it didn't because John Wayne was the pilot and he never crashed. "Do whatever you want."

She fell asleep with those words echoing in her head. "Whatever you want. Whatever you want. Do whatever you want."

She woke to an empty room and a note on his pillow, still dented from where it had cradled his head through the night. "Hunting breakfast. Back soon as I can." He had not signed the note or said he loved her. But who else would brave the dangers lurking behind the Salina, Kansas street signs to hunt down breakfast? And she knew he loved her. Why else would he have insisted on her moving to Utah immediately, not later when he was settled properly, knew for certain the move wasn't a mistake?

At the window, she parted the drapes smelling of mildew covered with pine spray. A light drizzle promised to last all day and into the night. Driving would be slow, signals even harder to remember today than yesterday.

Across the street a Dunkin' Donuts sign blinked temptation. She hoped he had resisted, not given in to immediate impulses. The sweetness on his tongue would be replaced by a heaviness in his stomach, worsened by the monotony of driving. For a man of systems, he often wasn't able to see beyond immediate pleasure.

She peered through raindrops, but couldn't see his car or him. A good sign, she thought.

She showered, dressed, packed her night case before he returned.

"You're up," he said.

"You're back," she said. "Back from the hunt."

He raised any eyebrow, having forgotten his note, the dangers of the breakfast quest disappearing with his safe return to the lair. "Bagels, O.J, apples and grapes. How's that sound?"

"Good. Sounds good."

"Had some trouble finding those bagels."

She envisioned small town dangers blocking his way.

"But I knew that's what you'd like."

She couldn't answer, her mouth full of hard-earned honey whole wheat bagel and a single grape.

"You'll like Colorado," he said, knowing her travels had been east of St. Louis, into Illinois and places beyond, never west. "The mountains. They're something else. You'll like that."

"Utah has mountains too," she said, remembering the map spread across the moonlit kitchen counter they'd left behind.

"Probably better than Colorado's. But I've never seen them, so I couldn't say for sure."

Then why are we going there, she considered asking. Why aren't we at least going someplace one of us knows?

He held an umbrella over her head while she slopped into her car. "Signaling will be trickier with the rain." He bent through her opened door, kissed her lips so lightly, it might've been the tickle of a single feather. "Pay close attention." He slammed her door shut.

The interstate wasn't far from the motel, so soon they were back on I-70, leaving farther behind every crevice of every place she'd ever known, abandoning everyone she knew. She didn't have to go. That's what her friends said, her mother and aunt, her two brothers and one sister-in-law. They weren't married yet, though they would be soon. That's what Evan said when anyone asked. Soon. But soon wasn't now and that meant she did not have to go with him. A wife has obligations. A girlfriend, even a fiancée, has choices.

Ahead, he slowed as the drizzle transformed into a harder rain. He turned on his lights. She squinted, trying the detect a message, but there seemed to be none, at least none she could read. So, she turned on her lights too, safety having become more important, even to Evan, than messages.

She cracked her window. The smell of rain mixed with earth from the tilled soil of farms they sped past. She was a city girl, the smells as strange as the flatness of Kansas, a state that seemed destined to never end.

"We love each other, I have to go." That's what she said each time a friend or relative suggested otherwise. "I'll find a job soon. Meet people. I'll be okay. You can visit."

They folded their arms then. No matter the person, folded arms accompanied their words, as if what she said demanded some physical sign of protest. And there had also been those unspoken words. You can find a job, meet other people, but you won't find us, meet us for dinner or a drink after work.

"You'll visit," she repeated, a weak answer to all they left unsaid.

They smiled at that for, like her, they faced the rising sun, not the setting one. Habits of perspective were hard to break. So were habits of love.

Now she was in her car, following a man halfway across a country so much larger in real life than in the confines of a map stretched across a kitchen counter, and she couldn't remember why she loved him enough to do this. She concentrated on the road, ignored the queasiness in her stomach reminding her she'd abandoned her old life without knowing whether she had chosen a proper new one.

As they drove farther west, traffic thinned. She watched her odometer when a car passed from the opposite direction, measured the distance elapsing before the next one appeared. Nearly two miles. Soon, she and Evan would be the only drivers on this road, the only remnants of a civilization that knew enough to stay put, detested wandering to unknown places. The west would never have been settled if the settling had been left to Anita or her ancestors. She smiled, thought of Evan agreeing with her, enjoying a laugh not quite at her expense, but almost. What was the signal for I've got something funny to tell you? She couldn't remember if there was one, so maybe there wasn't. Then again, the system was so complete, surely there must be a signal that substituted adequately.

She turned on the radio, but could only find two stations with clear reception. One was a farm report, the other a local talk show. She wasn't usually interested in talk shows, found the hosts boring, the callers even more so. But she left the station playing anyhow, a reminder that beyond this highway, these numbing raindrops, were other humans, many of whom left families and friends, ventured to unknown places, found niches of contentment. At least that's what she told herself.

"Takes a village to raise children. That's a good one. Who came up with that one? Somebody tell me that." His voice was thick, probably from too many cigarettes.

"Should I continue to Utah or go back home?"

She couldn't tell whether the speaker was caller or host.

"It's an African proverb or so I've heard." The voice was a woman's, soft and melodious, promising wisdom, understanding.

"Tell me this. Are we living in Africa? Does somebody know something I don't?"

The soft voice was silent, letting listeners supply the obvious answer.

"I guess that's all I have to say. We don't live in Africa."

"That's right. We don't." The voice was untroubled, settling.

"I'll hang up now. Give somebody else a chance." The belligerence was gone, left defenseless in the face of this balm of agreement.

"Thank you for calling, Jack. Always good to hear from you."

Anita searched for cynicism, an undertone of disparagement, but found none.

"We've time for one or two more callers. Today's open forum on KXKY. Anything you want to talk about, I want to talk about."

Evan turned off his headlights. Anita stiffened for a signal, then relaxed when none came. She turned down the wipers so they swiped the windshield only sporadically, the drizzle having nearly stopped, at least for the moment.

"The number is 744-1819. I'm waiting for your call." The voice was so patient, so inviting, so promising. "744-1819. Dial now."

Anita picked up her cell phone. 744-1819. The voice was waiting, waiting.

"You've reached Sonya at KXKY. What's on your mind, caller?"

"I'm just passing through. I'm moving to Utah with my boyfriend, fiancé. He got a great job there." She wondered whether Evan was tuned to the same station and watched for the signal that meant what the hell are you doing? But his lights stayed off.

"Utah is a beautiful state."

"You've been there?"

"I've never been. Neither has my boyfriend."

"Fiancé," Sonya corrected gently.

"Right. Fiance." He'd be insulted, if he were listening. A stranger, a talk show host no less, having to remind her what he meant to her, what he was to her.

"You're nervous about the move. Worried about what Utah will hold for you, whether you'll fit in there."

Was this a psychic talk show? Those were the worst kinds. But Anita didn't care, didn't want to hang up before getting some of the wisdom Sonya's voice promised. "That's it. That's it exactly."

"You've left your friends, family, everyone," Sonya said.

"Everyone," Anita echoed.

"Your fiancé has a job waiting, but you don't. You have nothing."

"Nothing," Anita said, reduced to repeating what radio Sonya, psychic Sonya, knew. She took a deep breath, steadying her voice for the question Sonya surely knew was coming. "Should I continue to Utah or go back home?"

There was a pause long enough to allow Sonya to tally the votes of the universe before she answered. "What's your name, caller?"

"I'd rather not say."

"Or course not." How could Sonya know Evan might be listening, that withholding her name was the only peace offering Anita could tender him at this moment? "Do you mind if I refer to you as Caller X?"

"That's fine." She spoke quickly, the snap of her words matching the static increasing in the phone connection as she drove farther from Sonya. "My question, though. Just answer my question, if you can."

"Patience is always a virtue, Caller X." The voice was an invitation to relaxation.

Anita inhaled deeply, knowing she must wait. A minute elapsed in silence. But the silence was nearly as comforting as Sonya's voice. Anita suspected regular listeners, and surely there must be legions of them, were very familiar with these pauses, looked forward to them as healing oases in days that, even in the middle of this vast emptiness, must have been filled with too much.

"No one can predict the future," Sonya said at last.

"We'd all be millionaires, if we could."

"That's right, Caller X. So instead, we must each of us, you too, learn to follow our heart's desire. Look into your heart, Caller X."

"I love Evan. Really I do." She spoke quickly, forgetting any duty to protect his identity or her own. "I'm a nurse or at least I was a nurse back home."

"Still a nurse. One of the great caring professions. You are a caring person. I could tell. My listeners could tell."

Anita flushed, embarrassed by how pleased she was with this compliment from a radio stranger. If she lived around here, she'd be a faithful listener, probably call on a regular basis, be a constant source of shame to Evan. "I'm Hispanic."

"We are sisters, Caller X." The voice was encouraging now, reaching out to lift Anita over this mountain of doubt.

"Mormons. I've read about them. They hate blacks, dark-skinned people. Me. In addition to everything else, there are the Mormons."

"No, no, Caller X. No one hates you. Mormons don't hate you or blacks or anyone of color. No. That's not the world any more. It's not what my listeners think and it's not what you really think either."

"It isn't?"

"No, Caller X. Do you want me to tell you the real concern you have?"

"Yes. Tell me quickly."

Sonya was fading rapidly. The drizzle returned to a steady rhythm. Evan turned on his lights again. Anita couldn't bother with lights.

"You are afraid the love of this man, this Evan, will not be enough to sustain you. That without your friends, your kin, you will wither and die. You must not . . ." The phone crackled twice, then Sonya was gone.

Anita jiggled the phone, pressed the talk button twice. Nothing. She hung up slowly. You must not . . . Must not what? Go to Utah? Go home? Keep driving? Follow Evan?

Drizzle changed to rain. She twisted the wipers to faster speed, turned on her lights. The rain answered with a heavier pounding. Water pelted the car until, even with the wipers at their fastest speed, the lights their brightest, she could not see where she was going. Evan had disappeared. Everything had disappeared. She pulled to the side of the road and waited.

After a few minutes, the rain stopped suddenly. Far ahead, a car blinked frantically, signaling "Where are you? Where are you?"

She turned off the engine but left the lights on, waiting to see how long it would be before he came back to her, willing to wait a long, long time, a well of patience growing in her heart.

Crab Orchard Review

Patience

Author's Comments ─────────

In passing, a colleague at my office mentioned her husband's driving code, using lights as signals when they travel in separate vehicles. That was enough to spark my imagination and provide the kernel for "Patience." As often happens, that idle comment grew until it encompassed an entire story. I should mention the characters appeared, as characters are wont to do, completely unrelated to the person who first mentioned the driving technique.

I worked to find that right balance between dialogue and narration. Also, I tried to explain the light code the characters used without becoming too repetitive. Throughout, I worked to maintain a consistent tone.

I did four complete revisions. I'm defining "revision" as the point when I've handwritten so many changes that another printing is mandatory. Otherwise, I stop being able to interpret what I've scribbled in margins. Usually, I do many more revisions, so for some reason, this story came together quicker than most.

Revisions consisted of everything from changing single words to eliminating paragraphs and adding others. One technique that works for me when editing is to read the piece aloud in a flat, quiet voice. Somehow, that lets me hear the clunkers my eyes miss. I did this on several occasions with this story.

I do very little planning, which is probably why my revising process is so extensive. Sometimes, I at least know where a story is ending up. Not with this one. Maybe that's why I had to be particularly patient as "Patience" evolved.

My advice is commonplace. Read and write. A lot. When you think your work is ready for publication, ask folks you respect to critique the piece. Consider the suggestions and decide which, if any, to incorporate in your work. Then review magazines where the piece might fit. Comply with magazines' guidelines.

Don't let yourself get too discouraged by rejections. Most of us writers get lots of those. Getting published is a matter of persistence. Resolve that you won't let yourself become one of those folks who gave up and dropped their efforts to find a public home for their writing. Remember, only you can write the stories you have inside yourself. If you don't write them, no one else ever will.

—Jacqueline Guidry

Killer Shift

by Michael Giorgio

Most people say I'm crazy for doing this work, but it's what I'm experienced at, and I'm damn good. This store, a Stop 'n Grab just off the interstate, is sort of far from the city, so we're the only business on the exit. Still, we have our regular customers, and that helps a lot. Overnight on a Saturday, it's quiet enough to think, busy enough not to have to. Just the way I like it.

Most cashiers call this the killer shift. Too lonely, too scary, they say, especially for a pretty young lady like me. Only I'm not that young anymore, and nobody can say I'm pretty and mean it, so this is perfect for me. It keeps my days free to decide where I'm traveling next because I'm one window woman who won't get stuck in any one place. Wherever I go, store managers jump at the chance to hire me when I tell them I've been cashiering for ten years. They don't even bother to check references since I can talk the lingo. Being an experienced graveyard shifter, I'm worth my weight in soda and chips to any convenience store.

Customer traffic's been steady tonight. It usually is on a Saturday. About eleven, when I start work, the high-schoolers are still coming, trying to score beer with fake IDs and settling for soda when they see they aren't getting anywhere with me. Around midnight, the college kids begin to show up, running in for a junk food fix and whatever brew is on special.

This is when the strange ones start showing up . . .

Other people come and go, too. Second shifters pick up smokes on their way home. Truckers stop, needing a caffeine jolt. Harried parents pick up cough drops and chewable aspirin for sick kids, bitching that it's overpriced, but paying just the same since we're the only place open. Guessing what a person will buy when he walks in is a game for me, a way to kill time. I'm usually right. I'm not psychic, just experienced.

Around three, the predictable customers stop coming. Until the morning regulars show up for coffee and early treats, a cashier learns the true meaning of 'graveyard shift' because it gets pretty dead in the store. This is when the strange ones start showing up, the loners and the losers, when the only comforting company a cashier has is the image on the security monitor, and that screen's as grainy as the 'authentic alien abduction' photos on the cover of the *Weekly World News* at the check out. It's now, in the dead of the night, that the fear sets in and makes this the killer shift.

A guy comes in around three-thirty,

Author Bio

Michael Giorgio lives with his wife, an author/teacher/editor, and his daughter in Waukesha, Wisconsin, where he teaches creative writing for All Writers' Workplace and Workshop. His fiction has appeared in such magazines as *The Strand* and *Mystery Time*, and in several anthologies. He has also had audio dramas produced in markets from New York to Los Angeles.

wearing a black jacket with a logo from some heavy metal band. He wanders around for a bit, looking at stuff, but doesn't pick anything out. When he comes toward the counter empty-handed, familiar, unwelcome jitters twist through me. I'm no stranger to holdups, and this guy's showing the signs. I've learned to trust my instincts.

Before the guy reaches the counter, a security guard from the factory in town shows up. He's a regular Saturday customer and a talker, a real motor mouth. I listen to him,

> ## *Your best chance to survive is if you cooperate with the robber.*

but never take my eyes off Heavy Metal lurking behind him. Before Security finished telling me the latest hassle with his boss, Heavy Metal gets discouraged and takes off.

I tell Security what almost happened. His look says it all—Holy shit. He gives me his money, nukes his sandwich, and warns me to be careful. He thinks I should call the cops, but I won't. Heavy Metal left and won't be back. That's been my experience with his kind.

Sometimes experience is wrong, I remind myself when Heavy Metal pulls into the parking lot around four. When he passes by me, he doesn't smell like he's been drinking or smoking grass to build up his nerve. Good thing. Sober and straight don't usually spell trouble. When they're stoned, you never know what'll happen.

The guy picks up a pack of gum from the display. When I go to ring him up, his hand shifts toward his jacket. I try to force down my fear, but the jitters demand life.

Your best chance to survive is if you cooperate with the robber, the convenience store owners always say. I've been at this long enough to know better. I slide my hand under the counter, carefully curling my fingers

around the little automatic, my special surprise for the likes of this guy. His hand inches closer to the opening of his jacket, and my grip gets tighter on my gun.

Then he starts to talk. Asks for directions. And all that's hiding inside his jacket is a map. I work the register one-handed, the other frozen beneath the counter, and get him on his way. Once he's gone, I start to shake. Violent, uncontrollable shivers.

It's not ten years ago. It's not ten years ago.

Heavy Metal's not the robbing, murderous scum who ended my husband's life, the only man who ever could call me pretty and mean it. It's today, and my instincts were wrong, and I can't stop shaking.

I pour myself a cup of hours-old decaf. Maybe it's time to switch to days, find out if I can sleep at night again. If I can't, I'm sure I'll be allowed to go back to overnights. Back to the killer shift.

Workers Write!

Author's Comments ————————

"Killer Shift" started when I wondered why anyone would want to work the overnight shift in a lonesome store. From that simple thought, the paranoid, revenge-seeking, lonely clerk was born. The story, initially, came easily once I let the clerk start to tell her story.

The complications came later, when the editor of *Tales from the Cash Register* made a simple request. He loved the beginning of the story, but hated the original ending (in which the clerk pulled the trigger, discovered her mistake, and ran . . . an ending I thought was cool) and asked me to change it.

No problem, I thought. I don't use outlines, preferring to let the characters go their own way rather than force my ideas on them, so I simply backed up to the pivotal point in the story and tried again. And again. And again and again.

Finally, with the deadline looming and my writing group as sick of my feeble attempts to finish the story as I was, I got it—from the character, of course. The key was that she feared her thoughts as much as she got excited by them. Once that realization came, the new ending not only came, but was stronger for it.

"Killer Shift" illustrates an important rule for writers: The story belongs to the characters. When the author gets in the way and imposes something he thinks is cool simply for the sake of placating his ego, the story veers off course and its chance of success diminishes.

—Michael Giorgio

One Life

by Kevin Brown

S ARS.
   Severe Acute Respiratory Syndrome.
   Begins with a high fever, 38° Celsius
or more, accompanied by headache, discomfort, and body pain. Ten to twenty percent of
patients get diarrhea. Within two to seven
days a dry cough develops, usually followed
by pneumonia.

Worldwide, 8,098 people are sick with
SARS. Of these, 774 are dead.

One of them, my wife Mei Lin.

Stepping off Cathay Pacific Flight 6121
at Hong Kong International, I breathe in a
chest-load of air, slide my hand along the tunnel rail, and wipe my mouth.

If there's a God, I'll be 775.

Leaving the terminal, I pass the luggage
carousels headed for immigration check-in.
This time, there's no suitcases or travel bags
so full they barely zip. No gifts from America
or tax free airport wine for Mei Lin's parents.
Everything I own is in a black travel pouch

Author Bio

Kevin Brown has published stories in
over 40 literary, satirical, and horror journals. He was nominated for a Best American Short Story Award and a Journey
Award and is the recipient of a Lily Peter
and Walton Fellowship. He wrote the
screenplay for a film that was accepted
into the Moondance International Film
Festival. He has also completed a novel,
Invisible Bodies.

strapped around my waist.

On your way to die, it's funny how the
things most important fit nicely into a travel
pouch.

At the counter, a thin man checks my
passport, staring at me over a baby blue surgeon's mask. He stamps the book beside the
stamps of other trips to Hong Kong—our
wedding. Christmas and summer visits. Mei
Lin's funeral.

He slides the passport back to me and,
muffled behind his mask, says, "Immigrant Entrance Card." I hand him the small yellow card
I filled out on the plane. The writing is barely
legible, and I'm not sure if that's from turbu-
lence or because my hands are still shaking.

"Enjoy your stay," he tells me, and I step
in. Cutting through the swarm of people in
the central lobby, I drop my passport in a
trash container near the exit, letting my fingertips smear the edge of its opening.

Outside the airport, I walk toward the
bus stop. Tai Mo Shan and the Eight Dragon
Mountains are wrapped around the back of
the island, dark and green and disappearing
into the morning skyline. Two years ago, Mei
Lin and I stood in this same bus line, huddled
against the wind coming off the South China
Sea. It was December, and we were staying
through Chinese New Year.

"The dragon dancers," she told me,
"come right into your home—even if you live
on the fortieth floor—and dance in each
room." Smiling, she said, "For good luck."

I board the KMB City Bus and spiral up
the stairs to the top level, sliding my hand

over the handrail to lift as many germs as possible. There are six or seven passengers, everyone spread out at least five seats apart. Except for an old man near the middle, they're all wearing surgical masks, their eyes following me until I pass.

I drop into the seat beside the old man, lean in close, and take a deep breath, patting him on the hand. His forehead bunches up. "Tsi sing, gwai lo," he says in Cantonese, calling me a crazy white man. He stands and plows over me, heading for the staircase. Over the hiss of the bus pulling away, he yells something else I can't hear, shakes his head, and drops down the stairs out of sight.

I breathe in deep through my mouth and hold it.

The other passengers are twisted toward me in their seats, all eyes and muffled breathing. A couple of their masks are blank, but the others are decorated with words and colors, pictures and symbols.

There's a British-Hong Kong flag.

A "Peace" sign.

A teenage girl a few seats up, her mask says: "NO KISSING."

The people are wearing these masks because it can be transmitted by air. If someone sneezes or coughs, the corona virus is released, back flipping in the air until it finds a

"One life, One love."

surface or is breathed in with your cologne or perfume. With the smell of your breakfast or green tea, your own oxygen leads it straight through the front door.

Sort of a new millennium Judas.

I take another deep breath and kiss the window glass. Outside, we're crossing the Tsing Ma Bridge, headed into the congested streets of the New Territories. The bus brakes hard every few seconds, squealing and stopping

inches away from the double-decker ahead.

I unzip the travel pouch and lay the contents across my lap. There's Mei Lin's wedding ring. An envelope with 45,000 Hong Kong dollars. There's a wedding reception photo of us standing above our red and gold cake, our arms hooked at the elbow, drinking after a toast. Her mouth is covered in red icing, her cheeks flushed from the champagne, the way they always did with alcohol. In the photo, I'm so nervous my glass is blurry from shaking.

I hold the wedding ring up and look at the inscription: Chinese characters meaning, "One life, One love." I slide it onto my little finger and twist it around, the light reflecting off the gold. The bus slips through a tunnel, and the ring and everyone staring goes black.

Tragedy and disease are educational. They teach you in a week what it takes months to memorize in any medical school. A son suffers massive head trauma in a motorcycle accident, give it a few days and his parents will be talking about brain injuries in words you can barely pronounce, much less spell. Your wife gets SARS, you learn she died without knowing she was dying. She's got a cold, then she's dead.

What's left are facts. The statistics. And you learn them all because now, that's your relationship with your wife. It's as close as you can get to being close.

And your memories, even after a few months they're just loose strings that used to have knots. Like medical facts you've heard of but never experienced.

With my wife, I remember washing dishes. Side-by-side, one washing, one drying. Me helping her with English, her teaching me Cantonese. I'd tell her the rules of "American" football, and she'd tell me about Chinese history and culture—legends and mythology. Superstitions. She told me that red is like their white, so it's worn at weddings for good luck. "White's our black," she said, rinsing a soup bowl. "It symbolizes death, so we wear it at funerals." She told how they avoid the number four because it's pronounced the same as "death." "So really," she said, "four's our thirteen."

I heard about the switchback from British to Chinese rule.

That street gangs fight with knives instead of guns, and that spitting is a good thing. "Spitting," she said, handing me a wine glass, "is our 'knock on wood.'"

One night, at the sink, she said, "My grandmother believes that to reunite with loved ones in the afterlife, those loved ones must die the same way." Standing at the sink, scrubbing fettuccini from a dinner plate, she said there's a different afterlife for every way of dying. "If a father dies of a heart attack and his son dies in a war, the real tragedy is they won't be together in spirit." Then she slapped me on the shoulder and said, "But that's bad luck talk," and laughing, we both spat into the sink.

I remember all this, but it's slipping. Becoming a fragment.

I also remember her sister getting breast cancer last year, starting treatment in January. And Mei Lin flying over to be with her. And me not being able to get off work. Her sister recovering and my wife contracting SARS, and not much else except for the facts and silence and everyone dressed in white.

I step off the bus in the Shatin shopping district, and everything's shoulder to shoulder. Cutting through the crowd, they move around me, just staring eyes over the tops of their masks.

One mask has puckered red lips.

There's buck teeth and freckles on another.

I walk through the shopping malls, running my hands along the escalator rails. Using the crowded restrooms, not washing my hands. Hoping to find the germ, I touch the toilet seats and wipe my nose. I force my way into overcrowded elevators.

All this, it's desperation. I'm running out of time. The news said the World Health Organization's found a cure, and by now all the hospitals have be quarantined off. Right in time to stop me, but not in time to save Mei. The window's closing. And if God closes one window and opens another, I'm fucked.

Outside, I take a mini-bus and get off in Tsim Sha Tsui in Kowloon and walk along Victoria Harbor, on the Avenue of Stars. It's starting to drizzle and, chilly, I take my coat off and let the wind eat at my skin. Catching a cold, my immune system would be weaker. Sort of a Welcome mat for the germ.

I place my hands in the cemented handprints of all the Asian film stars along the walkway, thinking how many people might have touched here recently. Thinking about the germs possibly waiting in the palm of Jackie Chan's hand. The viruses on Sammi Cheng's fingertips. Death in Bruce Lee's fist.

. . . if you fall in, it takes days to get the smell out of your skin.

I look out at the dark sea, the surface like dragon scales in the breeze. Mei Lin said this water is some of the filthiest in the world. That if you fall in, it takes days to get the smell out of your skin.

And behind me, I hear: "Sir? You want picture?"

I hear: "Clouds make good picture."

A man walks toward me carrying a camera and tripod, a mask tied over his mouth that says: "SMILE!" "Cheap picture," he says.

On my first visit, Mei Lin and I had our picture taken on the harbor at night, the city lit up behind us. The sky full of color from the light shows. It was probably this exact place. Maybe this exact man.

I lift my hand and shake my head no. I

pull out the envelope of money and slip out two thousand dollars. Pointing at the sea, I hold the cash up and say, "But, I'll give you this if you can get me a glass of that water."

I take the Star Ferry from Kowloon to Hong Kong Island. Usually, the ferry is spilling over with tourists, but now it's just me and an older Chinese lady sitting a row over. She's wearing a mask and watching me, an expressionless expression on the top part of her face. A few gray bands of hair mouse-tail over her eyes, and she glances down at the glass Coke bottle of seawater I'm holding.

Inside the bottle, trash and debris whip around like a shook snow globe, and some kind of thin, oily liquid is layered at the top. The man with the tripod and camera, after he filled the bottle I gave him an extra thousand dollars because his hand got wet.

I hold it up, say, "Water," in Cantonese, and take a sip, nearly gagging. The lady looks

White roses are spread out like a Chinese fan in front of the tombstone.

away and I spit something gritty out. It's risky, I know. Drinking this, there's all kinds of other diseases I could get. But like I said, I'm getting desperate.

Stepping off the ferry dock, I grab a cab and hop inside.

"Where you going?" the cab driver says in the rearview mirror.

"To my wife," I tell him.

He says, "Where she at?"

"She's dead," I say, and he spins around in the seat, his mask deflating over his mouth as he breathes. "Gallant Garden Cemetery," I tell him, and take another drink.

Cemeteries here, they're different than in the States. Space is limited where population is not, so the dead are buried on a steep slope. Like their houses, they go up instead of out. Mei Lin said after six years, the bodies are dug up for the space to be reused. One afternoon, staring at her grandmother's headstone, she told me, "If the family is wealthy, they can pay to have the skeletons cleaned and reburied in the same place."

She sat beside the grave, above where she'd be buried in under a year and, squinting at the sun said, "If they can't afford it, the remains are cremated."

My hands tremor and I slip the wedding ring off my pinky and hold it up.

I step through the gates and already there are four or five fresh mounds of dirt. Probably SARS, taking someone else's wife or husband. Mother or son. At one of the mounds, a lady is on her knees, her hands finger-to-finger, palm-to-palm and laced with Buddhist prayer beads, chanting, "*Namo Amituo Fo,*" over and over.

I walk to Mei Lin's grave and sit down. White roses are spread out like a Chinese fan in front of the tombstone, and at the foot there are three incense sticks burned to the stem.

It's the first time I've been here since the funeral.

I close my eyes tight and try to cry but can't. Those things are gone now. This is just a rock and a patch of grass. Below that, a sunken mound of dirt crushing a box with nothing like my wife inside.

It's not I'm moving on. I'm moving to.

"*Namo Amituo Fo,*" the lady behind me says.

I open my eyes and for a second, I see Mei Lin in front of me, like the day we saw her grandmother. She looks at me and, squinting her eyes in the wind, disappears.

My hands tremor and I slip the wedding ring off my pinky and hold it up. One life, one love, but all I need is one death. "I'm on my way," I say, and pop the ring inside my mouth. Throwing my head back, I turn the Coke bottle up and swallow the ring with the rest of the seawater.

It's getting late. The sky is the color of soaked newspaper and the buildings are blinking silhouettes. What's left of the light is sliding behind the mountains like a drop of dishwater on a wine glass.

I ferry back across the harbor to Tsim Sha Tsui. It's time to stop wasting time. To end this. Get through the window before the window shuts.

Leaving the shore, I place the envelope of money and picture in my shoe and walk toward Nathan Road. To where the dirty shit goes down and my odds go up.

To the Chungking Mansions.

Four towers of boarding houses, this place is seventeen stories high. Outside, air conditioners are knotted out of windows, and the façade is chipped and peeling like skin. Through the heavy glass doors, the first two floors are a maze of curry messes smelling like old chicken blood. Poorly lit sweat-shops and rundown sari stores.

Mei Lin said the Mansions are known for murderers and drug dealers. Prostitution and gambling. Illegal immigrants from India and Sri Lanka wander the labyrinth of halls and alleys. "And the poor," she said, "they're crammed together, sleeping in the alleys, begging for scraps of food like so many pigs."

And I feel the hands reaching into my pockets, clawing at whatever I may be carrying.

I step inside and the heat and sweat and food melts to my face. I walk through, letting my fingertips slide along the dingy surfaces.

The graffiti covered walls and snot-smeared handrails. Shoving through the hordes of people, I pass a shop where thin, patchy chickens flutter inside small cages. A fabric store where a stained Yin and Yang blanket hangs from a wire. The sign: "16 HKD" stapled to it. Neon signs reflect in the main hall's mirrored ceiling, where banners and Chinese lamps twist in a half-arc.

And I feel the hands reaching into my pockets, clawing at whatever I may be carrying.

Someone grabs the Coke bottle in my pocket, drops it, and pinches me.

Another hand, a ring gets caught and rips my pocket open. My travel pouch is clicked off and snatched away.

I keep my head down. If I take a knife to the guts, show's over. Curtain closed. My wife, any hope of seeing her again is out the wrong window.

I step inside a bric-a-brac shop and in the corner, an old fortuneteller watches me cross the room. His hair white and ratty, he stands and follows me down an isle.

"Fortune?" he says. "Fortune today?"

I hold my palm out flat and he takes it in his twitching fingers.

He looks up at me, then back at my hand. At me. My hand.

He smiles and shakes his head. "Good fortune, gwai lo." Patting my hand, he says, "Long life."

I snatch my hand away and tell him he's wrong. I say, "You're a liar," and step out, disappearing into the crowd.

At a food outlet, I stop and order a box of Indian curry.

"Something else?" the man taking my order says, and I tell him, "Not unless you'll touch the food with your bare hands."

I move on, taking large bites of curry and rice with my fingertips. It's cold and gummy inside my mouth, and the chicken meat's not chicken.

I turn down an alley that's empty except

for a pair of small legs sticking straight up out of a trash dumpster. Beside the legs, a baby carriage. After a few minutes, the legs seesaw at the waist and a frail girl slides over the lip of the dumpster, back to the ground. She's holding a glass bottle in each hand.

She places the bottles in a plastic bag hanging on the carriage handle. I walk toward her, licking slimy green curry off each finger. The light is weak, making the hall fluorescent green. When she sees me, she freezes, her eyes wide, and grabs the carriage, pushing it down the alley.

"Wait," I tell her in Cantonese. I say, "I won't hurt you."

Over her shoulder she's watching me, the carriage rattling on the rough floor. A wheel catches on a garbage bag, turning the carriage sideways, almost tipping it.

I run toward her.

Near the dumpster, something like rotting meat cobwebs my head and I cover my nose with my arm.

"Please," I tell her. "Let me help."

She rights the carriage, never taking her eyes off me. Her cheeks and clothes are smudged in something tar black and she smells like the dumpster.

"Dau tze," she says, her teeth rotten and knotted, and I tell her, "You're welcome."

Inside the plastic bag, there are several beer and wine bottles. Inside the carriage, a baby, completely covered by a dirty white blanket.

I've heard about these children. How the Chinese, the pregnant mothers, would come over and give birth to their babies, then after a while go back to the mainland without the children. Most die. Some are taken care of by other homeless children.

"The lucky ones," Mei Lin told me, "they have to find things to sell."

Like bottles. Cans and trash.

"Family?" I ask the girl, pointing at the baby.

And she says, "Sister," never taking her eyes off me.

Reaching real slow like into my pocket, I pull out the Coke bottle, hold it up, and place it in the bag.

She bows, watching.

And suddenly, I lean down and start digging through the piles of garbage. Looking for bottles—for anything—I tear holes in the bags and empty them on the floor. Every one I move, the odor goes through my nose and my eyes water. As bad as it is, the dumpster smell is worse.

. . . I reach down and lift the baby from the carriage.

I find a Blue Girl beer bottle and slip it inside the bag. She watches me a few seconds, then gets down and sifts through the junk beside me.

I find a bottle.

She finds a can.

I'm digging faster and faster, running my hands through dark wet trash, clawing for anything worth something. The smell getting stronger, I pull bottles out like babies from a womb. Saving them. Harvesting them.

After I've checked all the bags I stand, my pants cold and sticking to my knees and thighs.

The little girl is still digging, holding a bag bottom up and emptying it out in wads of muck that scatter like a virus.

I watch her, wiping my mouth with the back of my hand.

And then, all quiet, I reach down and lift the baby from the carriage.

And I find the smell.

I pull the blanket back from her face and can tell she's been dead at least three weeks. Not much is left of the cheeks and nose. The lips are gone, eaten away from the gums where teeth never got to grow.

The girl sees me and stands, again eyes wide. "Please give me sister," she says, "Please give me sister." She holds her arms out, her hands shaking so bad they're almost blurry.

I smile, hold my index finger to my lips, and say, "Ssh." Pulling the blanket over the baby's face, I lay it back down, slow and easy, into the carriage.

She puts her arm over her sister, still staring up at me. Reaching down to my foot, I slip my shoe off and take out the envelope of money. I lay it down on the baby's still stomach and walk back up the ally.

At the sink, Mei Lin told me how the Mongols were able to conquer most of the Eastern world by wearing silk shirts.

I laughed.

"Not kidding," she said, a soap bubble on her nose. If a Mongolian warrior was hit by an arrow, he'd just grab a fistful of shirt on each side of the shaft and pull in opposite directions. Rinsing a dumpling plate, she said, "Because it couldn't go through the silk, the arrow popped right out."

What's left are the facts. As if they really matter.

Leaving the Mansions, I grab a young guy by the arm, twist him toward me, and say, "If we just had silk shirts, the whole world could stay alive." The guy, he snatches his arm away and backs inside, watching me.

I walk back to the Avenue of Stars, still covered in wet black. Across the harbor, the light show's started, and red and blue, yellow and violet reflections are thrown across the dragon scales in the water. I sit at the railing and watch.

After a while, I pull out the wedding picture and stare at it. My shaking hands. Her red face. The lights throw shadows across me, then her. Me, then her.

Me nervous. Her laughing.

Everything red for luck.

A single tear slips over my cheek and snakes through the caked curry and trash on my face.

I wipe my eye and laugh. Things like crying are gone now. Like strings without knots. Warriors without silk.

The shadow covers me. Covers her.

Me.

Her.

And I put my fist to my mouth, close my eyes, and wait to start coughing.

Alligator Juniper

Author's Comments

My wife is from Hong Kong and she'd told me about several of her culture's superstitions. Around that time I'd also read that a huge factor in the Mongolian conquests was silk shirts—that arrows could not penetrate the silk and could be popped out, keeping the wounds minor.

Not long after, I saw an article on the Internet about Chinese children taken to Hong Kong and abandoned by their parents. There was a picture of a very young girl, her face smeared in dirt. She was collecting bottles from garbage cans to sell for food. Then, SARS happened. So I took these threads and tied them in a knot around a man on a mission.

I wrote the first draft of "One Life" and it was terrible. I had the left-to-right down, but there was no depth. I also didn't know the environment, the terrain, and since the country is really a character in the story, that was a problem. So my wife and I went to Hong Kong and stayed a couple of weeks. I learned quickly what was missing: the sights and sounds, the smells and rhythms of the city. I took notes.

I didn't use an outline. I knew I wanted the character to step off the plane, drop his passport in the trash, and enter the city where he wanted to die. I knew he'd visit his wife's grave and that he'd end up

Author's Comments *(cont.)* ━━━━━━

at the Chungking Mansions. I also knew he'd meet the little girl and her baby sister, but originally I had the ending in a theater. However, seeing the light show by the South China Sea when I was there changed that. It had to be used. And all the locations I chose came from visiting them. But the basic structure and events were always in my mind. Basically, I knew the destination and the roads I'd take, it was just the stops along the way that were a surprise.

I drafted the story twice. I kept some of the better lines and the structure of the first draft but started completely over on the second. After that, I carried a hard copy around and handwrote additional scenes. Deleted others. I typed up the changes, polished it the best I could, and sent it out.

I chose *Alligator Juniper* because a friend of mine had a subscription to it and I absolutely loved the journal. The content, the look and feel of the paper, the dimensions and thickness and weight, everything. It is a little-known gem in publishing, and I recommend it highly to writers who want their work displayed with care and quality. It is also the only journal to call upon acceptance.

My advice to writers beginning to submit is—DO MORE. Write more. Read more. Submit more and get rejected more. If you fail more, you will ultimately succeed more. If you're this far, you're serious about it. And if you're serious, you've obviously become aware that there's talent there. Do all this and it's just a matter of time before successes begin to appear. Spoken from pure experience.

—Kevin Brown

Stargazers

by David Michael Kaplan

Late one August night, when I was ten and my brother Jason only six, my father shook me awake. He put a finger to his lips, then raised his other hand. He was wearing a baseball glove.

"Get your mitt, Marcy," he whispered.

"Why?" I asked groggily.

"We're going to play catch." He was shaking Jason now, who woke quickly, blinking.

"But Dad, it's night," I said.

"I *know* it's night. Don't you hear how quiet it is?" He seemed nervous, skittish. "Jason, get your glove," he ordered. "And your sister's."

Jason plopped back on the pillow. "I don't want to play catch," he said.

"Don't you want to get better?" My father pounded his fist into his glove, over and over. "This is the time to do it."

"Where's Mom?" I asked.

"Asleep." He sounded as if I were foolish to ask. "Come on, let's go. We can't wait all night."

I tucked my night dress into my jeans. Sleepy and bewildered, Jason and I followed him out the side door into the night. Our streets had no lights and all the houses were dark. There was no moon, and most of the stars were obscured by clouds that passed like shadows on the sky.

"I want to see Mom," Jason said.

"You can't," my father said. "I told you, she's asleep." He raised the garage door and turned on the switch—light spilled onto the driveway and lawn, and I blinked. Moths quickly gathered around the bulb, circling it white and ferociously. My father cleaned his glasses on his undershirt, put them back on, and squinted behind the thick lenses—without his glasses, he was practically blind. He motioned to us to spread out. With only the spill of garage light for illumination, we began to play catch. My father grunted as he threw. He was a bulky man, and his shirt was soon damp with sweat.

"You have to practice if you want to get better," he said. He threw the ball to me, hard, and it stung. Jason wasn't very coordinated and was sleepy besides; often he missed the ball and had to run after it.

"Get your glove lower," my father snapped. "How many times do I have to tell you? Your sister catches better than you."

"It's hard to *see*," Jason said.

"He's trying, Dad," I said. I felt protective of Jason—he frustrated easily, and besides, he didn't want to be there.

Jason missed another ball, which rolled into the street, out of the light. He wouldn't go after it. "It's too dark," he protested.

"What are you afraid of?" my father asked. "There's nothing out there."

"I don't want to play anymore." Jason threw off his glove.

Author Bio

David Michael Kaplan's first short story collection is entitled *Comfort.* He has published a novel, *Skating in the Dark,* and his stories have appeared in *The Atlantic, Redbook,* and *Triquarterly,* among others.

"All right," my father said. "Go on, quit. Marcy and I'll play. We'll have a good time." Jason went inside, my father and I threw the ball in silence, the only sound besides the *thock* in our gloves the furious beating of moths around the light. And then, without a word, my father took off his mitt and shut the garage door, the light still on. Without a word we went back into the house, he to his room, me to mine. He seemed lost to himself and didn't even say goodnight.

Jason was asleep again. For a long time I lay awake and thought about it all, and it wasn't until I heard my father snoring that I could finally sleep. In the morning I ran to the garage and opened the door. My heart skipped—the light was off. It had all been a dream. But on the floor, moths lay like ghosts. Most were dead, a few still fluttered weakly. I stamped on the ones still alive, then swept them up and dumped them in the trash can outside, stuffing them underneath some newspapers so nobody could see.

"Come down here," my father called. "I want to show you something." It was a week later. I was in my room making an Indian bead belt for Girl Scouts. My mother had gone shopping, and Jason was at a friend's house.

My father stood at the bottom of the stairs, tool box in hand. He seemed agitated, as if some dark current were pulsing through him.

"Show me what?" I asked cautiously.

"We're going to take the wallpaper off in the bathroom. I'm going to teach you how."

I followed him into the bathroom. "Does Mom know about this?" I asked.

He winked slyly. "It's going to be a surprise." He handed me a scraper. "Do it like this." He scored the wallpaper, gently at first, then harder. "See?"

I held the scraper and stared at the gouge on the wall.

"When you get married someday," my father said, "you'll know how to do this. You can teach your husband something."

"I'm not going to get married," I said.

He grinned. "Then you should know this anyway."

"Dad . . ."

"Go on, scrape."

Hesitantly, I scraped. My blade was dull, and the paper only came off in small patches.

I watched him work, intensely focused on each scrape and gouge. Sweat glistened on his upper lip. Wallpaper shavings fell on the floor and in the tub, and I had a crazy urge to clean them up just as fast as they fell.

"Dad's tearing down the whole house!"

"This is taking too damn long," my father said. He threw the scraper on the floor and took a cold chisel from the tool box. He struck the wall. Paper and plaster tore off. He struck again, and the chisel point broke through the wallboard. When he worked it free, a small section fell out.

"Now you've done it," I said.

My father stared at the dark, jagged hole. He pursed his lips, then began stabbing the wall, again and again. Plaster dust exploded with each blow. Pieces of wall broke away, and I was frightened. "Dad, stop!" I cried. He shook his head.

A car pulled into the drive. "It's Mom," I said, moving toward the door. "Mom's home."

"Sure, go on, get her," he said. "I expect that." I ran. I heard him close and lock the door behind me, and then the furious pounding began again. I ran to the kitchen door, where my mother stood, grocery bag in arms. All she could say was "What . . ." before I blurted out, "Dad's tearing down the whole house!"

Everything after that happened in a blur.

My father wouldn't come out no matter how much my mother pleaded, and soon she started crying, and I could see she was as frightened as I was. She called my Aunt Wilma, who came over, saw what was happening, and called the police. Then she hustled me and Jason—who'd just come back from his friend's—to her house, where she fed us peanut butter sandwiches and Cokes.

"Dad's gone crazy," I told Jason.

"Marcy, you hush up," Aunt Wilma said.

"It's true!" My voice sounded shrill. "I was there!"

"You don't know that at all," she said, "so just don't be saying it."

It's true, I mimed to Jason.

Later, Aunt Wilma called my mother.

"They've taken your father to the hospital," she told us. "You'll stay with me tonight."

The shadows of the trees outside floated like ghosts along the window. I remembered the night we played catch, the dark and the silence, the oddly determined look on my father's face as he threw the ball and it stung my hand. I thought of the moths in the trash, the plaster chips falling on the bathroom floor. Everything will be different now, I thought.

"Is he going to die?" Jason asked.

"Jason, don't be stupid," I hissed angrily. "People don't die from being crazy."

"Marcy, will you hush!" Aunt Wilma said. "He's had a spell is all. He'll be just fine."

Years later I learned that when the police had forced open the door, my father had been sitting calmly on the edge of the tub, the ravaged wall behind.

"I'm waiting your guidance," he told them.

Suddenly, everything happened so suddenly, and then everything slowed down. He was gone for over a month, to a hospital south of us, near Pittsburgh. Every weekend my mother drove down alone to visit him while we stayed at Aunt Wilma's. Jason asked if we could go too, but she said No, the drive was too long. He was disappointed, but I wasn't: I didn't want to see my father in that hospital. "He's lots better," Mom told us after each visit, and I'd just nod. Aunt Wilma came over to help, and Uncle Lou and one of his men from the parts store replastered the bathroom wall. My mother and I spent a whole day painting it over. "I never liked that wallpaper anyway," she told me.

He should be doing this, I thought as I painted. He should fix it all.

And then one weekend my mother said we could come with her to Pittsburgh, that my father would be going out with us for the day. Jason was excited—a trip!—but I didn't want to go at all.

"I don't want to see him," I said.

"What are you saying, Marcy? He's your father."

I shifted my feet and wouldn't look at her.

"Marcy, it'll be good for him," she said. "He's different now. You'll see."

The "hospital" turned out to be a group of ugly brick buildings surrounded by a lawn of yellowing grass. My father was sitting on a bench in front of a sign that said ADMISSIONS. He grinned and waved to us. He and Mom embraced, and then he patted me on the head, and lifted Jason. He seemed quieter, gentler, and blinked a lot behind his thick glasses. I didn't know what to say, so I didn't say anything. I sat with Jason in the back seat, my hands folded tightly, while Mom drove us into Pittsburgh. I stared at the fine black hairs on my father's wrist resting on the seat top. A vein throbbed near the wristbone, and I thought, He is alive, his heart is beating like ours.

"You're real quiet, Marcy," he said, not looking back.

I tried to think of something to say, but I couldn't.

Still, it was a good day. We ate lunch at Stouffer's, and Jason got free balloons which he tried to blow up, but couldn't, so my father had to do it for him. One of them shot across the room, and we all laughed. After lunch we went to a skyshow at the planetarium. It was the first one Jason had ever seen, and he was frightened. "How do they get all the outdoors in?" he asked, and I had to explain to him that none of it was real.

The show was about how the first sailors used the stars for navigation. In a gravelly, professional voice, his illuminated pointer dipping and twirling through the artificial sky, the lecturer showed us the important navigational stars. The Zeiss projector wheeled and turned, and the constellations of four thousand years ago, when Phoenicians sailed the Mediterranean, appeared; the projector wheeled again, and the stars changed to how they would look four thousand years from now, when space ships traveled between galaxies. The show excited my father, and he bought a star map from the planetarium shop. On the drive back to the hospital, he kept talking.

"Did you guys listen?" he asked. "Wasn't that something? Did you understand it all?"

"He seems a lot better," my mother said on the way home.

"He better be," I said.

She glanced at me sharply.

"I don't want him busting down any more walls," I said. "I mean . . ." I felt my throat catch.

"Oh, he won't," my mother said. "The rest has helped him a lot. He's different now." She reached over and patted my hand. "It'll be good to have him back, won't it?"

"I want to see the sky show again!" Jason cried. "Next time!"

"There won't be a next time, Jason," I said. My mother looked at me quizzically. "I mean he's coming home, isn't he? You said so."

A week later, my father did come home. He walked more slowly, his movements hesitant and considered, as if he'd somehow gotten heavier, even though he really didn't look any different. He didn't go back to work—"not right away," my mother said—and often sat for hours in the backyard; or if it were too chilly—it was October now—in the wing chair in the living room. We moved around him as if he were an island which required careful navigation. He was quiet, and smiled in an absent way, and for the most part ignored us. "Just don't be a bother to him," my mother warned us. She seemed nervous, her face strained and tight, and spent a lot of time on the phone talking in hushed tones to Aunt Wilma.

I began waking up at night, breathing fast, expecting to see him standing by the bed. I'd listen for his snoring. If I heard it, I could go back to sleep; if I didn't, I'd lie awake until sleep finally came anyway.

And then it was November, and my father raked the leaves and Jason and I burned them in the rusty can behind the house. I put away my baseball mitt, took out my ice skates and waited for the pond to freeze over. Every cold morning I'd go down to test it. Sometimes it was covered with a thin layer of ice. I'd skate stones across, then throw rocks out, which always broke through.

"I don't even remember what the old wallpaper looked like," Jason told me one day.

"Me neither," I said, even though that wasn't true, because I did.

And then one evening, when my mother had gone out for her bowling league and Jason and I were putting together log cabins, my father appeared at the door of our room. His face was flushed and excited.

"Why don't we go look at the stars," he said.

I tensed. "What stars?" Jason asked.

"Constellations. Like at the planetarium, remember? Let's go look for some."

"What for?" I asked warily.

"What for? Because it's good to know where they are, that's why." He began pacing the room. "You kids should know something about the stars."

It's happening again, I thought.

"I don't want to see any dumb stars," Jason said.

"Come on, get your coats on," my father ordered.

"Mom's not going to like us going out without her," I said.

"Well, we just won't tell her, will we?" He grinned, and it all came back to me—moths and plaster dust and the night. "Now get your clothes on."

Jason looked at me, as if to ask what to do.

"Let's go," I said. In the hall I whispered, "Just don't get him mad."

Even though the night was freezing, my father wore only a light jacket, no hat or gloves. The car's heater didn't work well, and he had to keep scraping away the frost our breath made on the windshield. Illuminated by the dashlights, my father's face looked strange and green. He squinted at the road behind his glasses.

"Where're we going?" I asked.

"To the country."

"Why?"

"Because we can see better there. No city lights."

"This is stupid," Jason said, and slumped in his seat.

We passed houses and houses and then fewer houses and then only woods and fields. We turned from one road onto another, each one darker still. I shivered in my coat—it was so cold—and wondered if we were really going anywhere at all. I looked at my father's profile as he peered into the night, and realized that I knew nothing, nothing at all,

about what he was thinking. He was as strange to me as the face of the moon.

"There!" my father cried. "Back there." We'd been driving along bare, frozen farmland, but now he stopped, backed up and pulled off the road beside a large furrowed field that sloped gently to a rise. He took a flashlight from the glove compartment. "Let's go."

I was struck almost breathless by the air, so much colder here than in town. With the headlights off, the night seemed darker than I'd ever seen before.

"Just look at that!" my father cried, pointing to the sky.

I looked up. The stars, more than I'd ever seen before, were burning. I felt dizzy looking at them.

"It's just like the planetarium," Jason said.

"What do you mean?" my father said. "It's better than the planetarium! This, my buccos, is the real thing. Look!" He turned on the flashlight and pointed it skyward. I could follow its cone of light through the misty air right to the star at which he was pointing. "There's the Big Dipper. Remember what the man at the planetarium said? If you follow the line of those two stars in the ladle," he pointed to them, then moved the flashlight beam across the sky, "you'll come to the North Star. See?"

"Dad," I said, "it's real, real cold." I shivered and flapped my arms. How could he not be cold in his light jacket, with no hat or gloves?

"Let's go to the top of that rise. We'll see even better." He started across the field, the flashlight beam darting back and forth.

"What'll we do, Marcy?" Jason asked.

I didn't want to follow my father, but I didn't want to stay here either, without a light, by ourselves in the dark.

"Let's go," I said. "He's got the flashlight."

We stumbled across the frozen furrows.

Ahead, the beam disappeared, as if swallowed up.

"Dad?" I cried.

"Over here." He flicked on the flashlight. He was standing on the crest of the field. When we got there, he turned it off again. Beyond the field, the woods rose like a dark, frozen wave.

"Look at them," he said. "just look at them!"

The stars shone fiercely. I stared and stared and felt myself falling toward them, as if I were floating up and down at the same time.

My father pulled something from his back pocket and unfolded it. "Hold this," he told me. When he trained the flashlight on it, I saw it was the star map he'd bought at the planetarium. He pursed his lips and studied it, glancing from map to sky and back again.

"There." He pointed with the beam. "See that 'W' up there? That's Casseopaeia, the Queen."

"I don't see any Queen," Jason said.

"She's sitting in her rocking chair." He zigged and zagged the flashlight beam along the constellation.

"I don't see any rocking chair."

"My God, Jason, look!"

"I'm cold," Jason said. He chattered his teeth.

"Hold the map steady," my father told me. He retrained the beam on it, and his face seemed to float above us in the reflected light. Behind him, the woods shimmered, as if moving closer.

"Brrrr," Jason said. "Brr . . ."

"Jason, quit whining!" my father snapped.

"But I'm cold!"

"Well, why didn't you bring your cap? Haven't you learned that by now?"

"I don't like it here," Jason said.

My father slapped the map, and I jumped. "Goddammit, quit complaining! You could learn something here, you know."

"Jason, shush," I said.

Something shrieked. Jason yelped. Whatever it was shrieked again, and there was a fluttering downfield.

"Marcy . . ." Jason said plaintively.

My father turned the flashlight skyward. "There's Cepheus, the King. See him? Beside Casseopaeia?"

"Dad, let's go," I pleaded.

"Why? Why?"

"It's cold. And Jason's scared."

"What's he scared of? There's nothing to be scared of."

"I want to go." Jason sounded close to tears.

"Dammit, there's nothing to be scared of! Are you a fraidy-cat, Jason? Jason, look at me." My father held the flashlight beneath his chin, so that the upward-shining beam distorted his face like a Halloween mask. His glasses made his eyes bulge and gleam. "Broo-ha-ha!" he laughed spectrally. "Broo-ha-ha!"

"Don't!" Jason screamed.

He stepped toward Jason, his arms outstretched, like a movie monster. "I'm coming to get yoooou, Jason . . ."

"Run," I hissed. I dropped the map and we ran.

"Hey!" my father cried. "Hold on now . . ." I heard him stumble after us, then cry in surprise as he tripped on the furrowed ground and fell heavily, the flashlight tumbling from his hands. I ran back and grabbed it and shone it on him. He was on his hands and knees. "I tripped," he said disbelievingly. He blinked. "My glasses—my glasses fell off." He pawed the ground in front of him. "I can't see."

I cast the beam in wide arcs across the ground and saw the glasses a few yards away. I walked over to where they lay, hesitated, then stepped on them. They crunched secretly beneath my shoe.

"Here they are!" I cried. And then: "They're broken."

My father was kneeling. His hands fluttered. "Give me. Let me see." I handed him the glasses. He felt the cracked lenses, the twisted frame, then put them on. I held the light to his face. His eyes were obscured behind the shattered glass.

"I can't see," he moaned.

"What happened?" Jason had returned.

"Dad fell and broke his glasses."

"Well, how are we going to get back? He can't drive without them."

In my elation with having saved us, I'd never considered it at all.

"I can't see anything," my father said. He was standing now, arms heavy by his side, as if afraid to move.

"You mean we're *stuck* here?" Jason said.

We slowly crossed the field, my father holding onto my coat sleeve for guidance, and all the way across I wondered, What have I done?

"Maybe somebody'll come by," I said. "We'll flag them down."

"Nobody's come by since we got here," Jason said mournfully.

We were quiet then, and the night, which had seemed so infinite, closed in and breathed over our shoulders. We got in the car. My father fumbled with the keys in the ignition and started it. The heater fan roared, but only cold air came out. He turned if off. We sat.

"Dad," I whispered, "what'll we do?"

He grasped the steering wheel in both hands, but said nothing, as silent now as he'd ever been these past weeks. The hands of the clock seemed frozen. I told myself not to look at them for a long while. When what seemed like an hour had gone by, I looked again: only ten minutes had passed.

"I'm freezing," Jason said. And then, a moment later: "Are we going to die?"

"Oh, don't be stupid, Jason," I said.

But I thought, Maybe we would die. We would die and strangers would find our frozen bodies and not know why we had even come here, nor what I had done, which was to doom us all. Strangers would handle my body, and my mother would cry. I wanted to cry too, but couldn't because I'd have to confess everything.

Jason began to sniffle.

"Stop that!" my father snapped.

"I can't h-help it."

"Well, you just stop it. You whine all the time."

Suddenly, all of it, the darkness, the cold, the stars themselves, seemed to whirl and explode inside of me, and I was crying, "Don't you yell at him! It was your crazy idea to come here. You got us into this!"

My father stared at me, blinking.

"You're crazy," I cried. "Crazy, crazy, crazy! You—you're not a real father at all!"

I shrank back into the seat as if I might be struck. My father said nothing, just stared at me, then out the frosted window. Jason was whimpering. If the night had opened up and I could've fallen in and through it, I would've, gladly.

"Your mother'll be worried," my father said at last. His voice seemed as far away as the stars. "We should go home."

"But we *can't*," I wailed.

He closed his eyes, and I thought, to my horror, He is going to sleep. "Dad . . ." I murmured.

His eyes snapped open. "No!" he cried. "We'll do it! We'll just drive home."

"But you can't—"

He was shaking his head. "No, no, you'll drive, Marcy!"

I was dumbfounded. "But I can't!"

"You can steer," he said. "That's all you have to do." He took my arm. "Look, sit here between my legs. You'll steer, and I'll change gears and brake."

"I can't!" I said. "We'll crash!"

"No, we won't. We'll go slow. Come on, sit."

"No!"

"Do you want to stay here and freeze?"

"Marcy," Jason said, "I'm cold."

"It's just going to get colder, Marcy," my father said. "It's going to be a long night."

"Goddammit, goddammit!" I'd never sworn before my father before. I slid over his leg, sat between him and the steering wheel and gripped it. It felt huge in my hands. My father took the gear shift, put his foot on the clutch.

"All you have to do is steer," he said, "and tell me when to brake. Like at a stop sign, OK?"

I nodded. My heart was thumping.

"Jason, you look out for signs too." He adjusted his feet on the pedals and started the car. "We'll practice now. We'll go real slow." He put the car in gear, and it moved like a great boat off the berm and down the road. I clutched the wheel and tried to steer.

Crazy, I thought, all just crazy.

"Get the feel of it, Marcy," my father said, "OK? Better?"

I nodded, even though I didn't feel better at all.

"I'm shifting now, Marcy," my father said. Something grated, the engine roared louder, and we were going faster.

"Too fast!" I cried. It seemed like we were driving at the far edge of the headlights' beam, into darkness I couldn't see.

"Stop sign," Jason yelled. My father braked, and we stopped, hard. The car throbbed, and I kept gripping the wheel, as if to hold it back.

"It works!" My father was excited. "See?" And before I could protest, we were off again.

If we ever get home, I thought, I hope he goes back to the hospital forever and ever.

"Car," Jason said.

Two headlights, like angry bees, appeared over the rise of the road. My stomach rose to my throat.

"Get it to stop!" I cried.

"I can't!" my father said. "Easy, just go easy." He blinked our lights. The oncoming car did the same. It seemed like it was rushing straight at us, and I willed myself to steer a straight line.

"Easy, easy . . ." my father said.

But somehow, frightened, I oversteered, and our car veered toward the edge of the road. "Marcy!" Jason yelled. My father hit the brakes, the other car zipped by, and then we were bucking and stalling, and lurched to a stop near the side.

"I can't. I can't." I was almost in tears. "It's crazy, I can't."

My father squeezed my arm. "It's OK, Marcy. You did fine."

"No, I didn't!" And now I was crying.

"It's OK," my father murmured, his breath warm against my ear.

"Why did you do this?" I sobbed.

"What, Marcy?"

"Everything. Just everything."

He held me. "It'll be all right. We'll get home. We'll just have to do it together. We'll go a little bit at a time." He rocked me. "OK? Is that OK?"

I wiped my eyes, nodded, hiccupped. "Let's—let's just go slow."

"We will," he said. "No faster than you want to go."

Please, God, I prayed, please no more cars.

Soon we came to another crossroad.

"Which way?" I asked.

"I don't know," my father said. "I can't see, and I can't remember. What does it look like outside?"

"It doesn't look like anything," I said. "It's just dark."

He sighed. "I just can't remember how we turned."

What with everything else, I'd never thought of us as lost too, but now it seemed we were helplessly, hopelessly, lost.

"West," my father murmured. "If we

just go west, we've got to run into the main highway."

"Well, which way's west?"

"I don't know."

We fell silent. In any direction, the road seemed endless and doomed.

"Jason," my father said. "Remember I showed you the Big Dipper? Can you get out and find it?"

"I'm not getting out of the car," Jason said.

"Dammit, Jason," I hissed, "this is important."

"You come too, Marcy."

We got out. "Turn off the headlights," I told my father. Once again we were in darkness. I searched the stars, but everything seemed a jumble. I looked around frantically. "It's not there."

"It's *always* there," my father said. "Look again."

"There it is!" Jason shouted, and it was, right behind me. We got back into the car and I took my seat between my father's legs.

"If that's north . . ." he was figuring, "we'll go *right* then."

So we drove on, west by the Dipper, and when we came to other roads we took our bearings by it. I was uncomfortable sitting between my father's legs, gripping the wheel more in terror than in steerage while he blindly worked the pedals—yet I felt better somehow. We knew where we were going. We muttered to one another to "steer straight," or "slow down," and after what seemed like forever, we did find the main road. There were other cars now, but we drove very slowly, and somehow they didn't frighten me as much. They'd come behind us, slow down, honk. "Just wait, Marcy," my father said. "They'll pass." And they did. Once Jason spotted a gas station, but it was closed. "We're going to make it," my father declared. And I thought, Maybe we will.

"Keep on the lookout for Sandy Creek Road," he told us.

And as we went on, I grew more and more confident, so much so that when one car passed, and a woman stared at me through the passenger window, I even took one hand from the wheel and waved.

"There it is!" Jason cried. "Sandy Creek Road!" And then he spotted Franklin Street, and we were almost home. We turned onto our street, me steering and my father downshifting for the corner, and we all let out a big whoop.

"We got home. We made it all the way!"

"There's our house!" Jason said, and we all cheered again. The lights were on: my mother had returned. We pulled into the driveway, and I ran slightly onto the lawn as my father braked us to a stop.

"We did it!" he cried, flushed and happy. He patted me on the back, over and over. And I thought: I love him. In spite of everything that had happened and would come to happen—because his victory and joy would be only short-lived, and I suppose I knew that, but didn't want to know, even then—he had brought us home.

Jason and I jumped out of the car, and I looked at the stars, most of them obscured now by house lights, nothing at all as we'd seen them in the field and on the road, fiery and lost and furiously strange. But still, I knew they were there, and that was enough.

And then my mother was there, her breath steaming, bewildered and worried. Jason was jumping up and down, trying to say twenty things at once. My father reached out for my mother and, before she could ask anything, hugged her hard, excited as a boy himself.

"We did it!" he cried. "We got home. We made it all the way!"

Mirabella

Author's Comments

"Stargazers" started out some years ago as a poem, in which a father (not yet a mentally ill one) took his sons (not yet son and daughter) out to a country field to show them the constellations.

The poem was told from the older child's point of view and expressed his wonder that his father could, almost like a navigator of old, take them so "far away" and then get them home. (I suppose its deeper origins go back to the planetarium trips my father took me on when I was very young.) The poem didn't quite work, however, and I shelved it, only to resurrect it a few years later while searching for story ideas. (Just as stories can become poems, poems can become stories.) I decided it might make a better story than poem, and so began writing it.

I retained the older child's point of view, and originally—as with the poem—that child was a boy. At some point in mulling it over, I decided that the scene out in the field should be a frightening one to the children, that they should experience real anxiety as to whether their father would be able to get them home. That would provide the dramatic interest that was missing from the poem, and that was so essential for a story.

After I realized that, it was much easier to imagine the characters and situation that could create that anxiety—a mentally ill father, one who was frightening to his children and in whom they held little confidence, who had taken them, for his own strange reasons, to this country field. And the only way the father could redeem himself was by literally guiding them home by the stars, like a navigator of old: what was metaphor in the poem became plot in the story. Only then, in a sort of mutual sacrifice of the heart, could father and child learn to trust one another, and renew their capacity for love. In that sense, although the plot had changed entirely, the story remained very close to the feeling of the original poem.

The plot elements fell quickly into place, but after three or four drafts, I still felt something was missing. Everything seemed a bit flat. And then I realized how much richer the story would be if the narrator were a little girl instead of a little boy. That lent a poignancy to her desire to protect her younger brother—different from the usual brother protecting brother, or brother protecting sister—and it also made the conflict between daughter and father more allusive.

It was no longer a struggle over power, as father-son conflicts often are, but a struggle over love, one's desires for and distrusts of love—much more relevant to father-daughter conflicts and much, much closer to the story I really wanted to tell. And with that, the last key element of the story fell into place.

—David Michael Kaplan

The Lover of Horses

by Tess Gallagher

They say my great-grandfather was a gypsy, but the most popular explanation for his behavior was that he was a drunk. How else could the women have kept up the scourge of his memory all these years, had they not had the usual malady of our family to blame? Probably he was both a gypsy and a drunk.

Still, I have reason to believe the gypsy in him had more to do with the turn his life took than his drinking. I used to argue with my mother about this, even though most of the information I have about my great-grandfather came from my mother, who got it from her mother. A drunk, I kept telling her, would have had no initiative. He would simply have gone down with his failures and had nothing to show for it. But my great-grandfather had eleven children, surely a sign of industry, and he was a lover of horses. He had so many horses he was what people called "horse poor." I did not learn, until I traveled to where my family originated at Collenamore in the west of Ireland, that my great-grandfather had most likely been a "whisperer," a breed of men among the gypsies who were said to possess the power of talking sense into horses. These men had no fear of even the most malicious and dangerous horses. In fact, they would often take the wild animal into a closed stall in order to perform their skills.

Whether a certain intimacy was needed or whether the whisperers simply wanted to protect their secret conversations with horses is not known. One thing was certain—that such men gained power over horses by whispering. What they whispered no one knew. But the effectiveness of their methods was renowned, and anyone for counties around who had an unruly horse could send for a whisperer and be sure that the horse would take to heart whatever was said and reform his behavior from that day forth.

By all accounts, my great-grandfather was like a huge stallion himself, and when he went into a field where a herd of horses was grazing, the horses would suddenly lift their heads and call to him. Then his bearded mouth would move, and though he was making sounds that could have been words, which no horse would have had reason to understand, the horses would want to hear; and one by one they would move toward him across the open space of the field. He could turn his back and walk down the road, and they would follow him. He was probably drunk, my mother said, because he was swaying and mumbling all the while. Sometimes he would stop deadstill in the road and the horses would press up against him and raise and lower their heads as he moved his lips. But because these things were only seen from a

Author Bio

Tess Gallagher is a distinguished poet and short-story writer whose works have appeared in *Atlantic Monthly*, *The New Yorker*, *Glimmer Train*, and more. Among her writing credits are the short-story collection, *At the Owl Woman Saloon*, and a poetry collection, *Dear Ghosts*.

distance, and because they have eroded in the telling, it is now impossible to know whether my great-grandfather said anything of importance to the horses. Or even if it was his whispering that had brought about their good behavior. Nor was it clear, when he left them in some barnyard as suddenly as he'd come to them, whether they had arrived at some new understanding of the difficult and complex relationship between men and horses.

Only the aberrations of my great-grandfather's relationship with horses have survived—as when he would bathe in the river with his favorite horse or when, as my grandmother told my mother, he insisted on conceiving his ninth child in the stall of a bay mare named Redwing. Not until I was grown and going through the family Bible did I discover that my grandmother had been this ninth child, and so must have known something about the matter.

These oddities in behavior lead me to believe that when my great-grandfather, at the age of fifty-two, abandoned his wife and fam-

He walked from the house with only the clothes on his back.

ily to join a circus that was passing through the area, it was not simply drunken bravado, nor even the understandable wish to escape family obligations. I believe the gypsy in him finally got the upper hand, and it led to such a remarkable happening that no one in the family has so far been willing to admit it; not the obvious transgression—that he had run away to join the circus—but that he was in all likelihood a man who had been stolen by a horse.

This is not an easy view to sustain in the society we live in. But I have not come to it frivolously, and have some basis for my belief.

For although I have heard the story of my great-grandfather's defection time and again since childhood, the one image which prevails in all versions is that of a dappled gray stallion that had been trained to dance a variation of the mazurka. So impressive was this animal that he mesmerized crowds with his sliding step-and-hop to the side through the complicated figures of the dance, which he performed, not in the way of Lippizzaners—with other horses and their riders—but riderless and with the men of the circus company as his partners.

It is known that my great-grandfather became one of these dancers. After that he was reputed, in my mother's words, to have gone "completely to ruin." The fact that he walked from the house with only the clothes on his back, leaving behind his own beloved horses (twenty-nine of them to be exact), further supports my idea that a powerful force must have held sway over him, something more profound than the miseries of drink or the harsh imaginings of his abandoned wife.

Not even the fact that seven years later he returned and knocked on his wife's door, asking to be taken back, could exonerate him from what he had done, even though his wife did take him in and looked after him until he died some years later. But the detail that no one takes note of in the account is that when my great-grandfather returned, he was carrying a saddle blanket and the black plumes from the headgear of one of the circus horses. This passes by even my mother as simply a sign of the ridiculousness of my great-grandfather's plight—for after all, he was homeless and heading for old age as a "good for nothing drunk" and a "fool for horses."

No one has bothered to conjecture what these curious emblems—saddle blanket and plumes—must have meant to my great-grandfather. But he hung them over the foot of his bed—"like a fool," my mother said. And sometimes when he got very drunk he would take up the blanket and, wrapping it like a shawl over his shoulders, he would grasp the plumes. Then he would dance the mazurka. He did not dance in the living room but took himself out into the field, where the horses stood at attention and watched, as if suddenly experiencing the smell of the sea or a change of wind in the valley. "Drunks don't care what they do," my mother would say as she finished her story about my great-grandfather. "Talking to a drunk is like talking to a stump."

Ever since my great-grandfather's outbreaks of gypsy necessity, members of my family have been stolen by things—by mad ambitions, by musical instruments, by otherwise harmless pursuits from mushroom hunting to childbearing or, as was my father's case, by the more easily recognized and popular obsession with card playing. To some extent, I still think it was failure of imagination in this respect that brought about his diminished prospects in the life of our family.

But even my mother had been powerless against the attraction of a man so convincingly driven. When she met him at a birthday dance held at the country house of one of her young friends, she asked him what he did for a living. My father pointed to a deck of cards in his shirt pocket and said, "I play cards." But love is such as it is, and although my mother was otherwise a deadly practical woman, it seemed she could fall in love with no man but my father.

I refused to speak aloud to anyone until the age of eleven.

So it is possible that the propensity to be stolen is somewhat contagious when ordinary people come into contact with people such as my father. Though my mother loved him at the time of the marriage, she soon began to

behave as if she had been stolen from a more fruitful and upright life which she was always imagining might have been hers.

My father's card playing was accompanied, to no one's surprise, by bouts of drinking. The only thing that may have saved our family from a life of poverty was the fact that my father seldom gambled with money. Such were his charm and powers of persuasion that he was able to convince other players to accept his notes on everything from the fish he intended to catch next season to the sale of his daughter's hair.

I know about this last wager because I remember the day he came to me with a pair of scissors and said it was time to cut my hair. Two snips and it was done. I cannot forget the way he wept onto the backs of his hands and held the braids together like a broken noose from which a life had suddenly slipped. I was thirteen at the time and my hair had never been cut. It was his pride and joy that I had such hair. But for me it was only a burdensome difference between me and my classmates, so I was glad to be rid of it. What anyone else could have wanted with my long shiny braids is still a mystery to me.

When my father was seventy-three he fell ill and doctors gave him only a few weeks to live. My father was convinced that his illness had come on him because he'd hit a particularly bad losing streak at cards. He had lost heavily the previous month, and items of value, mostly belonging to my mother, had disappeared from the house. He developed the strange idea that if he could win at cards he could cheat the prediction of the doctors and live at least into his eighties.

By this time I had moved away from home and made a life for myself in an attempt to follow the reasonable dictates of my mother, who had counseled her children severely against all manner of rash ambition and foolhardiness. Her entreaties were leveled especially in my direction since I had shown a suspect enthusiasm for a certain pony around the age of five. And it is true I felt I had lost a dear friend when my mother saw to it that the neighbors who owned this pony moved it to pasture elsewhere.

But there were other signs that I might wander off into unpredictable pursuits. The most telling of these was that I refused to speak aloud to anyone until the age of eleven. I whispered everything, as if my mind were a repository of secrets which could only be divulged in this intimate manner. If anyone asked me a question, I was always polite about answering, but I had to do it by putting my mouth near the head of my inquisitor and using only my breath and lips to make my reply.

My teachers put my whispering down to shyness and made special accommodations for me. When it came time for recitations I would accompany the teacher into the cloakroom and there whisper to her the memorized verses or the speech I was to have prepared. God knows, I might have continued on like this into the present if my mother hadn't plotted with some neighborhood boys to put burrs into my long hair. She knew by other signs that I had a terrible temper, and she was counting on that to deliver me into the world where people shouted and railed at one another and talked in an audible fashion about things both common and sacred.

When the boys shut me into a shed, according to plan, there was nothing for me to do but to cry out for help and to curse them in a torrent of words I had only heard used by adults. When my mother heard this she rejoiced, thinking that at last she had broken the treacherous hold of the past over me, of my great-grandfather's gypsy blood and the fear that against all her efforts I might be stolen away, as she had been, and as my father had, by some as yet unforeseen predilection. Had I not already experienced the consequences of such a life in our household,

I doubt she would have been successful, but the advantages of an ordinary existence among people of a less volatile nature had begun to appeal to me.

It was strange, then, that after all the care my mother had taken for me in this regard, when my father's illness came on him,

There is a saying that when lovers have need of moonlight, it is there.

my mother brought her appeal to me. "Can you do something?" she wrote, in her cramped, left-handed scrawl. "He's been drinking and playing cards for three days and nights. I am at my wit's end. Come home at once."

Somehow I knew this was a message addressed to the very part of me that most baffled and frightened my mother—the part that belonged exclusively to my father and his family's inexplicable manias.

When I arrived home my father was not there.

"He's at the tavern. In the back room," my mother said. "He hasn't eaten for days. And if he's slept, he hasn't done it here."

I made up a strong broth, and as I poured the steaming liquid into a Thermos I heard myself utter syllables and other vestiges of language which I could not produce if I wanted to. "What do you mean by that?" my mother demanded, as if a demon had leapt out of me. "What did you say?" I didn't—I couldn't—answer her. But suddenly I felt that an unsuspected network of sympathies and distant connections had begun to reveal itself to me in my father's behalf.

There is a saying that when lovers have need of moonlight, it is there. So it seemed, as I made my way through the deserted town toward the tavern and card room, that all nature had been given notice of my father's predicament, and that the response I was waiting for would not be far off.

But when I arrived at the tavern and had talked my way past the barman and into the card room itself, I saw that my father had an enormous pile of blue chips at his elbow. Several players had fallen out to watch, heavy-lidded and smoking their cigarettes like weary gangsters. Others were slumped on folding chairs near the coffee urn with its empty "Pay Here" styrofoam cup.

My father's cap was pushed to the back of his head so that his forehead shone in the dim light, and he grinned over his cigarette at me with the serious preoccupation of a child who has no intention of obeying anyone. And why should he, I thought as I sat down just behind him and loosened the stopper on the Thermos.

The five or six players still at the table casually appraised my presence to see if it had tipped the scales of their luck in an even more unfavorable direction. Then they tossed their cards aside, drew fresh cards, or folded.

In the center of the table were more blue chips, and poking out from my father's coat pocket I recognized the promissory slips he must have redeemed, for he leaned to me and in a low voice, without taking his eyes from his cards, said, "I'm having a hell of a good time. The time of my life."

He was winning. His face seemed ravaged by the effort, but he was clearly playing on a level that had carried the game far beyond the realm of mere card playing and everyone

My father continued to win—to the amazement of the local barflies.

seemed to know it. The dealer cocked an eyebrow as I poured broth into the plastic Thermos cup and handed it to my father, who slurped from it noisily, then set it down.

"Tell the old kettle she's got to put up

with me a few more years," he said, and lit up a fresh cigarette. His eyes as he looked at me, however, seemed over-brilliant, as if doubt, despite all his efforts, had gained a permanent seat at his table. I squeezed his shoulder and kissed him hurriedly on his forehead. The men kept their eyes down, and as I paused at the door, there was a shifting of chairs and a clearing of throats. Just outside the room I nearly collided with the barman, who was carrying in a fresh round of beer. His heavy jowls waggled as he recovered himself and looked hard at me over the icy bottles. Then he disappeared into the card room with his provisions.

I took the long way home, finding pleasure in the fact that at this hour all the stoplights had switched onto a flashing-yellow caution cycle. Even the teenagers who usually cruised the town had gone home or to more secluded spots. Doubt, I kept thinking as I drove with my father's face before me, that's the real thief. And I knew my mother had brought me home because of it, because she knew that once again a member of our family was about to be stolen.

Two more days and nights I ministered to my father at the card room. I would never stay long because I had the fear myself that I might spoil his luck. But many unspoken tendernesses passed between us in those brief appearances as he accepted the nourishment I offered, or when he looked up and handed me his beer bottle to take a swig from—a ritual we'd shared since my childhood.

My father continued to win—to the amazement of the local barflies who poked their faces in and out of the card room and gave the dwindling three or four stalwarts who remained at the table a commiserating shake of their heads. There had never been a winning streak like it in the history of the tavern, and indeed, we heard later that the man who owned the card room and tavern had to sell out and open a fruit stand on the edge of town as a result of my father's extraordinary good luck.

Twice during this period my mother urged the doctor to order my father home. She was sure my father would, at some fateful moment, risk the entire winnings in some mad rush toward oblivion. But his doctor spoke of a new "gaming therapy" for the terminally ill, based on my father's surge of energies in the pursuit of his gambling. Little did he know that my father was, by that stage, oblivious to even his winning, he had gone so far into exhaustion.

Luckily for my father, the hour came when, for lack of players, the game folded. Two old friends drove him home and helped him down from the pickup. They paused in the driveway, one on either side of him, letting him steady himself. When the card playing had ended there had been nothing for my father to do but to get drunk.

"If you'd only brought him home from that card room."

My mother and I watched from the window as the men steered my father toward the hydrangea bush at the side of the house, where he relieved himself with perfect precision on one mammoth blossom. Then they hoisted him up the stairs and into the entryway. My mother and I took over from there.

"Give 'em hell, boys," my father shouted after the men, concluding some conversation he was having with himself.

"You betcha," the driver called back, laughing. Then he climbed with his companion into the cab of his truck and roared away.

Tied around my father's waist was a cloth sack full of bills and coins which flapped and jingled against his knees as we bore his weight between us up the next flight of stairs and into the living room. There we deposited him on the couch, where he took up residence, refusing to sleep in his bed—for

fear, my mother claimed, that death would know where to find him. But I preferred to think he enjoyed the rhythms of the household; from where he lay at the center of the house, he could overhear all conversations that took place and add his opinions when he felt like it.

My mother was so stricken by the signs of his further decline that she did everything he asked, instead of arguing with him or simply refusing. Instead of taking his winnings straight to the bank so as not to miss a day's interest, she washed an old goldfish bowl and dumped all the money into it, most of it in twenty-dollar bills. Then she placed it on the coffee table near his head so he could run his hand through it at will, or let his visitors do the same.

"Money feels good on your elbow," he would say to them. "I played them under the table for that. Yes sir, take a feel of that!" Then he would lean back on his pillows and tell my mother to bring his guests a shot of whiskey. "Make sure she fills my glass up," he'd say to me so that my mother was certain to overhear. And my mother, who'd never allowed a bottle of whiskey to be brought into her house before now, would look at me as if the two of us were more than any woman should have to bear.

"If you'd only brought him home from that card room," she said again and again. "Maybe it wouldn't have come to this."

This included the fact that my father had radically altered his diet. He lived only on greens. If it was green he would eat it. By my mother's reckoning, the reason for his change of diet was that if he stopped eating what he usually ate, death would think it wasn't him and go look for somebody else.

Another request my father made was asking my mother to sweep the doorway after anyone came in or went out.

"To make sure death wasn't on their heels; to make sure death didn't slip in as

The Lover of Horses

they left." This was my mother's reasoning. But my father didn't give any reasons. Nor did he tell us finally why he wanted all the furniture moved out of the room except for the couch where he lay. And the money, they could take that away too.

But soon his strength began to ebb, and more and more family and friends crowded into the vacant room to pass the time with him, to laugh about stories remembered from his childhood or from his nights as a young man at the country dances when he and his older brother would work all day in the cotton fields, hop a freight train to town and dance all night. Then they would have to walk home, getting there just at daybreak in time to go straight to work again in the cotton fields.

"We were like bulls then," my father would say in a burst of the old vigor, then close his eyes suddenly as if he hadn't said anything at all.

As long as he spoke to us, the inevitability of his condition seemed easier to bear. But when, at the last, he simply opened his mouth for food or stared silently toward the far wall, no one knew what to do with themselves.

My own part in that uncertain time came to me accidentally. I found myself in the yard sitting on a stone bench under a little cedar tree my father loved because he liked to sit there and stare at the ocean. The tree whispered, he said. He said it had a way of knowing what your troubles were. Suddenly a craving came over me. I wanted a cigarette, even though I don't smoke, hate smoking, in fact. I was sitting where my father had sat, and to smoke seemed a part of some rightness that had begun to work its way within me. I went into the house and bummed a pack of cigarettes from my brother. For the rest of the morning I sat under the cedar tree and smoked. My thoughts drifted with its shifting and murmurings, and it struck me what a

wonderful thing nature is because it knows the value of silence, the innuendos of silence and what they could mean for a word-bound creature such as I was.

I passed the rest of the day in a trance of silences, moving from place to place, revisiting the sites I knew my father loved—the "dragon tree," a hemlock which stood at the far end of the orchard, so named for how the wind tossed its triangular head; the rose arbor where he and my mother had courted; the little marina where I sat in his fishing boat and dutifully smoked the hated cigarettes, flinging them one by one into the brackish water.

I was waiting to know what to do for him, he who would soon be a piece of useless matter of no more consequence than the cigarette butts that floated and washed against the side of his boat. I could feel some action accumulating in me through the steadiness of water raising and lowering the boat, through the sad petal-fall of roses in the arbor and the tossing of the dragon tree.

That night when I walked from the house I was full of purpose. I headed toward the little cedar tree. Without stopping to question the necessity of what I was doing. I began to break off the boughs I could reach and to pile them on the ground.

"What are you doing?" my brother's children wanted to know, crowding around me as if I might be inventing some new game for them.

"What does it look like?" I said.

"Pulling limbs off the tree," the oldest said. Then they dashed away in a pack under the orchard trees, giggling and shrieking.

As I pulled the boughs from the trunk I felt a painful permission, as when two silences, tired of holding back, give over to each other some shared regret. I made my bed on the boughs and resolved to spend the night there in the yard, under the stars, with the hiss of the ocean in my ear, and the maimed cedar tree standing over me like a gift torn out of its wrappings.

110   Fiction

My brothers, their wives and my sister had now begun their nightly vigil near my father, taking turns at staying awake. The windows were open for the breeze and I heard my mother trying to answer the question of why I was sleeping outside on the ground— "like a damned fool" I knew they wanted to add.

"She doesn't want to be here when death comes for him," my mother said, with an air of clairvoyance she had developed from a lifetime with my father. "They're too much alike," she said.

The ritual of night games played by the children went on and on past their bedtimes. Inside the house, the kerosene lantern, saved from my father's childhood home, had been lit—another of his strange requests during the time before his silence. He liked the shadows it made and the sweet smell of the kerosene. I watched the darkness as the shapes of my brothers and sister passed near it, gigantic and misshapen where they bent or raised themselves or crossed the room.

Out on the water the wind had come up. In the orchard the children were spinning around in a circle, faster and faster until they were giddy and reeling with speed and darkness. Then they would stop, rest a moment, taking quick ecstatic breaths before plunging again into the opposite direction, swirling round and round in the circle until the excitement could rise no higher, their laughter and cries brimming over, then scattering as they flung one another by the arms or chased each other toward the house as if their lives depended on it.

I lay awake for a long while after their footsteps had died away and the car doors had slammed over the goodbyes of the children being taken home to bed and the last of the others had been bedded down in the house while the adults went on waiting.

It was important to be out there alone and close to the ground. The pungent smell of the cedar boughs was around me, rising up in the crisp night air toward the tree, whose turnings and swayings had altered, as they had to, in order to accompany the changes about to overtake my father and me. I thought of my great-grandfather bathing with his horse in the river, and of my father who had just passed through the longest period of his life without the clean feel of cards falling through his hands as he shuffled or dealt them. He was too weak now to even hold a cigarette; there was a burn mark on the hardwood floor where his last cigarette had fallen. His winnings were safely in the bank and the luck that was to have saved him had gone back to the place luck goes to when it is finished with us.

So this is what it comes to, I thought, and listened to the wind as it mixed gradually with the memory of children's voices which still seemed to rise and fall in that orchard. There was a soft crooning of syllables that was satisfying to my ears, but ultimately useless and absurd. Then it came to me that I was the author of those unwieldy sounds, and that my lips had begun to work of themselves.

In a raw pulsing of language I could not account for, I lay awake through the long night and spoke to my father as one might speak to an ocean or the wind, letting him know by that threadbare accompaniment that the vastness he was about to enter had its rhythms in me also. And that he was not forsaken. And that I was letting him go. That so far I had denied the disreputable world of dancers and drunkards, gamblers and lovers of horses to which I most surely belonged. But from that night forward I vowed to be filled with the first unsavory desire that would have me. To plunge myself into the heart of my life and be ruthlessly lost forever.

Zyzzyva

Author's Comments ―――――――――――

I wrote the initial draft of this story in a day. And it passed through probably five drafts after that. It was the first story I'd written which seemed to come in the way poems come to me—all in a rush and with a fateful surety. I had a terrible excitement about having written it and I remember the need to read it aloud, maybe to confirm the joy I was feeling. I had been working alone at Sky House, a place I had designed and built for writing on the Strait of Juan de Fuca near where I was born.

I drove across town to the house I shared with Raymond Carver, fellow short story writer and ultimately my husband. He was watching "Anna Karenina" on TV. I went over and switched it off and told him he had to listen to something. It was a very brazen thing to do, to substitute myself for Tolstoy, but writers probably have no shame when the gladness of creation is in them. It was late at night and Ray got comfortable to listen, picking up on my excitement.

We'd both put in a full day already, but I remember being grateful that he was listening in that way you listen in order to be inside something, to live it. I read the story aloud and he shook his head when I finished and said, "I hope that's as good as I think it is in the morning. That's just wonderful, I'd say. Wonderful!" he said.

Nothing so gratifying has happened to me since, in terms of that story, as Ray's praise after that late night reading with just the two of us in the cramped TV room. Of course I felt even better when he still loved the story the next morning, having read it to himself in the quiet of his study.

The story behind the story, so to speak, is that I had lost my father to lung cancer and I'd felt that I hadn't actually found the right rituals to honor that loss or even to fully experience it. In writing the story I used many details from his actual dying time, but I also used a voice which allowed me to widen his death so that it became almost mythological.

I told some things that were not true in order to make the truth more true. It seems to me that this story in some important way now redeems my father's life.

—Tess Gallagher

Love Spells

by Barbara A. Barnett

Cullych peered over Drielle's shoulder and stared at her as she prepared the potion. The girl's face, alluring in its simplicity, was creased with concentration; fierce intelligence flashed behind her eyes. Cullych wondered how difficult it would be to use a spell.

You would need more than one, he reminded himself.

He leaned closer, and the sweet scent of Drielle's hair filled his nose, overpowering the acrid stench of the myrfine root she had just dropped into the bubbling cauldron.

A reality-altering spell—just a small one—so the records say she has been studying under someone else. Luu, perhaps?

Standing this close, Cullych could see every imperfection. Drielle's lips were too thin, her nose was too round, and she wore powder to lighten the blemishes that girls of her eighteen years were prone to. The flaws didn't bother Cullych, though. He had too many of his own—the first hints of grey in his dark hair, and an absent-mindedness during his rushed mornings that resulted in a seemingly permanent amount of stubble on his otherwise boyish face.

A few memory-wiping spells. It won't do if anyone remembers her having been my pupil.

Standing this close to Drielle was maddening, but Cullych did it anyway, enthralled by the precision with which she prepared the potion he had assigned to test her. Every day he spent with her, his thoughts of propriety grew as inconsequential as a random bird song heard in the distance. He had once thought himself a man of fortitude, but the past few months had taught him otherwise as he found himself weakened by a desire that was as searing as it was inappropriate.

And one final spell for her—to make her love you.

"No," Cullych said, backing away.

Drielle turned with a start, her pale face crestfallen. "Did I do something wrong, Master Cullych?"

"No," he said again, then laughed nervously at his own embarrassment. "What I meant to say was, no, this test is too easy for you; beneath your talents."

Drielle smiled—a small, awkward expression accompanied by a slight lowering of her head and a blush across her dimpled cheeks.

"You're . . ." Cullych closed his eyes and took a deep breath to stop what had been about to escape his lips: *You're the most beautiful woman I've ever seen.* When he opened his eyes, Drielle was waiting expectantly, her eyes darting between him and the floor. Sometimes he imagined that such awkwardness was

Author Bio

Barbara Barnett made her first fiction sale when she was in college. Later she attended the Odyssey Writing Workshop. Her fiction has received an honorable mention in the Writers of the Future contest and has been published in markets such as *Shimmer*, *Hub*, *Flash Fiction Online*, and *Leading Edge*.

because of him—because he possessed her every thought, as she did his—but Luu had assured him that Drielle was like that with all of her instructors.

"You're going to have to wait until I can come up with a more appropriate way to test your skill," Cullych said at last, the words coming slowly. His following sigh of relief, however, was far too quick.

Perhaps what I need is a spell to make me a better liar.

Cullych sat on a stone bench in the courtyard, watching the students file out of the academy—a centuries-old castle that had been turned into a school of sorcery.

How many times did Drielle pass through here without my notice? he wondered.

She wasn't originally his student. She had been assigned to him after her first potions in-structor passed away, victim to one of the few things beyond magic's reach—old age. Cullych had only been teaching at the academy for a few months at that point; at thirty, he was the youngest instructor there. He had never no-ticed the wisp of a girl who roamed through the halls with her nervous smile and her silken black hair tucked behind her ears. It was only during their lessons that he realized just how brilliant she was, and after a few days, his world was disrupted by the first stirrings of passion, the beginning of an obsession.

Drielle passed by in a crowd of students on their way into town. She offered Cullych a small wave when she noticed his gaze, and his heart raced so quickly that he thought he might be sick. He smiled and returned the wave, inwardly chiding himself. He was too desperate for such minor attentions, and too infatuated not to dwell on what they might mean.

But it's not so impossible to believe. Luu said one of the female instructors finds me quite handsome.

"You're young," a woman's voice said,

"but not young enough for her."

Cullych looked up to find Luu standing over him. She was the only other instructor—the only one among his friends—he had dared tell about Drielle.

"You're not ruthless enough for this sort of thing."

And only after she plied me with a few drinks to find out if I had my eye on anyone. Probably wants to set me up with some friend's daughter.

Luu sat beside him and nodded in Drielle's direction. "It's been a decade or two since I've been that young."

"So which is it?" Cullych asked. "One decade or two?"

Luu smirked. "I'll never tell."

Cullych studied her, wondering how much of his inability to guess her age had to do with magic. She had certainly used a few appearance-altering spells over the years, but there was only so much that magic could hide. A few gray hairs poked through her thick blonde mane, and wrinkles lined the corners of her eyes.

Two decades, at least. More likely three.

Luu watched with pursed lips and squinted eyes as Drielle passed through the gates and out of the courtyard. "I still don't see what it is you're willing to risk your career over."

"Who's risking anything?"

Luu answered with a husky laugh. "Oh, I think that brilliant mind of yours has thought of a few spells you might try." She leaned closer and added in a conspiratorial whisper, "You would have to wipe a few memories. Would that include mine?"

Cullych laughed, troubled by how thin and nervous the sound was. "Of course not."

"You're not ruthless enough for this sort of thing." Luu sat back and crossed her legs, the hint of their slender form visible through the sheer red robes she wore. "What you need is a spell for yourself—something to make you forget this nonsense before someone on the academy board catches you staring after her a little too long."

Cullych sighed. "I don't think there's a spell strong enough."

"There's always a spell." Luu regarded him with a playful smile. "And for someone who the rumors suggest is on his way to becoming the youngest headmaster in the academy's history, there are always better options than some awkward little girl, no matter how gifted she may be."

Here comes the set up, Cullych thought, rolling his eyes and wondering why Luu insisted on hinting her way into it when she was always so blunt about everything else. "Just tell me who you have in mind already. Some homely niece of yours, perhaps?"

Luu's smile vanished, replaced by an injured expression so foreign to her character that it was startling to see.

"I'm sorry." Cullych shook his head, baffled by Luu's sudden lack of humor over the sort of remark she would have made herself. "I'm sure every niece of yours is perfectly attractive."

Luu stood to go. "You're hopeless, Cullych."

"Mind telling me what I've done wrong before you go?"

"I'll see you in the morning," Luu said, already on her way across the courtyard.

Once they passed the academy's gates, Drielle slipped away from the other students. She ducked behind one of the thick, marble pillars spaced every few feet along the fence before glancing back to see if anyone had noticed her disappearance.

Of course they haven't, she thought, watching with a tinge of bitterness as her classmates laughed and chatted with each other as if she had never been there. *No one notices shy little Dri.*

She peered around the pillar and through the iron fence posts. Master Cullych was talking to Mistress Luu now, smiling politely at times, but barely sparing the woman a glance, not even when she leaned closer to him or crossed her legs in that way that always had her male students gawking.

Shy, little Dri. If they only knew.

She had nearly sprinted through the gates when Master Cullych waved to her. It was silly, she knew, being driven into a panic by something that was all her doing.

A few of the other girls harbored hopelessly shallow crushes on Master Cullych, overlooking his brilliance and warmth; never quite getting his unexpectedly sardonic jokes. He was handsome, of course—his icy blue eyes were probably his most striking feature—but Drielle was more captivated by how unaware of his looks he seemed to be.

For a time, Drielle thought the spell hadn't worked.

Across the courtyard, Mistress Luu stormed away from the bench. Master Cullych was alone now, staring after the woman with a puzzled frown.

Drielle wasn't sure what she was waiting for. When she first cast the spell, she thought it would be all the effort needed. She expected him to proclaim his love as soon as she handed back the ring she had snatched from his desk the day before, pretending she had just found it on the floor of his study. He appeared disoriented when he first took it back, then shook his head and made some self-deprecating joke about always losing the ring whenever he took it off to mix a potion. For a time, Drielle thought the spell hadn't worked. Cullych paid her his usual teacherly attentions, complimenting her work and encouraging her to speak up more. Gradually, though, she noticed the changes—how much closer he stood during their lessons, his gaze lingering on her just a little longer than was necessary, the way he stammered around her, not as confident as before.

He's a good man, Drielle told herself, letting out a sigh that carried as much frustration as it did adoration. He was someone who would not want to ruin either of their reputations, no matter what he felt.

She watched him get up from the bench and walk across the courtyard, his gait slow and distracted.

No matter what I've made him feel.

Cullych snatched Drielle's bracelet from where it had fallen on the table. He turned it over in his hands, then glanced toward where she leaned over the cauldron at the center of his study, intent on mixing the potion just right. She hadn't seemed to notice that the bracelet was gone.

I could do it with this, he thought. *I could place a charm on it and make her love me.*

"Master Cullych?"

"I put the rithwort in first, and then the myrfine root . . ."

Cullych closed his hand around the bracelet, hiding it from Drielle's sight. "Yes?"

"I'm . . ." She stared at him a moment, her brown eyes as wide as a frightened animal's, then lowered her gaze to the floor. "I'm not certain I've done this correctly."

Cullych smiled, charmed as usual by how scared she was at the thought of not getting everything perfect the first time. "It's a difficult potion," he said, stepping closer to see what she had done. "It looks the right color."

"I put the rithwort in first, and then the myrfine root, but I'm not certain that I should have . . ."

Cullych stared at her as she continued,

his pulse quickening. He clenched his hand tighter around her bracelet, and the silver metal dug into his skin.

A few spells and I can be with her.

". . . and then I added the cullif powder," Drielle said, "but just a dash. I think that's what you suggested."

"I did, yes." Cullych took in a sharp breath. "You've done this perfectly—as always."

Drielle smiled, and the gleeful, wide-eyed look drained every bit of nerve Cullych had. He held out his hand. "You dropped this."

Drielle took the bracelet, and Cullych blinked with surprise, certain her hand was shaking as it brushed his.

"Thank you, Master Cullych."

"I've never been comfortable with you addressing me as *master*," he said, stepping closer to Drielle—closer than he knew he should.

"Oh." Drielle lowered her gaze, her glee now reduced to a nervous smile. "Why is that?"

"I . . ." Cullych closed his eyes, taking in a deep breath as he so often did to stop himself from making an ill-advised declaration of his feelings. He opened his eyes to find that Drielle had stepped closer. Cullych opened his mouth to say something, but the words were forgotten in a wave of surprise as Drielle darted her head forward and kissed him. A voice in the back of his mind screamed that this was madness, but he ignored it and pulled Drielle closer, pressing his lips harder against hers as the passion he had been fighting finally found a release.

The sound of footsteps in the corridor cut through his sudden euphoria like a knife through flesh. He and Drielle pulled apart and looked toward the door in alarm, but it was closed. Cullych turned back to her with a slight laugh, shaking with both fright and elation at what had just happened. Drielle's face was flushed, and she looked up at him with a shy smile.

"I need to see you tonight," Cullych said, cupping her face between his hands.

Drielle nodded. "Where?"

Who needs spells? Cullych thought as he told her where they could meet without fear of being seen. *Love is far more powerful.*

Cullych hurried out of his study, almost forgetting to lock the door behind him. He fumbled the key from his pocket, then nearly dropped it as Luu drew up beside him.

"Fancy a drink?" she asked.

"No." Cullych stared at the key in his hand, forgetting in his nervousness if he had used it yet. "I mean, I can't."

Luu regarded him with a slight frown. "Somewhere you have to be tonight?"

"Family obligation."

Cullych turned to walk away, but Luu grabbed his hand, tighter than he thought was necessary. "Tell me you're not going to see that girl."

Cullych yanked his hand free. "Don't be ridiculous." He glanced down the corridor, relieved to see that it was empty. "And keep your voice down."

"Your prize pupil seems upset."

Luu took his hand again, gently this time. "Sorry." She grinned at him in a way that had the unfortunate effect of accentuating the lines in her face. "Tomorrow for that drink, perhaps?"

"Perhaps." Cullych forced a smile, wondering at her sudden cheerfulness after her inexplicable huff the day before. "Could I have my hand back now?"

"Of course." Luu squeezed his hand before letting go. "Wouldn't want to keep you from that obligation."

Cullych arrived at the academy the next morning, certain there was something else he was supposed to have done the night before.

"Cullych," Luu said, hurrying across the courtyard to catch up with him. "Are you all right? You all but walked into the gate on your way in."

Cullych shook his head. "I've just forgotten something, I think."

Luu looked as if she was about to say more, but something across the courtyard caught her eye. "Your prize pupil seems upset."

Cullych followed her gaze to where Drielle stood, her face red and her eyes puffed, as if she had been crying. She stared at him a moment, her lips quivering, then turned and ran inside the academy.

"Now what was that about?" Cullych muttered, more to himself than to Luu. He turned to his colleague to find her holding a ring in her outstretched hand. "Isn't that mine?"

"Yes," Luu said as she handed it to him. "You dropped it yesterday."

Cullych slipped on the ring, then stared at Luu. "You look beautiful this morning." She hadn't done anything different—the same hair, the usual clothes . . . though perhaps a bit less makeup—and he wondered why he had never noticed how attractive she was until now.

"If you don't have any plans tonight," Cullych said, "perhaps we could meet for dinner after today's lessons."

He wasn't sure why, but Luu glanced in the direction Drielle had gone. Turning back to him, she smiled coyly before replying.

"I would love to."

Leading Edge

Author's Comments ───────────

Sometimes scene snippets pop into my head while listening to music—for "Love Spells," that music was Trevor Jones' score to *Merlin*. I finally wrote the story a few years later when an online group I belonged to used unrequited love as the topic for a monthly writing challenge.

Getting started was the hardest part. But once I gave myself permission to plow forward and figure things out as I went, it became surprisingly easy to write. The first draft went through minor polishing, but no major changes. Later, based on rejection comments I received, I changed the title and added some material. After running that draft by a critique group, I made a few more tweaks, resulting in the version *Leading Edge* accepted.

After trying a few professional markets, I moved on to semi-pro magazines, with *Leading Edge* high on my list. It's an established magazine with a good reputation, particularly in dealing with new writers, and I had received encouraging feedback from the editors on previous submissions.

Always follow the guidelines, brace yourself for rejection, and keep trying.

—Barbara A. Barnett

The Tree

by James M. Bellarosa

An old man answered a knock at his door one hot humid morning and a stranger, about 35, said he'd come to take down the tree in the front yard. The old man glanced out at his yard—a lush green lawn uncluttered by trees, shrubs, or flowers—and said, "There are no trees in my yard."

The visitor raised his eyebrows, turned and pointed outside.

"Then what do you call *that*?"

Puzzled, the old man gazed silently at his visitor—his snarled hair, dirty trousers, untied shoelaces.

"What do you call it?" he asked.

"That's a tentacle tree," the man replied, "and unless it's destroyed, it'll seize your house."

For a moment, the old man thought the visitor was joking, but the evenness, the gravity of his voice, and his intense unsmiling expression conveyed nothing but sincerity.

"I work for free," the stranger went on, "so you'd be foolish to leave that menace standing. Besides, I need the work."

Soon convinced that his visitor probably mingled often with moonbeams, the old man, by nature a humane and kindhearted individual, sensitive always to the frailties of others, replied, "I've tolerated that tree much too long. I'd be grateful if you'd remove it."

The stranger's lips thinned into a grin.

"Thank you!" he said. "I haven't worked for so long my self-esteem is trying to implode."

"Your tools?" the old man asked.

The stranger tapped his trouser pocket. "In my pocket," he said. "I'm eager to put them to work." And he bounded down the porch stairs and out to the lawn.

Inside, the old man watched from a window as the stranger, looking upward, began walking in circles in the center of the lawn, apparently assessing the "tree" and the job ahead of him. After a minute he dug his hand into his pocket, withdrew it, and waved it from side to side over his head, seemingly

> ## "He's taking down a tree he sees out there."

cutting away branches on the tree. For several minutes the "trimming" continued, then the worker stopped and appeared to collect the fallen branches into a pile a few yards away. Soon back at work, he picked up the pace, swinging, then flailing his arms ever more briskly in the air. The old man shook his head and wondered why it was that God would mix a man's marbles and then mock his malaise with mirages. He shrugged and went to perk some coffee.

As he sipped it minutes later, his next door neighbor and good friend phoned to ask

Author Bio

James Bellarosa has earned over 200 publishing credits (80 percent of those short fiction), including two short story collections and the humorous novel, *Virgil Hunter.*

about the stranger's shenanigans.

"He's taking down a tree he sees out there," the old man explained.

"But why is razzle-dazzle Quixote removing it? It seems to be minding its own business," the neighbor scoffed.

"It's a tentacle tree, George," the old man answered. "It's got its eyes on my house."

"Well, I have an abduction tree in my yard and it's got its eye on my wife," the neighbor cracked. "If Quixote comes anywhere near it I'll slug him."

The neighbor cackled until he couldn't speak, so the old man ended the call. He returned to his lookout window and noticed that the worker had become highly animated in his effort, bounding forward and chopping

"Go get help!" he screeched. "Hurry before it consumes me!"

at the tree, then hopping back quickly, then repeating the antic again and again. The old man sighed and sat down by the window with his newspaper. Soon after, the workman came to the door and asked for water.

"Have you run into a problem out there?" the old man asked, as he handed the man a glass.

"Nothing I can't handle," the stranger replied. "It's fighting back, trying to grab me, but I'm too quick for it." He stood at the door grinning. "Stay inside," he told the old man, "this fight is coming to a head and there'll be plenty of fallout when the showdown comes."

The elder promised he'd remain safely inside, and asked the stranger to finish up quickly. "The heat makes such hard work risky," he cautioned.

The worker finished his water and returned to the lawn, but after that brief interview, the old man called the local hospital.

When he explained his circumstance and asked a nurse if anyone was missing from their secluded ward, she laughed.

"We had someone harmless like that once, but when he began moving mountains, we had to put him to sleep."

The old man responded to her sarcasm by slamming the phone onto its stand.

Suddenly then, he heard calls for help outside and looked out to see the tree surgeon thrashing as if he were trying to free himself from some invisible restraint. Bent forward at the waist, legs pumping, arms flailing, he remained stuck in place. The old man shuffled out to the howling and struggling man.

"It's got me!" the man yelled. "Help pull me free!"

"What's got you?" the old man asked.

"The tentacle tree! Pull me away from it! Hurry!"

Stupefied, incredulous, the old man began wondering about his own sanity when he reached for the stranger's arm and pulled.

"Pull harder! Hurry!" the panicked desperate man shrieked.

Still unable to accept the lunacy of his circumstance, the old man almost turned away, but the stranger's resounding and unearthly pleas came charged with a terror he'd never heard before. He tugged and he tugged again, but despite the frantic efforts of both men, the stranger wouldn't budge.

"Go get help!" he screeched. "Hurry before it consumes me!"

Exhausted, the frail old man let go and trudged next door. He admitted himself, as he always did, and called for his friend to help with the "crisis" in his yard.

"Calm down, Charlie," said the friend, "and tell me again what's happening to Quixote."

The old man explained, his voice racing.

"I'm afraid he's working up to a heart attack. Come out and help!" he insisted.

The friend sighed, rose slowly from his easy chair, followed the old man back out onto his porch.

"Where is your Don Quixote, Charlie?" he asked.

The old man looked over at his property. The stranger had vanished.

"I swear to God, George, he was over there and he couldn't move," the old man muttered, as he gaped at his front yard. Finally, he turned to his friend, whose tongue distended his cheek.

"You don't believe he was even there, do you, George?" the old man snapped.

"Of course I believe he was there, Charlie," the neighbor drawled. "He left his windmill!" A raucous belly laugh exploded from the friend, and he staggered back into his house.

The old man turned to follow George inside, then thought better of it and headed home. He went to the lawn where the stranger had struggled so violently. There he noticed the sod chewed up, but he saw no exit line of grass depressed by the stranger's retreat. As he looked around for other signs of the man's departure, a breeze picked up and carried a tree leaf to his shoulder. Puzzled, tired of it all, he gave up, but when he tried to head back to his house he couldn't move.

The Storyteller

Author's Comments

For the past several years I've enjoyed crafting short stories in which rational people are seemingly placed in impossible situations, and by the time "The Tree" was completed I'd already published a dozen of these. So, once the idea of a dangerously possessive tree occurred to me, I'd already worked out the flow/structure of such a story. It just entailed making the premise seem more and more improbable . . . right up to the surprise ending.

"The Tree" didn't quite write itself, however. It went through four drafts (condensing, revisions of words and phrases, conversions to active voice, etc.) before I submitted it to *The Storyteller*. I chose *The Storyteller* because it publishes a wide variety of fiction, and because I like my work to appear in journals I enjoy and in those I subscribe to (editors know who their subscribers are!).

Mark Twain once said that writing is "the act of applying the seat of one's pants to the seat of a chair." That's great advice for all writers, and especially for beginning writers. It's helpful also to take a couple basic writing courses, important, too, to believe in oneself, and critical to think of rejection slips as confessions by editors that they've made a mistake!

—James M. Bellarosa

Fixing Larx

by Lou Fisher

It occurred to Matthew Wood at breakfast that Larx's share of the conversation did not contain the built-in brilliance of his former, glossier years. No longer did the robot come up with an assessment of Matthew's tie ("Indeed, sir—stripes?") or a decent rebuttal to the videoscroll news; now, for the most part, it was "yes, sir" and "no, sir," as if someone had squeezed the tips of his creative circuits. And there was the matter of the eggs.

"Larx," Matthew said from a seat at the table, "stop stirring the eggs."

"Yes, sir," replied Larx. And he stopped.

His arms fell. His face stiffened. His eyes went blank. But the eggs cooked on, with the wooden stirrer jiggling unattended in the pan. And Matthew, who was ready to leave for the office, was required instead to tap his fingers on the table, sniff the smoke in the air, and wait for Larx's timer to recycle. "Are you back with us yet?" he asked crisply. Talking crisply to a robot helped register the words as proper

patterns in the ear circuits. In this case it seemed to have an effect.

Larx's eyes rolled back down.

But as he restarted himself, his left knee jolted and banged into the stove. At the impact, the stirrer, with bits of egg still clinging to it, bounced from the pan to the floor. Unknowing, Larx kicked it across the room. Yet, to his credit, he managed after all that to slide the remainder of the eggs onto a plate and set them down in front of Matthew. "Good morning, sir," he said. "Good to see you."

"This is not the first you've seen me," Matthew told him. "I've been sitting here, all dressed, and quite late for work, you know."

"Yes, sir."

Matthew pointed to the eggs. "Tell me, Larx, do you consider this an ordinary breakfast? A number seven in your queue?"

"No, sir."

"Ah," said Matthew. Now he was getting somewhere. If Larx could only realize what had gone wrong, perhaps he could initiate some repairs. "Then it's not ordinary?"

"It's not a seven," replied Larx. "A six, sir."

"You'd never know it," Matthew said. With the tip of his fork he poked through the yellow-black mess and even tasted a piece of it. Like charcoal dust, after a rain. He stood up. "Well, six or seven, or twenty-nine—I can't eat this!"

Larx leaned over the plate. "Not hungry, sir?"

"This stuff is so badly burned," Matthew started to tell him, "that no human being, even one who was starving in a war zone . . ."

Author Bio

Lou Fisher's feelings for Larx are exceeded only by those for his wife. They live in downstate New York and take long walks together in the countryside. Though lately his stories have appeared in literary journals like *New Letters* and *Mississippi Review*, now and then he continues to justify his membership in the Science Fiction Writers of America. His earlier science fiction novels, culminating with *The Blue Ice Pilot*, were published by Dell and Warner.

But how could he go on? Larx's face had begun to turn gray with signals from the disappointment circuits, the very circuits that Matthew would have disabled, if he could. "Cancel the last message, Larx. Replace it with this—I'm just not hungry."

Unconvinced, Larx clicked his tongue noise and scraped the eggs into the disposer. Matthew watched them go down. Then with a finger pressed to his cheek, he studied the robot. But he saw only what he always saw. The head, without hair, was easy to inspect— no sign whatsoever of a nick or crack. The narrow body was, as usual, tucked inside Matthew's old blue sweater and other random leftovers of the upstairs wardrobe, while the feet, after years of being just feet, were now clad in a special pair of shoes they sold at Robotland. ("Indeed, sir—new shoes?" said Larx on the day they were bought.)

Matthew lowered his eyes and frowned. A bit of a problem with that left knee, that was for sure; but other than that Larx's legs could still bend and swivel in more directions than nature intended. So what exactly was

Larx had never needed any maintenance . . .

going on? Maybe nothing. Or maybe it was time to get some advice.

As he headed for the door, Larx came up behind him.

"Your briefcase, sir."

"Thanks. I've really got to get going," said Matthew, glancing at his watch. But when he reached for the briefcase, what he got decisively placed in his hand was the empty saddlebag from Larx's bicycle.

The moment Matthew walked into Robotland, his stomach began to hurt. A result, he thought, of skipping breakfast. And here it was lunch time, and he was looking at animated displays instead of having his soup and sandwich. The demos bored him. That tennis robot in the corner; a decent backhand, sure—but why buy it when he could rent one at the courts?

"Just looking," he said to the saleswoman who pursued him.

The young woman with the red hair folded her arms, then hung around, close by, with a bit of a hum to show she was there. Finally, Matthew asked her if she had much experience in the business.

"Trained at the company school," was her quick reply. "And Robotic Science in college—not my major but right up there with my computer courses." She unfolded her arms and pushed a strand of hair behind her ear. "My name is Nancy."

Pink suit. White blouse. He had to admit she was a pleasant-looking person to deal with. And her voice, though insistent, came with a smile that seemed to soothe the pain in his stomach. "I have a Larx," he said, more confidently, "who's twelve years old."

She lifted her brows. "That's old for a Larx."

"Well, I don't think so." Matthew moved over to a table of brochures. He'd been out of the market, out of touch, and long ago he had let lapse his subscription to *Robot World*. Now that he looked at the brochures, at the demos all around him—yes, there were new looks. New functions. But were they really made better these days? Larx had never needed any maintenance and, in fact, only one programming change—an option installed in the second year, at Larx's own request, a frivolous microchip that taught him to ride the bicycle. What more, Matthew wondered, could any new model offer?

The saleswoman—Nancy, he reminded himself—was at his heels, tapping him on the shoulder.

"Believe me, if you'd see what we scrap—" She waved her arm toward an unmarked door at the back of the display area, as if only the direction was important. Then she picked up a few brochures and fanned them out in front of Matthew. "I can let you try out anything in the store."

"No, I don't want a new one," he replied, taking a step back. "I just want information. About Larxes. Truthfully, what do the manufacturers say?"

Nancy gave it some thought.

Then she said, "The company that made your Larx is no longer in business."

"Well, I know that," Matthew told her. "But how long did they say, when they *were* in business, that a Larx should last?"

She touched her lips and stared into space. "The Larx, I remember, was way ahead of its time. Very popular, and very efficient. Thought of as a quality product. I didn't sell them back then, but the word was that a Larx was good for at least twenty years."

Matthew sighed. A pang of hunger turned up to get him ready for lunch.

"That's a relief," he said. "To tell you frankly, with some of the things going on with my Larx, I was getting worried about him. But he's only twelve." Matthew reached out to shake the woman's hand. "You've done me a lot of good. If you're still here someday when I'm ready for a new robot . . ."

"It seems to me," Nancy said, letting her hand rest warmly in his, "that you're more than ready right now."

He let her hand drop. "Oh, no. We just cleared that up. Larx is only twelve. You said he was good for twenty."

"You're mistaken. I didn't say that."

"Of course you did."

"Not me," Nancy explained. "That was the people who made the Larx. *They* said you could keep a Larx for twenty years."

"Then—"

"I'm sorry, do you want the truth?"

"Of course," Matthew said. He was thinking, however, that he should not have

come to Robotland. Not yet. Not, perhaps, for several more weeks until Larx could attempt some reprogramming.

"The truth," Nancy was saying as she looked directly into Matthew's eyes, "is that you've already had a lot more than you can expect from a Larx."

"But they said twenty years."

"About eight is the way it turned out."

"Eight!" He stared back at her. "What happened to twenty? They said twenty years."

The red-haired saleswoman spread her hands.

"That must be why," she said, "they're no longer in business."

Matthew was reading *Day* from the videoscroll when Larx came in with the coffee. By now he was watching every move the robot made.

Every move and every hesitation.

What was wrong? A little rust, Matthew thought, despite the guaranteed coating. Or— he could imagine worse—circuits grow brittle, microchips deteriorate, and here and there, unbeknownst to anyone, parts drop off inside. He sagged in the chair. The robot's aging could

"Robots are never sorry, sir."

not be overlooked. At the most inconvenient moments there were major delays in Larx's response time; annoying, too, as if when a friend stutters and you have to wait it out. And the performance, a mystery from swivel to swivel.

"Sorry, sir," said Larx, setting down the coffee.

Matthew looked first at the cup and then at Larx's face. "What about? I mean, I don't recall you ever being sorry before."

"Twice before," Larx replied, obviously reaching into his abundant memory banks.

"Is that so? Twice, you say? When exactly was that?"

"Sir?"

"The times you were sorry."

"Robots—" A click came from Larx's left knee. It buckled right afterward, and he crumbled to the floor. But at once, before Matthew could even try to help, he was back on his feet and taking up, more or less nonchalantly, where he had left off. "Robots are never sorry, sir," he said. "Seldom need to be."

Matthew nodded. "Well, now, Larx, that's what I thought, too."

"About what, sir?"

"About being sorry. We both know that robots can never be sorry. Why are you bothering me about it?"

Larx's knee shook but stayed together.

"*Bothering* you, sir?" he said.

Then he turned briskly and left the room. Minutes later Matthew spotted him speeding by the window on his bicycle.

Nancy looked perky, as bright as her red hair, and that, he was sure, reflected the sales spirit of Robotland.

"Well, we disconnect a few every day," she said. She pointed to the unmarked door, then turned back to Matthew with her same, soothing smile. "What *you* do," she went on, "is bring the robot down here on some pretext or other, and as soon as we get hold of it, you just turn and leave."

Matthew drew back.

"Maybe I can get him repaired."

"The robot won't feel a thing."

Nancy shrugged. "Not if it's worn out. Listen, all these years it's been repairing itself. That's what it does best. Believe me, if it can't handle its own circuits, it's beyond anything a service-robot can do."

Matthew looked away from her. Across the aisle, he saw an older couple testing a Dandy model, and for some reason his mind flashed back to the lonely years before Larx, when he stayed late at the office almost every night rather than coming home to an empty house. ("Good to see you," said Larx, at the very moment he was activated.) Of course, Matthew thought, companionship was not the reason for a robot. Cooking, cleaning, bringing in the mail, putting a log on the fire . . . Nancy's hand came onto his shoulder.

"We'll take care of everything," she said. Her eyes, by themselves, were a comfort. "We do it all the time. It's a standard procedure. Easy, believe me. The robot won't feel a thing. Not a thing. And it'll barely have time to realize it's being disconnected. A quick probe of the laser gun—*pttt*—and that'll be the end of your problem."

Matthew felt tired. "But Larx and I . . ."

"Sure. Nice. Ten years together, I know."

"Twelve," Matthew corrected.

"Well, you see? Far beyond the norm." Nancy looked knowingly at the door to the back room, then she turned to Matthew again. "Believe me, those Larx models gave out at six, and not a day over eight no matter how you took care of them. I can show you reports. Why, twelve years, that's outstanding. We might just want to write to the company about that, if only they were still in business."

"Dammit," Matthew said. He turned to her. "Nancy, I'll never have another one."

"You might think about," she responded, moving closer, "having a person instead."

Perhaps something only an owner could tell, but Larx was limping.

"Will there be anything else, sir?"

"You could get me my coat."

Larx swiveled, then swiveled back. Then he did it to the other side.

"The coat," Matthew reminded him, crisply again, to make sure he was understood.

Done swiveling, Larx backed away with some drag from the knee. "Exactly which would you want, sir? The stadium coat? Perhaps the raincoat, sir . . . or the warm-up jacket."

There was no need for Matthew to mull it over. "C'mon, Larx, it's the middle of January. You know I wouldn't go out without my wool-lined topcoat."

"Indeed, sir—January, is it?" Larx may not have been aware, but Matthew spotted it without trying, that there was a definite current coming from his puzzled circuit. In the twelve years they had been together, Matthew could have bet that the puzzled circuit, of all of them, of even anger and jealousy and other seldom active robotic traits, was the least used and the least required. Larx puzzled? So, because of that, was Matthew.

But a minute later Larx brought the topcoat, and slipped it politely over Matthew's arms. "Enjoy your day, sir," he said. Leaning to one side, he fastened the coat's buttons, from the collar on down. "I'll have dinner waiting."

Quickly Matthew told him, "I'm eating out, with someone named Nancy."

"But, sir, on Mondays I always cook for you. You eat out on Wednesdays, occasionally on a Sunday."

"Well, this will give you an extra day of rest."

"Sir?"

"Yes?"

"I'm not in need of rest. I'm programmed to do certain things, and those are the things I do."

. . . Larx seemed to be in fine control.

Matthew set down the briefcase and redid the front of his coat, where Larx had missed a button. "I know, Larx, I know. But it wouldn't hurt to let the chips get a little rejuiced. You're not . . . well, you're just not as young as you used to be."

"Not—" Larx paused for a second and his head fell into a tilt, from which angular position he said once more, "Not—" and then he stopped.

Matthew moved in and looked at him. Despite the lessening of duties, Larx seemed to have cut out. "Larx," he said, as crisply as ever, but there was no sign of a restart, even after a full minute or two. Matthew put down the briefcase again and walked around the robot. He considered calling Robotland. But they'd be of no help; Nancy had already said so. Yet something needed to be done. ("I take care of myself, sir," Larx was fond of saying, as if it were a matter of vitamins.) But Matthew was afraid to wait any longer—who knew what was going on inside? Facing Larx again, he raised an open hand, turned it, and pounded the edge of it into the middle of the breast plate.

Larx's head straightened and a few unfamiliar noises preceded the return to robot voice.

"Is that your final word, sir?"

"It is for now."

"Very well, sir."

"Very well, Larx."

"Then if you don't mind, sir, I'll list a few suggestions for your dinner," he said. "And some for Nancy as well." He seemed to imply by his professional tone that all things human could somehow be electronically comprehended. So when Matthew left the room, Larx seemed to be in fine control. But when he drove home from the restaurant that evening he found the bicycle a wreck in front of the garage, as if someone had taken a major fall.

The saleswoman—Nancy, of course—took Matthew aside.

"Shows all the signs," she whispered in his ear. It was the first she'd examined Larx. "You're doing the right thing. It's beyond repair, and soon it may not function at all."

"Still," Matthew whispered back, his voice unsteady, "I've never had a robot disconnected before. Maybe if I wait—"

"It's liable to set your house on fire."

"Oh, no. Not Larx."

"Could be."

"Not Larx," said Matthew. "Not Larx."

Nancy gripped his arm. "It's only a robot," she said. "And listen, believe me, it won't feel a thing. The laser probe is painless and as quick as a wink. *Pttt*, and it's gone."

"Just like that," said Matthew.

"All for the best. It's just a robot, they come and go."

"I suppose they do," Matthew said, and walked over to where Larx was waiting.

In the store's bright lights, Larx seemed a match for the old blue sweater, himself worn and faded, standing askew to favor the leg that had been giving him trouble. He swiveled toward Matthew and there was a delay while he appeared to search through all of his accumulated memory to create a feeling. "I'm a bit uneasy, sir," he said at last.

Matthew turned aside. From there he could see the unmarked door across the aisles; behind it the laser gun and probably a pile of scrap. But this was a moment to be realistic. The work around the house had to get done. Everyday mistakes by a robot could not be tolerated. The breakage, the time wasted, the constant apprehension . . . He turned back and straightened Larx's sweater around the shoulders. "Don't worry, Larx," he said. "Didn't I get a check-up myself last month?"

"Correct and correct."

"And wasn't it . . . You're a good robot, Larx."

"Thank you, sir."

"The best."

"If you say so, sir. Yes, I often try to please. Let me know when they're ready for me, and we'll soon be back home."

"Sure," Matthew said, glancing at Nancy.

She nodded. She took a step. She nodded again. Matthew looked away from her, to look back at Larx, but instead his head

dropped; he rubbed a finger under his nose and thought first about nothing and then about how lucky he was to have met Nancy at just this time, and so the lost blind moments passed . . . Until it occurred to him in a sudden stab of panic that he had managed to mumble, "Go ahead"—and he came out of it fast, fixed with the idea to scream.

Larx was gone. Gone!

But that couldn't be, Matthew thought.

He had meant, he told himself desperately, to take Larx by the hand, to stand with him against the probe, to reassure him, even falsely, that everything was all right. Just a routine service call, he was going to say. A bit of oil. A replacement for the knee chip. Whatever. He was going to try, above all, to leave a smile in the circuits. But there he was, having done none of it, having only looked to the floor, having deserted Larx at the end and given him to junk. But there he was, with a pain in his stomach.

And his hands were shaking.

A small, ugly weapon, a ruby laser, came spitting toward his robot. At that point, of course, Larx knew; Matthew saw the head swivel rapidly from side to side. *Too late*, he thought. He burst through the stacked cartons and crates into the center of the back room, expecting at any moment to hear the final *pttt* of the probe. Instead Larx said, "Sir!" and reached for him and his knee gave out and the narrow red beam passed over his head into the wall and Matthew grabbed him and fell over him and held up his hand to Nancy who was setting up for another try.

"We don't need that," Matthew said, puffing for breath. "We're just out shopping for a new bicycle."

Larx sat up. "Indeed, sir—a bicycle?"

"A slow one," Matthew told him crisply.

Aboriginal SF

Author's Comments

At one time I was a science fiction writer. The genre was at its height of popularity and I produced a couple of novels as well as short stories for various magazines and anthologies. When I heard that a new magazine was about to be launched, I wanted to make the connection.

The story's idea, however, came in a sad way. My beloved dog was euthanized at the vet. She was very old, truly ill, yet I opposed taking the action. It broke my heart. The next morning I sat at the keyboard while a complete draft of the story poured out of me along with an uncontrollable flow of tears.

At first Charles Ryan, the magazine's founder and editor, turned down the submitted manuscript, but he said if I would combine the characters of the girlfriend and the salesperson I could resubmit. When I made the change the story really took form. Ryan featured it in the premiere issue of *Aboriginal SF.*

Advice to writers: Often it pays to heed an editor's advice. As in this case, look over your story's supporting characters to see if any can be merged, perhaps turning two weakly portrayed characters into one who's more fully realized.

—Lou Fisher

The Knitting Madonna

by Julia Curcio

I never thought the sight of an old woman holding up a pair of baby booties would strike fear in my heart, but as Anne displayed the tiny knit shoes I was terrified of what Elda might do. Elda glared at the booties as if they had caused her bad back and the rising price of liverwurst.

"Frog them," Elda said shortly.

I didn't know what it meant to "frog" something. As funny as it would have been to see Anne paint her face green and hop around the choir room, I was pretty sure it was some kind of knitting term for ripping out the stitches. And that was not good.

"Elda, I worked really hard, and this wool is—"

"If you want to remain an upstanding member of this church and this choir," Elda said, "you will frog those booties."

Anne unraveled the first stitch. Elda resumed practice and pretended nothing was wrong.

That Sunday Mass was beautiful, and our rendition of "Hail, Holy Queen" sounded pretty good, but my heart just wasn't in it. Something was missing. Marisa was missing. And the Elda I thought I knew was gone as well.

Author Bio

Julia Curcio studied screenwriting and playwriting in college. Since graduating in 2006, she has concentrated mostly on short fiction and playwriting.

Marisa had been a member of the women's choir at Our Lady of Mercy for two years. She fit in wonderfully with Elda, Anne and me from the moment she showed up at her first rehearsal, ready to help out the members of the parish. Some members of our

I hated knitting.

choir had a tradition of knitting tons of baby gifts anytime a member of the parish was pregnant, and Marisa had come that day with a matching hat and blanket for Joyce, our organ player, who was pregnant with her second child at the time. I was thrilled enough that our new member was in my age bracket. It was even better that she could make up for my lack of yarn control in the group.

I hated knitting. In the previous five years, Elda had taught me to make the perfect baked ziti and to grow amazing tomatoes. She'd even helped me find my job in the library's rare books department. But, God love her, she couldn't teach me to knit. She'd learned that the hard way in an after-rehearsal knitting lesson that had ended with her using a letter opener to free me from the web of yarn tangled from my watch to my shoelaces.

Anyway, after rehearsal that day I gave Marisa a tour of the church and treated her to a cappuccino at Dean's Coffee. Marisa had been faithful to the choir from her first "Holy God, We Praise Thy Name," and she always joined me for an emergency caffeine fix right after "Come, Holy Ghost." When she called me for an emergency coffee meet-up and told me that her boyfriend, Joe, had proposed, I was thrilled. So thrilled, in fact, that I spilled caramel iced coffee all over my new white pants.

Three months later Marisa was planning her wedding and the choir was gearing up for the Feast of the Immaculate Conception. I showed up for rehearsal two hours before the seven o'clock vigil, armed with a ton of stories from my job to tell Marisa.

"You would not believe how old the book we—"

I stopped short. Marisa was not there. Her chair wasn't even there.

. . . I knew what I had to do.

Elda called Joyce in to begin rehearsal. "Aren't we going to wait for Marisa?" I asked.

"Marisa's not in the choir anymore," Elda said.

"She quit?"

"We will not discuss it," Elda responded.

"Oh, for Pete's sake, Elda," Anne interjected, "Just say it. Marisa's pregnant."

"What?" I exclaimed, dropping my sheet music, "Are you sure?"

"Elda ran into Marisa's neighbor. Marisa's gone out to the country to stay with her parents for a few days. She won't be back until Sunday," Anne explained.

"Let's not waste any more time," Elda said, signaling for Joyce to begin.

"Wait," I pleaded.

Elda gave me a deadly glare. I used to think I could ask this sweet old woman anything, but at that moment, I was afraid to open my mouth. After some thinking, I asked the most urgent and appropriate question I could: "Are you going to start making booties?"

Anne smiled. "Well, I picked out a nice yellow yarn from the—"

"We will not be making the child booties," Elda interrupted. "Now, let's begin the—"

"Why not?" I asked.

"We are not going to reward Marisa for her immorality or cast our pearls before swine."

Swine, I thought, *that's a little excessive.*

Anne reached into her bag and pulled out two perfectly knit yellow booties. "But I already made mine," she said.

Elda glared at the booties, and they soon met their froggy fate.

After rehearsal, I called Marisa's cell phone, but it was off. Her parents didn't have Internet access, so I couldn't even email her. I went to work the next day in a daze. I couldn't help but worry about Marisa, Joe, and the baby. It made me sad to think Marisa's son or daughter wouldn't nestle in one of Elda's trademark blankets.

I thought about buying a baby blanket, but I knew Elda would definitely kick me out of the choir if she knew I was running around behind her back "rewarding immorality." And how would Jesus feel about me if I chose my friend over literally singing his praises? I thought that maybe Elda was right. She was older and wiser and had always helped me when I needed her. Maybe it would be best to go on without Marisa. But somehow I still knew it was wrong.

That day one of the books I needed to re-shelve was a book of medieval religious paintings. I was flipping through it absentmindedly when I saw a painting of the Holy Family that made my heart skip six or seven beats. The Virgin Mary was in the foreground, and Joseph was gazing at her lovingly. The child Jesus was stretched out on the ground reading a book. And Mary! Mary was knitting a gorgeous blanket for Jesus. As I looked at the Virgin's patient and unconditionally loving face, I knew what I had to do.

When I got home, I went straight to my long-neglected yarn and how-to books. I stared at the never-ending instructions and diagrams, which would rival my 12th grade calculus textbook in complexity. But I pushed on, and after many tearful failures, I completed a stitch! I looked down at the pattern for the baby blanket. I had resolved to finish by Marisa's return in the morning. Only 2,876 stitches to go.

But I could swear I saw Anne smile just a little.

I enlisted the help of two pots of coffee and endless hours of late-night TV. By 4:30 A.M., my hands were burning. I couldn't tell where the yarn ended and the needles began. I felt like I could do no more. I needed help.

I knelt down and took out my rosary, but my thoughts were too jumbled even to say an Our Father. I tried as hard as I could to focus, but just counting the beads was too complicated at that point. I remembered the painting I'd seen of Mary working away effortlessly with her needles. "Show off," I muttered. But I realized she wasn't showing off; she was setting an example. And if I had any sense left, I would follow it.

I picked my needles back up and started stitching while repeating the Hail Mary. I found my focus all over again. I imagined the Blessed Virgin knitting her blanket right beside me. During each prayer I completed about sixteen stitches. Eventually, with the Madonna's help, the blanket was done.

When I woke up, I realized I had fallen asleep in my chair with the blanket on top of me. It wasn't perfect by any means—the rows were uneven and the ends were frayed—but boy, was it warm!

I was very nervous when I arrived at Marisa's doorstep. How would she feel?

What would she look like? When Marisa came to the door, she didn't look any different. She didn't look like an immoral person, she didn't look like someone who should be kicked out of the choir and she certainly didn't look like a swine. She looked like my friend.

"You heard?" she asked. She sounded like she hadn't slept in days. I nodded. "Elda left me a voice mail. I'm out of the choir. It just happened, Gina."

I shrugged. "It's ok," I said lamely.

"It just—it never happened before. I went to confession. We both did, and I—"

"Marisa," I said, praying to every saint above that I would think of something meaningful to say, "that's between you and Jesus. I'm just here to say congratulations." OK, not exactly Shakespeare, but I thought it was pretty good. This was as good a time as any to reveal my gift, so I took the blanket from my bag and handed it to her, tied with a red ribbon and everything.

"You made this?" she asked.

I nodded. She looked like she was about to cry. "It's beautiful," she said, giving me a hug.

"Why don't you come to Mass with me?" I asked.

"But I can't sit with you. Won't you be in the choir section?"

"We'll make our own choir. Bring Joe."

So Marisa called Joe, and the three of us set off for church. When Elda and Anne sang the opening hymn, Marisa and I sang along from our seats in the front pew. After the first hymn and before the start of Mass, Elda peeked down at us and frowned. But I could swear I saw Anne smile just a little.

When the organ was warming up for the exit hymn, I heard quick steps approaching our pew. Anne slid in beside me and leaned over to Marisa and Joe.

"Congratulations," she whispered and joined us for the "Hail, Holy Queen."

The Knitting Madonna

After Mass I snuck up to the choir room. Elda was already gone, but I left her a photocopy of the painting of the knitting Madonna and said a prayer for her heart to open up to Marisa and her growing family. Maybe she would be as inspired as I had been to knit side by side with Mary.

Marisa's wedding was beautiful. Anne and I worked together to make a white afghan for the lucky couple. I have to say my knitting has improved greatly. I've learned that it's called frogging because you take your knitting and you "rip it, rip it." Rip it, rip it, ribbit, ribbit. It's silly, I know.

The day after the wedding, a package from Elda arrived at Marisa's house. It contained two baby hats and a little holy card of Saint Gerard, the patron saint of pregnancy. I was so glad to learn that Elda had had a change of heart.

The baby, Maria, was born without a hitch and was met with countless little booties and hats from other parish members. Elda invited Marisa to come back to the choir whenever she was ready. I kept knitting and actually got kind of good at it. I found a charity nearby that accepts donations for parents of unplanned children. The choir organized a clothing and knitting drive for the charity, and it was so successful that we decided to make it an annual event.

On the last Thursday of every month, Elda, Anne, Marisa, and I all meet at Dean's Coffee and knit baby clothes. I can honestly say I now like knitting all because of Marisa and the knitting Madonna. And let she who is without sin frog the first stitch.

Liguorian

Author's Comments

I came up with the idea for "The Knitting Madonna" because I wanted to write a Christian story from a feminist perspective. I'm an avid knitter and have always liked the paintings of Mary knitting.

The biggest challenge in writing this story was making sure no one came off as a villain. I wanted it to be clear that all the characters were doing what they thought was right. I did about five drafts.

My advice to anyone submitting a story for the first time is that no matter how nervous you are to receive a rejection, remember you have nothing to lose by submitting your work. As a writer just starting out, I still receive many more rejections than acceptances. It's easier said than done, but don't take them personally. Sulk for an evening or so and then use the experience to refine your work and keep searching for the best market for your style. As long as you keep trying, you're making good progress.

—Julia Curcio

Road Gamble

by Scott William Carter

Whipping around the sharp bends, tires squealing on wet asphalt, Simon pushed his little Miata close to eighty. The wall of pine trees on both sides, as well as the black sky above, created a dark tunnel into the hills. He was thinking about making it to the coast before midnight, early enough to squeeze in a few hands with the late-night poker crowd at the casino, and he didn't see the motorcycle until he was almost on top of it. With no taillight, and with its rider clad in black, the bike emerged from the dreary gloom like a moth alighting on his windshield.

"Holy mother of—" he cried, stomping on his brakes.

The shoulder belt snapped taut against his chest. His car fishtailed, back tires screaming, front end coming inches from the bike's mud-caked license plate.

Up close, the Miata's headlights slashed through the rain and the dark, illuminating the man and his bike in vivid detail. The guy's glistening jacket bore a striking design: a white bear head in profile, glowing as if luminescent. It was the only thing on the rider that *wasn't* black; pants, boots, even the helmet melded with the stormy night, making the bear appear to hover over the road.

Simon didn't know much about motorcycles, but the bike was definitely too sleek and compact to be a Harley. It looked like it belonged on a racetrack, not a highway.

Heart pounding, Simon eased off the biker. He would have expected the commotion to startle the guy, maybe cause him to swerve, but the biker's only reaction was to turn his head halfway around, just far enough that Simon's headlights appeared on the helmet's mirrored faceplate like a pair of hot ember eyes. The guy looked for a moment, then turned back to the road.

And dropped his speed down to thirty.

Son of a gun. Simon could understand the guy being pissed—Simon *had* nearly plowed over him—but going half the speed limit, even in these conditions, seemed petty.

The squeaking wipers struggled to keep the windshield clear. Dashboard fans roared out a steady stream of warm air. There were few opportunities to pass on Highway 18, but Simon knew there was a passing lane in a few miles. He'd driven this road so many times, every pothole and mile marker was burned in his memory. He'd wait a few minutes, give the guy a chance to cool down. He really wanted to get to that poker game—he was already imagining the rush of tossing in his first ante—but he didn't want to get into some kind of stupid road game. In these conditions, one of them could end up dead in a ditch.

As his heart slowed, he felt a pang of

Author Bio

Scott William Carter has sold over two dozen stories to publications such as *Analog*, *Asimov's*, *Ellery Queen*, *Realms of Fantasy*, and *Weird Tales*, as well as to Pocket Books and DAW for use in anthologies. He is also the author of a novel, *The Last Great Getaway of the Water Balloon Boys*.

remorse. What if he had died out here? To-morrow—Saturday—was Jana's second birth-day. He could just imagine the look on her face as she sat on their crappy lima-bean couch in their mousetrap apartment—an apartment that should have been packed with children laughing and making noises with party favors, but instead would be empty and deathly quiet as her mother ex-plained why Daddy wasn't coming home.

She was so young . . . In a few years would she even remember him?

Guilt—it was the worst kind of feeling, a feeling Simon had come to dread because he knew it always lurked somewhere around the corner. The worst part, the absolute worst part, was that Tracy would know, if he died on this stretch of road at this time of night (when he was supposed to be hanging out at Steve's watching horror flicks) that he had broken his word.

Promising to give up gambling forever was the only way he had been able to keep her from leaving him. But what she didn't know couldn't hurt her. After all, he wasn't playing like last year when his losses forced them to file for bankruptcy. No, it was nothing like that. Just an occasional game here and there. For fun, really. Spare change he earned from his tips, money Tracy never saw. He'd never dip into his bank account again. He was in control now.

His radio, turned low, was losing its Rex-ton signal to static, and Simon clicked it off. When he did, he noticed his hand was shak-ing. Apparently the incident had gotten to him more than he thought it had. The biker went on puttering at thirty, the spray from his back tire misting in the beams from Simon's headlights. Not a single car passed from the other direction, but Simon knew the road was way too popular, even on nights like this, to chance passing with a double yellow.

Jana's birthday, he kept telling himself. *Jana's birthday.*

He honked his horn a few times, but the guy didn't react. A few minutes later, they crested a rise and rounded a bend, entering a brief downhill straight stretch. Ah, now here was the passing lane. The road opened up, the dotted white line appearing. Accelerating, Simon moved to the left. The biker stayed on the right and in a few seconds Simon was alongside him.

This was not a man you stared at, not for five seconds, not even for one.

For just a moment, no more than a few seconds, Simon eased off the accelerator to look at the biker.

From the side, it was easier to get a good look. He was a big guy, not tall but broad, wide across the shoulders, thick in the mid-dle. If he had a neck, Simon couldn't see it—his helmet sat right on his linebacker shoulders. His pants tucked snuggly into his boots, pulling tight around his bulging calves. His hands, covered with black leather gloves, were also huge. Clenching the handlebars, they made the bike seem undersized beneath him, like a toy.

Simon realized this guy didn't seem like a *guy* at all. He seemed more like the creature on the back of his jacket—a bear. He sud-denly wished he could see the guy's face. Would he look like Grizzly Adams, hair all over the place? He chuckled at the thought.

As if sensing he was being mocked, the biker turned and looked. It was then that Simon realized he had made a terrible mis-take, lingering like this; imagining the eyes staring at him from behind the face shield sent a chill up his spine. He did not know this man, had no idea where he was going or why, but he sensed that this was not some-body to mess with. This was not a man you stared at, not for five seconds, not even for one. He wasn't threatening in a Hell's Angel sort of way, all bravado and bullying. Most bikers acted tough because they didn't want to fight, hoping their image of toughness would be enough to scare you away. No, Simon got the feeling this guy didn't care about projecting an image of toughness.

He didn't need to act tough because he *was*.

As if he had just come face-to-face with a rattlesnake, Simon turned slowly toward the road, applying gentle pressure to the accelerator.

But as he accelerated the biker also increased his speed. Forty-five miles an hour . . . Fifty . . . Fifty-five . . .

The end of the passing lane was coming up in a hurry. The guy stayed right there, across from his window. Simon didn't dare look, but he saw well enough with his peripheral vision that the guy was still looking at him.

A yellow sign warned of the end of the passing lane. Sixty . . . Sixty-five . . . Seventy . . . For Christ's sake, the guy would not back off. The dotted white line vanished, the two lanes merging into one. His heart racing, Simon punched the accelerator and his Miata jerked forward.

He hoped one last burst of speed would propel him past the biker, but the guy stayed neck and neck. Worse, the road brought them together like two canoes in a narrowing river, and soon the guy was so close to his passenger-side window that Simon couldn't help but look. There, beyond the rain-streaked glass, lost in all that black leather, was the shiny faceplate still looking straight at him.

Cursing, Simon hit his brakes.

The biker sped past. Immediately the guy started to slow down—dropping, dropping some more, forcing Simon to keep tapping the brakes, until they were all the way back down to thirty again.

"I don't believe this," Simon said aloud.

He honked his horn a few more times. Again, the guy puttered along, not once turning to look back at his follower. There wasn't

another passing lane for at least ten miles. At this pace, the poker games would be shut down for the night by the time he got there.

Simon thought about taking his chances across the double yellow line, but as if in response to his thought, a pair of headlights emerged from the gloom and a van whipped past, rocking his car and spraying his windshield.

He laid on his horn, then gave the guy's back a double bird. Still nothing. Maybe the guy was deaf. He drummed his fingers on his steering wheel. He'd just have to bide his time. There was a place to pass in a few minutes, and if he had even a hint of open road, he'd go for it. Show this punk what real speed was all about.

But when he reached the area to pass, and started to make his move, the guy sped up again.

Totally unbelievable. The guy was determined to be an absolute prick. This went on for another ten minutes—slowing in the double yellows, speeding up in the passing areas—until finally Simon couldn't take it anymore. He was going to pass and damn the consequences. The jerk was on a motorcycle, for Christ's sake. He would have to back off or he'd end up flying over his handlebars.

The nachos and cheese he'd had an hour earlier now came back to haunt him; his stomach churned and gurgled. He'd need a bathroom before too long. He was halfway to the coast now, in one of the darker stretches; the dense forest on both sides crowded the twisting road, the branches reaching overhead, creating a canopy. They passed a wooden sign indicating they were in the Van Duzen National Forest. Simon knew that except for a rest stop and a campground, there wouldn't be any other sign of people for twenty miles.

At least the rain had lessened to a light drizzle, allowing him to turn down his wipers. He passed up a couple of opportunities to pass until he hit the spot he wanted—

another downhill slope with a passing lane. Then he bore down on the gas. His quick move got him alongside his companion, but as expected, the biker matched him.

The punk still wasn't backing off.

Simon clamped down on the steering wheel. He felt his pulse in his hands. They streaked down the hill, the forest a blur on both sides. The extra speed increased the moisture spattering his windshield, making the glass blurry for seconds at a time, but Simon didn't want to take his hands off the wheel to speed up the wipers.

They barreled along, his speedometer passing over seventy, then eighty, then ninety . . .

As his engine screamed, Simon held his breath. The dotted white line vanished. The road narrowed. The punk *still* wasn't backing off, and there was no way Simon was letting off the juice now. He took a quick glance at the biker and, with a chill, saw the guy look over at the same time.

The extra lane disappeared, and then the two of them shared a lane, Simon partially over the double yellow. A bend in the road loomed ahead, a wall of trees beyond it.

Knowing his Miata cornered well, he kept his speed high and squealed around the bend. The biker stayed right with him, leaning into the curve, his shoulder nearly touching Simon's passenger-side window. That's when a pair of headlights appeared.

Simon had only a second to react. The gap between the lights made him think the vehicle was a semi or a motor home, and he jerked his wheel to the right. He knew the biker was there, but he had no other choice. As the truck—and it was indeed a semi truck—rumbled past, shaking his little car with its wall of wind, the Miata bumped the motorcycle.

The guy swerved onto the shoulder and beyond, kicking up a shower of mud. Simon's momentum drifted him toward the shoulder, and for a second he thought he was going to hit the guy again, but the biker suddenly dropped behind. By then they had rounded the corner and Simon had the Miata under control.

He gasped for breath, finally remembering to breathe. Heart pounding in his ears, he roared up a hill in the storm, nothing but open road in front of him. The surge of adrenaline lit every one of his senses on fire. He'd done it. He'd actually done it. Glancing in his rearview mirror, he saw only blurry darkness behind him. The guy was gone. He must have pulled off, shaken up by the whole thing. Simon had actually proven the cooler customer.

"Hot damn," he said.

The glass splintered instantly into a spider web of cracks, the sound as loud as a gunshot. Simon yelped and ducked to the right, car swerving. He glanced up just in time to see a fist strike the window—a black leather fist wearing gleaming brass knuckles.

This time the glass gave way in the center, shards landing on Simon's lap. The wind roared in his ears. Wet air rushed into the car, smelling of pine and mud. Simon saw the outline of the biker outside the window, and seeing the shine of the leather through the broken glass suddenly made the guy more real—as if before he was merely a projection of Simon's tired mind, or a villain in a video game.

They neared the top of the hill. Leaning away from the window, Simon edged closer to the edge of the road, but the biker followed, punching the glass again. More glass went flying, and this time a piece struck him above his mouth.

Tasting blood on his lips, Simon hit the brakes, hoping his attacker would race by, but the guy slowed along with him. The fist came through the window again, and this time the burly hand struck him on the cheek. It was only a glancing blow, more leather than brass making contact, but it was still powerful enough to jerk his head to the right. Purple and red stars flashed in front of his eyes.

When his vision cleared, the Miata was halfway in the ditch. As it plowed over the uneven ground, the car trembled and shook. The side of his face throbbing, the skin around his left eye already swelling, Simon

. . . the biker barreled across the lanes.

steered the car back onto the highway. The biker was there, but Simon wasn't going to get punched again. As they roared over the hill, the night a swirl of black and green around them, he let out a primal scream and swerved at the biker.

The guy was too fast. He moved even farther to the left. They banked around a gentle curve, and it was then that a white motor home emerged from the night like a whale surfacing from the depths of the ocean.

Just in time, Simon whipped the Miata back into his own lane. He cringed, expecting to hear a sickening crunch.

But there was no such sound.

After the motor home roared past, blaring its horn, there was the biker on the far left shoulder, keeping pace. He turned and looked at Simon.

Simon's stomach churned even worse— now he really needed a bathroom. As they hit another straight stretch, not a car in sight, the biker barreled across the lanes. Simon swerved back and forth, trying to keep his attacker at bay, but these feints didn't fool him. He turned along with Simon, and then deftly sidled up to him. Simon leaned away, expecting another blow, but this time the fist grabbed his steering wheel.

The brass knuckles, shiny with moisture, were still there. The leather glove was cov-

ered with hundreds of pin-sized holes. Simon had no idea what the guy was doing until the wheel moved to the right. Along this stretch, the pine trees grew awfully close to the road, and if he hit one of them at this speed . . .

Slamming on the brakes was the most obvious thing to do, and he almost did it, but then he had a flash of insight.

With his left hand, he grabbed the door handle and jerked the door open, putting his forearm behind it.

It worked better than he expected. The door struck the motorcycle's handlebars, sending them careening in the other direction. The biker obviously hadn't expected this move; he held onto the steering wheel a split second too long. His weight was going one way, his bike the other, and the bike began to tilt.

In the next instant the biker was gone. This time Simon *did* hear the sound of a wreck—a series of bangs and thuds. Swerving into the center of his lane, he glanced in his rearview mirror and saw, through the smear of black and gray, a flickering headlight in the middle of the road, receding behind him. Then he rounded the corner and was alone with the rain and the highway.

In addition to his throbbing cheek, his whole body was trembling. Nobody could survive a crash like that. He had killed a man. He had actually killed. Dear God . . . His life was over. Even if it was manslaughter, he'd go away for years. His wife . . . his daughter . . .

He tasted bile. He clamped his hand over his mouth, and only through force of will did he keep from throwing up in the car. He descended a slight hill and, with fortunate timing, saw the sign for the Van Duzen National Forest Campground—and then another: Rest Area—1 Mile Ahead. He'd stupidly left his cell phone at home, so a pay phone was his best bet.

He could make it to the rest area.

The rain sliced into his car, dampening his left arm. The highway widened, a lane appearing in the center for a turnoff to the left, for the campground, and another lane on the right, to the rest area. Still shaking, he turned to the right, slowing gently, turning into the gap in the trees.

He'd never been to this particular rest stop. He'd passed it lots of times, even a few times when he had to take a leak, but by the time he reached it the pull of the casino had always carried him the last twenty miles. But this time he couldn't wait, and he was glad when he entered the pothole-infested parking lot and saw no other cars. He didn't want anyone to see him in his present condition—or his smashed window. He still hadn't decided if he was going to go back and fess up to what he did.

His mind raced, trying to understand how it all had happened. He had just wanted to pass. He didn't even see what he had done wrong. Honked the horn a few times, maybe. Had that really been enough for the guy to want to kill him?

The rest stop was a lonely place, a few chipped picnic tables and a drab concrete box in a small clearing carved out of the forest; the pine trees, with their long, slender trunks and thick green branches high above, loomed a few dozen feet beyond a grassy area like a wall of spears. A single lamp shed its pale yellow light on the area. As he parked in front of the little building, the rain turned into a fierce downpour, and it sounded so much louder when he turned off his engine.

He had killed a man.

Stomach clenching, he threw open the door and ran toward the building. The frigid rain instantly soaked his hair, cutting through his thin cotton shirt like icy needles. The wind whispered through the trees, stirring up the paper plates and cups on the ground near the overflowing garbage can. The phone booth was on the far side, near the women's door, but he couldn't wait. Dodging the puddles in the sidewalk, he sprinted to the green

door marked Men. When he grabbed the cold metal handle, the door opened (*thank God, thank God*) and he sprinted inside.

The room was dank and cramped, smelling of piss and mold. A single amber light above the cracked mirror and the metal sink was the only thing keeping the darkness at bay. There were two urinals to the left of the sink, two green stalls immediately to the left of the urinals. Gritty tile floor, lots of small white squares streaked with mud. Shoebox-sized vents near the ceiling. Stumbling into the first stall, he took it all in with a glance.

He barely made it down to the bowl before the contents of his stomach surged out of his mouth. Again and again, he threw up, until there was nothing left but dry heaves and the horrible acid burn in his throat and his nose. He hugged the cold metal, his head bent into the bowl and all its foulness, sobbing now. The damp ground soaked through his pants and chilled his knees.

The restroom door swung open.

There was no creak, just the distinctive swoosh of the door and the increasing loudness of the rain. Simon froze. The stall door had shut behind him, but he knew whoever it was could see his knees. They would have seen his car. Might have seen the wreck. Maybe it was a policeman, already come to haul him away.

Simon didn't make a sound. The restroom door swung shut, muting the storm. Only a dripping faucet broke the silence. After a few seconds, he heard footsteps, water dripping on the tiles, the rustle of heavy clothing. He half expected his stall door to swing open, but instead he saw a glistening black boot appear on the ground, only inches from his knee. The mud-coated toe pointed in the direction of the urinal Simon knew was right next to the stall.

A black boot.

Simon's despair was quickly washed away by an all-consuming dread. His breath caught in his throat. It couldn't be . . . The man could never have survived. It had to be someone else. *It had to be.*

As Simon remained absolutely rigid, he heard a zipper, then the tinkle of fluid hitting the metal urinal.

He felt himself relax slightly. It was just some traveler, stopping to relieve himself of his coffee. Maybe he hadn't even noticed Simon. If Simon just waited, maybe he would go away.

But then Simon felt a splash of warm liquid hitting his knee, and he realized, with a shock, that the man was pissing on him. With a startled cry, he scooted away from the line of piss, which continued splashing against the tiles. His heart thundered in his ears. The piss dribbled to a stop, and then he heard the zipper. He saw the boot turn, two boots appearing, both facing his direction.

Simon pressed his back against the other side of the stall, his body shaking. The boots didn't move for the longest time. Simon waited for a gloved first to smash through the stall, right in the middle of all the *Johnny + Suzie* and *For a Good Time Call* messages

He knew the sound. It was the biker.

scratched on the green metal. But instead, the boots turned away. As Simon sat rigid, waiting for his stall door to bang open, he heard the footsteps move away. The restroom door swung open.

Soon he heard nothing but the tinking faucet. Simon had no idea how long he knelt there, but it was a long time. Then, when he actually *wanted* to move, he found he couldn't. Would the biker be waiting outside? Or had it merely been a mistake, pissing on him like that? Maybe it wasn't the biker. Maybe . . .

The roar of an engine out in the parking lot made him jump. He knew the sound. It *was* the biker. He heard the screech of tires, and then the sound of the engine moving

away. He breathed a sigh. The guy was just toying with him one last time.

He was going away. It was over.

Shakily, Simon rose. He flushed the toilet, washed his mouth in the sink, then used damp paper towels to wipe off the piss on his pants. Breathing a sigh, he pushed through the restroom door and out into the rain. He didn't mind the water drenching him—he wished he could be submerged in it, like jumping into the ocean. He walked toward the phone booth, and as he neared, he saw that the metal cord had actually been severed. Had the biker cut it? The rain suddenly felt colder, and he turned, taking a few cautious steps down the sidewalk toward his car.

Until that moment, he hadn't realized that he was holding his breath. He took several long, shuddering gulps of air, then continued on to his car. Why would the biker cut the cord? Unless . . .

That's when he heard a roar from the trees.

He stopped. At first, he thought it was an animal, a mountain lion or a black bear, and he turned in the sound's direction.

It was coming from somewhere in the forest beyond the asphalt. Then he caught a glint of metal, and he saw a black shadow emerge from the darkness. A wheel appeared. Chrome. And then he saw the biker rolling out of the trees, like an apparition of death itself.

The rain created tiny white explosions on the blacktop between them. The biker, front tire poised at the curb, gunned his engine. His headlamp was smashed. Simon was halfway between his car and the restroom, and he knew this was exactly what the biker had wanted.

He broke into a run, heading for his Miata.

The biker gunned his engine, his back tire spitting up grass and dirt as he barreled into the parking lot.

Simon was only a few steps away from his car. He was going to make it. Remembering he had left the door unlocked in his haste, he grabbed the door handle and pulled.

But the door was locked.

He didn't understand. As the biker roared toward him, he fumbled for his key, but couldn't find it in either pocket. Then he remembered that he hadn't only left the door unlocked, he had left his key inside as well— and he realized, as he heard the sound of the biker's tires squealing, exactly who had it.

No . . . !

Sensing he had no time to turn, he jumped toward the front of his car. The biker, his back end swinging around as he banked into the turn, smashed into the driver's-side door. Simon landed on the pavement, scraping his hands, but he was up instantly and running.

He headed for the narrow line of trees separating the rest area from the highway. Through the darkness and the rain, he saw glimpses of the road, like a giant black serpent.

He would cross the road. Get to the campground on the other side. Find someone. It was his only chance.

> *The rain lessened, a gust of wind shaking the trees, starting as a whisper and ending as a low moan.*

He made it up over the sidewalk and onto the soggy grass, but then the roar was right behind him and something struck his shoulder. As he went sprawling, the biker thundered past, spinning around, his back tire carving a brown half-circle on the grass. Simon struggled to his feet, but a searing pain lanced through his right knee, and he collapsed onto the wet earth again.

He heard the engine die, the kickstand pop down. He raised his head to see the biker dismount. Simon rolled onto his back and scrambled backwards, the moisture soaking through the seat of his pants. Rain ran into his eyes,

blurring his vision. The biker loomed over him like a black shadow. Gloves descended, grabbed his shirt, pulled him off the ground.

Blinking away the water in his eyes, he looked up at the faceplate inches from the end of his nose.

The black helmet now bore a jagged silver scratch on the right side. Simon tried to peer beyond the mirror, but he saw only his own face reflected back at him: his left eye purple and swollen, a line of blood dribbling from his bottom lip across his chin, his soaked hair plastered against his scalp. It was the face of a small and frightened man. It was the face of a man Simon didn't know.

"Please," he begged. "Please . . . I have a wife . . . a daughter."

The biker's grip on his shirt tightened. For the longest time, he held Simon there, the faceplate so close Simon's breath fogged the glass. He got whiffs of motor oil and leather. The rain lessened, a gust of wind shaking the trees, starting as a whisper and ending as a low moan.

Finally, the biker released him. He fell hard on his backside, and looked up, too scared to move. The biker looked down at him another moment, then reached into his pocket and tossed a pair of keys between Simon's legs.

As if he was in a dream, Simon watched the man turn and walk back to his bike, a bike Simon now noticed was scratched, the fuselage dented, one of the handlebars twisted. He watched as the man started the engine and, without so much as a glance in Simon's direction, drove away.

Exhausted, Simon laid his head on the grass, listening as the roar of the biker's engine moved beyond the rest area, out into the road, and then blended with the storm. He lay there for a long time, then finally rose, retrieved his keys, and made his way back to his car.

As if he were floating outside his body, he watched as he put the key in the door, climbed inside, started the engine, and drove his car toward the exit. He thought the moisture on his face was rain until he tasted the tears on his lips.

With his car idling at the entrance to the highway, the road stretching into darkness on both sides, he knew he had a choice.

To the right lay the casino, where a group of strangers waited around a green felt table, the dimly lit room hazy with smoke. In his mind's eye he saw an empty chair, a stack of chips in front of it, five cards facedown. He saw himself sit, pick up the cards, and toss his ante into the pot. The pull was there. Even with his bloodied face and aching chest, he felt it. He wanted to go there. He wanted to join that table. There was still time. No-body would care how he looked. *Nobody*.

But to the left, somewhere beyond the shadowy hill, he saw something else: his daughter's dark room, the street lamp in the parking lot breaking through the gaps in the blinds. It was as if he were standing there in the doorway, his clothes still dripping. The room smelled so much different than the casino—no smoke, but instead the faint stench from her soiled diapers, an odor her diaper pail couldn't quite contain. It didn't smell bad to him, though. It smelled wonderful. He saw himself move quietly into the room, navigating around dolls and blocks and board books littering the floor. He saw himself ease down in the glider across from her bed, cringing when it squeaked. He saw his trembling hand reach for her sleeping form, his fingers inches from her hair.

He closed his eyes. He saw her so much more vividly this way. If he concentrated, he could almost feel his fingers brushing against her hair. Soft, like the finest silk. If he thought about how it felt, if he didn't allow himself to think about anything else, not even for a second, the feeling could save him. He knew it could. It had power. All he had to do was surrender himself to it. All he had to do was turn his hands to the left.

It should be so simple.

It should be so easy.

And yet, as he opened his eyes, and with a last convulsive shudder forced the wheel to the left, he knew it was both the hardest and the greatest thing he had ever done.

Ellery Queen's Mystery Magazine

Author's Comments

The genesis of "Road Gamble" was just a premise: a man driving to the coast during a storm plays a deadly cat-and-mouse game with a mysterious biker. I don't wait for inspiration. Often I'll play with words and phrases, do some brainstorming until I get an image or title that sparks a story.

I generally don't outline, though I often jot notes to myself as I write—images, plot points, bits of dialogue that I might want to include.

Usually, I just start with a premise and (hopefully) an ending, then work it out as I go along. Often the ending changes. The longer I've been at this, though, the more of the story I see in my head from the start.

No major revisions were necessary, just minor tweaking. I write until the story's done and then mail it to the best possible market for that particular story. I rarely change a story except by editorial request.

My advice is to start at the best possible market, then work your way down. Keep the story in the mail until you've gotten at least two dozen rejections. Make it a process. Don't let your own insecurities stop you. What's the worst that can happen? An editor says no! Think of how much worse you'd have it if you were trying to make it as a stand-up comic. People sometimes throw drinks! We writers actually have it easy.

—Scott William Carter

Petri Parousia

by Matthew Hughes

A research scientist is someone who cannot rest content within the confines of existing knowledge, but always itches to know what is over the horizon.

Or it's somebody who doesn't know to leave well enough alone.

Either definition would fit Wally Applethorpe. So it was natural for him to stay on at Yale School of Medicine on a research fellowship, while I couldn't wait to get out and start cutting people open to give them new knees and hips and other useful parts in return for a six-figure income.

In our last year together, Wally had got interested in DNA. Nothing wrong with that, of course. There are plenty of useful things to do with DNA, from catching serial killers to editing congenital diseases out of the gene pool. I suppose you can even make a case for the idea of "improving" the species by making people stronger or more germ-resistant, or whatever he was getting up to in his lab over behind the red brick Farnham Building.

I admit, I could never totally fit my mind around what he was doing. If I could have, maybe I wouldn't have become a surgeon. To me, the human body was not a quasi-

metaphysical mystery to be unraveled. It was a kind of soft machine whose parts could be repaired when they broke down, or—even better—replaced entirely with materials God would have used if He'd only had access to Teflon and stainless steel.

But to Dr. Wally Applethorpe, full-weight genius and Bentham Research Fellow Extraordinaire, the human being was an infinite series of nesting boxes, like those wooden Russian dolls, one inside another. As soon as he got one open, he'd discover another, smaller one inside, and he'd get busy trying to find his way in, world without end.

I moved up to Boston, joined an existing medical group as their bone man, and got busy in my own way: marriage, mortgage, membership in a decent country club. I received regular emails from Wally—"Keeping in touch" was always the subject header—to which I replied as briefly as I knew how. You may not know many real geniuses, but let me tell you: close up, over the long term, they can truly get on your nerves.

Then late one morning he showed up at my office. Sharon, the receptionist, was still buzzing me to ask if I wanted to receive an unscheduled visitor when he walked right through my door and said, "Jimmy-boy, you've got to see this."

By reflex, I said, "Don't call me Jimmy-boy. It's Jim, or James, or what the hell, Dr. Feltham."

He gave me that look he always used to give me, the *Let's not make a big deal out of nothing look* (although it seemed to me his whole

Author Bio

Matthew Hughes writes science fiction and suspense fiction. His work frequently appears in *Fantasy & Science Fiction*. He was formerly a freelance speechwriter for Canadian political leaders and corporate CEOs. His website is www.archonate.com.

life was about making big deals out of next to nothing), and said, "I've got to show you this!"

Now, someone who didn't know Wally Applethorpe might think that the logical response to his statement would be, "What?" But I'd spent three years in a grungy New Haven apartment with him, so my question was, "Why?"

He blinked and put on that expression of astounded innocence that went with the clear blue eyes, perpetually pink cheeks, and shock of corn-yellow hair. "Because you're my friend," he said.

"I'm not your friend, Wally," I said. "I'm just a guy who wound up rooming with you because I couldn't find anything cheaper. Why don't you try to think of us as strangers who got stuck in an elevator and then happily went their separate ways?"

With Wally, I had found that control was the key to maintaining sanity.

At which he gave me his *You old kidder, you* look and launched into the matter that had brought him here. "Give me some blood," he said, pulling a specimen kit out of his pocket.

This time, my response was the same as anybody's would have been. "Why?"

"So I can show you what I've been doing."

"Why?"

He sighed indulgently. "'Cause you're going to want to get in on the ground floor of this. I'm launching a company, got some backers, going to make some big buckazoids, do a lot more research. Sky's the limit. So naturally I thought of my old buddy, Jimmy-boy."

It was on the tip of my tongue to say, "I'm not your old buddy," but another part of my brain weighed in and said to me, *Just*

'cause he's an annoying little twerp doesn't mean he isn't brilliant. How many people could stand Bill Gates before he was a multi-billionaire?*

I rolled up my sleeve and he efficiently took ten ccs out of me. "Now what?" I said.

"I'll be back tomorrow," he said, "to show you."

"That's kind of a long commute from New Haven."

"Didn't you get my email?" he said. "I'm just six blocks from here now. Hey, you free for lunch?"

I pleaded an urgent, though imaginary, consult with Jag Sharma, our geriatrics specialist. And, thank God, I did genuinely have a couple of hip replacements scheduled for the afternoon, which allowed me to ease him out the door while he was still bubbling about how it was just like the good old days, the two amigos back in the saddle again. But after he had gone, I wondered how I would keep him at a manageable distance.

I went out front to plot strategy with Sharon. "What a sweet guy," was her opening comment, which was just what girls always said about Wally. Of course, they hadn't had him at full strength and close quarters for three years. Or maybe it was just me. Either way, and notwithstanding the puzzled look she gave me, I worked out a system with Sharon: she would buzz me the moment she saw Wally out in the elevator lobby and heading for the glass doors. That would give me time to get into somebody else's office and close the door before he could inflict himself on me at will. With Wally, I had found that control was the key to maintaining sanity.

But, of course, he was beyond control, so the system failed on its first test. Impatient with the slowness of our elevators, Wally came up the fire stairs and was past Sharon and halfway to my office before she could buzz me with the code words, "Mrs. Arkwright to see you."

So Wally caught me, my desk spread with insurance forms, which meant I couldn't plead any urgencies to justify shortening his visit. He carried a small plastic case, like an insulated lunch box, from which he removed a set of petri dishes with transparent covers. They were marked with numbers and names. The names were familiar.

"What is that?" I said.

He touched one of the covers. Its label read STANLEY FELTHAM. "That's your grand-dad," he said.

Next to it was a dish labeled ROSE (MAGUIRE) FELTHAM. "And your grandma."

The two other dishes were labeled with the names of my mother's parents.

"What is this?" I said again.

"I've isolated each of your grandparents' DNA," he said, giving me that wide-eyed, farm-boy look that meant he had cracked open another doll.

"How?"

So now, finally, he explained. He could unravel a subject's DNA to separate what each of that person's parents had contributed to the mix. It involved microlasers and several kinds of enzymes—cutters, movers, and assemblers, he called them—and the whole process was handled by a super-fast computer that could sort through all the possible combinations and find the one that was true.

"I patented the process and we're going public in a few weeks," he said. "Write me a check for five grand and I'll give you stock warrants that will be worth two percent of the company."

"And what will the company be worth?" I said.

"Why, billions," he said.

"Why?" I said. "What will people do with their grandparents' DNA?"

He shrugged. "I suppose some of them will put it into an egg, insert it into a womb and give birth to grandma or grandpa. Most people have fond memories of their grandparents—

from childhood, that is—but by the time the kids are old enough to really get to know them, the old folks are getting ready to shuffle off this mortal coil. Or they're senile."

"Okay," I said, and thought about it. My mother's parents had died before I was born and the world would thank me for not creating another Stan Feltham: there was already an oversupply of sourpusses. "Supposing there is a market for grandparent clones. It can't be worth billions."

He waggled his hands on either side of his head. "Think, man," he said, then he spread them wide as if offering the whole world. "We're not just talking grandparents. We can go way back. Way, way back."

"How way?"

"Wa-a-a-ay, way."

"Give me a for instance," I said.

I wasn't actually thinking about me raising a young Ben Franklin.

He moved the petri dishes aside and sat on the corner of my desk. "Got any famous ancestors?"

There was a legend in the family on my mother's side that we were descended from one of Benjamin Franklin's illegitimate sons. My mother had never been sure whether she should brag about it or hush it up. I told Wally about it.

"Ben Franklin?" he said. "Really? How come you never mentioned this?"

"I guess it never came up."

I probably had mentioned the Franklin connection at some point, but I wasn't surprised that Wally had missed it. In any discussion, he usually did most of the talking; listening was not among his alpha-level attributes.

"Well," he said, picking up one of the dishes that contained my maternal ancestors, "how'd you like to have Ben Franklin as your own son?"

I thought about it and he read my face. "And how much would you pay to be able to do that?" he said.

I wasn't actually thinking about me raising a young Ben Franklin. Chances were he would have been a handful and a half. I was thinking about all the people who named their kids Jared or Jessica some other J-name just because it was that year's fashion. They never thought about what it would be like for the poor kid to be one of four or five identically named people in every group they'd ever join, never thought about how the kid would feel knowing that that most personal of possessions, one's own name, had been chosen merely because it was popular and because their parents were irredeemably shallow.

I was thinking about just how many such people existed and how many of them were willing to spend their bank accounts to remain in vogue. "Should I make the check out to you or the company?" I said.

And so we were in business.

"I'm just a bone cutter."

And a very good business it was. Wally's company—Ancest, he called it—caught the world's eye and the world's ear. The backers had poured in plenty of start-up money, a good portion of which went into a saturation ad campaign on network television. Within days, Leno and Letterman were making jokes about their imaginary ancestors, Regis and Kelly were interviewing Wally live, and the stock price hit two hundred a share, then split. It was structured as a straight-out franchise operation and the prospective franchisees were fighting each other to get in the door.

"Come work with me," Wally said. He offered me a salary that was one figure more than the six I'd been getting as an orthopedic surgeon, plus options, expense account, corner office, company Lexus.

I said, "What on Earth can I do for you?"

"It's medical research. You're a doctor."

"I'm just a bone cutter."

He gave me his bashful Tom Sawyer look and said, "You're my touchstone. Everybody else, they're always slapping me on the back and telling me what a brilliant researcher I am. You don't do that. You're the only one keeps my feet on the ground, Jimmy-boy."

I should have run for the hills. Instead, I took the corner office with the title of Executive Vice President on the mahogany door behind which I did a lot of not very much, while being well paid for my exertions. It turned out, though, that there was one chore Wally wanted me to take over.

"I'd like you to interface with backers," he said. "Give me less time in meetings, more time in the lab. I've got some interesting projects on the burners."

"Okay," I said. I figured it wouldn't be too onerous a task to schmooze the money people, dazzle them with a little science and set visions of sugar-plum dividends dancing in their heads. Thus armored in my innocence I walked into the Wednesday afternoon board meeting with a fat folder of glowing results from the first few weeks and even shinier projections for the next three quarters.

"We've blown right through the granddad and granny market, and we're into a serious run on major historical figures," I said. "Now that the federal court has ruled that DNA from more than four generations back is public domain, it's not just Robert E. Lee's descendants who can have him for a son; we estimate we'll sell him to about five percent of the population below the Mason-Dixon Line. Plus the interest in European monarchs is picking up, particularly the Bourbons."

I had plenty more, but I was strongly sensing that the five men in black suits on the other side of the table didn't give a damn. I set aside the bar charts on eighteenth-century poets and nineteenth-century composers and said, "Gentlemen, am I missing something?"

"Project Parousia," said the Chairman of the Board. He was a big, stone-faced man with eyes that had had a lot of practice at weighing and winnowing his fellow human beings. I had the feeling I was close to being assigned to the giant bin labeled *Chaff.*

I shuffled through my papers but I knew there was nothing in there about any Project Parousia. I'd never heard of it, although the name rang a faint bell.

"I don't have any information on that project," I said.

"Then get some," said the Chairman. "Or get Applethorpe up here." The other board members nodded, their jaws grimly set, and I realized that they were all cut from the same block of close-grained hardwood as the Chair-

"I think we've made it all the way back to Cro-Magnon man."

man. Now that I inspected them closely, I saw that they didn't have the sleek, well-nourished look common to the upper links of the corporate food chain. Instead, each had the aspect of the zealot; they might have been carried over from some previous era when the most popular pastimes were burning witches and crushing heretics under piles of boulders.

"We'll be back tomorrow," he said. "Be prepared to tell us what we want to know."

I went down to the lab. It was below ground and behind a number of thick steel doors and an even larger number of men who wore uniforms and sidearms. At the last door, even my senior executive pass was not enough to get me through, but I managed to convince the head guard to buzz Wally and

he told them to admit me.

When I came into the lab he was bent over the monitor of a scanning electronic microscope, humming to himself. Without looking up, he said, "I think we've made it all the way back to Cro-Magnon man. In a week or two, I should be ready to clone a prehuman hominid. After that, Jimmy-boy, I'm going to get some birds and work back toward the dinosaurs."

"What's Project Parousia?" I asked. My teeth chattered a little. The air was chilly; the large room was designed to keep its banks of super-fast computers happy. Humans could put on a sweater.

"Oh, just a bee in the board's bonnet," he said, looking up for a moment. "Don't worry about it."

"No bee would survive a second in any bonnet of theirs," I said. "Who are those people?"

He had turned back to his monitor. "Backers," he said. "Money people."

I put a hand on his shoulder and pulled him down to my lowly plane. "No," I said. "They're not. Tell me how you found them."

I could see him consulting the part of his memory where he stored irrelevant details. "I didn't," he said, after a moment. "They found me. After I published my paper on retrogressive DNA sequencing, they came to see me."

"It was their idea to set up the company?"

"Uh huh."

"But they're not interested in our actual results and revenue projections."

He looked mildly puzzled. "They're not?"

"No, the only thing they care about is Project Parousia."

"Hmm," he said, and gestured to a lab bench across the room. "It's over there."

His microscope was pulling him back to wherever he went when he was working, but I exerted a more immediate level of force and pushed him over to the Parousia bench. He examined a series of petri dishes connected to sensors and probes that were in turn linked to one of the big computers, then checked a stream of data that was zipping across a monitor.

"Almost done," he said. "Of course, it's just fantasy."

"What is?"

"Their idea."

"Tell me about it," I said.

Wally said he figured that the board had gotten themselves all wrapped up in that goofy book about a secret society that had protected the descendants of a union between Jesus and Mary Magdalene through two thousand years. I hadn't read the book but I had heard about misguided enthusiasts trying to dig up church floors to get at supposed clues.

I saw it now. "They want you to work backward through the DNA until you've got a clone of Jesus." And now I remembered what parousia meant. It was Greek for the Second Coming.

"They want to bring on the end of the world," I said.

Wally was the only person I'd ever heard use the word "Pshaw." He used it now, then added, "It's just a myth."

"Work with me a moment," I said. "Suppose it isn't a myth. Suppose there really is a secret society. 'Cause I'm thinking if there ever was a secret society of religious fanatics they'd look an awful lot like our board of directors."

"Still," he said, "what are the chances they could be right?"

"I don't know," I said, "but how much research could you get done if the seas are boiling and we're all being pitched into a lake of fire?"

"That's not going to happen."

"Okay, suppose all you give them is a mild mannered carpenter—aren't they likely to think you've teamed up with the Antichrist to wreck their plans? 'Cause they

don't look like the kind of people who would get their lawyers in and sue. I'm thinking, they're more the pitchforks and torches kind."

At that moment the Parousia Project's computer emitted a discreet *ding*. Wally leaned over and picked up the last petri dish in the series. He peered into it. "There it is," he said then looked around. "But I don't see any angels or wise men."

"Fine," I said. "Tomorrow I'll give it to them and maybe they'll go away happy." Though I didn't think so. But planes left for obscure corners of the world every hour, and I would have enough time to pick a good one.

Except that I noticed how Wally was looking at the dish with that expression I'd seen so many times before. He had found another doll he could crack open.

"No," I said, and reached for the dish. "For once, leave well enough alone."

But he had already slipped it back into its connective armature and his fingers rippled across the computer's keyboard.

He turned to me with that smile of genius I'd seen so often before, the one that is a virtual twin to the grin of madness. "I can prove it's a myth," he said. "You see, if that's really Jesus, the Son of God, then half its DNA is Mary's and the other half is . . ."

Ding went the computer.

Behind him, from the lab bench, a light glowed.

I turned to run, but the floor shook and the walls cracked and I was thrown down.

I looked up and saw that the petri dish was enveloped in a flame that burned yet did not consume, and a voice that came from everywhere at once said, "Put off the shoes from thy feet for the place where thou standest is holy ground."

"Oh, God," I said.

Fantasy & Science Fiction

Author's Comments ───────

At the time I came up with this idea, Dan Brown's *The Da Vinci Code* was in the news. Its premise inspired me to write a spoof around the argument that Jesus had living descendants. I created some characters to carry the story, and wrote the opening. The rest followed naturally.

There are three things I try to din into the heads of anyone I'm teaching/tutoring: character, theme, and conflict. Each of these can be boiled down to the following words of wisdom:

1. You think it's your story because you're writing it; in fact, it's the characters' story, and you're just writing it for them. In other words, start with the characters' situations and needs, and your story will stay centered.

2. If you know what your story is "about," at the thematic level, well below plot, you'll know how it has to end, and you won't get lost in the plotting. For example, a love story ends with the lovers united forever or tragically separated; a revenge story ends with the hero taking or forsaking revenge; a quest adventure ends with the hero reaching the goal or discovering, through the life-changing events of the journey, that the goal is not the true grail.

3. Conflict is the universal tool of fiction writing. Every story is built around a conflict, posed as a dramatic question and ultimately answered by the climax. Every scene is built around a lesser conflict, the answer to which is *yes*, *no*, or *not yet*. Conflict—character vs. character, character vs. environment, character vs. him/herself—is what makes story.

—Matthew Hughes

A Box Full of Nothing

by Arthur Sánchez

B rian sat dejectedly in his lawn chair as a single persistent housefly buzzed around his head. By anyone's standards it would be a perfect afternoon; the sun was shining, big puffy clouds were floating across the sky, birds were singing in the maple tree behind the house. But for Brian, who sat nursing the early stages of what would surely become a nasty sunburn, it was his own personal version of Hell. Brian was running a yard sale.

It wasn't that he'd never run a yard sale before. In fact, he'd run several for his parents after they'd decided to retire down to Florida. It wasn't just that he truly hated yard sales—which he did. (You would too if some woman insisted on spending twenty minutes haggling with you over a twenty-five cent ashtray.) No, it was that he was running a yard sale for his Uncle Max—a man he'd barely known and who had never seemed much inclined to get to know him. Not that there was much of a chance of that happening now. Uncle Max had the misfortune of dying and having had

that misfortune decided to share it by naming Brian his sole heir and beneficiary. Which meant Brian was responsible for all his stuff.

Uncle Max wasn't a bad man. On the contrary, he always remembered to send Christmas presents and birthday cards (albeit they sometimes arrived a month late). It's just that Uncle Max had been a scientist (a theoretical physicist, whatever that was) and had lived for his research. For that he'd sacrificed everything—including family. Brian figured that's what hurt the most—being less important than a bunch of theories.

So there he sat—hot, tired, and about ready to call it a day. He'd done the honorable thing. Now it was time to bring it to a close. If it weren't for one middle-aged woman who, despite having spent the last two hours building up a small cache of treasures, was still rummaging through the boxes; he would have.

It was just as Brian looked over to check the woman's progress that the conservatively dressed, modest-looking lady turned her head to glance at him. Brian nodded politely. She nodded back. Then, as if sensing that she'd overstayed her welcome the woman snatched up a wooden box she'd just pulled from the discard pile and began to pack her treasures in it—though there probably wasn't enough to require a box. Brian closed his eyes and groaned. Ah geez, he thought, not another one.

One of the things Brian had learned from this yard sale is that people are essentially crazy. He discovered that it's not enough that the items are being offered at a fraction of

Author Bio

Arthur Sánchez has written over 100 stories published in collections as diverse as *Chicken Soup for the Romantic Soul* to *Dead Men (and Women) Walking* to *Catty New Year*. He's also produced two paperback collections of short stories: *Digital Daydreams* and *Digital Daydreams II: The Dreamer Dreams On*. His website is www.arthursanchez.com.

their original cost. It's not enough that he was practically giving the stuff away. No, some people want a bargain so bad that they'll do almost anything for it—including cheat and steal.

Brian watched as the lady began walking primly across the yard towards him in a tailored gray suit and reasonable shoes. She was probably a banker or a lawyer in the world beyond his uncle's picket fence. But put up a

"How much for the box?"

yard sale sign and suddenly she's Ma Barker about to go on a major crime spree. Unfortunately for her Brian had seen this con at least three times before.

The pros will hit a yard sale late in the day, when the owner is burnt out and the really valuable stuff has been left behind by those too cheap to pay the price. They'll stroll along, pick up an empty box, stuff some choice pieces of jewelry in the bottom, then fill it up with old dish towels, lace doilies, and broken toys, before asking for a price on the whole box. The homeowner, distracted, tired, and grateful to be rid of the stuff doesn't even bother looking past the first layer and names a price for the towels—never realizing that grandma's silver teaspoons are also going along for the ride.

The woman, who did seem a little nervous, smiled at Brian as she stepped up to his folding table and placed the box down. She then reached into her purse and produced a wallet. And right on cue, like an actress doing her lines, asked: "How much for the box?"

Brian gave her a tight smile as he rose to his feet. "Well, I don't know," he said, "let's just check what you've got." He saw her stiffen as he pulled the box towards him. Yup, it was the box scam all right.

Yanking off the stained dishtowels Brian stuck his hand straight into the pile and began pulling things out. He wasn't about to

get taken. Not when he'd worked this hard. "Right," he said as began to lay things out, "a couple of ashtrays, five textbooks on . . . Physics and Thermo-Dynamic Principles," he looked at the woman, "a little light reading?" She giggled politely at his joke. "Two pipes, an open bag of pipe tobacco, a box of three-penny nails, and . . ." Brian hefted a misshapen cobalt-blue pottery bowl up into the sunlight. "A really ugly ceramic bowl."

The woman, who up to now had been standing there placidly, reached out quickly for the bowl and took it from him. "Please," she said, "be careful. That was Max's one and only attempt at artistic expression."

Brian's eyes narrowed. "Max? You knew my uncle?"

The woman, who was cradling the bowl, looked startled. She hadn't intended to reveal that fact. "Ah, yes, we ah . . . we were colleagues. We worked together at the university."

For a brief moment Brian saw something in her eyes that said she and his uncle shared more than a mutual interest in physics. So Uncle Max did have a life beyond his lab. To Brian's surprise, that revelation made him feel a little better. Uncle Max might not have been much for family but at least he'd found someone to share his obsession with science. And that meant that someone had gotten to know him.

Brian felt ashamed of his suspicious thoughts and pushed the box to one side. He was about to tell the woman she could have it all for free when something caught his attention. The box, though empty, felt heavy. Brian glanced at the box. It was wooden, sturdy, built well but not that well. He tipped the box on one side and glanced inside it again. It was still empty. Yet, for it's size, it was heavier than it should be. "Hold on. What's going on here?"

The woman glanced at Brian and then at the box. "I'm sorry. I don't know what you mean." But she wasn't a very good liar. He could see in her expression that she was hiding something.

Brian reached into the box and felt around. Still nothing. But then he realized that the inside was shallower than the outside. A false bottom? All of Brian's good feelings disappeared. This woman might have known his uncle but she was still trying to pull a fast one. He began tapping on the bottom of the box.

"Please don't do that," the woman said.

Brian glared at her. "Why not? Afraid of what I might find?"

To his surprise she nodded her head and answered very softly: "Yes." That caused Brian to pause. The yard sale pros never admit to knowing that there is anything else in the box. Was this her first time?

"Look," she said, staring at him earnestly. She had large green eyes. He hadn't noticed that before. "I'll give you a hundred bucks for the box. That's more than fair, isn't it?" She opened her wallet and began counting out twentys on the table. "Just, just don't bang it around."

That really confused Brian. Half the stuff in the yard wasn't worth a hundred bucks. Why then was the box worth so much? Did his uncle hide some priceless relic in here? Were there notes on a secret invention? Or perhaps, he thought sadly, had his uncle had an adulterous affair and hidden his love letters to another man's wife in this box. Brian looked at the woman. Was she that other man's wife?

Brian shook his head. That was ridiculous. In the span of twenty seconds he'd gone from believing his uncle had found love to believing that his uncle had found forbidden love. No, there was a more practical reason for this woman's unease. "I'm sorry," he told her, "but I think I should I find out what you're hiding." He reached for a screwdriver that was lying on the table and jammed it into the bottom of the box.

"NO!" The woman screamed as if he'd plunged the screwdriver not into the aged wood but into her chest. She reached frantically for the box. Brian held it away from her as he wedged the screwdriver between two slats and pulled. There was a satisfying cracking as the wood snapped. "No, you mustn't," she continued, grabbing a hold of the box. "Your uncle warned against—" But Brian wasn't listening. The slat popped up and he broke the piece off with his bare hand. Staring down into the dark gap he'd created he saw nothing. It was empty.

Something grabbed Brian's hand. It wasn't a physical something.

The woman, who was also staring down into the box, released the lip and backed up a step. "See," she said, "nothing. Just empty space." A light breeze picked up and the collar of her white blouse began to flutter. "There's your money," she said, pointing at the small stack of bills on the table. "I'll just take my things." She held out a hand for the box.

"Yeah," Brian said doubtfully, "I guess." Not quite willing to give up Brian hefted the box over his head and peered into the hole again. It was completely dark and, except for a few dust particles that were beginning to swirl around it, completely empty. He put the box down on the table. He could have sworn he was being scammed. He jammed his hand into the hole and felt around.

"Please," the woman urged, "don't do—"

"Look, lady," Brian began, feeling rather irritated, "I'm just making sure—"

Something grabbed Brian's hand. It wasn't a physical something. It was more like a force. Like placing your hand over the mouth of a vacuum cleaner. He could feel his hand being sucked down into the hole.

"What the—"

The woman reacted instantly. She grabbed a hold of the box and pulled. Brian's hand partially emerged from the opening but not before the suction increased tenfold. Suddenly, he felt like he was being pulled off his feet. Air began to swirl past his hand with a hissing sound.

"Your uncle warned of this," she cried. "Pull your hand out before it's too late!"

Brian didn't need to be told twice. Holding the box out in front of him he waited till she got a grip on it then pulled as hard as he could. They must have looked like they were engaged in some bizarre tug of war over an old fruit crate. But it was to no avail. It felt like he had wedged his hand into a pipe. Pain shot up his wrist as the opposing forces stretched the tendons in his hand.

"Hurry," the woman said as she let go of the box. Brian nearly fell over as the box dropped like a rock and bent him over double. The woman grabbed him around the waist from behind. "If you brace it with your foot and we pull together we might overcome the suction." Brian did as he was told. Placing

> *"It was your uncle's greatest discovery— and his greatest regret."*

his right foot on the lip of the box he leaned back while pushing off on it. This time his hand did slowly begin to emerge. It was barely perceptible at first but by varying degrees they were able to wrestle it free so that it eventually popped out like a cork. They fell back as air suddenly began to swirl past him and into the box. Debris and papers were swept up and sucked into the center of an invisible vortex.

"This isn't possible!" Brian shouted over the storm. "It's just an empty box!"

The woman wasn't listening. Snatching up one of the heavy tomes on physics that Brian had put aside, she jammed it into the box flat side down in order to cover the hole. Remarkably, the dusty old book acted like a patch on a balloon and the air stopped moving. As quickly as it had begun the freakish storm ended.

Brian stared at the now disheveled woman. Her suit and hair were mussed up. Her glasses were askew but there was relief written all over her face. "What was that?" Brian demanded.

The woman, who was now kneeling next to the box, brushed a stray lock of hair from her face and rose slowly to her feet. "That," she said with impressive dignity, "was nothing."

Brian shook his head. "Don't tell me that was nothing. That was ***something***."

"No," she corrected him as she gathered up her belongings, "that was nothing." She then took a slow deep breath as she tried to compose herself. "That," she said with a shrug, "was literally the absence of . . . anything. It was, for the lack of a better description, complete and utter nothingness."

Brian tried to wrap his mind around what she just said. He vaguely remembered some of the topics his uncle had loved to discuss. "You mean it was some sort of Black Hole or Gravity Well?"

The woman gave him the same sort of smile she might give a first year grad student. "Black Holes and Gravity Wells aren't nothing. On the contrary, because of their gravitational pull they are usually full of elements that couldn't escape them." Brian stared at her as if she were speaking a foreign language. "Look, you probably didn't know this but your uncle was a brilliant man. He spent his career searching for the physical equivalent of the number zero—a natural state in which nothing exists. When he found it, he realized he'd made an enormous mistake. Nature abhors a vacuum. Empty a space, any space, and nature will insist on filling it. And," the woman said with a chuckle, "nature won't be too particular about what she uses. It was your uncle's greatest discovery—and his greatest regret. All those years spent on . . ." she smiled at the irony of her own words, "nothing. It was too dangerous to reveal and impossible to destroy. So your uncle placed his discovery in a box, a small wooden box without openings or gaps, and he left it there. He just forgot to tell me which one it was and it took me all afternoon to find it."

Brian stared at the box in her hands. It looked like any you'd find at the local hardware store. "Th-that's not possible."

The woman smiled again. "Of course it is. Everyone has a box full of nothing. Your uncle just had more of it than most." Then she cocked her head to one side as if the absurdity of it all no longer mattered to her.

> ## *"Everyone has a box full of nothing."*

"So what do you say? A hundred bucks for an empty box—sounds like a bargain to me."

Brian nodded his head without even thinking it. He didn't want it. Best let a scientist deal with it. "Agreed." Then, realizing how much of an ass he'd been towards her he added: "I'll even throw in some old textbooks. Not much of a read but I understand they're great for plugging up holes." He gave her a shy smile so as to let her know he was making a joke. This time the woman let out a genuine laugh as she turned to gather up her things and though she hadn't said it, Brian had the distinct impression that she'd just saved his life. "And this," Brian said as his brain began to function again, "is from me— a gift." He picked up the ugly bowl that had been his uncle's one attempt at art and handed it to her. "I think," he said softly, "that Uncle Max would have liked you to have it."

The woman's eyes misted over as she accepted the pottery and gingerly laid it in-

side the box. She lingered for a moment over its polished surface before quickly grabbing the other things she'd selected and adding it to the pile. "Helen," she said as she draped a dishtowel over the top.

"Excuse me?"

"My name," she explained. "I never gave it to you. It's Helen."

Brian gave her a nod. "Nice to meet you. My name is Brian." They stood in an awkward silence: family and friend of the deceased meeting for the first time. Where did one begin? Then a thought occurred to him. "Excuse me, Helen, but . . . but would you like to come into the house and have a cup of coffee? I didn't really know my uncle that well. I was wondering if you could tell me about him."

Helen's face brightened. It was as if he'd answered a secret desire of hers. "Yes, I would like that, I'd like that very much." To Brian's amazement he discovered that he would too.

Brian looked around. Despite the fact that the world had nearly ended the only evidence of their little adventure was the fact that his yard sale sign was now hanging from one corner. Brian tore off the sign and threw it down on the grass. "Glad that's over," he said with enthusiasm. He flexed his hand. The feeling was beginning to come back into his fingers.

"I know what you mean," Helen said. "I try to avoid these things myself. The time, the bother, and some of the people you get!" She rolled her eyes dramatically.

"Tell me about it," Brian said as he carefully picked up the box and carried it in for her. "I had one lady tell me my prices were too high. Can you believe that? Fifty cents is too much for a wool overcoat." And together, with a box full of nothing between them, they went inside to remember a man Brian was just coming to know.

Anotherealm.com

Author's Comments

I conceived of "A Box Full of Nothing" in response to an online writing challenge. I never answered the challenge but I did end up with a story I liked. The toughest part about writing this story was slipping in the science fiction. The line between reality and fantasy had to be blurred to the point where the reader wouldn't see it coming but would still accept it happening.

The story underwent three or four revisions for structure and numerous adjustments to language. Since I prefer to write using a rough outline, the story was free to take unexpected turns.

Anotherealm.com was selected as the target market because it pays, has a decent readership, and an active bulletin board for reader feedback.

The best advice for someone starting to submit: don't fear rejection. It isn't personal and can be incredibly useful. At first you'll get stock letters that are of no help. Then you'll get short notes scribbled by the editor. Pay attention, they're telling you what to fix. Eventually they'll be saying that your work is good but not right for them. Pay attention, they're telling you what they buy. Eventually, you'll sell your story and get to start the whole process all over again.

—Arthur Sánchez

Blood Lilies

by Robert E. Vardeman

Alan Mitchell had come to the SeaHarp Hotel to die.

He leaned back in the sleek, comfortable white Lincoln Town Car the hotel had sent for him, too tired to even look out the smoked-glass window. The driver opened the door. Mitchell heaved himself out and smiled wanly.

"I'll see to your bags, sir," the driver said. Mitchell thanked him with a vague wave of his hand. He found it increasingly difficult to concentrate. The doctors said it was his imagination, that the real ordeal lay ahead.

Mitchell refused to linger for months or even years. He had chosen the SeaHarp Hotel as the most luxurious spot he could find for his last week. Then he would take his life. Mitchell was nothing if not thorough. He had researched poisons to find the best, and had rejected it as an alternative. All involved risk and the possibility of lingering or outright failure. He shuddered at the notion of the pain when some virulent poison ate away at his stomach. The slightest gastric upset put him into such a state.

Author Bio

A popular and prolific writer, Robert E. Vardeman is the author of more than 90 novels and the ghostwriter of more than 100 additional titles. His short story collection is *Desert Bob's Reptile Ranch*, and a film, *Gimme Skelter*, is available on DVD. He is also an instructor for Long Ridge Writers Group.

Asphyxiation. That was his researched choice. He would put a clear plastic bag over his head and securely fasten it. To keep the carbon dioxide level from rising in his blood and giving him even a moment's distress, he would pump helium into the bag. His lungs would be tricked into thinking all was well.

He had brought a small green-painted cylinder of the inert gas, with appropriate valves and regulator, in his larger suitcase.

Mitchell closed his eyes and imagined the event. The plastic bag fastened with a length of duct tape around his neck. Inelegant, undignified, but necessary. The rubber hose. The hissing tank of helium. A few barbiturates to prevent him from backing out when the moment came, but not so many that it would nauseate him. A soft and gentle death, slipping off into eternal peace without pain.

He winced as he moved. Something pulled loose inside him. Again, Mitchell pushed it out of his mind. The doctors said it was nothing. Kaposi's sarcoma didn't have symptoms like this. At least, he didn't believe so. He would have to look it up in his medical encyclopedia when he got to his room. Or perhaps in the most recent issue of *Morbidity and Mortality Weekly* he had sent to him from the CDC in Atlanta.

The driver fussed behind him, getting the luggage from the trunk. Mitchell stretched and looked out over Greystone Bay. The sunlight fought a heavy fog and won by slow inches. Here and there whitecaps danced on the bay, but it seemed too sullen to interest Mitchell. He had never enjoyed water or water sports.

He turned his attention to the six-foot-high fieldstone wall that ran along Harbor Road. He smiled. The top of the fence had been adorned with more varieties of flowers than he could identify. Dying in the spring had advantages. The beauty of the flower-and-hedge-topped wall pleased him.

He stopped along the stone walk leading to the hotel's porch and drank in the beauty of the grounds. The SeaHarp's groundskeeper had not littered the fine lawn with the usual

> ## *"I take care of the flowers and hate to see them bothered."*

icons. Mitchell saw only neatly kept grass, not swing sets and chairs and boccie ball courts or even the ridiculous bent wire wicks of a croquet field. Just green, lush, well-tended grass. Mitchell liked the hotel more and more.

"I'll have the bags sent up to your room, if you want to look around first," the driver said.

"Um, yes, thank you." Mitchell hadn't realized it. He did want to explore. The Sea-Harp's four stories of gingerbread front needed paint. The sea air tore away at the wood constantly. Mitchell wondered what riding out a storm inside the grand old hotel would be like. He wished he would live long enough to discover the mysteries of creaking boards and howling wind and hard-driving water against bulging windowpanes. He had lived too long in the dirty hustle of the big city.

"Don't go walking there," came an irritated voice. "You'll disturb the plants. They don't like it."

"Sorry," Mitchell said, stepping back. In his reverie he had walked across the lawn and blundered into a flower bed. The gardener pushed back thick glasses with a dirty, cal-

loused finger. He stared up in what Mitchell considered a belligerent manner unbecoming to the hired help of a resort hotel.

"Didn't mean to sound so brusque," the gardener apologized. "I take care of the flowers and hate to see them bothered." Almost as an afterthought, the small, sun-browned man added, "You wouldn't want to get your shoes dirty."

"You aren't from this area, are you?" asked Mitchell. He had always prided himself on identifying accents. Even if the gardener had spoken with the same clipped tones the others in the Greystone Bay area did, the suntan set this man apart. The heavy fog and winter storms didn't permit any native to get this tanned.

"From down South," the man said. His eyes looked like giant brown fried eggs behind the thick lenses. Pushing back and getting off his knees, he struggled to his feet. Mitchell saw his first impression was right. The man stood a head shorter than he.

The accent didn't match any Mitchell had heard. Wherever the man did come from, it wasn't the South. Yet the tan suggested as much. And the gardener had no reason to lie.

"What kind of flowers are these? They look familiar but . . ."

"All kinds," the gardener said hurriedly. "These are a strain of marigolds. And those, the ones with the light red centers, are daisies."

"I've never seen daisies with such pale pink petals and red middles."

"My hybrid. I developed them myself."

"And those?" asked Mitchell, curious in spite of himself. He had the city dweller's love-hate relationship with flowers. They were pretty to look at but too much trouble to bother with.

"Those are Byzantine Roses."

Mitchell bent over and examined the delicate, involuted petals. They had fine red etching like veins inside pure white.

"They're lovely. You must be very proud of your garden."

The man nodded and smiled almost shyly. "They aren't the best I have to offer. The lilies are better. Want to see?"

Mitchell followed silently as the gardener led him to the rear of the hotel. He had thought the other flowers were gorgeous. These defied description.

"These are prize winners. I don't know much about horticulture but from an artistic standpoint, they're unparalleled." Mitchell heaved a deep sigh. The world had so much to offer. He would miss it after he killed himself.

The lilies thrust up bold yellow trumpets. Tiny crimson spots decorated their interior. He blinked. They seemed to follow him heliotropically as if he were the sun. He reached out. The trumpet flared and the bloom dipped toward his hand. The image of jaws opening flashed across his mind. He jerked back, embarrassed at his reaction. It was only a flower, after all.

"The insects like them," the gardener said.

"How do you grow them?"

"That's a secret." The gardener turned furtive and scuttled away. Mitchell shrugged. The flowers were as spectacular as the Sea-Harp Hotel itself. Following a small path around the side of the building, Mitchell returned to the front stone steps. He passed between two large stone vases with more of the gardener's handiwork inside.

Mitchell opened the French doors leading into the hotel lobby, wondering why they didn't leave them open to catch the cooling, fresh breeze off the bay. He stopped and stared. If he had entered another world, the feeling couldn't have been much different.

Quiet fell over him like a blanket. He couldn't imagine what would shake the sense of serenity inherent in the room. A tear came to Alan Mitchell's eyes. This hotel would provide a fitting final week for him. He went to the registration desk to his left.

"Welcome to the SeaHarp, Mr. Mitchell," the clerk greeted.

He started to ask how the man knew his name, then remembered the driver had already brought his luggage in. A good hotel—a first-class one—hired a friendly, intelligent staff. Of course the clerk knew his name. How many others would be arriving in the span of a few minutes?

"Thank you. I'd like a room on the second floor, please."

"That's been arranged. Your luggage is in suite 207."

"How did you know I'd want a room on the second floor?" Mitchell disliked the notion of being trapped in a burning building higher than he could safely jump out. It had been difficult living and working in New York with such a phobia, but he had managed.

"The lady told me." The clerk lifted a pen and pointed discreetly toward a writing desk with a Tiffany lamp. Mitchell tried to penetrate the darkness caused by the light.

"Hello, Alan."

He knew the voice instantly.

"It's been six years, Elizabeth." His heart almost exploded when she rose and moved around the writing desk and came fully into the cone of light from the lamp. Elizabeth Morgenthal hadn't aged a day, an hour, even a second, in the years since he had seen her.

She took both his hands in hers and pulled him close. The fragrance of her perfume was as he remembered. He closed his eyes and inhaled deeply, savoring the moment. Transported back to happier times, the spell was broken when she kissed him. He recoiled slightly, unable to stop himself.

"What's wrong, Alan? Still angry with me?" Eyes so green they made emeralds envious stared up at him. He sought the tiny gold speck in her left eye and found it. The cute upturn of her nose and the pixy smile that quivered on her lips, threatening to break out into a laugh at any instant—he remembered them all.

"You *have* forgiven me?"

"I . . ." He had no answer. He had seldom thought of her in the intervening years. Seeing her, feeling the heat from her nearness, he wondered why he hadn't. "How did you know I'd be here?" he asked, trying to change the subject.

"You haven't forgiven me." She let out a deep sigh of mock regret. "Let me buy you dinner. You always did enjoy a good meal. The SeaHarp has the finest chef, not only in Greystone Bay but anywhere within a hundred-mile radius."

He would kill himself in one week. He would!

"No, no," he said, "the meal is on me. I insist. And you didn't answer the question. Did you peek at the reservations?"

"Nothing so elaborate. I saw you coming up the walk. I wondered what happened to you when you didn't come in."

"The gardener . . ."

"I saw. I decided to play a little prank on you." She stared at him with those fabulous green eyes. "You still don't like upper stories?"

"You remember my foibles. I hope you remember my better points, too."

She hesitated. Then Elizabeth's face broke out in a sunshiny smile. "I do, Alan. Thoughts of you have never been too far from my mind."

He swallowed, suddenly uncomfortable. "What brings you to this particular hotel?"

"My best friend got married last year and came here on her honeymoon. She made it sound so pleasant I decided to take my vacation here. I've been here a week."

"Are you staying on?" he heard himself asking. Mitchell fought down the memories—and Elizabeth's presence. He had a mission.

He had decided. He would kill himself in one week. He would!

"For another week. It is expensive but restful. I've found it has restored my faith in the world. I was getting a little burned out and other things weren't going well."

"Personal?" he asked.

"Naturally. The agency grossed two million dollars last year and will double that this year."

"You always were a fine businessman."

"Businesswoman," she said. "You always were such a fine sexist man." Elizabeth gave another of the deep, almost shuddering sighs. "Business is fine. Personally, I'm a wreck."

"What was his name?"

"You always saw through to my soul, Alan. I hated that and loved it at the same time." Elizabeth took a step back and swayed.

"Are you all right?" Mitchell's arm went around her waist. He was still strong enough to support her. He got a chair and guided her into it. A ray of light slanted through a beveled glass window, sending gentle rainbows across her pale cheek. For the first time he noticed how peaked she was.

"It's why I came here. I work twenty-hour days. The doctor said I was killing myself and needed a vacation."

"After a week you're still faint?"

"Always the hypochondriac. When you can't fuss over yourself, you fussed over me," she said. In a low voice, she added, "I always enjoyed the attention."

"I have something in my suitcase . . ."

"I'm fine, Alan. Please. And the fainting spells only started a day or two ago. Stress. Or the relief of stress. Have you seen the porch? It stretches completely around the hotel. I enjoy sitting and watching the sunset."

"Do they serve a decent drink?"

"The SeaHarp? You've got to be kidding," she said, looking stronger. The paleness in her face remained. "The best, just like everything else in the hotel."

"Let me get settled, and I'll join you in an hour," he said.

"Not one second later," Elizabeth warned with mock severity.

"I'm always prompt."

"It's nice seeing you again, Alan. Really. And don't be mad at me."

"I'm not," he said, meaning it. What had drawn them together seven years ago was gone. Those days could never be recaptured. Mitchell felt a bleakness inside when he realized he would never see Elizabeth again after the end of the week. She would leave, return to the city and her job, find a new lover, and repeat endlessly the same drama she had written for herself.

And he would be dead. Mitchell considered using the elevators to one side of the lobby, then decided to take the stairs. The sweep of the stairway reminded him of old movies about grander times, more elegant times. When he reached the head of the stairs, he was out of breath and had to rest.

He leaned against the highly polished mahogany railing and stared out over the lobby. Elizabeth still sat in the chair. The clerk had brought her a glass of water. From this distance, he wasn't hypnotized by her personal energy. She seemed frail, as if wasting away.

Mitchell pushed such nonsense from his mind. He was the one who was dying, not Elizabeth Morgenthal. She had always been the health fanatic, working at exercise the way she worked at her job. That had been part of her problem, he remembered. She met muscle-bound jocks in the health spas who invariably loved themselves more than they ever could her.

Rested, he sought out Room 207. The key given him by the clerk slid into the lock and turned quietly in the well-oiled lock. The suite on the other side was everything he had hoped for. He could die peacefully in such a room.

Mitchell heaved his suitcases onto the bed and worked at the intricate locks he had put on them. Minutes later, he opened one and decided what needed hanging and what could be put in the wardrobe's single bottom drawer. Only then did he open the larger suitcase. Fastened inside was the bottle of helium, a thick plastic bag, the roll of sticky gray duct tape, the brass fittings he needed and a long, single-spaced typewritten letter explaining his suicide. He leafed through the document, his eyes dancing over the will he had appended.

"How times change," he muttered to himself. He considered finding a lawyer in Greystone Bay and changing the will to include Elizabeth. She would share his last days, just as she had already shared fourteen months of his life. She deserved more than his company. "No," he told himself firmly. He had carefully weighed what to do. Altering his plans now would only introduce error.

"Let's just enjoy the sunset."

He took a long, hot bath that relaxed the tension knotting his shoulders and upper back. Dressing carefully, wanting to impress Elizabeth, he studied himself in the full length mirror. The light wool jacket and shirt collar hung loose. The weight loss would continue, but only this small hint betrayed his secret. He pressed out nonexistent wrinkles in his chocolate-colored slacks and studied himself even more critically. He decided he would pass all but the most penetrating of inspections.

He took the elevator to the lobby, saying nothing to the elevator starter. Mitchell tried to remember when he had last seen a human operator. The elevators in the Port Authority had men who sat on their stools in make-work projects, but he had no need to go to the rooftop parking garages.

The sun was dipping down over the high

wall with its foliage when he walked onto the porch. Elizabeth had staked out a spot with a small table and two comfortable chairs. She waved to him. He couldn't restrain the smile that came to his lips. He *had* missed her and hadn't known it.

"You are right on time. You're a constant in the universe, Alan. Never a second late."

"Some people call that a compulsion. Or is it properly an obsession?"

"You haven't changed in other ways, either," she said in exasperation. "Don't try to be so precise. It doesn't matter if you're not in complete control. Really."

"Is this the New Age philosophy? Let previous lives intrude on the here-and-now?" He ordered a dry Gibson when the waiter came and silently stood beside his chair. "Never mind," he went on. "Let's just enjoy the sunset."

"Such beauty," Elizabeth said, sighing. "I've come out here every night for a week and it still awes me."

They sat and chatted about old times, the people they knew together and apart, the threads that had bound them. After awhile, they fell silent, content to watch the stars turning into hard diamond points in the velvet black sky.

Mitchell turned slightly in his chair and stared down the length of the long porch. Twin lights flared. He cocked his head to one side and got a better look. The gardener stood at the end of the porch. His thick glasses reflected pale yellow light coming from inside the SeaHarp's lobby. The man studied them. When he saw Mitchell returning the stare, he stepped back and vanished into the shadows.

"Let me buy you dinner. Anything you want."

"No, Alan. I'm the one with the successful business." Elizabeth's thin hand shot to her lips. "I'm sorry. I don't know what's happened in the past six years."

"The bookstore isn't grossing four million this year," he said, with a laugh. "But I'm comfortable. I can afford a brief vacation here."

"This is so nice running into you here," Elizabeth said. "And you may buy me dinner."

"Only if you have a steak. You need the protein." He reached out and touched her cheek. The flesh was porcelain-cold.

She laughed and held his hand close, giving the palm a quick kiss. "Whatever you say, Alan."

After dinner, they had another drink in the bar. They entered their own private world when they sat in the high-backed booths.

> ### He saw the sadness in her eyes—and a curious haunted expression.

"It's nice finding a bar without loud music. I hate shouting to make myself heard," she said. Elizabeth giggled, then belched. "Sorry, Alan. Too much to drink."

"You've only had two glasses of wine, unless you had more before we watched the sunset."

"I just had a Perrier. I can't hold my liquor like I used to. I hate to break it off. This has been so nice seeing you again, but I'm too tired."

"I'm a bit sleepy myself. It was a long trip down on the train. May I see you to your door?"

"Always the gentleman. Of course you may." Arm in arm they left the bar and took the elevator to the top floor.

Mitchell's heart raced when Elizabeth stopped outside the door and handed him her key. He opened the door.

"Thank you," she said. She stood, head slightly tilted and eyes closed. The kiss he gave her was hardly more than a quick peck.

She hid her disappointment well.

"Good night," Mitchell said.

"Breakfast?"

"Not too early," he said. "Let's say nine?"

She nodded. He saw the sadness in her eyes—and a curious haunted expression. Elizabeth spun around and closed the door behind her. The click of the deadbolt sliding home started Mitchell on his way back to his room.

He was drowsy, but he couldn't sleep. Rather than returning to his room, he went back outside onto the porch. A few other guests sat about in twos and threes, quietly talking. He didn't want their company, even if they had desired his. He walked across the dark, dew-damp lawn until he found the high wall. From here he started pacing slowly, intending to circumnavigate the SeaHarp's grounds.

Mitchell stopped and found Elizabeth's room on the fourth floor. He watched until the light went out. Six years ago there might have been more between them. Now, it was impossible. He started on his lonely walk again when the light in Elizabeth's room came on again.

He frowned when he saw that it wasn't the room light. A beam bounced and bobbed against the windowpane, as if someone with a flashlight had entered. Mitchell considered alerting the room clerk to the possibility of a sneak thief in the hotel. The light snapped off. Mitchell found himself unsure if he had seen anything important or if his active imagination played tricks on him.

Starting for the lobby, he paused when he heard a door at the rear of the SeaHarp open and close. Mitchell walked on cat-quiet feet until he saw the circular yellow disk of a flashlight moving on the ground. He stood beside a tree, indistinguishable from a distance.

The gardener hurried toward his flower bed. In one hand he held the flashlight. In the other he carried a small capped jar. He dropped to his knees beside the bed of lilies and carefully unscrewed the lid. Mumbling to himself, he poured the liquid onto the flowers, being sure each got a measured amount. A lewd sucking noise echoed through the stillness of the night.

Finished, he stood and tucked the jar under his arm. The gardener left, whistling off-key.

Mitchell waited several minutes after the man had gone before approaching the flower bed. The lilies tracked him like radar. Kneeling, he avoided their questing stalks and ran his finger along the damp soil, then lifted and sniffed what he had found.

"Blood," he said, startled. In the past few months he had come to loathe the sharp, coppery smell. Involuntarily he rubbed his left arm where so much had been removed for tests. Oh, yes, he knew blood. And he knew why the gardener's lilies and other flowers grew so lushly.

The Egyptians had used slaves' blood to fertilize their crops. Mitchell wondered how many other guests besides Elizabeth Morgenthal contributed their lifeblood to the SeaHarp's thirsty flowers.

He returned to his room but sleep wouldn't come. He sat in an overstuffed chair staring at his opened suitcase holding the paraphernalia of his death.

At breakfast he watched Elizabeth eat double portions. "You're hungry," he said, knowing the reason. Blood loss would do it. His real questions were how the gardener

"It doesn't have to end."

entered her room when she had thrown the deadbolt and how he drew the blood without waking her.

"The past few days I've been famished." Her cheeks burned with a fever. The paleness was greater this morning than it had been. Mitchell wondered how much blood the gardener had sucked from his victim.

"Did you sleep well?"

"I have since I got here," Elizabeth said, smearing homemade preserves on her fifth piece of toast. "That's odd, really. I have insomnia. That's one reason I work such long hours," she said between bites.

"It might be the other way around," pointed out Mitchell.

"The doctor said that, too. It doesn't matter. Not at the moment, Alan. I'm sleeping like a log." Her green eyes locked on his. She didn't have to add that she wished he had been with her.

They spent the day walking along the shore of the bay, skipping stones like small children, examining sea shells and discarding them, finding a peacefulness that hadn't existed for either in many years. They returned to the SeaHarp Hotel at sunset.

"It's been a wonderful day, Alan," Elizabeth said almost wistfully. She reached across the small table in the bar and touched his hand. His fingers twined with hers.

"It doesn't have to end," he said. Her eyes glowed with an inner light.

"I hoped you'd say that." She smiled almost shyly. "Your room or mine?"

"Yours," he said without hesitation, remembering the suitcase he had so carefully stored in his wardrobe. Even being in the same room with the implements of his destruction seemed wrong now.

They took the elevator to the fourth floor and entered her room, arms around each other. She flipped on the light switch. Mitchell noticed her room was much smaller than his, but still larger than the standard hotel room. He studied the room as she fussed about, dropping purse and kicking off shoes. He saw nothing to indicate how the gardener had entered.

"Aren't they thoughtful, Alan?" she asked. "They leave a fresh flower for me each night." She lifted the bud vase from the dresser top and sniffed at the delicate blossom. He watched as she weaved slightly. Her eyelids drooped the barest amount. She took another deep whiff. "I so love fresh flowers."

"You're giving your life for them," he said in a low voice, understanding one part of the riddle.

"What?" She sank to the bed and tried to unfasten her blouse. She fell to one side, sleeping deeply. The combined exertion of the day-long walk and the potent effect of the flower's narcotic perfume had caused her to fall into a light coma.

Mitchell struggled to get her off the bed and into the bathroom. He put a blanket down in the tub and rolled her onto it, hoping she would be comfortable. He didn't want her to awaken in the morning with a kink in her neck. It took longer than he'd thought it would. His strength had been taxed, too. That was the progressive nature of his disease. The T-cells in his blood turned traitor. Infections took hold more easily and conquered with little struggle.

His entire autoimmune system had betrayed him. AIDS. Tears formed at the corners of his eyes at the outrageous fortune that had visited him. He pushed the knowledge of a lingering, painful, ugly death from his mind and concentrated.

Mitchell went to Elizabeth's wardrobe and opened the door. At one end of the fragrant, redwood-lined cabinet hung a frilly nightgown. He stripped off his clothing and donned the gown. It was too tight across the shoulders but should pass in the dark. It hid the different flow of his muscles—what remained of them—and gave him a hope of stopping the gardener.

Before he lay down in the bed, Mitchell returned to the bathroom to check Elizabeth. Her deep, regular breathing showed she was all right. He took a few minutes to shave the hair from his left arm. Even in the dark the gardener might notice the hirsute difference.

No longer. Mitchell thrust out his thin arm and knew it might pass for a woman's.

He returned to the bedroom and turned out the light. Crawling under the covers, his needle-marked left arm dangling over the edge of the bed, he waited.

The light going out gave the gardener his cue. From the ceiling came scurrying sounds, as if rats had infested the century-old hotel. From half-closed eyes Mitchell watched as a piece of the intricate plasterwork turned into utter blackness. The gardener dropped down to a chair from the exposed crawlspace. The flashlight's beam darted around, checking. The gardener hummed to himself as he came over and gripped Mitchell's arm.

A thin rubber hose circled Mitchell's upper arm. The needle sank into veins almost collapsed from too much blood being drawn. The gardener didn't notice. He had been milking Elizabeth heavily. Mitchell almost protested the amount of his blood taken. Even lying down and feigning sleep, he felt dizzy from the loss. To have taken this much from Elizabeth would have killed her.

Only when the jar was filled to the brim did the gardener remove the rubber constrictor hose and retreat. Mitchell watched openly as the gardener jumped from the chair and into the dark square overhead. Like a monkey, the man vanished. Seconds later, the ceiling was again whole.

Mitchell had to fight to sit up. The bloodletting had taken too much from him. An hour later he had wrestled Elizabeth into bed and left quietly. In two he had made his calls. In four his phone jangled for long minutes. He didn't answer it. He knew he would eat breakfast alone.

He slept fitfully, nightmares of grotesquely twisted blood cells chasing him. The sound effects accompanying the nightmares were worse. The sucking noise, the awful obscene sucking.

As Mitchell went into the dining room, a bellman stopped him. "Sir, the lady left this for you."

"Thank you," Mitchell said, knowing what Elizabeth had put in the note. He opened it and read anyway.

"Darling Alan," it began. "I'm so embarrassed about last night. I remember nothing—but do know it had to be as wonderful as you. I wish we could have spent more time together, but it's not possible. I received a call last night. There was a fire in my office and

Mitchell felt no triumph.

my manager was severely burned and is in critical condition. The quickest way back to New York was the 5:10 train. I tried to call your room but you didn't answer. Please, Alan, call me when you get back to the city. With all love, Elizabeth."

He tucked the note in his pocket. She would be angry and confused when she learned there hadn't been a fire and that none of her staff had been hurt.

Mitchell sat in the main dining room and stared out at the blooming flowers.

As he sipped his tea, white-uniformed men rushed past the window. Mitchell turned in his chair and craned his neck. They went to the bed of lilies the gardener had tended so carefully. In a few minutes, they returned, pushing a gurney laden with a black plastic bag large enough to hold a body. A body the size of the gardener.

Mitchell felt no triumph. What the lilies had become, he didn't care to know. He shuddered, thinking of them propagating. But that was no worry of his. He finished his Earl Grey, put the cup down with a steady hand, and returned to his room.

The suitcase opened and Alan Mitchell began his journey to the undiscovered land, from whom no traveller returns.

The SeaHarp Hotel

Author's Comments

I started writing science fiction and fantasy after working as a research physicist at Sandia National Laboratories. A journalist friend asked me to co-author a story with him for the fun of it—I did. It sold. The thrill was incredible. Writing has been my sole career since 1975; I now have more than 200 novels published, in addition to scores of short stories and nonfiction articles.

The great horror writer Charles Grant asked me for a story set in his Greystone Bay universe for an original anthology. Quiet horror was called for because of the tone of the series, and a man intent on suicide after enjoying a final week of luxury suggested itself. My protagonist had to face a death worse than anything he could inflict on himself, but this was not enough. The complication of a friend being used in a diabolical fashion entered the plot. As a last act, he confronts horror more fearsome than his own contemplated death and finds ultimate peace with his situation.

I always do a synopsis and "write" the story in my head before going to the keyboard. "Blood Lilies" was completed after one rewrite and then submitted. All research on AIDS, flowers, and blood was done over two months prior to writing the story.

—Robert E. Vardeman

The House Spider

by Kurt Newton

I was nine years old when the house spider came to live with us. Back then, our doors were always open, and living near the woods, there was always the opportunity for uninvited guests.

No one noticed it at first. It found a comfortable niche underneath the stairway leading to the basement. Only when I was sent down to fetch a jar of pickles one day was it discovered, but by then it had already "moved in."

Its "nest"—which is what I called it, it seemed too involved to be called a web—inhabited the underside of the top tread of the stairway, not quite as thick as cotton candy, but unnavigable by any other insect standards. In fact, a few of those unfortunate insects were already imbedded in the nest and wrapped up tight like tiny corpses. Where the house spider was at the time, I could only guess. The dim light of the basement was of little help. And it was only when I got the idea that the house spider perhaps didn't live in the nest at all, and in fact most likely lived outside of it, that the hairs on the back of my neck began to tingle, for it could have been right overhead.

I nearly dropped the jar of pickles I was holding and quickly scrambled up the stairs to my mother, who wondered where I'd been.

I didn't tell anyone of the house spider's presence. It seemed a shame that all the work that went into building such a nest would have to be destroyed. That and the fact that the only harm the house spider did was capturing other uninvited guests. Which didn't seem to be much harm at all. In fact, it seemed quite useful.

But as the summer months came and went, the house spider's nest grew.

My two sisters seldom entered the basement, if at all. For them it was too slippery and icky down there to begin with, let alone think of what might be living in all those damp, lightless corners. My father spent a lot of time out of the house, and when his footsteps were finally heard, it was usually in his study, away from us children. So that left only my mother and I. She canned tomatoes in the fall and made jellies and jams. Her canning jars and pans sat to one side beneath the one bulb which spread light in progressively dimmer degrees to the farther reaches of the basement. The light that made it to the stairway was enough to see what the house spider had been up to.

The nest now included the top three stair treads. A series of near-invisible wires helped to keep the nest suspended. The densely spun bodies imbedded in the mass were now the size of mice. At any other time this would have worried me, but there were other, more pressing, concerns on my mind. Because it was also the summer my father lost his job.

I remember low arguments at night which seeped through the walls as I tried to sleep; a

Author Bio

A former editor at a small press, Kurt Newton is the author of two short story collections, *The House Spider and Other Strange Visitors* and *Dark Demons*, as well as a poetry collection, *Life Among the Dream Merchants and Other Phantasies*.

day I happened to catch my father sitting at the kitchen table staring at the magnets on the refrigerator, his breakfast gone cold; and the two weeks he stayed upstairs in bed, not once getting out, except to go to the bathroom. First, "Your father's taking a vacation," our mother explained to us. Then, "Your father's got a flu bug." But after a while she stopped trying to explain and told us just to hurry up and do our chores or hurry up and eat our dinner or just plain hurry up, as if there was something after us and if we weren't careful it would soon catch up to us.

As a result, by the start of the new school year, our home became both brooding and quiet.

Eventually, Dad moved out of the bedroom and came downstairs to live in the living room. He sat in his favorite chair and watched TV most of the day, while Mom vacuumed under his feet. A doctor came to visit him once a week. My two sisters were seldom seen. They took to spending more and more time in their rooms and over their friends' houses. Mom didn't bother with the canning that year and left the vegetables to rot in the garden.

I didn't feel it was necessary to tell anyone about the house spider living underneath the basement stairs, and at times forgot it was even there.

The entire underside of the stairway was now home to the house spider.

The years passed. My sisters exchanged their girl friends for boy friends and eventually got pregnant and married and moved out of the house. I tried to keep up with the chores and general maintenance Dad would have done, but after a while the house began to take on a lazy, unkempt appearance. Door hinges squeaked, windows became stuck in their casements. The interior paint faded and the heads of nails showed through the plaster until it looked as if the walls were fastened together with shirt buttons. Mom did the best she could, working several jobs to help support the house. Her hair turned grey and, like the nail heads, the wrinkles on her face, which had only been ghost lines before, began to show through.

There was hardly a reason for anyone to enter the basement anymore, what with Mom not canning, my sisters gone, and myself working odd jobs and not always available to do the fetching. But on certain days, with nothing else better to do, I would excuse myself from the dinner table and go down into the basement to check on our uninvited guest who decided to stay all these years.

The entire underside of the stairway was now home to the house spider. Its collective web had grown into a massively intricate structure stretching from floor to ceiling, with support strands extending upward and along the ceiling's floor joists in all directions, like the branches of a tree.

I remember one particular day, as I stood marveling at the nest's structure, I wondered just what had kept it going all these years. Surely it had exhausted its habitat of flies and beetles and mice by now? There came a scuttling behind me—a shifting in the degrees of light and dark in the deeper recesses of the basement—which prompted me to abandon this train of thought and return upstairs. Perhaps it didn't want me to know. Or perhaps it was just something I shouldn't have thought to ask.

It's been twelve years now since I've been home. At seventeen, I enlisted in the Army and have since served three successful tours of duty. I have served in many parts of the world, large wealthy countries and small struggling ones with no food, no economy and no form of stable rule, where apathy rules instead. It is in these countries that I've come across the nests—the house spiders. It is rare for a hut or hovel to be without one. They are as common as our domesticated dog or cat. The people who live in these dwellings defend their spiders' right to be there, and in some cases even help to feed it. Much like I allowed ours at home to thrive under the protection of my silence.

Twelve years. Until today. I had to see my parents one last time. I had to see *it*. I had to know how far it had spread.

When I pulled up to the curb, I hardly recognized it as the same house I'd left. The clapboards were nearly colorless; some had bowed with weather damage and pulled free from their placements. The bushes in front had grown untrimmed for decades now. The walkway was thick with weeds, the lawn gone to seed. The front door was a patchwork of blistered paint and cracked wood grain. It took several knocks before the door opened and an old woman stood squinting in its place.

The recognition was slow, like a trickle of water from a rusty well pump, but it finally came, the rusty water turning more fluid. The grey of her hair formed a mist around her face. Then I realized the mist was a thin veil of spun thread, like a cobweb, only much more coherent. A caul for the elderly.

"Paul . . . Paul is that you?"

"Yes, Mom, it's me."

My mother gave me a fragile hug and led me inside. So this was the house I grew up in, listening to my sisters argue and watching my father waste away. The rooms were thick with webbing. Grey macramé patterns wove themselves over doorways and across furniture. The webbing seemed to emanate from the very walls themselves. The TV, with its rabbit-eared antenna, sat beneath a circus tent of spun thread; my father, sedentary in his favorite chair, himself entombed. From where I stood, I could see he was still breathing.

"Will you be staying, Paul?" my mother asked, leading me into the kitchen. She put the kettle on for some tea. As I passed by the basement, I noticed the door was wide open, the dark stairway impassable. The thick stench of rot and decay wafted up from below. This was where it all began, I thought. And this is where it will end, if I don't leave. Leave now. I saw what I had come to see.

"No, Mom, I can't stay. I—" I ran out of words then. Everything failed me. Everything but my sense of urgency. "You understand, don't you?" I asked her, hoping.

For a moment her faded blue eyes seemed to register the web-infested rooms that surrounded us. Then her eyes floated back and met mine. "I'll tell your father you stopped by."

She hugged me then and I kissed her on the cheek—webbing stuck to my lips like chewing gum. "Hurry up, now," she whispered into my ear.

And I hurried—I ran—those words echoing in my head from some long forgotten time when things first began to go bad . . . when the doors were left open and an uninvited guest crawled in. I ran before the exit was sealed shut, before my ankles became tied to the floor and my opportunity passed. I ran back to my car and drove away.

And now, as I drive along these suburban streets, I see the houses—one here, another there—the houses with the peeling paint and the neglected front yards; the houses whose children have probably moved away and will never return, and don't know why; the houses whose dark hollow spaces are most likely home to the house spider . . . I see these houses and I consider myself lucky. Lucky to be alive and moving. Lucky enough to have seen what I have seen. Lucky enough to still care.

So, a word of caution. Please, check your basement stairs or your attic eaves. It begins small, almost unnoticeably—the spun dust in the corners, the hairline cracks in the walls, the stains on the ceiling that weren't there yesterday, but were always there. It takes over if you let it. So don't let it.

Pirate Writings

The House Spider

Author's Comments ──────────

As a child growing up in the country, I came in contact with all manner of hidden household pets: spiders, beetles, mice. Our house had a fireplace with a large woodbox beside it. There was always great fear when reaching inside the woodbox because sometimes there were some very large spiders inside it. Wood spiders. I remember calling them wolf spiders because of their hairy bodies and long, hairy legs. They were as large as my open hand.

This experience—this shared coexistence with something fearful—was commonplace in my childhood. Add a family caught in its own web of dysfunction and the disassociative ambition of one of its members, and you can see how easily the metaphor can be applied.

Originally written as a series of loosely connected scenes charting the destructive process of age and decay, I sent the story to Ann Kennedy, editor of *The Silver Web*, who returned it, advising that I should ground the reader in a more concrete time frame. Using this advice, I added specific seasons and events (such as going back to school, working a first job, etc.) and sent it out once again, this time to Ed McFadden, editor of *Pirate Writings*, who had previously published another story of mine.

—Kurt Newton

Rumple What?

by Nancy Springer

To take first the point of view of the miller's daughter, her father is just the sort of consummate jackass who *would* brag to the king that his girl can spin straw into gold. So when she is unceremoniously escorted to a shed full of straw, locked in there with a spinning wheel, and told to do her thing or die, she weeps—but not pathetically, as the tale would have it; rather, she howls with rage. No matter how dire her fear, no miller's daughter has ever been able to weep the dewy, snot-free tears of a damsel in distress; our wench bawls with messy, grimacing fury, all the more so because crying is *not* what she wants to do. It is one of the Seven Most Unfair Fates of the female condition that when you really want to thunder, threaten revenge, scare your asinine father and his new crony the king shitless, what happens? You goddamn cry.

Even so, when the shed door opens and the most peculiar little man comes in, she does not seize the opportunity to thump someone smaller than she, for quite sensibly she wonders what the hell is going on. The king locked the door himself. By what power did this dwarf, who is too short to reach the handle, open it? And what does he want? The miller's daughter has heard some nasty rumors about what really went on with Snow White. Perversely, because there is now clear and present danger, her weeping ceases. Wiping her face and blowing her nose upon her apron, she tries to study the visitor, but through her traumatized eyes she can see only that he is sharp, all points, including his face. Pointy nose, steeple brows, wishbone chin, skinny birdy arms and fingers, chicken legs in velvet trousers tailored to fit. Peaked velvet cap, curling feather. Probably never went heigh-ho off to work in his life.

"What's the matter?" he wants to know. His voice is thin and pointy too, like a needle.

She replies very politely, in case he might be somebody, "Thank you for asking. It's my allergies. I'm horribly allergic to dusty places, straw, stables, that sort of thing." This happens to be true, making her whole rotten day even rottener.

"What will you give me if I spin the straw into gold for the king?" Of course he knows all about it; otherwise, why would he be there?

The miller's daughter offers, "Um, my necklace?" and is puzzled when he accepts that commonplace string of beads without further bargaining. As he spins all the straw, quite quickly, into gold, she feels relieved, naturally, that she need not die in the morning, but also apprehensive, for there's no getting around it: she's dealing with the supernatural, and has not yet paid a sufficient price. Even

Author Bio

Award-winning author Nancy Springer published her first novel in 1977. Since then she has published more than 50 novels for adults, teens, and children, in genres including mythic fantasy, contemporary fiction, magical realism, suspense, and mystery.

as she thanks the little man effusively for saving her butt, even as he takes his leave, she is hoping she will never see him again, yet has a miserable feeling that she will. These things happen in threes.

Bingo. She doesn't even get to go home for her second-best necklace before the greedy king, with the inevitable death threat, sticks her into another, bigger shed full of straw. At nightfall, sure enough, just like a mucus machine she starts weeping—this time with tears appropriately wretched, due to her allergies plus the fact that, while she does not miss her father, she does miss breakfast, lunch, and supper—and right on cue, the little man shows up.

She gives him her ring—again, the cheapest of baubles, yet once more he accepts without demur. Once more, not unkindly, he sets to work. He is an odd sort of midget, thinks the miller's daughter as she watches, maybe not a dwarf after all, too slender, more like one of the pixies, but lacking their beauty, perhaps an elf . . . with a face like a wedge of cheese? No, he seems to fit no known category of little people, but it hardly matters, so long as he spins straw into gold.

Which he does. She is saved. But oh, no, day three, huge shed this time, huge pile of straw once more, death if she fails. Only this third time the king, that total oinker, adds that if he doesn't kill her, he will marry her, as if this were supposed to be an *inducement*?

So this time, when the little man shows up, the miller's daughter is weeping wearily, for no matter what happens, she's out of

This is the prize he has sought all along . . .

luck. When he asks what she'll give him to spin the straw into gold, she replies, "I have nothing left," which is, of course, not true. She could offer him the oldest of incentives,

quite expects him to request same, and really doesn't care, although she supposes that, for the dubious sake of survival, she will—

So she is totally taken off guard when, instead of bargaining for the pleasures of her body, he says, "Oh, that's okay. Just promise me your firstborn child."

She is astonished; what on earth does the little man want with a baby, all that noise and filth? But of course she agrees; who wouldn't? A firstborn child, which might or might not happen sometime down the road, is the merest abstraction when one is a teenager faced with death at sunrise.

To take now the little man's point of view: Eureka! The baby! This is the prize he has sought all along, caring nothing for the baubles, the necklace, the ring, and as for the girl herself—yes, indeed, she is quite appealing in her peasant-wench way, and he knows she is desperate enough to let him embrace her, but within his strong, solitary mind he also knows that such intimacy would provide only the most temporary of respite from his terrible loneliness.

For he is uniquely alone. It is one of the Seven Egregious Unfairnesses of his life that he is out of place even among supernatural manifestations. He is neither dwarf to delve in the earth with other dwarves, nor pixie to dance in the moonlit mushroom-ring with other pixies, nor elf, sprite, fetch, bogy, nixie, leprechaun, brownie, or any sort of acceptable faery-goblin. And his is a situation most unjust, for, while giants sometimes live alone because of their grisly habits, and ogres because they are odious, the singular little man has committed only kindness, namely, the spinning of straw into gold.

Yet he could save the miller's daughter's life a thousand times and she would still give him the same wary look, like a barn cat. Because she is an ordinary person, and he is not. In the minds of those who consider themselves normal, who *are* normal, otherness is suspect. Deformity (being auger-nosed, chicken-limbed, and only three feet tall) signifies evil. Doing impossible things means the devil's help, reason for fear.

But the baby will know none of this! Never will the baby look at him with misgiving; the baby will not only accept him, but love him! No baby can help but love, completely and helplessly and forever after, the one who nurtures it. And nurture it he will, as well as any mother; he will give it magical milk to drink, and what are a few soiled diapers to a being with the power to spin straw into gold? He will provide well for the child. And once he has possession of it, and especially once it grows a bit and can talk with him, he will be no longer a misfit, alone, but he will belong to a clan of two.

The king does not care about being loved.

Now he must wait for the miller's daughter to give birth, that is all. And even if it takes a few years—which seems unlikely, given the buxom bloom of that girl—but even if she has the sagacity to delay the inevitable, the singular little man will pass the time in patience, as he has already passed many, many years, tens of hundreds of years.

To the king, who scarcely deserves a viewpoint, it's about time something went right. One of the Seven Most Unfair Grievances on his rather limited mind is that he had no choice what to do with his life, no options other than to be king after his old man croaked, yet he never got to be a Handsome Prince (he is an oinker in face as well as in heart) and therefore he never found a Beautiful Princess willing to be his bride. Or a Fair Lady. Or any female the least bit suitable to wed His Exalted Highness. Now he's a

middle-aged Majesty with an ale belly, up to his triple chin in debt for doublets and hose and ermine codpieces and all the other ridiculous, expensive trappings of his regal job, and with vassals grumbling that he needs to provide an heir, and—and lo and behold, here the dumbass miller puts him onto a reasonably attractive girl who goes and makes him rich.

The king does not care about being loved. He does not feel alone in the world; there are plenty more like him, heading up nations and corporations. He considers that he can be very happy with gold to pay the bills, plus a wench with whom to rumple the bed sheets. Why not marry her? While she lacks the sort of pedigree that is usually required, she shows every promise of being quite fertile—almost certain to pop out an heir—and then there are the financial considerations. If he needs more money, he can always threaten again to kill her.

Not that he really thinks she has spun straw into gold. No, if he believed that, he wouldn't touch her; what if she could turn other things into something elses? But the king doesn't worry, because he knows about the little man. He is no fool; he has his spies, his guards, his people keeping watch. He figures that whatever she—the miller's daughter; even though he is going to marry her, the king can't recall her name—whatever she gave the little man doesn't count because of the minuscule size involved, and absolutely can be overlooked in the light reflected from a pile of gold.

And if the little man comes back into the picture, well, it depends whether he, the king—who does not deserve a name either—whether he wants more gold at the time, or would rather take the freaky bastard, who has been described to him as twig thin and no more than three feet tall, and whack him in half with one blow of his sword.

At first the miller's daughter thought it would be fairly yucko, having to deal with His Ugliness, but she soon adapts. When he comes to her bed, she spreads her legs and thinks about necklaces made of real jewels, not beads. Thus, aside from her dealings with His Porcine Highness, being queen turns out to be a blast—getting to dress up, and spend money, and order people around, no more scrubbing and cooking and messy flour for her! Relief from hard manual labor is ample compensation for being married to the king, for the miller's daughter is no dreamer; she had never thought to find love. Least of all in wedlock, but not in any other way, either.

So it startles her to the heart of her heart, indeed it startles and astonishes her to discover such a heart within herself, when, most unexpectedly and all in a moment, she falls in love. Deeply. Irrevocably. Completely. Under the most unexpected circumstances, when she has just gone through the most harrowing pain she has ever known.

When the midwife places the baby in her arms.

When she lays her face against the soft spot atop the baby's downy head.

One breath of that primal infant essence, and the queen is no longer the miller's daughter or the king's wife either; she is woman, and she is mother. She is weak and invincible and happier than a butterfly yet fiercer than a wolf, for she will defend this tiny person, this newfound love, with her life, against anything that threatens—

And then she remembers.

What she promised.

Oh. No.

No. Never. No matter what.

But—surely it won't come to that; surely the freaky little man didn't mean it, really. Or he has forgotten. She hasn't seen or heard of him for a couple of years.

Still, alarm bells of hell ring through her, agitation that will not cease for any soothing, so relentless that, within a day, she breaks down and asks to speak with His Royal Ego, her husband.

For the simple reason that the king gives not a rat's sphincter about the fate of the baby, one can tell that the newborn is a girl. One can assume this even though the child's gender is undocumented.

When his wife begs him for guards because someone is likely to take the baby, he laughs at her and asks who would want such a bawling parcel of stink. She does not know that he knows about the little man, and it costs her all the courage she never knew she had to tell him that she did not herself spin straw into gold. Will he kill her now? No; he laughs again, this time in quite an ugly way,

"But you promised me this baby . . ."

because it has been necessary for her to admit that the little man spent three nights with her, and that she promised him her firstborn. He asks her what the gold-spinner wants with the baby. She whimpers that she does not know. Again she pleads with him to safeguard the child. "Why should I?" he demands, shouting with cancerous laughter. "It might not even be mine!" He says this not because he thinks it true, but simply because he can. He says it to press his advantage, to consummate his power over her, to complete her despair.

Triumphant, exit the king.

When the little man opens the locked door to the queen's chamber and goes in, he is unprepared for the emotional maelstrom that greets him, for he had assessed the miller's daughter as the most pragmatic of peasants. Yet there she sits in the great canopied bed, hugging the infant to her velvet-robed bosom and weeping as he has never seen her weep before. And offering him all the riches she has, necklaces of emerald and ruby and diamond, rings of sapphire and gold, if he will only let her keep the child.

"But I care nothing for necklaces and rings," he says.

"You did before!"

"Only because the narrative demands a sequence of three."

"Let me give you my third child, then!" Fierce, desperate, this time she does not weep in a messy mucus-prone manner; today, hers are the tragic, crystalline tears of a true queen.

"But you promised me this baby," he insists, knowing that he is in the right, although her tears pierce his heart.

"Please!" She knows, also, that a queen must keep her promises. "Is there no power that can persuade you otherwise?"

"No power can prevent me except one: if you should guess my name."

His own compassionate honesty drags this truth out of him, for it is a very serious matter, the naming of names; as he is something more than a normal Tom, Dick, or Jane, anyone who knows his true name would possess power to command him. This is how wizards control genies and demons, by the naming of names.

The queen realizes what a chance he has offered her. "Grant me, then, three days—" It must, of course, be *three* days. "—to discover your name, I beg of you."

He can't believe what a doughnut he is being. Yet, "Very well," he replies, turning away.

"A hint! At least give me a hint!" The queen cries as the baby starts to whimper at her breast. "Is yours a short name or a long one?"

"Outlandish and multisyllabic. I will be back tomorrow to see how you are

doing." And off he goes, knowing himself to be a soft-hearted fool, and knowing just as well that she nevertheless considers him an imp of evil, and that he will be so depicted in human retellings of his story for the next millennium or two.

Along with love and womanhood, the baby has taught the queen the awesome power and significance of names, for she must name the child, and feels all the responsibility of the nomenclature not yet accomplished.

But far greater is the weight of divining the name that will save her baby—for so she perceives the matter; she cannot imagine what the bizarre little man could want with her child other than to eat it, perhaps, or sacrifice it in some fiendish rite, or starve it into a bony monster like himself, or whatever it is that fairies do with the babies they steal from cradles.

All day, hugging her child, she sets herself to thinking of names. That night she lies awake nursing the infant and trying to remember all the outlandish, multisyllabic names she has ever heard in her life. In the morning she summons the court scribe to begin a database—she herself can neither read nor write—and she sends out messengers to bring her more names, and more. But in the darkest hollow of her heart she knows that so many possible names are far beyond her ken; even a computer naming all the names of the deity would take a few minutes before the stars would begin to blink out.

When the little man whispers the name of the door and walks in, the queen is ready for him. She tries first some fairytale-type names she made up during the night. "Is your name Goldenhands? Is it Goldfingers? Goldspinner? Treasurewright?"

"No, no, no, and no." Marveling anew at his own idiocy, the little man gives her another hint. "Your majesty, my name makes no sense."

"Moon Unit? Dweezil? Madonna? Rosencrantz, Guildenstern?"

"No, no, no, no, no."

And so it goes all that day and the next. Kasper, Melchior, Balthazar, Schwarzenegger, Engelbert, Humperdinck, ad infinitum and ad nauseum; wearisome to the max for all concerned, especially the little man. He nearly decides not to show up for the third day, but he grits his pointed teeth and reports to the queen's chamber.

And he senses at once that, overnight, something has immensely changed. That royal woman, with babe in arms, welcomes him with dry eyes that emanate a strange gleam. "Rumplebedsheets," she greets him.

"I would like to give the little one a name."

Oh, no. He begins to feel alarmed. "My dear little miller's daughter—"

"It's Rumple something. Rumple-for-skin?"

"No." Then he repeats, shocked, "No!"

"Rumplestockings? Wait! Rumple—Rumple-shins-skin?"

"You are still trying to make sense out of me." When nothing makes sense. He feels his own eyes as sharp as knives begin to drip the clear blood that is tears, for he knows what she has done, like generations of mothers before her, for the sake of her child.

"Rumple-stilts-skin!" she cries.

He feels weak, he feels her power over him, he has to sit down. "Almost," he admits. "Not quite. You're spelling it wrong."

"Spelling? I know nothing of spelling! But I know your name is Rumpelstiltskin!"

"In the original German," he hedges, "it is Rumpelstilzchen." And in the French Grigrigredinmenufretin, in the Swedish Bullerib-

asius, the Finnish Tittelintuure and the Italian Praseidimio, and there are many more, in Estonian, Czechoslovakian, Hebrew, Japanese and so on, for like any self-respecting supernatural being, our oddling has many names, of which the miller's daughter knows only one.

"What did you want with my child?"

"Rumpelstiltskin," she repeats in vast and bitter triumph, for it is just as the little man says in the story; the devil has told her. She has made a pact with the devil, bargaining away her soul to save her child, trading it for the knowledge of Rumpelstiltskin's name. So she belongs to the Prince of Darkness now. But her baby does not. Her baby, body and soul, belongs to no one but her.

Rumpelstiltskin has been defeated. But he does not, as the devil and the tale expect, stamp off in a suicidal rage. There is no longer any need for him to rip himself in half, as it has been proven that he is not an evil being.

He sighs in great, everlasting sadness and makes a strange request. "I would like to give the little one a name."

"What?" The mother is startled, for she had thought his interest in her baby was culinary. "How come?" For the first time she really looks at the little man. "What did you want with my child?"

Such is his weary sorrow that he does not even try to explain. Yet, now that she has shaken hands with Lucifer, she sees the light.

"Oh, for crying out loud," she whispers, "you wanted the exact same thing that I have."

Unspeaking, he stares back at her with spindle-sharp eyes.

"You get out of here," she orders. Recent events have made her a fitting mate for the king; they will be two of a kind from now on.

Her command lifts him to his feet, but before he departs he asks again, "Allow me to gift the little girl with a name."

And in her shameless greed the mother agrees to let him bless with the power of a faerie name the child he cannot possess.

He touches the babe's rose-petal cheek and names her, "Softasilkskin."

Then he goes away with his head hanging, his woodcock nose directed toward the ground, and is never heard from again.

But Softasilkskin, despite her deplorable parents and to the devil's disappointment, grows up to be the good and beautiful Princess Silkskin, meets a Handsome Prince and Lives Happily Ever After, even though everybody else in the story is royally screwed.

Fantasy & Science Fiction

Author's Comments

Some of my novels and short stories have been based on classic material such as the Arthurian myths and the legends of Robin Hood. Therefore I was asked to contribute a workshop on "Reshaping Classic Tales" to a writer's conference. As an example, I thought of ways to reshape the Rumpelstiltskin fairy tale, and the idea took hold of me by the throat.

I felt playful while writing this story, mischievously so, and therefore I broke a lot of rules. I pointed out viewpoint. I allowed my fairy tale characters a self-conscious knowledge of the traditions of the fairy tale. I threw in anachronisms for humorous effect. I refused to worry about whether any of this would work.

"Rumple What?" was one of those blessed stories that simply came to me. Of course I had my plot already laid out for me by the Brothers Grimm, so all I had to do was to play games with what already existed.

I did my usual first draft, let it age for a few weeks, looked at it again and smoothed it out a bit, then sent it off with no idea whether it was a gem or a dud. Apparently my spontaneous approach succeeded, because the story was accepted for publication. *Fantasy & Science Fiction* editor Gordon Van Gelder suggested a few revisions, which helped the story work even better.

Although I have won two Edgar Allan Poe awards from the Mystery Writers of America, I think fantasy remains my first love. I have been sending my fantasy stories to *F&SF* for the past 30 years; why go elsewhere?

It takes a lot of guts to submit writing for publication. Don't make it any worse than it has to be. Don't pin all your hopes on one piece. Send it out, forget about it, write another to the best of your ability and send that out to another publisher. Then if the first one comes back with a rejection slip, send it out someplace else, and start a third story.

The more you write, the better you will get at it, and the more work you keep circulating, the more likely that something will find a home. This approach will work only if you continue to grow as a writer, but it's certainly better than getting "stuck" for years trying to publish one flawed story.

—Nancy Springer

Nonfiction

TheGreatGreenberg's Gift

by Philip Stein

Dad was ever boasting about Hank Greenberg's exploits on the ball field. He always referred to him as "TheGreatGreenberg," running the words together as if they were, in fact, one word. "TheGreatGreenberg!" he'd say. "What a terrific ballplayer he is, always getting that clutch hit, always knocking in that winning run!"

During his heyday, TheGreatGreenberg was a hero to thousands of baseball fans, especially to Jewish fans who needed one of their own to show the world that they could play ball with the best of them.

Living in Los Angeles, Dad never saw TheGreatGreenberg play ball. But he followed the 6-foot, 3½-inch slugger's career from afar, reading the sports pages and baseball magazines, and occasionally watching TheGreatGreenberg whack a homer on a movie newsreel.

I saw TheGreatGreenberg in person several times during one Saturday and Sunday in the spring of 1948. The place was Los Angeles' Wrigley Field, the home of the Chicago Cubs' number one farm team, the Los Angeles Angels of the Pacific Coast League.

Greenberg had retired from playing baseball after the 1947 season, but he was about to become a special assistant to Bill

> *He skipped out of the batting cage, laughing and tipping his cap . . .*

Veeck, principal owner of the Cleveland Indians. The Indians and the Cubs had traveled to Los Angeles from their Arizona spring-training camps to play two exhibition games.

That Saturday, before the first game, I was standing in the box-seats section near the first-base dugout, pestering the Indian players for their autographs. Then, suddenly, there he was, TheGreatGreenberg, emerging from the dugout in an Indians uniform.

Making his way to the batting cage, he laughed and kibitzed with the players about getting older and being past his prime. He hit a few balls here, a few balls there. Then, one after another, he launched—in his trademark towering-skyscraper style—five or six shots over the left-field wall.

He skipped out of the batting cage, laughing and tipping his cap to the Indian players who were standing around, whooping it up and applauding. Some Cubs across the field

Author Bio

Philip Stein writes regularly about baseball for a variety of publications, including *Looking Back, Spitball: The Literary Baseball Magazine, Good Old Days Specials,* and *Elysian Fields.* A former student of Long Ridge Writers Group, he has also published more than a dozen professional journal articles about the criminal justice system during his long career as a Los Angeles County probation officer.

and in and around the third-base dugout were applauding, too.

"Hey, Hank, how about an autograph?" I called to him as he walked past me on his way back to the first-base dugout. "Not now, kid," he said. "I'll get to you next time."

After the game, I saw TheGreatGreenberg again. He was outside the ballpark, about to get into a taxicab. Dashing up to him, I shouted, "Please sign my autograph book, Hank!"

"I'm in a hurry now, kid. Catch you tomorrow."

I was amazed. How did he know that I'd be at the ballpark the next day?

The next morning, before the gates opened for the fans, I was outside the players' gate, pestering the Indians for autographs as they arrived. I rushed up to TheGreatGreenberg when I spotted him getting out of a taxicab and shoved my autograph book at him.

"Please let me talk to TheGreatGreenberg."

"How many autographs do you want from me, kid?" he asked, recognizing me from the day before.

"You haven't signed my book yet," I assured him, flipping quickly through the pages and showing him all the autographs. "See, I kept this page blank. It's especially for you."

TheGreatGreenberg smiled down at me as he scrawled his signature. I cherished that autograph for many years. I even incorporated the way he wrote the letter E into my own signature.

During the late innings of that Sunday ballgame, my kid brother Ronnie and I snuck into the box seats right next to the Cubs' third-base dugout. After the game, Ronnie leaned over the short railing separating the stands from the field to peer into the dugout.

The players were gone. But there, on the bench, Ronnie spotted a cardboard box. He beckoned me to the railing. I looked into the dugout and saw the box. Ronnie and I knew that it could be a great find.

He climbed over the railing and ducked into the dugout. He shook the box. Then, certain of our good fortune, he lifted the lid. We beamed. Lined up in that box, in four rows of three, were 12 shiny National League baseballs, brand-new Spaldings, their horsehide as white as the veritable driven snow, their stitched seams as red as maraschino cherries.

Ronnie and I looked at each other. Should we or shouldn't we? Of course, we shouldn't. Of course, we did. As we ran from the ballpark, Ronnie concealed the box of baseballs under his jacket.

When we got home and Dad saw the box of baseballs, he blew his stack—an act that was completely out of character for him. Then he quickly checked the telephone directory for the number of the Biltmore Hotel in downtown Los Angeles. The sports pages had reported that both the Cubs and the Indians were staying there.

"Please, it's urgent," Dad pleaded when someone at the hotel answered his call. "I need to talk with anybody affiliated with the Chicago Cubs."

Dad was silent for several moments as he listened to the person on the other end of the line. Then he said, "Good! Please let me talk to TheGreatGreenberg."

The next words that Ronnie and I heard went something like this: "Hello, Mr. Greenberg. My boys were at the ballpark today. They stole a box of brand-new baseballs from the Cubs dugout. I want to take them to the hotel right now so they can return the baseballs."

Ronnie and I stared in stunned disbelief. There Dad was, talking with TheGreatGreenberg as pretty as you please, as if the slugger were just anybody—as if he weren't a cinch for a spot in the Hall of Fame!

Dad listened silently to TheGreatGreenberg's response. Then he replied, "Yes, Mr. Greenberg. I understand. Thank you. Thank you very much for your time."

After Dad hung up, he glowered at Ronnie and me without uttering a single word. Finally, when our anxiety was at its peak, he said with considerable disgust, "Nobody's at the hotel to receive the baseballs. The Cubs have already gone back to Arizona; the Indians too. TheGreatGreenberg's checking out of the hotel right now. He said that the two of you should do special chores to earn the baseballs, one ball at a time."

And that's what happened. Ronnie and I did scores of special chores over the next two years or so. Before each chore, Dad lectured us about the evils of stealing. But after each chore, he plucked one of the new baseballs from the cardboard box, flipped it to us and said, "Here, catch. And don't ever forget: This ball is a gift from TheGreatGreenberg."

Good Old Days

Author's Comments

This true story honors my father. My children knew him; my grandchildren didn't. This piece gives them a written snapshot of the kind of man he was.

The initial draft came quickly. It usually does for me. The writing I enjoy the most is revising and polishing and getting it to say precisely what I want it to say. I revised the article three or four times in three or four drafts.

I wrote the article completely from memory, just as it happened—no outline, no notes, no special planning.

The piece is a nostalgic one. *The Best of the Magazine Markets for Writers* indicated that *Good Old Days* publishes articles about personal experiences between 1935 and 1963. The article and the magazine seemed to be a perfect fit. As it turned out, it was.

I always advise writers submitting work for the first time to get it to the right market. It's critical. There are a number of references that describe the needs of different markets. Don't get discouraged when your work is rejected. Rejection comes with the territory.

—Philip Stein

Home Remedies for the Sick Season

by Kris Franklin

Stuff a cold and starve a fever.

Or is it the other way around? I keep forgetting, so I usually claim it's stuff whichever I happen to have, since starve is a concept I can appreciate only during a bout of stomach flu. Besides, what if you have a fever with your cold? You could end up driving your innards totally schizoid.

The reason for my concern is clear. Winter has arrived, and the Sick Season's upon us again. It's a time when you don't know who to trust . . .

"Gimme a big kiss!" exclaims your spouse or significant other, or someone you like enough to go mouth-to-mouth with. So you're semi-puckered, but then this unworthy thought creeps into your mind:

Say, didn't I see this character sneeze, or cough, or make one of those sounds like a chainsaw starting—where you snort the contents of an entire sinus cavity down your throat—a few minutes ago? Give you a big kiss, huh? Right, bub. Shortly after I empty a can of disinfectant all over you.

(I once visited a friend who'd married and reproduced with admirable enthusiasm. One of his heirs had the mumps and kept try-ing to climb into my lap until his wife handed me a can of Lysol with instructions to set the button on Stun and blast the little bugger every time he got close.)

> *Once winter rolls in, every kid below the age of 13 is carrying some form of Loathsome Disease.*

According to *Consumer Reports* (hey, you're gonna get scientific research with this one), evidence shows the common cold occurs only in the presence of an infecting organism. This comes as no surprise to anyone who deals with kids—with or without a spray can—and knows what Infection Factories they are. Once winter rolls in, every kid below the age of 13 is carrying some form of Loathsome Disease (past 13 this doesn't seem as common, since raging hormones probably boil away a lot of the germs), plus enough post-nasal drip to fill Lake Michigan.

As I recall from my teaching days, this is equally a hazard to any adults they encounter. My second grade teacher, Miz Nazlerod, used to put down masking tape on the floor, enclosing her desk within an imaginary box with about three feet of space on all sides. Kids hauling around any form of Loathsome Disease had to stay outside the tape. I remember Miz Nazlerod never got sick, though we figured it was because viruses were scared to go near her. My wife Kathy was far less forbid-

---

Author Bio ———————

Kris Franklin is a former English teacher who has spent the past 20 years as a professional writer. He has authored more than 100 articles and several novels of suspense, and is an instructor for Long Ridge Writers Group.

ding during her teaching days, and therefore caught everything, which she was generous enough to pass on to me, including my personal fave, that famous stomach flu, which'll motivate you not to wander.

So, what are we to believe? Research indicates a lot of the over-the-counter stuff we consume for winter sickness may not do all we think. My own perennials, Nyquil and Vicks Formula 44, are each about twenty-five percent booze, which is fifty proof and no

Have fun with garlic.

doubt the reason I like them. But it's depressing to wake up still sick and with a hangover to boot, and I've heard other items like Listerine and Aspergum aren't as effective as I'd thought, either. Maybe if we're in that intermediate stage—too sick for the Bedroom Friskies but not sick enough to visit the doctor—it's time to consider an age-old method of treatment: the home remedy.

Notice: The author assumes no liability for results—ranging from mildly bizarre to behavior out of a Tarentino flick—which may accrue to the following remedies. Go sue my grandmother.

1) Moan a lot. This gets me hot soup, tissues by the bed, and occasionally gourmet desserts (hey, stuff a cold, after all), as well as sympathetic quotes like, "Poor baby! Does it hurt? Let me rub your back" and so on. Don't carry on too much, though. Once or twice I've moaned my way right into the downstairs bedroom. Moderation's the key.

2) Watch soap operas. These teach us that, no matter how miserable we think we are, there are a bunch of characters named Eden and Dakota and Silver (no, not the horse) who are much worse off. On one soap there's a character named Erica who's either been married to or Bedroom Frisky pals with

every male on the show, all of whom have six-pack abs except for the ones so filthy rich they hire pool boys to do crunches for them.

3) Have fun with garlic. You can eat it, wear it, or rub it on your door frame to keep vampires away. I know this works because I frequently don't see anyone for weeks, supernatural or otherwise, after its use. It also clears the sinuses better than anything except Twinkies dipped in jalapeno sauce.

4) Take Vitamin C. Back in the 1970s, Nobel Prize winner Linus Pauling stirred up the drug companies with his notion that megadoses of C did more for colds than the stuff they were selling. This made him about as popular as the Surgeon General is with Philip Morris, and there are those who say spending money on C is a waste. Personally, I take it every day when I'm sick, and I believe it works really well, especially if you wash it down with Nyquil or Formula 44.

5) Rub gunk on your chest—or better yet, have it rubbed on by someone you lust after. Since Kate Beckinsale won't return my calls, Kathy usually does this (or she did until she read the last sentence). I don't

The full ingredients must remain secret to protect your sanity . . .

know if the goo actually opens up the chest and throat, or if it just smells so gawdawful we think it must be good for us.

6) Drink terrible things—like cod liver oil, or hot tea with hunks of honey that slide down your throat like a raw oyster. Or anything made with so many lemons that your teeth get sharp as a werewolf's and your gums squeak each time you speak. To qualify in this category, the drink must fulfill the following criteria: (a) someone must tell you it's for your own good, (b) the full ingredients must remain secret to protect your sanity

(not to mention your gag reflex), and (c) it must taste so vile that you get zit-sized goosebumps all down your arms.

Okay. So you've moaned and drunk and been rubbed. You've swallowed vitamins with hunks of garlic while watching Skye tell Rory that her baby is really her uncle because Sequoia and Autumn were actually amnesiac Siamese twins joined together at the eye-shadow. But you still have that cold, and you're considering coming to visit me with a blunt object. As it happens, I have one more home remedy, sent to Joseph Graedon, author of *The People's Pharmacy*, by a reader from Minnesota:

". . . and if that doesn't work, place hand over nose and mouth and do not breathe for several minutes . . ."

That should do it. At least until I can get out of town.

Rx: Take with a grain of salt and call me in the morning . . .

Pagosa Springs Sun

Author's Comments

When I left teaching to pursue a writing career, my perceptions of the process were both idealistic and unrealistic. I initially cranked out short fiction—primarily horror, some mystery/suspense—and soon discovered the capricious nature of little fiction magazines and their editors. One of them had me rewrite a story three times, including his own view of how the plotline should play out. I was desperate; I had no pride; I retooled the whole thing to match his preferences. He rejected it anyway.

Then I saw an ad in the local newspaper for a features writer. Early on everything was assigned, until I slipped in a humor piece, which got a favorable response. From there I evolved into writing primarily humor, and eventually into writing what I wanted in what became a weekly features/column hybrid. Over a couple of years I wrote close to 100 pieces in this vein.

Most of the nonfiction came from my own experiences, usually exaggerated a bit for humor. I learned that a self-deprecating persona worked well with readers, so in most of my stories I made fun of myself. Some attempts at satirizing other targets weren't as well received.

"Home Remedies for the Sick Season" was based on my experiences with a persistent case of the flu one winter, exaggerated but with reality at its core. It was written straight through in longhand—always my first draft format—with only some cross-outs and rewording here and there. I don't necessarily recommend this seat-of-the-pants, non-outlined, non-organized approach, but it often worked for me in short form writing, though not as much with novels.

A writing position with a newspaper can be difficult to obtain, especially at larger papers, which often consider only college grads with degrees in journalism. And once on staff, it can be equally difficult to move from reporting assignments into any sort of regular column format.

Clearly there was serendipity involved in my connecting with a small town newspaper—possibly the best way to break in for a would-be columnist. No credit to me in terms of persistence or initiative, and all credit to my editor at the time for loosening the reins and letting me take the original format in a different direction.

It was a highly enjoyable time, and a good learning experience.

—Kris Franklin

My Mom's Song

by Barbara A. Stoughton

Bless this house, O Lord, we pray
Make it safe by night and day

The familiar refrain flows directly from the radio into my heart. As always, it paints me a picture—not the one my mother dreamed of, but one precious to me nonetheless.

Researchers tell us the sense of smell is our most potent memory trigger, but for me it's always been music. Just a few bars of an old song instantly transport me to another time or place, a recollection as clear and bright as if projected on a movie screen. Often, they're not important events, but snippets from ordinary days.

I first remember hearing *Bless This House* during World War II, when all the world wished for firm and stout walls that would keep "want and trouble out." We sang it at school and heard it on the radio. This was a time when everyone was acutely aware how precious homes and families were, and the lyrics spoke straight to my mother's soul.

Author Bio

Barbara A. Stoughton writes fiction and very occasional poetry, but is most successful with the personal essay, either serious or humorous. Her work has been published in travel and camping magazines, and frequently appeared in what was formerly the *Detroit Free Press'* Sunday magazine.

Poignant Message

She probably found it especially meaningful because she'd lost her own mother before age 5, and was cared for by an assortment of housekeepers and stepmothers. She'd envied friends with "normal" families, and was determined to create for her own children the ultimate snuggery.

Mother, in her apron, sits at the piano, softly singing and playing.

So though she wasn't particularly musical, Mom resolved to learn to play *Bless This House* on our piano, which wasn't particularly musical, either. Enthralled with the square baby grand's handsome ebony finish and the notion of a piano in the house, she'd paid the princely sum of $5 for it at auction. But the carved grapevines adorning its generously proportioned legs couldn't make up for its cracked soundboard.

Mom read music haltingly, identifying notes one by one and then counting up and down the keyboard until she hit the right one. But she persevered day after day until she was able to play *Bless This House* from beginning to end—with both hands!

Musical Gathering?

Looking back, I'm sure she cherished hopes that if she learned to play it well enough, we might all spontaneously gather around her, perhaps on Thanksgiving or Christmas, and sing together—a perfect Norman Rockwell moment.

At the time, I was a typically self-involved young teenager, and the idea never occurred to me. I wish we'd done it. I'd cherish that memory now as much as she must have wished for it.

She succeeded, though, in creating another indelible memory. Hearing that nostalgic song, it's as if I'm once again standing in the entryway of my childhood home, just back from school.

The glow from the lamp at the piano holds back late fall's afternoon shadows, and supper's cooking in the kitchen. Mother, in her apron, sits at the piano, softly singing and playing. And I'm surrounded by a sense of home as comforting as a warm embrace.

Country Woman

Author's Comments

I began writing as a bored nine-year-old who had run out of things to read and decided to write my own stories. I haven't stopped scribbling (and reading) since! I was on the staff of my high school paper and college literary magazine. Here in our medium-sized city I belong to an active group of about ten writers, all of whom work in different fields. We meet once a month to share and critique one another's creations, and find it extremely helpful.

"My Mom's Song" originated as a short bit of memorabilia for my mother's funeral, and was later expanded for possible publication. As with most of my pieces, I find it hard to re-read without making some changes, so it would be difficult to say how many revisions it has had.

—Barbara A. Stoughton

Lake Superior, Winter Dawn

by Gustave Axelson

"Come, let's go down to the lake to see the sunrise."

The words wake me from contented early morning slumber. Opening my eyes just slightly, I see that predawn light has cast silhouettes of the dresser and chair, strewn with winter clothing, on the bedroom wall.

"Come on, I've got some coffee brewed. If we leave now we can still catch it." This time the words are accompanied by the frosty fog of the speaker's breath. That tells me it's cold in the cabin. Damn cold. And, no doubt, colder still outside.

The speaker is my friend Ruurd, who along with his wife, has joined my wife and me for a weekend getaway. The lake Ruurd speaks of is mighty Superior, notorious for frigid waters even in July. In December it lashes out with a frozen arsenal of snow, ice, and gales that penetrate even the thickest pair of long johns. The day before, with the sun at full mast, I went down to the lake and came back with my nose hairs frozen and my eyelids nearly sealed by frosted lashes.

"Well, you can stay here and sleep if you want, but I'm not going to miss the sunrise," Ruurd whispers with just a hint of annoyance in his throaty Dutch accent.

I'm now awake enough to fully appreciate how warm and snug I am under my blankets, my wife's head buried in my shoulder. She yawns, rolls over on her side, and nestles her head deep into her pillow for a few more hours of sleep.

In one hurried motion, I pull back the covers and leap out of bed. My bare feet hit the wooden floor with a resounding slap and report back that the cabin is indeed quite cold.

Ruurd seems pleased with my decision. "There you go," he says, "you won't be sorry. Now get dressed, let's get going, we don't have much time."

Moments later, I'm swishing down a wooded ridge to the lakeshore. I don't really remember getting dressed, or stepping into my cross-country skis. I do remember the thermometer's reading on a tree outside the cabin—minus 20 degrees.

At this point, all I'm aware of is the stinging numbness of my cheeks and nose. With a stiff arctic wind, the lake warns me to turn back. Cold air fills my lungs, and they protest with a choking cough. I momentarily stop to lean against a tree and regain my breath.

"What's wrong? Are you alright?" Ruurd yells from 50 yards ahead. "Let's go. We're almost there."

The last stretch down the ridge drops

Author Bio

Gustave Axelson is the full-time managing editor of *Minnesota Conservation Volunteer*—the official magazine of the Minnesota Department of Natural Resources. He is also a part-time freelance writer who has been published in *Men's Journal*, *Backpacker*, the *New York Times*, *Minnesota Monthly*, *Wisconsin Trails*, *Minneapolis Star-Tribune*, and the anthologies *Voices for the Land* and *The Talking Stick*.

nearly 200 feet. It requires little effort from me, other than keeping my skis in Ruurd's tracks. But the brisk pace of coasting downhill amplifies the wind chill. My teeth are chattering as I reach the bottom of the ridge. Ruurd mentioned none of this when he asked me to go see the sunrise. Then, I find out what else he failed to tell me.

He didn't say anything about the magnificent diamond sculptures the lake carves along its shore. Each sharp point of rock is perfectly rounded by several inches of ice.

I'm reclining on the icy rocks just as if I were at home on the couch, watching football on a Sunday afternoon.

Shafts of ice the diameter of a baseball bat shoot down from the rocks, forming spectacular icicles.

He didn't mention the ice-glazed birch trees that face Superior, with their thin branches bowed by heaps of snow. Chickadees and nuthatches and downy woodpeckers flit among the trees as they carry on their morning business. I'm sure they've something to say, but their chatter is muted by the relentless crashing of the lake's waves.

Ruurd never said a word about the giant, jagged boulders of ice floating in the lake. The bergs collide with a brittle crack each time a new wave readjusts them. Above all, he is guilty of not telling me about the sun's lakeside magic—the rays of glorious rose and orange and blazing gold. The rays refract through the ice on the trees and rocks, filling my eyes with brilliant, piercing white sparkles and glints.

"Care for some coffee?" Ruurd offers. "I made it with steamed milk and chocolate, just like we used to do in Holland."

I take off my gloves so my chilled hands

can feel the toasty steel thermos; the steam rising from its mouth looks as inviting as a roaring fire. I hold the thermos close to my face for a moment to thaw my cheeks before taking a swig and feeling the coffee's pleasant burn roll down my throat.

"You see how wide the wolf's paws are . . ."

"Is it too strong?" he asks.

It is on the bitter side, despite its milky shade of brown. But it's also hot. And my teeth are no longer chattering.

"No, it's perfect," I say.

We speak in hushed tones. Amid this crystalline palace, it almost seems inappropriate to speak at all. I take a second sip of coffee, then remove my hat and untie my scarf. The stiff wind blowing off the lake has mellowed into a gentle breeze.

Ruurd points out the tracks of a timber wolf that wind along the tree line on the shore. A former wildlife preserve director, he knows about the north woods and its inhabitants.

"You see how wide the wolf's paws are, how his tracks only depress a few millimeters into the snow? Their paws are designed to give them excellent flotation," he says. I nod in agreement, though I don't think he noticed.

"Now you see these deer tracks? Look how their hooves sink so deep. They don't have a chance, struggling through the snow while wolves run on top of it."

He pauses to stare out at the lake for a moment.

"Then again, deer don't really belong up this far north. This is supposed to be caribou country."

I listen to Ruurd's story about the hardships of timber wolves and deer in winter. Then our conversation wanders to other topics—the canoe trips we hope to take this summer, what a great life it would be to work as a sailor on a Lake Superior freighter ship, how we met our wives.

As the talk dwindles, I notice the coffee thermos is empty and I have taken off my jacket and balled it up under my head as a pillow. I'm reclining on the icy rocks just as if I were at home on the couch, watching football on a Sunday afternoon. The only chill I feel is at my fingertips, wrapped around the thermos that is now filling with falling snow.

"Well, we better get going," Ruurd sighs. "The girls will be up soon." My jacket and hat, gloves and scarf, feel heavy now. The sun has been sucked into the gray, snowy clouds that have moved over the lake. I push on my pole to start the ski back to the cabin, and a gust of wind sneaks down my collar to send a shiver down my back. A few swishes of my skis, and my cheeks are numb again.

Minnesota Conservation Volunteer

Author's Comments

The idea for this essay was spawned by my desire to experiment with using fiction story elements (dialogue, symbolism) in a nonfiction essay. As I reflected on skiing down to Lake Superior's shore at dawn, and read over my notes (I always keep a pad of paper handy and write down notes from any experience that even remotely could end up in my writing), I saw a parallel pattern between removing my gloves, scarf, and hat and how I emotionally "warmed up" to the idea of skiing down to Superior on a bitterly cold day.

I also tried to get vivid and rich with the descriptions of the lake, the ice, the cold, the birds, yet I didn't want to get too syrupy or self-absorbed in flowery writing.

My first draft was much longer, but in editing I deleted all detailed descriptions that didn't advance the story. Sometimes first-person narratives are stuffed with compound adjectives and pretentious verbiage seemingly because the author is impressed with their own creative writing ability.

The final version of the essay was intended to be a gear-shifting experience for readers—from lots of details about the cold cabin to a brisk account of skiing down the hill to a vivid portrait of the icy crystalline creations by the shore—all flowing in the direction of a central point: When the opportunity presents itself to get up and watch the sunrise, no matter how inclement the weather, you better damned well get up and do it.

—Gustave Axelson

A Christmas Farewell

by Diana M. Amadeo

I grew up in the cornfields of Iowa in a community so tiny that it rarely made the maps. Nestled between then rural Des Moines and the farms of Ankeny was Carney. The community was composed of a handful of well-spaced homes, a white clapboard chapel and a tiny grocery store. Most of the town was cornfields. Acres and acres of cornfields. There was also a tavern, where some of the local people hung out, but my parents simply used it as a focal point for out of towners to be aware of the turn of our road. The tavern was usually decorated for Christmas. Our old house on the gravel road was decorated, too. Especially that last Christmas.

Our last Christmas at the old house was planned well in advance, as many of us had to travel a great distance and coordinate busy schedules. My folks, looking a bit grayer and more frail than our last visit, greeted us warmly at the front door and ushered us quickly in from the frigid outdoors. My nine brothers and sisters, their spouses and children were already there. The large two-and-a-half story farm house was filled with laughter, hugs and chatter. It was to be our last great hurrah. The old house had been sold.

That big old white house with the blue shingles and matching trim was three quarters of a century old. Mom and Dad bought it along with its dormant fields and adjacent apple orchard before I was born. They planned to fill it with children and memories. And they did.

Near the giant swing set was a "clubhouse."

There was a railroad track that ran alongside the dormant field. It was lined with trees, barbed wire and raspberry bushes. Each summer we'd put pennies on the tracks and in the fall, show off the results to our friends in the city school where we were bussed. The squashed pennies were done when we were supposed to be picking berries for Mom. When we finally did tend to our duties and competed with the bees for the berries, Mom would reward us with raspberry jelly, jam or pie.

Dad built a fifteen-foot swing set with his own hands from the remnants of metal and chains obtained from the welding shop that he ran. He placed the swing set next to the clothesline pole on the edge of the yard. We spent hours aloft on the swings during the long hot summers. Near the giant swing set was a "clubhouse" with sliding windows and a door that padlocked shut that Dad constructed from scrap lumber. The boys painted it to match the house. From the clubhouse,

Author Bio

Award-winning writer Diana Amadeo received the 2006 Catholic Press Association Book Award. Her essays have appeared in five *Chicken Soup for the Soul* books. She also sports a bit of pride in having 450 published pieces with her byline. Her book, *My Baby Sister Is a Preemie*, for ages four to eight was published by Zonderkidz.

we fought wars between ourselves and neighborhood kids, often using the building as a fortress against the onslaught of flying green apples from the orchard.

The big old house with its worn wooden steps and inviting front porch embraced its occupants like a warm cloak. Its distinctive odor, rustic charm and antiquated beauty made everyone who entered feel safe and secure. Each room held a special significance. The back entryway, with its saggy floor and worn threshold, reminded me of the time, as a teenager, that I missed the 11 P.M. curfew and found the back door locked. At 6 A.M. my mother found me shivering, huddled next to the door. Concerned and apologetic, she awoke each sibling on the "out" list to determine who was the last one in that had locked me out. Under pressure, my brother blurted out that he had arrived home after 5 A.M. and that I wasn't asleep at the door then. Needless to say, we were both grounded.

> ## For eight years I had tortured the rest of the household with my lessons.

In the kitchen next to the stove was a worn enameled sink, its basin blackened by years of washing away the porcelain. Being a chauvinistic household, after meals, the girls would grab a towel to wipe the dishes that Mom washed, while Dad and the boys retired to watch black and white TV. Many great conversations were held at that sink. And lots of lectures, too. I probably learned more about the evils of sin, sexual promiscuity and Catholic Doctrine at the sink than in all my years of parochial school.

We had three large bedrooms dubbed appropriately, *The Girls' Room*, *The Boys' Room* and *Mom and Dad's Room*. Mom and Dad's Room wasn't all that private. There always seemed to be an occupied crib in the room.

Sometimes, there were two.

In the dining room, beside the two large wooden tables, there was an old, upright piano. For eight years I had tortured the rest of the household with my lessons. But I wasn't alone. All ten of the children took lessons on piano, steel guitar, flute, trumpet, recorder, clarinet, drums or accordion. None of us became masters, but there was a secret wish we all shared: to be half as good as we were in our prime. Like now.

"It's time, Diana," my mother said, finding me deep in thought next to the lighted painted nativity. "Everyone is ready."

Sure enough, I could hear the laughter and giggles of the family gathered around the piano. Some were warming up their vocal chords, others hamming it up for photographs.

I gave my Mom a quick kiss and walked dutifully through the living room, passed the lighted tree whose pine scent left me heady. The crowd of family members parted with cheerful comments like, "It's about time," "We've been waiting for an hour" and "Fashionably late as always." I grinned as I sat on the piano bench and fumbled through the music to find just the right song. And then I began to play, with my family joining in song.

"There's no place like home for the holidays."

Teachers of Vision

A Christmas Farewell

Author's Comments ───────────────

I can't recall ever not writing. I grew up scribbling my thoughts on paper and my parents, thank heavens, encouraged it. As a child, I had a favorite writing spot in the girls' bedroom behind the dresser next to the heating vent. I could completely shut out all the sounds of the noisy, busy household while writing in my journal. After many calls for supper, my parents knew just where to look when I failed to come to the table.

It's no surprise that "A Christmas Farewell" came from a place where I felt so safe, secure, and creative. The greatest challenge I had writing this piece was keeping within a 1,000-word limit. (Magazines are requiring much shorter essays these days.) Having published with *Teachers of Vision* before, I kept the simple, folksy style that landed me an acceptance there previously.

Usually with short pieces like this, I put all my words on paper and then edit. I work from an outline only on larger pieces. (For example, the book I am working on now was completely outlined before the story began.) Manuscripts under 1,000 words I usually send out cold. For larger pieces, I query the publisher before wasting time, energy (gas and my own!), and shipping costs on a story they don't care to see.

I write from the heart for myself and for those I love. For me, technical pieces have no soul, and it shows in my writing. I'd rather draw you to tears, make you sigh, or find you speechless after reading my piece than attempt to dazzle you with my perceived intelligence. In a world of chaos, I wish to convey peace and hope through my actions and words.

—Diana M. Amadeo

Mind the Migraine

by Judy Gruen

From the time the earliest cave men and cave women scraped their knuckles across the savannah, people have suffered from headaches. I bet that even way back then, many of these afflictions were induced by job stress. After all, cave people lacked many of the modern amenities that make careers today so relaxing, such as computer solitaire and company-mandated diversity training. Experts suspect that other headaches may have been caused by the sneaking suspicion that indoor plumbing was still 6,000 years away.

As a chronic headache sufferer, I am exceedingly grateful that medical science has evolved from the days when headaches were cured by drilling a large hole in the skull to ward off evil spirits or demons. Sure, this was an extreme treatment, but it had its own weird genius: after the cave doctor aimed his non-sterilized spear at your cranium, you would never have another headache as long as you lived, which was probably about three seconds.

However, it didn't take long for clever Cro-Magnon physicians to perceive that this approach to pain management also put a serious crimp on their monthly billables, so they began to devise other headache treatments, such as Lydia Pinkham's Vegetable Compound and Ray-Ban sunglasses with anti-reflective coating. Yet inexplicably, headaches continued to plague mankind, and especially womankind, who out-headache men nearly two to one.

Having My Head Examined

I have had headaches—and their big, ugly brother, migraines—since the Reagan administration. Some of them even seemed to last as long as the Reagan administration. Lately, however, they have gotten a lot worse, so I decided to go to the doctor.

"What brings you here today?" the doctor asked.

"Migraines," I answered.

"How long have you had them?" The doctor held her pen aloft, poised to write my answer.

"Since the Reagan administration," I answered.

She stared at me in disbelief. "That long?"

"I was waiting for my HMO to approve the office visit," I explained.

I hoped that my doctor would offer some relief for my noggin-banging, vision-blurring, nausea-inducing plague, so I asked her to order lots of expensive tests. Even if the tests yielded no helpful information, at least it would make me feel that I was starting to get my money's worth out of our crippling monthly health insurance payments. They don't call them "premiums" for nothing.

My doctor obliged me by sending me off for an MRI, which made me feel important. After doffing my street duds and donning

Author Bio

Judy Gruen is the author of three award-winning humor books, including *The Women's Daily Irony Supplement*, and several hundred essays and features.

the kind of flimsy medical gown that makes you feel deep regret at the invention of the fluorescent bulb, I followed the technician into the lab. The MRI was a huge machine that would suck me into its narrow tunnel and take photos of my head. The test results

Eliminate stress? Put the kibosh on MSG and chocolate . . . ?

would determine whether I was doomed to live with migraines for no reason, or whether I was just plain doomed.

I lay down on the table, and noticed with some anxiety that my young technician wore a sweatshirt emblazoned with "Nightmare on Elm Street" on the front, surrounded by a medley of ghoulish skulls.

"You're not claustrophobic, are you?" she asked.

"Who me? Of course not," I said as she pressed a button that zipped me deep into the bowels of the machine. But once inside, I immediately discovered that I was absolutely, clinically, and irredeemably claustrophobic. There wasn't even enough room for oxygen molecules, let alone a human being.

"You okay in there?"

"No!"

"Great!" she said. "Get ready for the first photo. It'll last about forty-five seconds and it may be a smidgen loud."

"Help!" I cried from the depths, forcing myself to take deep, slow breaths to avoid a total freak-out. The technician instructed me to lie still (as if there were room to even blink) and close my eyes. The "smidgen loud" noises were in fact blasts of jackhammers in my ears. Over the next half-hour, my Nightmare on Elm Street technician gave me gentle warnings about each upcoming photo and the "slightly loud" noises I might notice.

I had always thought of photography as

a quiet process (except for when the people being photographed all shout "cheese!"), but these photos sounded like car alarms and jam sessions with Metallica and Iron Maiden, each vying to see who could snap one another's eardrums the fastest.

Although I hadn't had a migraine when I arrived, the jackhammering and heavy metal symphony in my ears ensured that I left with a whopper.

Two Aspirin and . . .

For several days afterward, I waited anxiously for the results. Finally, the doctor called.

"Your MRI is fine," she said.

"Are you sure?" I asked. If this were true, I could stop divvying up my good jewelry among relatives. "What else do you recommend?" I asked.

"Try to avoid stress. Also, try eliminating caffeine, wheat, cheese, MSG, nitrates, and chocolate from your diet. Then call me in two weeks."

Eliminate stress? Put the kibosh on MSG and chocolate, two of my favorite food groups? The very idea made the ancient cave doctor remedy of spearing my cranium look good in comparison. On the other hand, if I had to live with migraines, perhaps I'd ask to become the poster child for the National Headache Foundation. Who knows? It might at least help with book publicity.

I am happy to report that since my MRI, I have not had a single migraine. I know it won't last, but based on my self-diagnosis, I attribute this felicitous trend to a surge in my consumption of MSG and chocolate.

Just don't tell my doctor.

Stitches for Patients

Author's Comments

This story emerged as all my stories do: from my own life. I'd suffered from migraines for more than 20 years—why not at least try to squeeze these painful lemons into lemonade?

I don't remember how I found *Stitches for Patients*, but I keep up subscriptions to online newsletters for writers, and I also sometimes Google various topics I'm writing about, because you never know what you'll find.

I hate outlines and never use them, but I revise each piece at least three or four times before sending it out. Let a column sit for a day or two after you think it's finished and don't look at it! You'll be amazed at how much you can improve it when you return to it with fresh eyes.

I also welcome the challenge of reslanting older material for newly discovered markets. For example, I write for a lot of websites and magazines featuring Jewish content. I can add some Jewish references to almost any piece and re-sell for these markets.

One of the biggest mistakes beginning writers make is sending material to a market that has no use for it. You have to know the readership, whether the publication takes freelance work, and what its editorial needs are. This information gathering takes time. Don't rush your work. Take the time and care to show you're a pro!

—Judy Gruen

The Tortilla Cycle

by Rebecca Allen

Rosa can, and does, make tortillas in the dark. The ancient generator needs a new belt and a prayer and can't always be counted on to power the light bulbs of Unión Victoria, the Guatemalan village where I live with Rosa and her two young daughters. Rosa's husband works in Florida. In his absence Rosa carries on, feeding her pigs, hauling firewood, planting crops, and making three meals a day. In the midst of all this, she insisted on teaching me to make tortillas.

Guatemalan corn tortillas bear almost no resemblance to the machine-made flour variety sold in U.S. grocery stores. Each tortilla requires a careful process of patting and turning the dough by hand into a pliable disc approximately three inches in diameter. When this is done to satisfaction—no thick center, no cracked edges—Rosa places the dough on a *comal*, a hot clay griddle balanced on three stones above a wood fire. After thirty seconds or so, she flips the tortilla by pressing her calloused fingers into the dough until they stick, allowing for a quick inversion. The comal fills quickly as Rosa scoops another egg-sized ball of dough from the grinding stone with a practiced swipe and begins to slap it flat between her palms. She's fast: the average Guatemalan woman prepares 170 tortillas each day. And she's a patient teacher. After four months of minor burns, singed arm hairs, and irregular blobs suitable only for the pigs, I could produce—albeit slowly—a consistently circular and even stack of steaming tortillas.

Making the tortillas is only one in a cyclical series of tasks. Rosa plants the corn. She harvests and dries the cobs, tying the husks into pairs to dangle like ballet slippers under the tin roof blackened by years of smoke. Every afternoon, she shells corn into a pot of

Here, corn is the stuff of life.

boiling water where it cooks for over an hour until it is soft enough to be ground into dough, or *masa*. The electric mill down the road grinds the corn in thirty seconds; otherwise, when the generator fails, Rosa bends over the grinding stone, passing over and over the kernels until she's satisfied with the consistency. Finally, she begins to pat out the tortillas that give her strength to plant more corn for more tortillas.

At first, my body rebelled against facing yet another meal of beans and tortillas, or greens and tortillas, or anything at all and tortillas. Little distinguishes breakfast from lunch and lunch from dinner besides the position of the sun. But our simple meals have

Author Bio

Rebecca Allen returned from Guatemala in 2006 and makes her home in Seattle, Washington. She works at a local community organization, El Centro de la Raza, as an advocate for people applying for U.S. citizenship. Much to her chagrin, Rebecca hasn't made tortillas in months . . . but she still knows how.

quietly grown on me. I imitate Rosa as we eat with our hands, breaking off pieces of steaming tortilla to scoop the food from our bowls to our mouths.

Here, corn is the stuff of life. According to the K'iche' Maya creation legend, the gods formed human beings of masa. Now, to strengthen their bodies and show respect for the gods, the people must plant, tend, harvest, dry, grind, and eat their sacred plant. In K'iche', *wa*, the word for "tortilla," also means "food." To invite a guest to the table, the host says, "Let us eat our tortillas." The other food is inconsequential.

Yet much to the astonishment (and ultimate disbelief) of my Mayan friends, the vast majority of U.S. Americans don't eat corn tortillas, much less at every meal. Then just what *do* we eat, they want to know. I try to explain that we combine several different types of food for the same meal, assign certain foods to specific meals, and rarely eat the same food twice in one day. Despite my elaborate verbal platters, they remain puzzled. "But aren't you hungry?"

As we eat together, Rosa occasionally asks me what I'll do when I return to the United States. Initially, I failed to understand her. "Where will I live? Or work?"

A giggle escaped her. "No, for your tortillas," she reminded me gently as I took one from her outstretched hand. "You'll miss them."

Orion

Author's Comments

Other than short prose pieces published in school and church publications, "The Tortilla Cycle" was my first attempt at professional publishing. I write mostly narrative nonfiction, and this piece evolved during two years I spent in Guatemala as a human rights accompanier. I don't remember any particular challenges with the writing process; it was an idea I'd been mulling over for a while, and the material came naturally.

I chose *Orion* on a whim—I had limited access to reading material in Guatemala, and I'd recently seen a beautiful issue of the magazine. In hindsight, I wish I had used *Orion*'s submission guidelines during the writing process instead of afterwards. With *Orion*'s helpful editing staff, I cut the piece in half and eliminated a political paragraph about NAFTA's connection to corn tortillas. In about five revisions, the article evolved from a political piece into a brief, detailed description of something very specific: the centrality of corn tortillas to the Guatemalan life.

As you prepare to submit your work, I recommend patience (it took six months to hear back from *Orion*!) and passion. I care so much about Rosa and her tortillas that every part of the long publishing process was worth it to tell her story.

—Rebecca Allen

Turning Heads

by Sharon Wren

If you drive this summer along Interstate 5 near East Moline, Ill., you may want to bring your camera to capture an amazing sight—rows and rows of sunflowers, their yellow heads offering a sharp contrast in color from the usual corn and soybeans. For the past few years Steve and Michael Urbaniak have planted the half acre of organic sunflowers on part of their farm. "It's just mainly off the highway so people can see them when they go back and forth to work," says Michael. "We've had so many people want to take pictures as they were driving by."

The National Sunflower Association (NSA) reports that the combination of demand for healthy oils for producing potato chips and the growing popularity of in-shell sunflower seeds has pushed new-crop sunflower prices to an all-time high. "The demand for sunflower has never been stronger," says Lance Russell of Hays, Kan., president of the Kansas Sunflower Commission and an NSA board member.

The Urbaniaks' sunflowers started as an experiment. "About three or four years ago I asked Dad if we could plant sunflowers for the heck of it," says Michael. "I went to pick up the seed and they said my 10-pound order

would cover 10 acres. We just planted them and experimented. If it does work out that we can harvest them, we'd like to start selling them as bird seed to neighbors."

Sunflowers have a long history of being part of people's diets. Native Americans who lived in present-day Arizona and New Mexico may have cultivated sunflowers as far back as 3000 B.C. Besides snacking on the seeds, they used the flower to make dye for textiles and body paint and used the oil for skin and hair. Spanish explorers brought the sunflower back to Europe, where it became immensely popular in Russia. While the Orthodox Church of Russia forbade the use of many foods during Lent and Advent, especially those with high levels of oil, it did not forbid the consumption of sunflower oil. By the early 1800s, Russian farmers were growing over two million acres of sunflowers yearly. Today Russia is an international leader in the production of sunflower seeds.

Sunflower seeds are good sources of vitamin A, protein, folate, selenium, copper, zinc, iron and fiber. Nutritionists recommend eating a 3-ounce serving of seeds every day to help maintain heart health. A quarter-cup serving of sunflower kernels (the seeds minus the shell) contains 190 calories, 4 percent of the daily recommendation of calcium, 20 percent of the daily recommendation for vitamin E, 15 percent of the daily recommendation for folic acid and 2 grams of fiber.

Besides being a healthy snack, "sunflowers are easy to grow, and there are lots of great colors out there, not just the yellow ones,"

Author Bio

Sharon Wren has been writing professionally since 1995, but she has enjoyed writing since grade school. Her writing has appeared in numerous magazines and local newspapers.

says Duane Gissel, Iowa State University Extension Horticulturist in Scott County, Iowa. The Burpee catalog alone has 31 varieties, including pink and double dwarf red. Sunflower seeds can be started indoors but are easier to plant directly in the ground after the last spring frost. Seeds for large flowers should be spaced about six inches apart and about two inches deep in full sun. Seeds for smaller varieties can be planted closer. Sunflowers can withstand some dry weather, but deep, regular watering will encourage deeper roots, which will help keep the plants upright. A good, slow-acting fertilizer will encourage larger flowers and staking will keep them standing tall. Be careful if you plan to use sunflowers in bouquets, as sunflower pollen stains just about anything it contacts.

Naturally, birds are attracted to sunflowers. They just can't keep away from those yummy seeds, whether they're in a home garden with just a few plants or in a field of sunflowers like the Urbaniaks'. "Birds are a problem—probably every wild canary (goldfinch) in Rock Island County comes out for a free meal," says Michael Urbaniak. "We get lots of gigantic bumblebees around the field, too."

Michael says he and his dad still have a few bugs to work out in their sunflower field. "Sunflowers are supposed to turn with the sun but ours only face one way. We're trying to figure out why they don't turn."

For more information, visit the National Sunflower Association website, www.sunflowernsa.com.

Easy Healthy Granola Bars

1/2 cup raw sunflower seeds
2 cups old-fashioned rolled oats
1 cup almonds, sliced
1/2 cup wheat germ
1/2 cup honey
1/4 cup dark brown sugar, packed
1 ounce unsalted butter, plus extra for pan
2 teaspoons vanilla extract
1/2 teaspoon kosher salt
6 1/2 ounces chopped dried fruit, any combination of apricots, cherries or other favorites

Butter a 9x9-inch glass baking dish and set aside. Preheat oven to 350 degrees.

Spread the oats, sunflower seeds, almonds and wheat germ onto a cookie sheet. Place in the oven and toast for 15 minutes, stirring occasionally.

Combine honey, brown sugar, butter, extract and salt in a medium saucepan and place over medium heat. Cook until the brown sugar has completely dissolved. Once the oat mixture is done, remove it from the oven and reduce the heat to 300 degrees. Immediately add the oat mixture to the liquid mixture and the dried fruit. Stir to combine. Put mixture into the baking dish and press down, evenly distributing the mixture, and bake for 25 minutes. Remove from the oven and allow to cool completely. Cut into squares and store in an airtight container for up to a week.

Source: National Sunflower Association. Recipe courtesy of Chef Bob Holloway, Eggland's Best Eggs, Platteville, Colo.

Radish

Turning Heads

Author's Comments ━━━━━━━━

"Turning Heads" was an example of what can happen when you turn in quality work on or before deadline. This article was actually an assignment from *Radish*, one of the first they gave me (and not the last). I had pitched them a couple of article ideas previously, and one on the stress reduction benefits of crafting hit the editor's desk right after he had read an email from a reader, suggesting that someone write a similar article.

My biggest challenge was making sure this article was as good as the previous ones I'd written for *Radish*. A close second was writing an article on a sunflower garden that would be gloriously in bloom when the issue hit the newsstands, but was a big plot of cold mud when the article was written! Fortunately I had pictures of the plot in bloom from the previous year, so I just had to use my imagination and hope there wasn't a natural disaster in the meantime.

—Sharon Wren

An Out-of-This-World Rescue

by Kristin Grant

When Ryan Ballard said goodbye to his orange tabby, Galaxy, on August 27, 2005, he had no idea that within 48 hours, 10 feet of swirling water would fill his New Orleans home. Before leaving, he set out large bowls of food and water and locked the doors and windows, expecting to return two days later as he had done so many times before.

However, once at his evacuation destination, he turned on the news only to discover that the "impossible storm," Hurricane Katrina, had become a reality and New Orleans was right in its path. "I saw that the levees broke, and I thought, 'Oh no, Galaxy!'" he recalls.

For two months, authorities would not allow residents to return to their homes, and Ballard settled in Manitou Springs, Colo. He spent hours on the Internet desperately searching rescue sites. Although he pored through hundreds of photos of orange tabbies, Galaxy was not among them.

Ballard finally got to enter his house the day after officials permitted residents to return. Searching through the rubble of his belongings, he found no signs of life but still helplessly clung to one glimmer of hope.

"There was no Galaxy in the house," he says. "But there was no body, either."

After days of searching throughout the neighborhood for Galaxy to no avail, Ballard had to return to Colorado where he was settling into a new home.

"The moment I saw it, I knew it was him."

Nearly six months after Katrina struck, Jeanette Althans of Animal Rescue New Orleans, who rescued hundreds of pets after Katrina, began feeding a scraggly, orange cat in the Lakeview area. She posted his photo on a rescue website, and received an immediate response from a family from that area who believed the cat to be theirs.

When Althans took the cat to the family, they realized it was a case of mistaken identity, yet they offered to care for him nonetheless. A few weeks later, Althans was going through letters and photos in an attempt to reunite more pets with owners and decided to email Ballard a photo of the recently rescued kitty, who seemed to fit the description he had posted. Ballard was ecstatic. "The moment I saw it, I knew it was him. I emailed her back and said, 'This is Galaxy. This is my cat. Where is he?'"

At the end of April 2006, Ballard went to Galaxy's foster home, and the two were reunited nearly eight months after they last saw each other. "At first he was really happy, and then he was really mad at me," he laughs.

Author Bio

Kristin Grant has more than 150 published articles to her credit, and has won seven national awards for writing, including "Best Magazine Article in 2006," awarded by the Missouri Writers' Guild.

After a few weeks in Colorado, Galaxy was back to his normal self again.

Ballard owns and operates a company that produces magic and puppet shows. His latest venture is a show in the Denver area called Galaxy the Cat's Hurricane Katrina Adventure, which he calls a "glitzy, pyrotechnic experiment in political satire" about the kindness of individuals and the hindrances of bureaucracy.

Cat Fancy

Author's Comments

After meeting a veterinary student who had volunteered at a makeshift animal shelter for evacuated Hurricane Katrina pets, I immediately wanted to document one pet's journey. I located the director of a New Orleans animal league who had orchestrated numerous rescues, including that of a little cat named Galaxy. *Cat Fancy* magazine was my first choice of publication, since it reaches more cat owners than any other "pet-centric" magazine.

Getting in touch with owner Ryan Ballard one year after the query was difficult. He had moved, so I had to contact several people in New Orleans to track him down, which I finally accomplished via email.

The biggest challenge in writing the story was keeping it under the 500-word limit, since I could have easily written 2,000 words about Galaxy's incredible journey. I cut out the parts I thought were too graphic, including how Ryan thought the cat survived by floating in a snake aquarium (and eating the contents!).

I set up the article as a series of chronological events to keep the reader "in the moment" as the story unfolded.

My advice to writers trying to break into freelancing is to make sure the first sentence of their query letters features a solid "hook."

—Kristin Grant

The Conspiracy

by Kathleen Thompson

Until I met Billy Summers, I was convinced that I was a freak: I only wore shoes that were brown or black. No reds, aquas, or pastels for me—persons with wide feet do not wear those colors. Ask any woman you meet what her foot size is, and if it is anything beyond a B width, you can convince her you are clairvoyant, even if her shoes are concealed underneath a luncheon table. You need not see her shoes; they will be brown or black, or a shade thereof. You see, there is a conspiracy in the shoe business: the manufacturers do not like wide feet. Consequently, the few shoes they do make in wide sizes are limited to brown or black.

Because of my handicap I have become a frequenter of shoe stores and quite an authority on shoe salespersons. Those persons fall into two categories—those totally unaware of the conspiracy, and those who are in on it, but who will attempt to sell you shoes of any size anyway, whether they fit or not.

The first category is far more prevalent. I walk into a shop, The Glass Slipper, dreaming of walking out in Cinderella shoes. A young lady in fuschia flats rushes over to me.

"Could I help you, m'am?" I must be her first customer; she is still very happy and anxious to sell shoes.

"Yes, I'd like to try a pair of flats, perhaps in the color you're wearing."

"Of course. What size would that be?" she asks.

"I'm not sure."

She is not sure what to make of this response. She is not programmed beyond fitting concrete sizes. She stares at my brown sandals that are spread out and comfy now after two summers of constant wear. She begins to wring her hands ever so slightly. I realize that I must say more to stop her flustering and floundering.

"Maybe we could try a seven or seven-and-a-half in a C width if you have it," I suggested.

There is no point in trying to explain to her that my foot measures six-and-a-half D with a narrow heel. In her training no such foot exists.

Relieved to have a size to look for, she races off to the back. She returns before I have had time to even start drooling over the new spring pastels that line the display shelves.

"I'm sorry, ma'am, but we don't have that shoe in fuschia in seven or seven-and-a-half C width."

And that's that. No offer to bring out another shoe. No attempt at another color. She's quickly off to seek a more normal foot to fit into a fuschia flat. I leave wearing my brown pumpkins.

Author Bio

Kathleen Thompson writes in various genres. "Nothin' to Cry About" appeared in *REAL: Regarding Arts & Letters*; and "Mother and Child" in *Christmas Is a Season! 2008*. She has published two poetry chapbooks: *Searching for Ambergris* and *The Nights, The Days, 2008*, winner of the Negative Capability Press Chapbook Series. Her full-length poetry book, *The Shortest Distance*, was released by Coosa River Books in January 2009.

The second category of salespersons has had years of coping with freaky feet.

"No problem," one says as she hurries away to the back.

This time I am looking for a pair of dress pumps at The Universe, a very classy store in spite of the odd name. The dress pump is an item usually nonexistent in the shoe wardrobe of folks with wide feet. For dress shoes we must resort to slingbacks, in a size too long, of course, but at least we can tighten the heel strap to keep the shoe from flopping up and down when we walk.

This woman is older and wears her too-dark-for-her-age hair pulled back into a severe bun. She has the air of a person who has had the same job for so many years that customers had better tread softly. Not one to despair easily, I revel in this thought while she is in the back, hoping that her years of experience will benefit me in finding a shoe that fits.

> *"We'll just put this one on the stretcher for a few hours while you finish your shopping."*

I am still holding the Bally pump in burgundy that she is searching for in my size. I touch the curve of leather at the instep. My knees weaken at the idea of wearing this nifty number with my navy suit whose jacket is bound in a burgundy trim. But this one was made for a midget; it is stamped five AAA. I continue to caress its smooth heel as I wander among silver and gold tennis shoes, scores of huaraches in a prism of fall colors, and the skin shoes—alligator, eel, lizard—all with matching bags. I could forego the burgundy for the eel with its inserts of burgundy on the toe.

"And here we are," the fine salesperson says.

My reverie is interrupted, and I try to control my breathing which has become quick and short at the sight of her. She is car-

rying six, maybe seven, shoe boxes. She must have the Bally, and she has probably brought the eel, too, since she knows I am interested in burgundy. I practically knock the boxes from her hand trying to get into the chair to be fitted. She opens the Bally box.

"We didn't have this one in burgundy, but maybe you'd like to try this milk chocolate one. A nice, neutral color. You can wear it with anything."

Yes, I am thinking. I have been wearing brown with everything all of my life. But not to worry. It's only the first box.

I slip my foot easily into the milk chocolate pumps. I stand. There is a one-inch gap between my foot and the back of the shoe.

"No problem," she says. "We only had this in an eight, but we can add an extra innersole and a pad at the heel to keep your foot from slipping."

My hope is slipping now more than the shoe itself, for I recognize the first trick of the trade with this group of salespersons: padding. They have pads of every shape and size made to correct any imperfection in the fit of a shoe. I have tried them all. If they cannot succeed with padding, they can always resort to their second ploy: stretching.

"No problem," she says while forcing my foot with the metal shoe horn into a sassy slingback with a red satin bow on the toe. The heel strap has been loosened to its last notch.

"We'll just put this one on the stretcher for a few hours while you finish your shopping."

A verbal reply is impossible. The pain shooting through my toes is too great. I nod no as I grip the shoe to remove it.

Finally we have only one box left. The burgundy Bally is only a memory, and hope for the eel is diminishing.

"Now this last shoe is a winner. It is a six-and-a-half D, the only one we have left in the store. Every customer who has tried this one returns every fall for another pair. Open stock, you know."

She draws the treasure carefully from its bed of tissue. A black oxford, laces up the front, wedged heel, with an inch-thick crinkly sole. A treasure for bird watchers, maybe. In the tropics, maybe.

And so the conspiracy goes. My conclusions are based on having tried on shoes in every city where I have lived, or even visited.

In London I felt certain that my freaky foot problem could be handled with ease. Friends had said that almost any shop in London would custom make shoes. But the clipped response was always the same.

"Yes, mum, we do make shoes to your individual requirements. But you must return in three months for a proper fitting."

Well, if I could afford a return trip for a proper fitting, perhaps I could just seek a proper cobbler. Surely somewhere on this planet there lives a cobbler with a desire to pound the leather on the last as his ancestors did.

So far I have not met such a cobbler, but I did meet Billy Summers.

Tempting styles were not necessary to lure me into the Naturalizer store on Canal Street in New Orleans: the treasured black oxford had already worn blisters on both my heels.

Having been dismissed by a girl in the first category already (she did not have the pink canvas shoe in my size), I glanced wistfully at the array of summer sandals as I started to leave.

"Have you been waited on, m'am?" Billy asked.

He was nice looking young man, of college age, I thought. He has seen my shoes. He has guessed that they contain freaky feet. He already has boxes of brown and black shoes lined up next to his cartons of pads and his stretching machine.

"Yes," I said weakly. "The shoes I wanted come only in narrow sizes."

Billy smiled as he looked again at my black shoes.

"My mother has wide feet," he said.

I left the store wearing a pair of lavender flats that had no pads and had not been stretched. I did not bother to ask Billy what size they were.

Later in a thank-you note from Billy, he indicated that he had been transferred to a store closer to Tulane with a promotion. This move would make working and going to classes a little easier for him.

A letter of commendation was the least I could do for Billy. He had found shoes for me that fit. Lavender shoes, not brown or black. After all, his mother has wide feet.

And we are not freaks, Billy assured me. We are sisters in this fight against the conspiracy.

Georgia Guardian

Author's Comments

During the early nineties I became bold enough to call myself a writer. I bought a cheap business card saying so, thereby casting off my teacher persona of previous decades. I had a few poems published, a drawer full of potential chapters for a novel, and a few prizes for poems and short stories. When the *Georgia Guardian* began publishing local writers on its Pen & Ink page, I saw this as a byline possibility and began to shape some essays for submission. I chose subjects on which I was an expert, for example, my lifelong search for shoes that fit.

The first draft of this essay was written after a trip to New Orleans where I did buy lavender shoes from Billy Summers. More a journal entry than essay, the original draft was verbose and flabby. Typically, I revise and revise again. At the top of my revision checklist is oral reading. This simple exercise spotlights the deadly writing sins I tend to commit in the haste of early drafts.

—Kathleen Thompson

The Man Who Carved Lincoln

by Richard Bauman

I f you look at it using a magnifying glass, you can discern, between the center columns of the building, the image of President Lincoln seated. On the penny this image is just one-fiftieth of an inch tall, but at the Lincoln Memorial in Washington, D.C., the actual statue is 19 feet high.

While millions of Americans have visited the Lincoln Memorial, and millions of others have seen photos of the seated Lincoln, most people don't know that it was Daniel Chester French who conceived the idea for this unique statue.

French was born in Exeter, New Hampshire, in 1850, but he spent most of his youth in Concord, Massachusetts. There he met and associated with numerous other creative persons including Ralph Waldo Emerson, Henry David Thoreau, Henry Wadsworth Longfellow, and Louisa May Alcott.

There's little doubt that his friendship with these talented persons stimulated his interest in the arts, but his talent for sculpturing seems to have been a natural blessing. In fact, he had minimal formal training in the art of sculpting. May Alcott, Louisa May's sister, taught him the basics of art. He studied for a short time with Dr. William Rimmer in Boston where he learned the principles of anatomy and refined his talent for producing life-like images of persons.

His first opportunity to create a major piece of sculpture came in 1874 when a wealthy member of Concord society left $1000 in his will to the town for the creation of a statue as a memorial to the Minute Men of the American Revolution.

Learning of the gift, French boldly approached the town council and offered to do the statue for no pay if the $1000 was used to buy materials and pay the rent on a studio in which he could work. It took French over a year to finish the seven-foot-tall statue, which like the seated Lincoln, has also been seen by millions.

The Minute Man statue depicts a soldier of the Revolution holding a rifle in his right hand, his left hand resting on a plow handle. His eyes seem to be focused on a distant horizon as if he can hear the sounds of battle and is about to join his comrades in their struggle against the British. The likeness of that statue has appeared on U.S. Savings Bonds, being first used on War Bonds during World War I.

When three million dollars was budgeted by Congress to build a suitable memorial to President Lincoln, French was selected to create the statue that would become the focal point of the shrine.

The most common depiction of Lincoln

Author Bio

Richard Bauman has been writing and selling magazine articles since the early 1970s. He writes travel, history, health, and general interest spirituality articles, and has been published in hundreds of periodicals. *Awe-Full Moments: Spirituality in the Commonplace* is his first book. For more than 12 years, he authored a page-a-day calendar, *Legal Lunacies.*

used in statues at that time was of Lincoln standing. French, however, was determined to create something totally different. He studied hundreds of photos, paintings, and statues already made of Lincoln in order to produce the most life-like image possible. He wanted to show Lincoln as a man of warmth, but one of strength and courage, too.

The assembled statue weighs 175 tons.

Lincoln seated satisfied him more than any other pose, and after completing preliminary sketches, he spent three years making an eight-foot model of the statue, perfecting and refining the details so the full-size version would look as much like the President as possible.

The 19-foot-tall statue was to be carved from white Georgia marble, but that presented a problem. It was impossible to find a single flawless piece of stone large enough for the job. Rather than diminish the quality of the image by using flawed stone, French decided to chisel the statue from 28 smaller but perfect pieces of marble, and then fit them together to create the finished work of art.

Upon completion of all the statue pieces, they were moved to the memorial in Washington and put together. The assembled statue weighs 175 tons, yet French's artistic skills were so fine that the seams between the individual pieces of the statue are invisible unless one knows just where to look for them.

French was 72 years old when the statue of Lincoln finally went on public display. Yet he never retired and continued to create statues and other works of art, in stone, until his death in 1931.

While the Lincoln Memorial is a tribute to a great President, it is also a tribute to Daniel Chester French, one of America's least known, yet finest artists. Incidentally, Daniel Chester French's summer home and studio is located in Stockbridge, Massachusetts, where many of his best-known works were designed. The house, studio and gardens are open to the public.

Journal Plus, The Magazine of the Central Coast

Author's Comments

"The Man Who Carved Lincoln" was the result of visiting the Lincoln Memorial. I was intrigued with the strength of Lincoln evident in the immense statue. I wanted to know more about Daniel French, the man who created it, so I did a lot of research to find out what motivated him to create this particular sculpture.

I overwrite my articles. First drafts are crammed with information. The challenge is to make the final revision interesting and lively, and still within word limitations. I try to see the piece through the eyes of the readers—what information they need from me in the article. It usually takes me three or four revisions before I'm satisfied with an article.

Journal Plus is a regional magazine (Southern/Central California), but I knew the editor sometimes uses national pieces, especially when it relates to a holiday. Lincoln's birthday is in February, so it seemed like a natural tie-in to me. Obviously, the editor thought so too.

Be confident. Act like a professional writer, even if you don't feel like you have "arrived." Submit your writing expecting it to be accepted. But if it is rejected, find another market for it, and send it out again. And write about things that interest you—others will be interested too.

—Richard Bauman

No Place Like Home

by Shirley Raye Redmond

Petals of ash fell softly around me in odd contrast to the brisk wind and the ferocious flames nearby. The sky was so dark and ominous with smoke that the streetlight in front of our house flickered off and on and off again. It was only 2:00 in the afternoon. All of the residents in our small mountain community of Los Alamos, New Mexico, were told via emergency radio broadcasts and automated telephone warnings to evacuate immediately. But this would be no small feat, I knew. Approximately 18,000 of us had to evacuate from the mountaintop that May afternoon. There were only three possible means of escape—and one of them was already cut off by the raging wildfire.

Glancing at the pillars of billowing black smoke, I quickly finished filling all of the birdbaths with water. Already my backyard was a sanctuary for soot-covered robins and squawking, frightened Stellar's jays.

As I was home alone at the time of the evacuation, I knew it would be up to me to save my family's most valued possessions. I scrambled to pack the car, mindful even in my panic of a pattern of paradox. I had abandoned my computer (too big) and seven years of tax papers (who cares?) to make

room for family photos, a zither that had belonged to my husband's Polish grandmother and my recent book contract with Random House that had just arrived in the mail. Then I made a beeline for our teenage son's room.

Jordan was away at school—a cadet at New Mexico Military Institute. I rescued his collection of *Star Wars* cards and the shadow box hanging on the wall near his bed that contains his grandfather's bronze star and other World War II medals. I knew he'd have chosen the same items. At least I hoped so, as I cast a regretful glance at his pinewood derby trophies and his matchbox cars. When I'd crammed everything I possibly could into the car, I called my out-of-town husband to assure him that I was leaving and that I was all right.

Life is more than possessions.

Then I coaxed our aging Scottie into the front seat of the car. Although deaf and nearly blind, Wimsey had been nervously sensing the imminent danger for hours and he didn't hesitate to leave. I was the one that paused in the driveway, taking one last long look at the modest house we'd called home for so many years. I swallowed hard and glanced at the newly planted pansies, their sad faces drooping in the parched breeze. Life is more than possessions, I reminded myself, blinking back tears.

As I joined the long line of evacuees snaking steadily down the steep Main Hill Road, I knew I could and would survive the

Author Bio

Shirley Raye Redmond has sold more than 400 magazine articles, stories, and essays to a wide variety of publications. She's also written a number of award-winning children's books.

destruction of our home. But later that night, reunited with my husband in a motel in Albuquerque, I recognized the incinerated house of a neighbor on the evening news and burst into tears. Never before had I felt so vulnerable, so definitely miserable.

The next morning, longing for coffee and comfort, Bill, my husband, and I staggered wearily into a donut shop. Other Los Alamos evacuees with the same needs were already

"When we're together, that's home."

gathered there. "My place is gone," one man wept. "Everything. We lived in that house for nearly 50 years."

Bill squeezed my hand as my eyes filled with hot tears. Was our house gone too? The fire on the mountain was still blazing out of control. Were we homeless? Would the bank with our checking and savings accounts be burned to the ground as well? How would we be able to start up our home business again? What would we do? Where would we go?

It was a phone call from our son that finally restored perspective for me. Having completed his final exams for the semester, Jordan was anxious to leave school. "I've been watching the fire news on television," he told us. "Can you and Dad please come get me? I want to come home this weekend. Sunday is Mother's Day," he reminded me.

"Honey, we can't go home," I replied with a ragged sigh. "We don't know if we even have a home."

"Is Wimsey with you?" Jordan asked. I assured him that the dog was with us, safe and sound.

"Then the three of you come get me," he said. "And when you get here, we'll all be together. When we're together, that's home."

For a moment, I was speechless. "When we're together, that's home," Jordan had said.

I knew then that no matter what happened, no matter what the fire consumed, I was the most fortunate mother in the world.

Author's note: While our home suffered only minor smoke damage, sadly, more than 400 families—many of them our friends and neighbors—lost all they owned in the Cerro Grande blaze, which raged through the mountains for over two weeks.

Romantic Homes

Author's Comments ———

I selected *Romantic Homes* as a market when I read in a writer's magazine that the publication was looking for essays with holiday themes other than Christmas and Thanksgiving. As our town was evacuated right before Mother's Day, it seemed an appropriate topic for a holiday essay.

This essay was "recycled" from a feature article I did for a Santa Fe newspaper immediately following the fire—which I wrote while still living in an out-of-town hotel, unable to move back home. I basically cut out the general interest facts about my hometown evacuation and focused on the personal aspects of that evacuation.

—Shirley Raye Redmond

Snakes Alive!

by Dean Henson

I think it's safe to say that most people don't like snakes. Virtually nothing in the outdoors is as feared or misunderstood, and the widespread fear of snakes—long nourished by a steady diet of distortions and exaggerations, borders on the irrational.

Snakes are probably maligned and abhorred for a variety of reasons, but it doesn't help that they lack the aesthetic appeal of birds and mammals and tend not to be cuddly creatures. An aversion to reptiles might arise from one's in-home nurturing; if the parents revile snakes, chances are their children will, too. The stealthiness of snakes is unnerving to many, for the thought of a snake lurking about one's feet on a woodland trail or slithering unseen among sleeping bags in camp evokes strong feelings of fear and loathing.

In Kentucky, we have snakes a plenty. They have adapted themselves well to the wide variety of habitats afforded by the state's varied topography. In fact, it is the great diversity of niches, ranging from the cypress swamps of the Jackson Purchase to the rolling hills of the Bluegrass to the mature forests of the Cumberland Mountains that have significantly contributed to their overall abundance.

Author Bio

Dean Henson has been a professional naturalist for more than 20 years. He writes almost exclusively about natural history subjects and his preferred form is the essay.

Behaviorally, these inconspicuous prowlers go their way, quietly living out their lives on their bellies. They appear essentially helpless except for the ability of some to bite. Many smaller species do not even have that recourse, and all are effectively deaf. They have no limbs to aide them in fleeing and must meet all their needs by movements of the head and body.

Nevertheless, though they appear to be discouragingly handicapped and ill equipped for survival, they are, in fact, the most successful of all the reptiles. A highly complex physiological structure amply compensates them for what they lack in visible external attributes.

While snakes are without eardrums and external ear openings, they make up for this insufficiency by being remarkably sensitive to odors and physical vibrations. The forked tongue is a highly specialized organ to aid the snake's ability to smell. It is lightly touched to objects in the snake's path or waved in the air and then retracted for sampling by smell-sensitive organs in the roof of the mouth. As well, being unable to pick up airborne sounds, they detect vibrations through the ground by way of their belly scales.

Depending on the species, some snakes are egg-layers while others are livebearers. In either case, there is no parental care of the young and they are left to fend for themselves from the start. Hatchling constrictors are capable of overpowering prey comparable to their size. Poisonous types are born fully equipped with fangs and venom and are capable of delivering a dangerous bite. From the beginning, young snakelets are well prepared to take on the business of living entirely by their own resources.

The jaws of a snake are unlike those of any other vertebrate. Owing to elastic ligaments and double joints, their construction assures that they have more or less independent movement in all directions.

Copperheads may well be more dangerous than rattlesnakes.

This unique skeletal-jaw structure coupled with extremely distensible skin makes the business of eating more a matter of "crawling around food" than of swallowing.

Of particular interest is the life history of some of the more noteworthy snakes found in Kentucky. Kingsnakes commonly consume other snakes as a significant portion of their diet and will even eat their own kind. Though they don't deliberately seek them, they can consume rattlesnakes and copperheads, if large enough to physically subdue them, and are apparently immune to the venom of both.

The hog-nosed snake has a taste for toads. Though fish, salamanders, frogs, lizards and chipmunks are also on the menu, toads are tops. This works out great for the snake, since nothing else in the natural world wants to eat a toad. Toads have a mildly poisonous secretion covering their skin that makes them unpalatable to the mouths of would-be predators.

Also known as "puff adder" or "blowing viper," hog-nosed snakes are well known for defensive posturing when threatened or disturbed. At first approach, the head is raised and the neck is flattened to double its size. Next come loud hissing sounds and repeated forward striking. If pressed, it will try another tactic—play dead. They roll over on their backs and lie motionless with mouth open and tongue dangling out. This ruse is

accompanied by the smell of decay supplied by vented fluids—all of this from a snake that is completely harmless.

Garter snakes are probably the most common and widely known snakes statewide. It's a bit of an oddball, being one of the few non-poisonous snakes that bear live young (water snakes account for the rest). Though savage when first captured, they become quite docile with a few minutes of handling.

Of the 40-plus species of snakes in Kentucky, a few are poisonous but most inhabit locales less frequently visited by humans. As copperheads frequent a larger variety of habitats than do rattlesnakes, they are the poisonous variety more likely to be encountered by people. Though not considered deadly, copperheads may well be more dangerous than rattlesnakes. While rattlesnakes possess lethal venom, copperheads are notably more irritable and easily disturbed. As a result, they are more likely to bite with a minimum of provocation than the more subdued and passive rattlesnake.

. . . people are learning to respect these marvelous reptiles.

Snakes are often encountered in the most surprising places, especially when water is in short supply. Since most Kentuckians live in rural or semi-rural settings, snake sightings and run-ins are not uncommon. Kentucky's varied snake populations annually suffer much unnecessary persecution at the hands of the misinformed and unknowledgeable. Fortunately, attitudes are beginning to change and people are learning to respect these marvelous reptiles. So, before you reach for a stick or the garden hoe, calmly assess the risks. You may even begin to respect and admire them.

Back Home in Kentucky

Snakes Alive!

Author's Comments ─────────

Much of my work as a naturalist finds me interpreting nature in outdoor settings to the public. These outdoor excursions are often themed or have a specific interpretive goal in mind. Still, every guided hike or outdoor adventure produces unexpected moments of discovery. Encountering a snake is just such a moment, and the occasion is always immersed in a great deal of excitement and, just as often, irrational fear.

As a naturalist, I acknowledge that encountering a snake can be unnerving, and it's wise to exercise caution, as some snakes are poisonous and potentially harmful. However, the overreactions I've observed coupled with erroneous ideas suggest that there is a great deal of misinformation and misunderstanding among people about snakes in general.

It is the job of a naturalist to speak on behalf of natural things that cannot speak for themselves. So, I saw an opportunity to try and elevate the lowly status of snakes in hopes of diminishing their undeserved reputation.

The biggest challenge in writing any natural history piece is getting beyond the science and complexity to reveal the heart of the matter. How can you tell the story that needs to be told without getting bogged down in dry details?

In this way, nature writing is more akin to poetry than prose. If a nature essay is presented as merely a parade of disjointed facts, its power is lost. The author should become a storyteller.

So the primary challenge was to convince readers that snakes are not vile, evil creatures, but rather just another wonderfully specialized life form that seeks only to survive and multiply like all other animals.

I'm essentially an essayist; I write about subjects that almost anyone can relate to so long as they enjoy the outdoors, live in a rural or semi-rural environment, or are concerned about the future of our natural world. Full-color magazines that include feature articles accompanied by "departments" covering subjects like food, books, history, travel, gardening, and nature are tailor-made for well-written essays.

—Dean Henson

Sneaker Obsession Is Baffling

by Karen Kaufman-Orloff

There's something in this country that's getting out of hand and I'm not talking about the presidential race. This is way more important.

I'm talking shoes. Yes, shoes, the things you put on your feet. Or, more specifically, sneakers.

The obsession with sneakers is taking over America. I recently saw a news report about people standing all night in line just to get their hands (or should I say "feet") on a limited edition pair of Nikes.

Another report showed a store in a secret, underground location that sold expensive sneakers. Catering to a specific clientele, who all apparently knew the location of this store, the owners said they didn't want word to get out as to where they were because that would ruin the ambience for their customers. The store didn't even have a phone.

And the prices? Some of the sneakers sold were so high-end, they had to be kept in a locked showcase. One pair was priced at $3,000.

Author Bio

Karen Kaufman-Orloff is the author of three picture books for children, *I Wanna Iguana*, *If Mom Had Three Arms*, and *Talk, Oscar, Please!* A former editor, she has been published in regional and parenting magazines. She writes a weekly column for *The Poughkeepsie Journal* and lives with her husband and family in Dutchess County, New York.

For sneakers? Come on, these aren't exactly Jimmy Choo shoes, although I don't really get that, either—maybe because if I wear anything higher than a one-inch heel I fall off them.

Old Sneakers Modernized

I see the sneaker obsession in my own family. On any of our excursions to the mall, my daughter's eyes often drift to the new lines of Converse sneakers, her current shoe of choice.

These are not the Converses of old, the ones I remember, which, along with Keds, came in about three colors—white, black and maybe navy blue if you could find them in your size.

Now Converse sneakers come in more colors than a bag of Skittles and patterns that can rival a Jackson Pollock painting. There are stars, stripes, hearts, dots and zebra zigzags. Some have pictures of bugs, flowers, people or city skylines on them. Others come in lattice looks or patchwork prints. I even saw a pair of sneakers made out of see-through plastic.

It's all very creative, I guess.

Sometimes, I admit, I even sneak a look at the colorful new foot apparel, wondering if I—a middle-age mom—can pull off wearing that cute little pair of pink and white gingham slip-ons. I get as far as the checkout line before I decide to put them back.

I'll stick with my boring old brown leather loafers.

The Poughkeepsie Journal

Author's Comments

"Sneaker Obsession Is Baffling" came to me, as most ideas do, by observing life and finding humor in just about everything. I had been watching a news program and was struck by how silly it was that an "underground" high-end sneaker store even existed.

Because I write a weekly column for *The Poughkeepsie Journal* there's little time for revisions. I have to be quick! My work process is this: Once I come up with a theme, I jot down various ideas and phrases I want to include. Since they're almost always based on true happenings, I have to brainstorm about the real events that took place and make note of them.

Once I write a first draft, I re-read the piece many times and change, add, or delete unnecessary words. Since I have to keep my columns to a specific word count (400 words), editing is important.

My advice to aspiring writers is to keep a notebook handy, observe everything, and write down interesting tidbits of life. You never know when you'll be inspired to write about them!

—Karen Kaufman-Orloff

Chicken-Necking on the Bay

by Cynthia Rott

Looking for something fun to do with your out-of-town guests or special little friends who are bored? Crabbing with a drop line is the answer. Known around the Bay as chicken-necking, this is a great way to get outside, have some fun and learn some patience. After all, this is one reason why we live in the great state of Maryland. It is also definitely something that is more fun with friends.

The materials needed are few:

1. **String.** We use kite string, or any other all purpose string.

2. **Chicken necks.** They are available at grocery stores, but if we can't find them, we'll use anything handy: liver, hotdogs, etc. It helps to have some little washers or other small weights available because not all baits sink. When desperate, we have tied rocks to the string to sink the bait.

3. **A pole net.** If you do not have one, your neighbors probably would be glad to lend you theirs.

4. **A big bucket or basket.** Your caught crabs don't need water in their bucket, since they will quickly deplete the oxygen in it, but do keep them out of the sun. You don't want to cook them yet.

(Optional items to increase the fun: cold drinks, snacks, a good book, wet wipes, life jackets for the little ones and crab tongs—salad tongs work too, but you might want to retire them from their salad days.)

First, find a place to go. Many communities have piers. If you invite members from a waterfront community for a fun day on their pier and let them know you'll supply the bait and cold drinks, I bet they would love to join you. You can also crab from a boat, if you choose. Or you could find one of the few public piers for this purpose. There is no license needed to be a chicken-necker. And you can take up to two dozen hard crabs per person per day.

> The county's park and recreation department can tell you where a local pier is located that allows crabbing. Sometimes local marinas and waterfront restaurants allow crabbing off their piers if permission is asked—chances of gaining access increase dramatically if the kid makes the request.

The early morning hours seem to prove most fruitful. Start by cutting your string a little more than the depth of the water (10-15 feet seems to work well), tie your bait to the string and drop it in. Remember to tie the other end to the piling or a cleat. Then wait, and wait, and wait . . . I like to rig 8 to 10 lines to increase my odds.

Author Bio

Cynthia Rott has been enjoying chicken-necking in the Bay area since her high school days. Rarely catching enough for dinner, she finds joy in the catching. Her work appears regularly in *Outlook by the Bay* and other local publications.

When you notice the string is taut, slowly, very slowly pull it in. Have the net ready, or a helper to scoop the crab when it's visible from the surface. Quietly and slowly get the net underneath your catch or you'll lose it. That's it! Make sure you measure it if you want to keep it. For males or jimmies, a keeper must be at least 5¼" after July 14. I always let the females go. They are legal to keep, but more regulated. Letting the female go is my way of helping the crab population, and it is easier to just remember 5¼" for males. It is easy to tell which is which, since the males have an elongated apron on their underside . . .

The small ones or the females get gently released back to the water, well away from my bait unless kids are with me, in which case I release next to their bait . . . it is fun to catch them, even if you don't keep them.

When the day is done, if our catch is not enough, I will run to Annapolis Seafood Market to supplement our bounty with more crabs, or for those who don't feel like cracking their meal—crab cakes.

Outlook by the Bay

Author's Comments

The editor of *Outlook by the Bay* requested articles focusing on local appeal or technology. Before I write an article, I find out when the issue will be published and if there is a theme for the issue. "Chicken-Necking on the Bay" would be placed in a summertime issue.

The primary audience of this magazine is "active seniors," so I tried to think like a senior. What fun things could seniors do with their grandkids that both parties would enjoy? As the mother of small children, this part was easy for me: What would my kids like to do with their grandparents? I was keeping with the mantra: Write what you know.

This particular article has a very local appeal and is truly part of summertime in Maryland. I have chicken-necked many times and enjoy writing articles on topics that I am knowledgeable about. Subject expertise reduces the amount of time I must spend researching.

Since I was familiar with the subject, I quickly wrote my first draft. I jotted down a couple of talking points and then began typing. I skipped to the second paragraph as I usually do, because introductions often stump me. (I always return later to write the intro.)

After my rough draft, I went online to see what others had to say about chicken-necking, and to make sure I correctly stated the appropriate regulations. Finally I let the article "sit" overnight, did a final rewrite, and submitted it.

—Cynthia Rott

Plant a Second Season Salad

by Barbara Pleasant

Easy to grow—and beautiful to boot— salad veggies are easy to love. Lettuce and other salad makings are among the first crops to plant in spring, yet their fondness for cool weather also makes them great encore crops for fall. As a self-confessed salad addict, I often spend $5 a week on ready-to-eat gourmet greens when I can't get them from my garden—reason enough to work up a little sweat planting a second season salad garden. It's a simple project that leads to fast rewards. Clear off a patch of ground in a spot that's convenient to water, sow some seeds, and a fall salad patch will start spewing out tasty tidbits in only a few weeks.

What to Grow?

The major player in any salad garden is lettuce (*Lactuca sativa*), which comes in an amazing array of colors and textures. If you have partially used seed packets of lettuce leftover from spring, start with those varieties, because shard-shaped lettuce seeds often lose viability after only a year. Did your spring crop get tall and bitter before you could eat it all? Some of the frilliest lettuce varieties can't wait to bolt when days are getting longer and warmer in spring, but in the fall garden they hold much longer. If you need to buy lettuce seeds, start-

ing with a mixture of varieties is an effortless way to turn your salad garden into a tapestry of colors and textures. All of the mail-order seed companies (See "The Seeds You Need") sell various lettuce blends, often called mesclun, that include a palette of leaf colors and forms.

Spinach makes a great fall salad green, too, and in many climates fall-sown spinach can be left in the garden until spring, when the cold-ravaged plants bounce back with amazing energy. Fast-growing radishes also plump up quickly when grown in the fall, and autumn is the best season to grow buttery-tasting baby beet greens. Scallions are a bit slow to grow from seeds, but you can be assured of a ready supply of tender green onions if you buy a slender bunch at the supermarket, trim the tops back by half their length, and stick them into moist soil. See "Fall Garden Standouts" for even more great greens for your second season salad garden. Finally, stud your patch with a few fast-growing annual herbs including dill, cilantro, and chervil, which sprout and grow quickly enough to provide flavorful snippets for the salad bowl.

Ready, Set, Grow!

All the books say that salad crops need full sun, but up to a half day of shade is beneficial when you're planting in warm, late summer soil. If the best site you have bakes in the September sun, install a shade screen on the west side of your salad patch. A short length of snow fencing or a piece of burlap attached

Author Bio

Award-winning garden writer Barbara Pleasant is the author of *The Complete Compost Gardening Guide*. Her website is www.barbarapleasant.com.

to stakes will do the trick.

Lettuce and other salad greens have shallow roots, so soil preparation is a simple matter of clearing the space of weeds and withered plants, working in a 2-inch deep blanket of compost, and then mixing in an organic fertilizer at the rate given on the label. Spinach is a heavier feeder than other greens, so be generous with the plant food when preparing its fall home.

Caffeine is a neurotoxin that makes slugs writhe to death.

Some say that lettuce seeds need light to germinate, but the light that comes through a one-eighth-inch layer of soil will coax the seeds to life quite nicely. The easiest way to sow the seeds is to scatter them on the surface of a prepared bed, barely cover them with soil, and then pat the surface lightly with your hand. If you have clay soil that tends to form a crust over germinating seeds, cover the seeds with potting soil or compost instead of garden soil. Plant other salad garden crops about a quarter inch deep and at least half an inch apart.

Early fall is often a dry season, and salad greens thrive on moisture, so keeping the soil constantly moist is an ongoing challenge. Immediately after planting, the easiest way to keep the seeded bed from drying out at midday is to cover it with an old blanket or cardboard box on sunny days. Once the seedlings are up and growing, keep a watering can stationed at the edge of your salad patch, and give your babies a cool drink first thing every morning and again just before sunset.

If you think of leaves as solar panels, you'll understand why thinning plants so that leaves of adjoining plants don't overlap is so important. Begin thinning your salad patch as soon as the seeds sprout, and continue to pull up (and eat) crowded babies every few days. Thoughtful thinning also

deters slugs, one of the few pests that bother lettuce and other leafy greens. Unlike large "garden" slugs, which are best trapped with shallow dishes of beer, lettuce slugs tend to be so small and numerous that it's more practical to drench plants with cold, caffeinated coffee or tea at night, when the slimers are active. Caffeine is a neurotoxin that makes slugs writhe to death, but you must get it on them for it to work.

The key to enjoying crisp salad greens is to harvest them early in the day, when the leaves are plumped with water. You can harvest lettuce or mixed salad greens by pulling whole plants, picking individual leaves, or using scissors or a sharp knife to gather handfuls of baby greens. As long as you cut them off one inch above the soil line, the crowns left behind will quickly produce a new flush of leaves. Gather spinach, baby herbs and arugula by pinching off perfect leaves.

Don't worry if an early freeze sneaks up while your salad patch is in full bore. Until the cold weather passes, throw an old blanket over the plants or cover them with a cardboard box held in place with stones or bricks. With protection, your salad veggies can easily survive several nights in the mid-20s. With luck, you may even have fresh salad greens for your Thanksgiving table.

Fall Garden Standouts

Autumn is the perfect season to get to know great greens that are at their best when enjoyed fresh from the garden. These four off-the-beaten-track greens really strut their stuff when grown in the cool, short days of autumn. All are extremely easy to grow.

Arugula (Eruca vesicaria ssp. sativa), also called rocket or roquette, bears dark green leaves packed with savory flavor. When

(cont.)

sown in spring, the thrifty plants quickly bolts a days become longer, but fall-sown arugula seedlings grow into dense, bulky plants that often survive Zone 7 winters. Use young leaves in salads; cook older leaves like spinach.

Corn salad (Valerianella locusta), often called mâche, is a petite little green known for its remarkable cold hardiness. It's safe to let the plants stay in the garden well into winter; they can freeze and thaw repeatedly and still make great additions to salads or sandwiches.

Cress (Lepidium sativum) has a peppery flavor that's made more palatable by consistent cool temperatures. Leaves may be smooth and flat, frilled and curly, or somewhere in between, depending on variety. Tender baby leaves are ready to cut less than a month after planting.

Watercress (Nasturtium officinale) is phenomenally productive when grown in a moist garden bed in the fall. The exuberant plants bear bumper crops of dark green leaves with a mild peppery bite that are great for salads, sandwiches, or as last-minute additions to stir-fries. Plants withstand light frosts but are killed back by hard freezes.

The Seeds You Need

The sources listed here offer collections that make choosing seeds for your fall salad patch less confusing.

Kitchen Garden Seeds (CT), 860-567-6086, www.kitchengardenseeds.com. The "Fall Salad Garden" collection includes packets of 7 great fall salad crops, including a painterly lettuce blend.

Nichols Garden Nursery (OR), 800-422-3985, www.nicholsgardennursery.com. The "Eclectic Eleven" is an economical blend of almost a dozen assorted salad greens.

The Cook's Garden (PA), 800-457-9703, www.cooksgarden.com. The "Salad Fresh Mesclun Cutting Mix" collection includes six excellent salad greens, including arugula and two red and green lettuce.

Grit

Author's Comments

The "Second Season Salad" assignment began as a one-paragraph summary sent to the managing editor of *Grit* along with several other ideas. This was the only one chosen. Because *Grit* is a general interest magazine for rural property owners, it was important to make the material easy for non-gardeners to understand.

Like most articles I write, it began as a simple outline and underwent two major rewrites. Before the final revision, I always let stories rest for two to three days, and then check each sentence for strong verbs and weak adverbs, and review each paragraph for cohesion and flow. It is this kind of attention to detail that wins assignments.

—Barbara Pleasant

The Time Machine

by Kim Kunasek

Last week I grabbed an armful of brown suede and a package of straight pins and set out to finally finish the panels for the French doors in our bedroom. I plugged in the 1968 Singer Selectric, lowered the foot, and joyfully anticipated the five minutes it would take to sew the hems and the opening for the curtain rod. Eager to cross this off my endless list of half-finished household projects, I stepped gently on the pedal. A dull whirr, like a record playing on the wrong speed, followed. To my chagrin, I realized the motor had died.

I felt like a dear old friend had passed away. More than any other household appliance, sewing machines have always played an important part in my family's history. After all, my mom, newly arrived in the United States from Germany, had used a Brother to make curtains, pillowcases, bedspreads, and slipcovers for my parents' modest first apartment above a little grocery store in Deal, New Jersey. A few years later, pregnant with me, she got the Singer and designed and sewed the most stylish maternity clothes imaginable out of odds and ends of material: an avocado green coat with half-dollar-sized black buttons and Peter Pan collar; a chocolate brown mini-dress with white polka dots; a white sundress with ladybugs and black piping and little bows at the straps. She taught me how to sew on that Singer. It took a couple of tries but I finally got it, and the rich tradition of almost-finished projects and visits to the fabric outlet was born.

Money was sometimes scarce when I was growing up, so clothing fell into the "occasional purchase only" category for my immigrant family. Mom sewed most of our clothes. In almost every family photo of my sister and me, I can find something she made. I've by no means carried on her tradition of being a great seamstress, but I love stitching pretty grosgrain ribbon along cloth diapers as baby gifts, taking scraps of fabric and making little wine bags, and sewing fabric onto blank note cards.

At 73, my mother finally got her state-of-the-art sewing machine. It threads the needle automatically, as most of them do now. She wouldn't be able to see the eye of the needle otherwise. It has a buttonhole function and shows you a picture of the stitch you've chosen. If she wants, she can take her foot off the pedal for "cruise-control-sewing" and let the machine run along at a set speed.

I inherited her old Singer and its worn, two-toned carrying case. Now that its mighty motor has finally died, I'm not sure what to do with the machine that made my crib bumper and little hooded baby towels.

But I can't throw it away. It reminds me too much of the countless hours my mother spent sewing, bravely stitching together a life for her family in a new land by making something out of very little.

Mary Engelbreit's Home Companion

Author Bio

Kim Kunasek has a law degree and is a freelance writer living in Paradise Valley, Arizona.

Author's Comments

I write a lot of creative nonfiction with a sentimental, nostalgic tone. I love family history and childhood memories, particularly the way kids process things. I have the greatest mom—she inspires me in her generous spirit and immense creativity, and I write about her quite a bit.

My mom taught me to sew when I was 25, and I loved it right away. She gave me her old sewing machine, which she'd owned since before I was born. It worked great, but only had about four functions, which was really all I needed. The day it konked out on me in the middle of a project, I was flooded with a sense of nostalgia. I just knew I had to write about it as a link to the past, but even more, as a symbol of our family history. I read the piece at a Mother's Day reading that our writing group holds each May, and many people approached me afterward to compliment me on it.

I probably did about three revisions of the piece. It was really difficult to get it down to 240 words—I had to kill off so many of my beloved memories!

I had read *Mary Engelbreit's Home Companion* for years and loved the way artists, crafters, and designers were profiled and how their work was shown. I saved several of the "Home Is Where the Heart Is" essays that appeared on the last page of the magazine. They were usually inspiring, somewhat bittersweet, occasionally nostalgic essays about life.

As a challenge to myself, I decided to send my piece about the sewing machine to *MEHC*. It would build up my courage, keep me honest, and keep me writing. I literally opened the magazine, picked the second name down, and wrote an email to that person explaining that I thought my piece was well-suited to the "Home Is Where the Heart Is" section.

To my surprise, he wrote back the next day, saying he liked my essay and was trying to find an issue for it. About four months later, he sent me a contract stating that the essay would appear in the April/May 2008 issue. So it was published about a year after I sent it out the first time.

You should know the publication you are submitting to well, and have a sense of the type of material it features. There is a lot of consistency in these publications.

Local publications such as parenting magazines or religious community publications are a great way to start to get your name out and get you in the habit of writing and submitting.

—Kim Kunasek

Things We Do for Love

by Laurie Klein

"Reach for the blue one," the stranger says. "Take your time." We are eye level, even though he leans over the first floor balcony. I cling halfway up the rock climber's practice wall, jaws clenched, chest heaving.

"Blue," he repeats, "and don't look down."

If I disregard his advice, I'll glimpse Kevin, our mountaineering guide here in Canada's Purcell Mountains. Blond, compact, and confident, he's on belay—the rope attached to my harness. His stance and attitude remind me of Jeff, a young man I've loved like a son these past few years. He'd be all grins and admiration today, seeing me try this. Angling my gaze sideways, I spy the blue synthetic foothold. I have to heft my right foot 18 inches. I can do this. Despite my white-knuckled fear of heights, I've already survived daily helicopter rides, hiking with my husband at 8,500+ feet—an anniversary brainstorm embraced for his sake. Earlier this

summer, when he'd first handed me the brochure, I had misread *Heli-Hiking*, seeing *Hell-Hiking* instead—which turns out to have been prophetic. Grateful for my effort and proud of my grit, for three days my husband has helped me traverse loose shale and mud, boot-wide switchbacks, and grizzly runs. He's a seeker of peaks with a taste for the glacial. I, however, lack the adventure gene. Give me an armchair, a stack of books, shortbread and tea, and I'm transported, albeit through someone else's story. Instead, each morning this past week we've choppered through tummy-torqueing winds to some new cliff. Oh, the things we do for love. Then we trekked for hours through snow and fog and hail that only partially obscured how far we might fall. Talk about turbo-charging one's prayer life. Hiking provided one benefit: it distracted me from recent sorrow as fear edged out grief. I often felt like crying while shuffling along a ledge, but I needed my wits and clear vision. I rediscovered both every time I looked to my husband, who glowed with well-being.

After the final hike, we had feasted with the other climbers in our group: goat cheese in puff pastry, orzo and tenderloin with onion confit, snow peas and asparagus followed by hazelnut chocolate mousse with blackberry ice cream. I had staggered away from the table.

"Let's try the climbing wall," my husband said.

"Go ahead," I told him. "I'll pray."

In his raggy striped sweater, Kevin, our

Author Bio

Laurie Klein's prose and poetry have appeared in numerous publications. Winner of *New Letters'* Dorothy Churchill Cappon Nonfiction Award and a two-time finalist in the *Writer's Digest* essay contest, she also won the Thomas Merton Poetry of the Sacred Award and the Predator Press chapbook award for *Bodies of Water, Bodies of Flesh*. She is a co-founder and consulting editor at *Rock & Sling*.

guide, stood at basement level to belay the man I'd married 31 years ago. He clambered partway up, grinned and waved, then rappelled down with a whoop. Meanwhile, a second beginner, assisted by the Swiss guide, failed to sufficiently *hug* the wall. Out she swung, hurtling through space like a wrecking ball. The Swiss fellow expertly reeled her in, but vicarious panic shunted through me.

"Your turn," Kevin said, motioning. His forearm was lean and smooth, not nearly as muscled as Jeff's. For no reason I could explain, I wedged my feet into the purple Rock Jock shoes, even joked as Kevin politely cinched the harness around my nether regions.

Slack-jawed with disbelief, my husband had waved me on, then run for the camera.

Now, I'm frozen here, halfway up the wall. The stranger across from me catches my eye. "Go," he urges.

"Blue," I mumble, eyeing that next foothold. *Blue.* My throat aches, as if I've swallowed a pound of rope, fraying more with every breath. One foot edges onto a fist-sized hump of plastic, and I strain for the next handhold. Why am I trusting this guy in the balcony?

"Doing fine," he says. "Embrace it; breathe; le-e-ean in."

Above me the wall looks diseased, a rash of multi-colored lumps.

My groin creaks. Torso-to-wall, I feel like an insect in someone's collection: thorax pinned, legs splayed. I have an audience too. Ranged across three floors of landings in the stairwell behind me, fellow hikers have gathered, cheering each move as I venture higher.

The Swiss guide motions the next in line to wait, so invested in my exertions is he. "Higher," he calls. "*Ja.* Go all the vay!"

Above me the wall looks diseased, a rash

of multi-colored lumps. Aren't I too old for this? A year shy of senior meals at Denny's, cheap seats from Fandango, I should be *watching* Hollywood thrills, not tempting death.

As with any near-death experience, scenes from my past unspool. Lashed to stilts at age nine, I tottered across the lawn toward my father. Segue 15 years to bushwhacking up a ridge with my husband. Chin lifted, hair blowing, he straddled a ledge over the canyon while I molded myself to lichened rock—in fetal position. Fast-forward to 2002: Jeff striding into my kitchen, that slightly tilted eye of his catching mine.

"Come climbing with me," he said, an oft-repeated invitation. For Jeff, mountaineering embodied faith, creative risk-taking, committed teamwork. It meant doing

"Sit deep in the harness . . ."

whatever it took to avoid falling. Above all, it meant freedom. Joy. Why do the men in my life crave heights?

"You'll be safe with me," Jeff always said, that mega-watt grin washing over me like a hot flash. "Brave this, and nothing'll faze you."

Pitons, grigris, screwgate carabiners—the lingo alone gave me the heebie-jeebies. So I had declined his invitations, forcefully, and repeatedly.

Now, a camera flash yanks me back to the present. "The kids won't believe this," my husband calls. "Keep going. It's easier than three decades of marriage!"

Some of the spectators chuckle at this, a few applaud. I'm tired, though, and press my forehead against the wall.

"Sit deep in the harness," the balcony guy advises. His quiet confidence calms me. It also kindles untapped nerve. There's a patch of ceiling above me that needs my sweaty handprint. I yearn to touch it, as if in doing so I can somehow redeem fear, those refusals to climb with Jeff. Sweat pools in the small of my back; it seeps through my shirt. Energy flags and everything quivers.

The balcony guy clears his throat, and I glance down at him. "You can do this," he says. He sounds just like Jeff.

I reach for a yellow handhold, slide my fingertips around its lip. Tendons flex. Strength surges through my knee as it straightens, catapulting me upward.

"She's a natural," someone says.

I eye the red rock shape, gauge the stretch and go for it, surprised when foot and hand fluidly coordinate—a fluke, but it feels good. Savoring the illusion of balance and finesse I spider up a few more yards. Our camera flashes again and again. The ceiling seems

> *. . . I huddle against the wall, shaken and numbly passive.*

alive, a presence, leaning down toward me, and the remaining distance compresses with every reach, each step. I'm a mountain goat: pliant, springy, sure-footed. If Jeff could see me now.

"Terrific," Kevin says, and I risk a downward glance, seeing Jeff again in our guide's short hair and dazzler grin. "Just a little farther," he says.

The crowd eggs me on; my brain says, Quit. Much as I want to wow my husband, the crowd, myself, everything stalls and jitters.

"I'm done, Kevin. That's it."

"Okay," he says, adjusting the rope. "Let go."

Let go? I'm three stories high, nearly five times my height.

"I've got you. Let go and kick out from the wall. This is the fun part."

My pulse accelerates, blood hammering ribs and lungs as the crowd yells encouragement. I glance up. Then down. I search the room for a second opinion.

The balcony guy quietly says, "Hold the rope lightly with one hand if you need to."

But I huddle against the wall, shaken and numbly passive. Sometimes even simple activity demands monumental effort. Walking, for instance, requires negotiating that pause between each foot's rise and fall, an interval of trust when one's full weight is suspended. I have to believe in physics as well as the ground meeting my shoe—an everyday act of faith which helps me believe I can also meet and be met by Grace, right here and now.

I wipe my hands on my shorts until they stop trembling. It will come to me now, in my fear, my grief. I smile, and my husband snaps another picture, recording the moment.

Tomorrow, I'll realize my bizarre compulsion to brave this wall was not about facing fear or impressing my husband. It was about the freedom I'm meant to enjoy, in spite of my fears and resistance. And the week after that I'll understand I kicked free from having let someone down, someone I loved—Jeff, who had recently died in Baghdad. Eventually, I will glimpse the lengths the Maker of Mountains goes to sometimes to give us another chance at joy as well as making things right. But that will take more time.

For now, I hold the rope lightly and dangle one foot over emptiness, waver, thinking *Dear God* . . . exhale, then push off with the other foot. Faces blur, the floor balloons toward me, but I am breathing again, unafraid as a goldfinch scalloping thin air, weightless, bounding. A girl on the moon. Applause erupts when I touch down, and I throw my arms around Kevin.

My husband claps, too, louder than anyone, his eyes glassy and bright as the faithful lens of our camera.

Passager

Author's Comments

A workshop assignment inspired this personal narrative. Dazed with both grief and exhilaration from recent experiences, I had grist in spades: The story would explore humor riding shotgun with sorrow, maybe navigate regret.

Problems ensued. Take pronouns, for instance. Five essential male characters, three of them unnamed, blundered in and out of time and place as mini-flashbacks and flash forwards interrupted the present-tense scene. Would readers track with me? I also wrestled with what to include, and when, concerning Jeff's death in Iraq.

Outlines save time but limit discovery. I plunged into that first white-knuckled moment, between handholds, then sketched in backstory, upping the ante "on the wall" as well as relationally. Themes emerged: climbing how-to's, embracing second chances, facing fear and loss, sustaining long-term marriage, opposing the war. I had to choose.

"Things We Do for Love" survived half a dozen structural revisions, not to mention chronic tinkering, out loud and line by line, with each pass. Teachers often advise gagging one's inner editor in the work's embryonic stage; I egg mine on. Revising en route keeps me engaged, curious. Energized.

The finished story, too religious for most literary magazines, too literary for Christian periodicals, fell between markets. I wanted a general audience. *Passager* intrigued me with its celebration of mature writers rich in life experience.

—Laurie Klein

Pickles and Salsa

Grow Your Own Ingredients for Exceptional Taste

by Cathy Schneider

My husband loves dill pickles. Also sweet pickles, bread and butter pickles, beet pickles, and salsa. As a young bride I was determined to satisfy his taste buds. I collected recipes, experimented, gardened, and canned. I'm not sure to this day if I realized what I was getting myself into.

Canning and gardening can be very time-consuming and a lot of work. But if you're going to can produce, it's best to have as many of your own fresh ingredients as possible. I can assure you that the tasty rewards are worth the effort.

Let's Start In the Garden

For pickles and pickled beets I grow my own cucumbers, dill, beets, and garlic. Salsa garden staples are tomatoes, garlic, onions, cilantro (if desired), and either jalapeño or habañero peppers. I buy seedlings of tomato and pepper plants and grow cucumbers, beets, dill, and cilantro from seed.

Garlic and onions are planted from bulb transplants. I prefer "Vidalia" or "Sweet Red" onions. Garlic should be a mild soft-necked variety. Plant these in rows with enough space between each plant to allow a three- to four-inch growth. When leaves form small bulbs at

the ends, press them into the soil to promote more root growth. Harvest onions when two to four inches in diameter. Storage is sometimes tricky; they tend to rot. I quarter mine into the blender, add a small amount of water and blender-chop. The onions are poured into pint freezer bags and flattened to freeze. I just break off the amount of onion I need for any recipe.

Cucumbers should be a pickling variety, one that's somewhat fat and not too long. Look for a bushy or vine type with bumpy, pale green skin. Do not buy burpless cucumbers, as they tend to be long and skinny with very dark skins.

When planting cucumbers, allow plenty of vining space. (A cucumber vine can completely take over your garden.) Make a mound of dirt and plant several seeds evenly spaced. Dig a trench around the mound for watering purposes. It will take time for the vine to develop and the flowers to form. But watch out, once the cucumbers begin to form they can become large in the blink of an eye. If they get too large they'll be porous and bitter. Cucumbers for dill pickles, as well as for bread and butter pickles, should be picked when they reach four to six inches long. If making sweet pickles, harvest when two to three inches long. Harvest, and store them in the refrigerator until you have enough for canning.

Tomato plants should be the types that lean toward flesh and less pulp, such as "Roma" or "Jetstar." Buy seedlings six to twelve inches high. After planting, make a

Author Bio

Cathy Schneider is a receptionist in a minor emergency office in Wichita, Kansas, and a graduate of Long Ridge Writers Group.

large trench around the plant for watering. Place wire cages over the plants. This allows the plant to grow up the cage (and keeps the vines off the ground) and makes it easier to find ripe tomatoes.

Peppers are planted in the same manner, but without the cages. Store harvested peppers in the refrigerator. They also can be frozen whole.

Beets need to be the dark red globe variety, such as "Ruby Queen." Beets are planted in rows. Here I trench along both sides for watering. Plant seeds three to four inches apart to allow growing space. Beets are a root crop and best when harvested at two to three inches in diameter. Do not let them get too large or they will be woody and tough. Store in the refrigerator till used.

The last garden items are the herbs. Cilantro, a type of parsley, is best grown in a large container (mine is an old stock tank). Clip stems and leaves when the plants are about six to eight inches tall. When allowed to grow much taller, they start to flower and seed and tend to be tough. In addition, clipping encourages new growth.

Dill should be a flowering variety; do not get fern leaf dill. I plant dill in a row next to a tall windbreak. These plants have been known to grow four feet tall or taller and will buckle in hard winds. This herb is best when it starts to go to seed and dry. Don't let it get too dry, however, or you'll lose the seeds. Harvest whole stalks and either tie them together and hang them upside down or cut the stalks into pieces and store in large plastic bags.

KOSHER DILL PICKLES

3 cups vinegar
3 cups water
6 tablespoons canning salt
Fresh dill
Garlic
Mustard seed
Cucumbers (washed)

Place brine of vinegar, water, and salt in saucepan. Bring to a boil. Place a generous layer of dill, 1 to 2 cloves of garlic (sliced), and 1 tablespoon mustard seed in bottom of each jar. Pack with cucumbers, and add more dill. Fill washed and scaled wide-mouthed jars to half an inch from the top with brine. Wipe jar rims, put on canning lids (always use new lids), and screw tight. Process 5 minutes in boiling water bath. Use regular canner, not a pressure canner. Remove jars, and set aside to cool. Lids will seal as they cool.

BEET PICKLES

Beets
1 cup white vinegar
3 cups water
1 teaspoon salt
3 cups sugar
1 tablespoon mixed whole pickling spice (tied in cheesecloth bag)

Wash beets, cook until just firm, and cool enough to peel. Slice beets about ½" thick. In large pot, bring vinegar, salt, water, sugar, and pickling spice to a boil. Add beets to boiling brine and let boil gently 15 minutes. Pack in washed and scalded jars with brine. Lids will seal as they cool.

SALSA

Tomatoes
2 cups onions (peeled)
20 jalapeño peppers* (stem removed)
15 cloves garlic (peeled)
3 tablespoons canning salt
Cilantro to taste (optional; it has a strong flavor)

Peel tomatoes: drop into boiling water 15 seconds; remove, and put into cold water; peels slip right off. Chop tomatoes in blender. Fill 8-quart pot half-full with tomatoes. Cook over low heat until reduced by half. Chop onion, peppers, and garlic in blender. Add with salt to tomatoes. Cook 30 minutes more. Fill washed and scalded jars, and process in boiling water bath 10 minutes. Set aside and cool. Lids will seal as they cool. Makes 8 pints.

*Habañeros can be substituted for jalapeños. They impart a slightly fruity flavor, but use only half the amount as they are very hot.

BackHome Magazine

Author's Comments

My writing experience began with Long Ridge Writers Group when I was accepted into the course, *Breaking Into Print*. It continued with the second course, *Shape, Write, and Sell Your Novel*.

"Pickles and Salsa" was submitted to *BackHome Magazine* in March 2005. My research was done with the aide of *The Best of the Magazine Markets for Writers*, and an online search into the magazine's requirements. The article was contracted in April 2005 and was to appear in the spring of 2006, but due to an overload of material, they regretfully had to cancel publication. In March 2007 the editor of *BackHome* contacted me via phone requesting permission to publish the article in the May/June 2007 issue.

Now I am concentrating on writing fiction. I love the process of writing; it relaxes me. All of my first drafts are handwritten and my stories go through at least three revisions before the final draft is typed and ready to submit.

My advice to new writers is to never give up. If your story or article is rejected, dig deeper and make improvements. Submit to other magazines, and keep trying until you are accepted. It's a great feeling to have your work printed for everyone to see.

—Cathy Schneider

Nights at the Round Table

by Matthew Hutson

As dining out overtakes gathering 'round the hearth, we fill ourselves with unhealthier food, and more of it. Meals at restaurants typically contain more sodium, saturated fat, and calories than home-prepared food and come in larger portions. And when we stay in, we often forage on our own. A frozen pizza here, some left-over Chinese there. But few rituals have such far-reaching effects as the family dinner; breaking bread together not only encourages healthy eating habits but also bolsters kids' intellectual development and bonds families via rich social narratives that can last for generations.

Family meals are a great way to model good eating behavior, with long-lasting consequences: Young adults who had more family meals as adolescents consume more fruits and veggies, according to a 2007 report from the University of Minnesota. And the benefits don't stop with diet. Other studies show better grades, higher self-esteem, and less substance abuse in kids who dine four or more times a week with their families. It's hard to say for sure whether meals are responsible for these effects, but the researchers have made efforts to control for overall family connectedness.

If you've got teenagers, you can expect some grumbling, but there's a dirty little secret you should know: They *want* to hang out with you. Maybe not at the mall, but definitely at the dinner table. National surveys show that teens want to spend more time with their families and that family meals are one of their favorite family activities.

So get everyone involved. Kids who help prepare dinners tend to have healthier diets, and learn responsibility. "We no longer live in a world where the mother stays home and cooks," says Dianne Neumark-Sztainer of the University of Minnesota. "So if we're going to have more family meals, we need to find creative ways of making it happen."

The average meal lasts only 20 minutes.

Scheduling and preparing group meals encourages you to include all the food groups in decent proportions. "It doesn't have to be an elaborate meal," Neumark-Sztainer says. "You can pick up a rotisserie chicken and a bag of salad at the grocery store. Or use just basic foods, like bread and cheese and vegetables to make sandwiches, and maybe some soup."

"People feel, 'I don't have time to do this,'" says Barbara Fiese, a psychologist at Syracuse University. "The expectation is that

Author Bio

Matthew Hutson has a master's degree in science journalism and is the News Editor at *Psychology Today*. He has written for *Discover, Scientific American Mind,* and *The New York Times Magazine*. He lives in New York City.

it's going to be a long, drawn-out, elaborate affair, but in reality it's not." The average meal lasts only 20 minutes. "A lot happens in that very brief period of time." Everyone feels included, lines of communication open, concerns leak out. It's a great opportunity for problem solving.

According to Fiese, "It's also a time when family members tell jokes, family stories are created, and kids learn about family history. That's really how a family identity is created."

Psychology Today

Author's Comments

I was looking for something to write on the topic of childhood obesity and came across a health article on the benefits of family meals. I looked up the research and interviewed the researchers to find out what was new and what practical advice they had for families.

The hardest part was sifting through the research to figure out what factors were responsible for other factors, and what factors were merely correlated with each other. For example, is it accurate to say that eating together makes you healthier, or is it just that the amount of TV watching influences both family meals and health?

I did not use an outline because the article was only about 500 words. I glanced frequently at the notes from my interviews and the research papers and had an overall organization in my head.

I wrote one draft, and another editor suggested some changes. The main changes were to move the research findings closer to the top, and to change the intro so that it appealed to people's concerns about their own health, not simply about the health of their teenagers. Then once the text was placed in the design layout, I cut some small things here and there to make it fit perfectly. Next, all the other editors looked at it and it was copyedited and more small word changes were suggested.

Writers submitting their work to a publication for the first time should read previous pieces in the publication carefully so they can match its style. And if you're covering science, it's important to get the facts right, and to explain the science clearly, but it's also good to inject a little bit of humor and personality.

—Matthew Hutson

Peggy Hedman Is Driven to Keep Her Charges Safe

by Tricia Booker

On what began as a typical summer day, NYCONN Horse Transport professional driver Peggy Hedman picked up a horse in Florida for the long drive up I-95 back to the Northeast. She knew this trip would be a little different because this particular horse wasn't a show horse returning home from winter competition. Instead, this was a stolen horse being returned to its owner in Connecticut.

"The horse had a rare medical condition, and I really didn't think it would make the trip," Hedman recalled. "It was traveling poorly."

She worried about the outcome as she crossed the Connecticut state line and eventually approached the owner's barn. "Then, when I turned a corner and onto the street, I heard horses outside starting to scream," Hedman said. "And the horse in the truck started to scream too. That horse knew he

was home and couldn't wait to get off the truck.

"It's beyond me that the horses all knew, even the ones in the field," she continued, shaking her head. "They knew something special was going on. Everyone there was ecstatic, from the people to the horses. It was a very emotional reunion. It's amazing the power of communication between horses."

Hedman, 53, New Fairfield, Conn., has experienced many wonderful and literally moving adventures over the course of her 12-year career working for NYCONN as a professional driver. And although she said there are no typical days in this job, some are more memorable than others as her jobs range from local jaunts to and from one-day horse shows to cross-country excursions to the West Coast and Spruce Meadows in Calgary, Alta.

They're All Mine

Like many lifelong horse lovers, Hedman grew up wanting to be with horses. Her early years in New Jersey included working at a nearby farm in exchange for lessons and the opportunity to ride other people's horses.

She attended Sullins College (Va.) and after graduation started working as a groom for Hunterdon in New Jersey. When Hunterdon and Beacon Hill split, Hedman moved on to Beacon Hill with Frank Madden. She eventually rubbed horses for Old Salem Farm (N.Y.), where she worked with international

Author Bio

Tricia Booker is the editor of *The Chronicle of the Horse*, a weekly equestrian news magazine that was established in 1937. She began at the *Chronicle* as an intern while in college, and she returned after graduation as a member of the editorial staff. She worked her way up to assistant editor, managing editor, and to editor over a 20-year period.

Nonfiction 231

grand prix rider Katharine Burdsall and renowned hunter rider Charlie Weaver.

Throughout her grooming career, Hedman regularly transported her charges from show to show so it was a natural next step for her to move into driving full-time in 1995.

"I had been a groom my whole life. And honestly, I grew tired of longeing horses," she admitted. "I love the horses and the showing, but I knew it was time for me to do something else. I'd always taken care of other people's horses, but in the horse transportation industry it's different. They're mine when they're on the truck. I feel totally responsible for them."

Geoff Teall of Montoga Inc., in Wellington, Fla., regularly employs Hedman to transport his show horses. He's known Hedman since her days working as a groom and has trusted her to ship his hunters, jumpers and equitation horses for more than 10 years.

"You can feel when they're fighting in the back; the truck rocks."

"The best thing about Peggy is that you don't have to worry about a thing," he said. "The horses are taken care of, she shows up on time, and if there are any questions she calls you right away. Unless you hear something, it's all going smoothly."

Each day Hedman receives instructions from NYCONN owner Tony Baxendale from the company's home base in Wilton, Conn. She's told where to go, when to go and which type of truck she needs to take—from six horse van to tractor-trailer. On long-distance trips two drivers are employed and one drives while the other rests. Hedman said one of her greatest challenges has been to learn to sleep in 5- to 10-hour shifts at all times of the day or night.

When traveling long distances, Hedman stops every five hours to check the horses, stuff haynets, water the horses, change sheets if needed and open or close windows as the weather dictates.

"Much of what I do is really common sense," said Hedman. "But I'm very careful to monitor each horse. For instance, as we drive back up from Florida and we stop in the Carolinas, I close the windows and put sheets on. The horses have been in Florida for months, and even the mild changes in temperatures as we travel north really affect them."

As a busy trainer, clinician and industry leader, Teall is particularly grateful to have his horses under the care of a true horseman when they make the stressful long distance relocations from Florida to the Northeast and back again. It's one less responsibility he has to take on while coordinating his own business demands.

"Most of the time the drivers are not horse people, and you worry about their loading and unloading and their feeding while on the road," noted Teall. "Peggy knows horses and knows if they're not shipping well. And if something goes wrong, she can handle the situation."

Adding video surveillance cameras to the rigs has been one of Hedman's favorite new technologies in transportation. She's now able to observe the horses as she drives and can recognize when a horse is having difficulties, such as fighting with its neighbor or becoming lethargic.

"You can feel when they're fighting in the back; the truck rocks," she said. "In the past, I'd have to shorten up everyone's crossties. Now I can watch them during transport and know which horse I have to shorten up. You don't have to punish them all."

After reaching her destination, Hedman's work is far from complete. She unloads the horses—sometimes with help from owners or grooms—and then must unload all of the equipment she's transported with the horses, from tack trunks to feed and show equipment.

"It's very physically demanding, but I'm proud to say I can hold my own," she said smiling.

A Smooth Trip

Because there's more to Hedman's job than just sitting behind the wheel, she said that the relationships she's developed with the horse owners, trainers, barn managers and grooms makes a huge difference in whether her day runs smoothly or with bumps in the road.

"One thing that really makes my job nice is the customers. I really try to take care of the grooms too, to make sure they have enough to eat and drink. And one of the nicest things is when we arrive and everyone is ready to go, all the horses are wrapped and the equipment is waiting to be loaded."

A gratifying aspect of Hedman's job is when she transports young children or novice adults to the local one-day horse shows. After arriving, she helps unload the horses and assists as they're groomed and tacked up for their classes.

"We try to encourage the kids, and even the adult amateurs, to learn about safety in loading and unloading the horses," she said. "For example, you load the passenger side horses first and then the driver's side. That way no horse is putting its backside in front of another horse."

During the show, Hedman usually remains at the truck (sometimes reading a book), where she can monitor the horses remaining on the rig and can assist in getting horses on and off.

She's also especially patient with the difficult loaders. While many men can manhandle horses onto the rig, through experience she's learned that philosophy isn't likely to work for a woman. Instead, she prefers to

spend time working with the horse so he'll learn to trust the process and can then become a reliable shipper for anyone who loads him.

Another lesson Hedman insists every horse person should learn is how to compassionately drive a horse trailer. "Before you drive a horse, you should have to ride in the back with your hands in your pockets and try to stand up back there," she said. "People who trailer horses should be especially aware of their stops and starts.

"Before exiting the highway I give the horses a little warning, such as a tap on the brakes, so they know something's coming up," she explained. "Then I take everything much slower. If the exit ramp says 35 mph, I slow to 25. I like telling young drivers that you have to throw your watch out the window. You have to let the horses tell you how fast to drive."

Being a veteran caretaker has also allowed Hedman to better monitor her horses for signs of illness or injury. She's careful to track the amount of hay each horse consumes, the number of drinks he takes and his overall alertness. One of the first signs a horse is feeling ill is his lack of interest in his surroundings.

> *"It's not an easy life and not the life for someone with a family."*

Making the decision to leave the highway and head for a veterinary clinic is one of the most difficult situations she faces in her career. Perhaps the horse is fine, but then again she could save a horse's life through taking the more conservative route. "It's often a judgment call," she said. "You have to make the decision and stand by it."

Like many jobs in the horse industry, transporting horses is a seven-day per week job. Hedman doesn't have a set day off, and because she lives in close proximity to NY-CONN's home base, Hedman is regularly the one called for a emergency trip to the veterinary clinic. "It's not an easy life and not the life for someone with a family," she said.

Transporting horses is considered one of the least appreciated jobs in the horse industry, but Hedman is very much appreciated for her commitment and ability. "She's almost conscientious to a fault, if there's such a thing," said Teall smiling. "If there's any question, Peggy will give too much care than not enough. And that's truly invaluable."

Despite the long hours and the challenges the job entails, there's nowhere else Hedman would rather be than sitting in the cab of the truck with her trusted co-driver Cindy-Lou, her Jack Russell terrier, by her side. "I truly love my job," she said. "It's the horses and the people who make it what it is. And it's great."

The Chronicle of the Horse

Author's Comments

The idea for this story was generated in one of our weekly editorial staff meetings. For our annual Horse Care issue, we wanted to profile some behind-the-scenes caretakers who help show horses in ways other than training or riding them. One of our staff members (who had worked as a groom) knew Peggy and suggested her.

I interviewed Peggy by telephone and had never met her, so I spent the first part of the interview asking about her background and how she became involved in horse transportation. In addition, I didn't know much about commercial horse transport, so I asked Peggy lots of questions about the process so I could more easily picture her at work as we spoke.

As a novice writer, I outlined my articles and then developed a first draft. Now, with hundreds of articles under my belt, I generally develop the story line in my head and write a first draft. I find this process allows the piece to flow into directions I might not have considered as I was developing a formal outline. I usually let the article "breathe" for a day or two and then return to it with fresh eyes and polish it up before submitting it for editing.

—Tricia Booker

Old Man on Campus

by Ehud Havazelet

Last spring I spent four days visiting my son, then a first-year (don't call them "freshmen") at the University of Chicago. There were no hotel rooms available; the National Restaurant Association (the "good N.R.A.," two different cabbies said) was holding its annual convention. But Michael was able to arrange a room for me in his dorm, a crumbling former hotel from the golden age. Al Capone stayed there, and Elvis Presley. Jimmy Hoffa used it as his base of operations when in town, and rumor has one of his attachés strangling a hotel employee who had the nerve to inquire about the bill.

The Shoreland's thirteen floors, hundreds of rooms, will be a dorm for another year or so before it's transformed into high-end condominiums. Meanwhile, plaster sifts from the ceilings, and the lobby is a mishmash of couches, stacks of student publications, a big-screen TV and handbills covering the walls. A friendly, bored staff of desk attendants watches as students—listless, sleepy, harried, running late, dressed to the nines, falling down drunk, depending on the day and hour—file past.

Aside from a few unused rooms I'd been given while teaching, this was the first dorm

I'd stayed in since my college days, back in the Nixon years, at Columbia. Livingston Hall, our local fading remnant, was about as well maintained as the Shoreland. Now, three decades later, my son was living 10 stories above me. I was in a ground-floor version of his room except much, much cleaner: two twin beds stiffly made up, two desks, two bookcases and bureaus, two desk lamps (one working) and, in the bathroom, two i-Pod-size hotel soaps: Welcome. Enjoy your stay.

> *No father would say his son's trajectory was utterly normal.*

I had taken my computer and enough reading matter for a month, but the first morning, while Michael rigorously kept to his academic schedule—no class before noon, sleep till 11:30, sprint for the bus, eat and shower God knew when—I couldn't concentrate. The 10-foot windows opened onto the circular drive, where students gathered to meet the shuttle to campus. I glanced up from my reading, back again, then finally gave up all pretense, lifted a window to hear better, drew the curtain and openly stared.

Snatches of conversation filtered through—"Don't know. He never made it back last night." "I thought that was due *next* Friday!"—the various Dudes and What's Ups and Wait Ups.

No father would say his son's trajectory was utterly normal, and perhaps my son's was

Author Bio

Ehud Havazelet is the author of two story collections and a novel, *Bearing the Body* (Farrar, Straus & Giroux). He teaches writing at the University of Oregon and the Warren Wilson MFA Program.

not as unusual as I think. My early separation from his mother set us on a course of travel, long-distance calls and stays in hotels of varying seediness and safety, until I found a wonderfully generous couple who rented us a room in Philadelphia for my visits and became, over the years, another set of grandparents to my son. We read all of Narnia and half of Tolkien over the phone. We went to Yankee Stadium, to Disney World. I grieved, raved, tried to learn how to do better.

Then, when Michael was 14, I became seriously ill. He was visiting for the summer and, facing the possibility of losing a parent, had to face, equally suddenly, the burden of caring for one. Through the drugged haze of this time are memories of him smiling bravely and of caresses clumsy and no doubt excruciating for a teenage boy to deliver to his dad. We got through.

Who will take care of him now?

And now he was launched. My son—smart, gentle, open-hearted to the point of worry (mine, not his)—was moving forward. "Care" was the word repeating itself in my head. Take care. Be careful. Whatever you do is fine as long as you're safe. Walking home from dinner the night before, as he was discoursing on Nietzsche's "Genealogy of Morals," I couldn't resist telling him to tie his shoe. There is nothing unusual about this—though every parent has perhaps felt the uniqueness of its poignant sting: Who will take care of him now?

Outside, patterns emerged dependent on the shuttle schedule. Women were usually in plenty of time; men rushed, hair still wet. Some boy was invariably last, running after the bus, disheveled, inexpertly dressed, maybe a half-eaten Pop-Tart hanging from his mouth as he flailed at the bus already moving from the curb.

One of these boys, misreading the time perhaps, was early. He bore a slight resemblance to my son, curly-haired, with the same calculated slovenliness in dress, his backpack half-open. He sleepily approached a group of three young women waiting for the bus, groomed, alert, ready for the day.

They saw him and immediately went to work. One buttoned his shirt, one patted and tugged his hair into place, one zipped the backpack so nothing would tumble out. They gave him the grief he deserved, and one leaned up to kiss his cheek. It was all I could watch. Moved, obscurely relieved, wondering who these young ladies were and how I could introduce them to Michael, I got up, closed the window and went off to shower.

The New York Times Magazine

Author's Comments ━━━━━━━━

I came to writing rather late, because I was one of the people Flannery O'Connor referred to when she said, "Many people want to be writers, but few actually want to write."

I don't work from outlines, though I do take notes, a lot of them. This piece came directly from my experience visiting my son in college, and while the writing, as always, took work—editing, revising, revising again—the organization came pretty quickly.

The biggest challenge was tone. I worried about sentimentality, a liability I'm rarely accused of in my fiction. But this was my son, he was in college, I was in a dorm room, what I felt was, well, sentimental. I tried to find a balance between the emotion and the need for it not to clutter, abase the experience itself.

I did two or three original drafts before sending it in, trimming, focusing, dealing with the issues mentioned above. Once it was accepted by the *Times* they asked for cuts, made some, I made some more. Most of these were about space constraints.

Learn what you can about where you're submitting. *Field and Stream*, I'd venture, wouldn't have been interested in this piece. A lot of time and anguish is wasted simply because people don't send material to magazines that might be interested.

Writing is hard, so is getting published. Hope for everything, expect nothing (counsel easier to espouse, I know, than to enact). Write what you can as best as you can; when it's ready (and only then) send it out, try to forget about it, write something else.

—Ehud Havazelet

When 'Tis(n't) the Season to Ride?

by Aida Elder

Sleigh bells ringing . . . Jack Frost nipping . . . chestnuts roasting . . . and mountain biking? No, it's not the sour eggnog talking. You really can include mountain biking in this special catalog of all things winter. Who uses a sleigh anymore, anyway? On two wheels you can experience your own unique and exhilarating winter wonderland.

Most mountain bikers would agree that the fall season offers some of the best riding conditions. Cool weather, dry trails, and toned legs from miles of summer riding can make for a pleasurable biking experience. But once snowflakes fall and temperatures plummet, many riders reluctantly hang up their bikes for the winter. Luckily, with a few simple modifications for winter riding, you can continue mountain biking right into spring.

Cold temperatures mean frozen precipitation, resulting in conditions that are often too icy and slippery for standard mountain bike tires. The answer lies in studded tires, which give traction on frozen surfaces where even walking would be impossible. A hasty dismount will promptly remind you of this fact as your feet fly out from under you.

Too strapped for cash to afford costly studded tires? You can make your own with two mountain bike tires, about two hundred half-inch-long sheet metal screws, two new mountain bike tubes and two old bike tubes.

Screw about 100 screws through each tire from the inside. Each tip should protrude through the outside of the tire by about a quarter of an inch. Take care when handling the tires once the screws are in place. Sheet metal screws have razor sharp tips.

Then, cut along the inner circumference of the old bike tubes and install the resulting circular piece of rubber within each tire. This layer functions as a barrier that will protect the new bike tubes from the screw heads. Now, place the new bike tubes inside the tires and fit the tires as usual on your rims.

Granted, these homemade tires are not as light as factory-made studded tires, but they will allow for traction over icy surfaces that would otherwise be off limits.

Disc brakes are a definite must in the winter.

There are other simple but important modifications for winter riding that can make the experience safer and more enjoyable. Toe spikes added to bike shoes can provide you with necessary traction on ice while off your bike. Although they can make clipping in and out of pedals more difficult, they are well worth this extra hassle when you need to walk your bike down an especially icy section of trail.

Disc brakes are a definite must in the

Author Bio

Aida Elder is an emergency medicine physician and has been writing for about a year. Mountain biking is one of her passions. She was a student of Long Ridge Writers Group.

winter. Water on the trail can cause ice to form on the rims, making it practically impossible to slow down or stop with rim brakes.

To prevent your drink from freezing inside your Camelback hose, use an insulated hose cover, or simply blow air into the hose after each sip.

Along with colder temperatures come shorter daylight hours, so make sure to carry a headlamp in case of emergencies. As always, pack enough food and hydration, and, especially in the winter, ride with a buddy.

Optimal Winter Riding Conditions

The beauty of winter riding is that you can do it when it is too icy to do anything else. If the weather isn't conducive for skiing or snowshoeing, then give biking a try. A lot of rain followed by a deep freeze is perfect.

Morning rides are generally best.

On the flip side, if there's fresh powder out there, then forget the bike and go skiing. Biking in soft snow is like biking through loose sand—traction is nearly impossible and the whole experience becomes thoroughly exhausting. If it has been a dry winter and the trails are frozen, then leave the studded tires at home. In these conditions the ground has a sandpaper texture, allowing standard tires to grip with ease.

Snowmobile paths and any other well-traveled trails covered with firmly packed snow and ice are ideal for winter riding. You will find that a blanket of frozen precipitation can completely change the character of an otherwise familiar trail. Obstacles such as small rocks and logs disappear, while subtle elevations and dips become level.

Be wary of riding in deep ruts of ice at high speeds, though. The front tire will in-evitably hit one side of the rut, risking a spectacular fall.

Selecting the right time of day to ride is important. Trails that are frozen in the morning can become slushy as temperatures rise throughout the day. For this reason, morning rides are generally best. Of course, riding through slushy mud for miles is no fun and destroys trails, so if the temperature is simply too warm, resist the urge to mountain bike and try a refreshingly cool road ride instead.

Protect Yourself From the Elements

As with other winter sports, winter riding requires appropriate apparel for colder temperatures. Even in the cold, pedaling uphill causes perspiration, which can create quite a chill on the downhill sections of the trail. Layering the torso with thermals, fleece and a jacket allows you the flexibility to shed and layer as necessary.

Much of the same clothes used for skiing—thermal underwear, insulated ski gloves, a neck gator—can also be used for winter biking. For head protection, a beanie that covers the ears will fit comfortably under a bike helmet.

Lycra bike shorts with a chamois can be worn as usual under fleece pants or insulated, wind-block tights. Ski socks work well, and can be worn under Gore-Tex socks to keep your feet dry.

Shoe covers can offer added protection to summer shoes, but for the ultimate luxury in warmth and comfort, treat yourself to insulated winter cycling shoes. As with skiing, chemical toe warmers will keep feet toasty on particularly cold days.

So, instead of dust gathering on your mountain bike this winter, why not a dusting of snow? A few simple bike modifications and an adventurous spirit are all that are required.

Jingle bells, optional.

Silent Sports

When 'Tis(n't) the Season to Ride?

Author's Comments

This article was the lemonade I managed to squeeze out of a sour point in my life. A ruptured disc in my back left me unable to walk, let alone even think about mountain biking. The summer biking season passed before my eyes, and I wondered if I would ever ride again. I was blessed to have had a successful surgery, and when my doctor told me I would be free to pursue my usual recreational activities in three months, I took him at his word. Three months meant that on the first of December I would be mountain biking.

In the meantime, I had a writing assignment due for the Long Ridge course that I had put off until the last minute. Although I had missed the summer biking season, the winter season was just around the corner. The thought of reuniting with my bike for a winter ride elevated my spirits during my recovery, and I harnessed this enthusiasm to write the article.

An outline was crucial. My brother Pat, a lawyer, has a knack for ruthless editing. He read through some drafts and indicated areas that needed clarification, such as the section describing how to create a studded tire. A fresh pair of eyes can be indispensable for highlighting weak points.

I thought the article was too general for hard-core mountain biking magazines, so I queried outdoor/recreational publications via email instead. Editors who accept email submissions seem to be more receptive and respond promptly.

In this case, the editor of *Silent Sports* initially rejected the piece because it did not have a Midwestern slant. He surprised me a month later with an email stating that my article complemented another one he was using for the January issue, and he had decided to include it after all.

One piece of advice—write about topics you love. Passion is that extra ingredient that will make an article stand out.

—Aida Elder

Colonial Cuisine and the Road to Revolution

A Q&A with Historian James E. McWilliams

by Paulette Beete

How did food "fit for swine" become a staple of the Colonial diet? Why do Colonial kitchens suggest that the colonists were reluctant revolutionaries? How did Colonial America's thirst for beer pave the way to the Declaration of Independence? Historian James E. McWilliams answers these questions and more in *A Revolution in Eating: How the Quest for Food Shaped America* (Columbia University, 2005), a lively investigation of Colonial eating habits and how they shaped the revolutionary views of the new Americans.

Food and politics might seem like strange bedfellows, but McWilliams says the link isn't surprising at all. "Food is central to life, and if a nation cannot fulfill a basic need like its food supply, its independence will be compromised."

McWilliams says his interest in the nation's past sprung from an intense interest in the present. "I was living in Washington, D.C., (as an undergraduate at Georgetown) and reading lots of newspapers and getting well versed in current events," he explains. "It occurred to me that I knew very little about the background to these events. This pulled me into the past, and I started reading history on my own."

McWilliams collected food-related evidence over several years while working on his graduate degree, eventually amassing enough to write *A Revolution in Eating*. McWilliams cautions, however, that he's not a culinary historian. "I'm not necessarily a fan or advocate of being a food historian because I think it misses the larger context in which food was produced. You have to understand how and why particular foods were eaten. You have to look at the agricultural situation, the trade situation and intercultural situations."

The movement of corn into a staple of the Colonial American diet, McWilliams explains, is an example of how an intercultural situation shaped American eating habits. In the 17th century, the English would have thought Indian corn was a crop fed to pigs. However, when these white English settlers found themselves in a new world, they realized how dependent they were on Native Americans for everything—including food. "Everyone was soon eating corn, whether they wanted to or not," McWilliams says. "Thus the adjustment to eating Indian corn was huge one, and one that speaks powerfully to the adaptive nature of American food."

McWilliams is a past winner of the Whitehill Prize in Colonial History, awarded annually by the *New England Quarterly*, in which he has published extensively. His articles on food history have appeared in the *Christian Science Monitor* and the *Texas Observer*. He spoke with *American Spirit* about *A Revolution in Eating* from Texas, where he is an assistant professor of history at Texas State University, San Marcos.

Author Bio

Paulette Beete is a literary writer, primarily of poetry. She writes regularly for *American Spirit*.

A Revolution in Eating **illuminates the link between Colonial cuisine and the road to revolution. Why is this connection important?**

I don't argue that food caused the American Revolution. All I'm saying is that food and attention to food and the food supply was a critical factor in the American Revolution. It's obviously far more inspirational to focus on the revolutionary rhetoric. My question is what had to be in place to even have the luxury of embracing those political ideas? Americans had to be able to feed themselves. They took an enormous amount of pride in the fact that they were dependent on nobody else for food. What were they thinking when they thought about independence? One important aspect of that was material independence; they could provide for themselves.

A troubling element of [the colonists'] material independence, however, is that a great percentage of the food production in the United States was done with slave labor. If food was central to the American Revolution, and if that food was being produced by slaves, it's hard to avoid the conclusion that slavery was a critical element to the quest for independence.

How did you go about researching exactly what the colonists were eating prior to the American Revolution?

I looked at all kinds of documents, such as farmer account books, so I could see what kind of food farmers were bartering. I also looked at a fair number of probate records, which would include the kind of food settlers had in their barn or cellar or kitchen and also the cooking utensils that housewives owned. Any type of travel narrative was also important. At a time when people couldn't take their food supply for granted, they were diligent about recording what they ate. And since people didn't travel a lot, they paid a lot of at-tention to what people ate in different regions. This was critical to my thesis that there wasn't any one American way of eating. Instead, it was intensely regional. I used quite a bit from letters from Europeans visiting the Colonies because they would remark about the agriculture and different crops they were observing, such as West African crops growing in gardens belonging to slaves.

Did you discover anything in your research that you found particularly surprising?

I was definitely surprised by how intense the regional differences in food were. I had not expected to find such clear differences between the lower South and the Chesapeake, and I didn't expect to find such dramatic differences between the middle Colonies and New England. Also, although I was well aware that the colonists drank routinely and by our standards, quite heavily, I wasn't prepared for how central alcohol was to the Colonial diet. The emphasis on beer, cider and rum was all encompassing. The emphasis on rum was so heavy that it was the rum trade that sparked a larger and more systematic trade of food up and down the coast.

Wasn't alcohol a factor in fomenting the colonists' rebellion?

It would be misleading to say alcohol led to the American Revolution, but it's interesting to point out that the taste for alcohol led to a public venue—the tavern—where people could talk to each other and make sure they were all on the same page ideologically. It's important to keep in mind that there weren't many public venues where people could get together and discuss ideas in the 18th century. During the Revolutionary era, colonists would not only talk politics in taverns, but also read the popular political pamphlets of the day.

Historians traditionally focus on the importance of the triangle trade to the Colonial American economy, but in *A Revolution in Eating,* you point out that inter-Colonial trading of food was equally important—if not more—to establishing a thriving economy.

As so often happens in historical study, the overemphasis on one side of the story obscures the other side of the story. What's been completely obscured in this emphasis on transatlantic trade is just the day-in and day-out patterns of local trade. The vast majority of trading that was done in Colonial America—in some estimates 90 percent—was local. For example, people in Massachusetts traded with people in Massachusetts and sometimes with people in Pennsylvania. It was that kind of trade that kept the economy going and supported transatlantic trade.

What do you think historians will say about our nation in 2007, based on contemporary eating habits?

The way we eat today is quite consistent with the way that colonists ate with respect to the attitude we have about food. The colonists had an incredibly pragmatic attitude about food—they were radically open to eating anything. I think today's Americans are also incredibly pragmatic, flexible and open-minded about their food.

The difference, and I think really what historians 100 years from now will focus on, is that what has happened in the last 50 years in American cuisine has been a radical disruption between the consumption of food and the production of food. I think historians are really going to seize on that disruption as a critical and a detrimental characteristic of how Americans eat today. The implication of this difference is that it diminishes an important environmental awareness. One reason Americans can be fairly casual about dangerous environmental habits is because we're fairly ignorant about how the ecosystem around us works because we're not intimate with it.

American Spirit

Author's Comments

While in graduate school, I was an editor on the literary journal, which involved interviewing established authors. I enjoyed doing background research in preparation for the interviews, and started looking for additional publication opportunities.

I have written about visual artists, inventors, and tobacco, but my primary interest is learning about other writers, so I get a lot of ideas from scanning bookstore shelves. Since I have had regular success with *American Spirit*, I always keep its subject area in mind when browsing.

There's a two-fold challenge with interview-based articles. The first is digesting enough of the background material to craft questions that will elicit substantial answers from your subject. The second challenge is discerning what to include in the draft, and how to build a narrative if you're using a Q&A format.

I don't write from an outline. I think of my articles as investigations. As I conduct each investigation—through interviews and research—the narrative, or what I call "the real story," appears.

It's important to know the magazine you're pitching to. It doesn't matter how great a writer you are, if you pitch off topic, the editor will automatically hit "delete."

—Paulette Beete

Sharing Memories, Sharing Lives

Arlene Silverman

The latest thing seems to be videotaping one's parents and quizzing them about their lives. My daughter and I thought we had a better idea. For my 65th birthday, I told her, I'd like a notebook with questions that she'd always wanted to ask me about my childhood.

The idea seemed like a winner. After all, how many of us bemoan the fact that we learned little about our parents before they died or become too ill to communicate? My own children ask questions from time to time, though their late father was much better than I in going into detail about his up-bringing in Rhode Island (but said precious little about his being in a German prison camp during World War II).

I have found that my son's and daughter's eyes glaze over easily when I talk about my Aunt Sarah's habit of asking questions about the one thing you didn't want to talk about, like "So, how is that weight-loss plan coming, dear?" Or Grandma Esther, an otherwise devout and demure type, who embarrassed me in front of my friends when she sang loudly, in her Polish accent, "Where was Moses when the lights went out? Down in

the cellar eating sauerkraut."

To my delight, on that birthday my daughter, Becky, presented me with not a Walgreens' special but a thick book she'd put together with care. There were drawings to go with questions such as: What did you read when you were a child? What did you and Auntie Susie (Susie and I have known each other since we were 5) talk about when you got together? What was Sunday like in your house? How did you and your siblings get along? What did you and your mom fight about? How did you celebrate holidays? This was, I thought, so much better than sitting down at a tape recorder or a video camera and putting together a memento that might be titled, "Where Was Mama When the Lights Went Out?"

What did my mom and I fight about?

What I didn't count on, though, was how hard it would be to answer the questions. What was Sunday like in my house? The fact is that I remember little about Sunday at my house, because I was rarely there. My parents were busy putting food on the table. My life was on the street. There was no such thing as a "play date." Rather there was simply play, from morning till night.

Question: What did my mom and I fight about? How could I tell my daughter that we fought about everything? We fought about my clothes. We fought about my grades, es-

Author Bio

Arlene Silverman is a freelance writer and communication consultant whose work has appeared in a variety of publications including *The San Francisco Chronicle*, *San Francisco Bay View*, *The Potrero View*, and *The Richmond Review*.

pecially when in junior high I somehow managed to fail both sewing and gym class in one semester. "How can someone fail sewing?" she'd yelled. My three siblings and I also fought, particularly the sister nearest my age who, when stuck babysitting for me, threatened to send me to "Bad Girls' School." (Actually, the idea seemed kind of attractive. I was that kind of kid.)

What will my own children remember about their childhood?

The question that sent me reeling was, "What did you read as a child?" How could I say, "Not much"? My house contained a couple of copies of *Reader's Digest* and *Ladies' Home Journal* and maybe a book or two on how to crochet or make a pot roast. My friend Susie and I spent hours on Saturdays at the main library. How could I tell Becky, though, that our favorite room there contained listening booths where we could dance, looking like manic puppets to passers-by, to the latest hits? How could I tell her that my joy in unassigned reading didn't happen till I started college and opened up Albert Camus' *The Stranger*?

I guess the memory book that Becky so thoughtfully gave me has had an interesting effect on me. I've realized that questions about childhood can bring up more troubling memories than one would like. Do I tell her that Auntie Susie and I had a big fight in high school over her active social life and my lack of same? (I had no answer for Becky's question "Who was your first date?")

Do I tell her that I envied my cousin Helen Ruth because her mother seemed nicer than mine? Do I tell her that my mother and I really didn't enjoy each other's company until she was in her 70s? That my memories of my father land on an image of his snoring

in a chair, exhausted at the end of a day at a low-paying job?

I think the answer to all those questions has to be yes. There has to be a truth somewhere between that gray-haired grandma in those Norman Rockwell pictures, appearing complete with Thanksgiving turkey and beaming children, and the memoir writers who recall dreadful childhoods that make Charles Dickens' visits to his father in the poorhouse look like a walk in the park.

And, believe me, there are happy memories: I remember holiday celebrations with my mother's ten sisters and brothers that featured raucous singing and Uncle Moishe playing his version of Santa: a guy we all called Hanukkah Charlie. I remember the time Aunt Sarah stuck up for me in front of another aunt, my mother's tearful apology to me years after she'd yelled at me about something unimportant, and an English teacher who, despite the lack of books in my home, taught me to write a decent English sentence.

Which leads me to the inevitable question: What will my own children remember about their childhood?

Norman Rockwell Thanksgivings? Doubtful. A turkey brought to the table tougher than shoe leather? Probably.

Jogging the Memory

The secret to having a fulfilling conversation with one's parents or grandparents, either in writing or in person, is to ask questions about specific events. It's difficult to respond to general questions, such as "What was it like growing up in the 1940s?" or "What was your mother like when you were a boy?" Instead, aim for occasions or everyday occurrences that will jog the memory, such as the following examples from my daughter's gift to me of a memory book.

(cont.)

Jogging the Memory (cont.)

- What was it like being the oldest/ youngest/middle child in your family? How did you and your siblings get along?
- What was a typical weekday dinner like at your house? What kinds of foods did your mother make? What foods did you like? Which did you hate?
- What movies did you like? What television shows?
- What books did you read when you were a kid?
- What kinds of rules did your parents enforce in the household when you were young?
- Did you ever break the rules?
- Tell me about a best friend.
- What were holidays like as you grew up? Thanksgiving? Christmas? What about birthdays?
- What was the happiest memory from your childhood? The saddest?
- Where did you and Dad/Mom meet? Was it love at first sight?
- Tell me what you remember about your wedding.
- Tell me one lesson/thought that you'd like to pass on to the next generation.

Saturday Evening Post

Total Recall

by Gary Marcus

How much would you pay to have a small memory chip implanted in your brain if that chip would double the capacity of your short-term memory? Or guarantee that you would never again forget a face or a name?

There's a good reason to consider such offers. Although our memories are sometimes spectacular—we are very good at recognizing photos, for example—our memory capacities are often disappointing. Faulty memories have been known to lead to erroneous eyewitness testimony (and false imprisonment), to marital friction (in the form of overlooked anniversaries) and even death (sky divers have been known to forget to pull their ripcords—accounting, by one estimate, for approximately 6 percent of sky-diving fatalities). The dubious dynamics of memory leave us vulnerable to the predations of spin doctors (because a phrase like "death tax" automatically brings to mind a different set of associations than "estate tax"), the pitfalls of stereotyping (in which easily accessible memories wash out less common counterexamples) and what the psychologist Timothy Wilson calls "mental contamination." To the extent that we frequently can't separate relevant information from irrelevant information, memory is often the culprit.

All this becomes even more poignant when you compare our memories to those of the average laptop. Whereas it takes the average human child weeks or even months or years to memorize something as simple as a multiplication table, any modern computer can memorize any table in an instant—and never forget it. Why can't we do the same?

Much of the difference lies in the basic organization of memory. Computers organize everything they store according to physical or logical *locations*, with each bit stored in a specific place according to some sort of master map, but we have no idea where anything in our brains is stored. We retrieve information not by knowing *where* it is but by using cues or clues that hint at *what* we are looking for.

In the best-case situation, this process works well: the particular memory we need just "pops" into our minds, automatically and effortlessly. The catch, however, is that our memories can easily get confused, especially when a given set of cues points to more than one memory. What we remember at any given moment depends heavily on the accidents of which bits of mental flotsam and jetsam happen to be active at that instant. Our mood, our environment, even our posture can all influence our delicate memories. To take

Author Bio

Gary Marcus is a professor of psychology at New York University, and director of the NYU Center for Child Language. He is the author of *Kluge: The Haphazard Construction of the Human Mind*, which was a 2008 *New York Times Book Review* Editor's Choice. He is also the editor of *The North Psychology Reader*, and author of *The Birth of the Mind*, a look at the role of genes in the development of the brain.

but one example, studies suggest that if you learn a word while you happen to be slouching, you'll be better able to remember that word at a later time if you are slouching than if you happen to be standing upright.

And it's not just humans. Cue-driven memory with all its idiosyncrasies has been found in just about every creature ever studied, from snails to flies, spiders, rats and monkeys. As a product of evolution, it is what engineers might call a kluge, a system that is clumsy and inelegant but a lot better than nothing.

If we dared, could we use the resources of modern science to improve human memory? Quite possibly, yes. A team of Toronto researchers, for example, has shown how a technique known as deep-brain stimulation can make small but measurable improvements by using electrical stimulation to drive the cue-driven circuits we already have.

But techniques like that can only take us so far. They can make memories more accessible but not necessarily more reliable, and the improvements are most likely to be only incremental. Making our memories both more accessible *and* more reliable would require something else, perhaps a system modeled on Google, which combines cue-driven promptings similar to human memory with the location-addressability of computers.

However difficult the practicalities, there's no reason in principle why a future generation of neural prostheticists couldn't pick up where nature left off, incorporating Google-like master maps into neural implants. This in turn would allow us to search our *own* memories—not just those on the Web—with something like the efficiency and reliability of a computer search engine.

Would this turn us into computers? Not at all. A neural implant equipped with a master memory map wouldn't impair our capacity to think, or to feel, to love or to laugh; it wouldn't change the nature of what we chose to remember; and it wouldn't necessarily even expand

the sheer size of our memory banks. But then again our problem has never been how *much* information we could store in our memories; it's always been in getting that information back out—which is precisely where taking a clue from computer memory could help.

The New York Times Magazine

Author's Comments

I came to writing relatively late in life, not in grade school, or even in college or graduate school; my principal mission had always been to be a scientist. But as it happens, my scientific mentor, Steven Pinker, is one of the world's leading science writers, and I watched over his shoulder as he made the transition from writing for scientists to writing for the broader public. If Pinker gave me a model, practice—five years of concerted efforts to make every email sparkle—gave me the needed skills.

"Total Recall," is about the perils of human memory and what we might do about them. In some ways, it's an extract from my most recent book, *Kluge: The Haphazard Construction of the Human Mind*, but it's not a straightforward first serial pulled directly from the book. In fact, the key idea in the essay doesn't appear in the book at all. The book tried to answer the question, "If evolution is so powerful, how come the human mind is so clumsy?" "Total Recall" is really about a different question: Will we ever be able to use technology to work around the mind's most serious limitations?

The hardest part in writing the article was in achieving a sort of acceptance: the recognition that (a) the essay that I would be writing wasn't the straight-from-the-book-piece I originally had envisioned but that (b) changing focus was a great way to explore new territory.

—Gary Marcus

Deadlines and Diapers and Dinner

by Heidi Drake

I was talking to a colleague this morning, verifying information in a report we were collaborating on, when my 20-month-old daughter reached for the phone, crying, "Miiine!" while her older sister proceeded to spill juice on the carpet. Thank goodness the person I was talking to laughed and complimented me on my multi-tasking skills, rather than finding it to be horribly unprofessional.

Being a freelance writer allows me to be home with my kids, but the term "office distractions" has taken on a whole new meaning since I left the office where I'd worked for over ten years to become a contractor. My house often feels like a three-ring circus, with me juggling my job, the girls, and domestic responsibilities. Still, I have no desire to return to the corporate world. After much trial and error over the last five years, I have settled into a work-and-life style that fits my personality and my family's needs.

In 2005, *USA Today* reported that there were over 10 million female-owned businesses in the USA. A growing number of these are home-based. I noticed this trend personally as I became acquainted with other moms in my neighborhood and found myself in the company of a realtor, a speech therapist, a book publisher, and another freelance writer. When we have time to get together, we often discuss how to survive—and even enjoy—being business owners as well as taxi drivers to school and swim lessons. What does it take to be successful at both without losing your mind?

Consider Your Personality Type

Do you thrive on interaction with colleagues in the workplace or does the thought of "commuting" down the hall and working in relative solitude sound appealing? I was spurred on by my desire to be home with my kids while they were young, and my productivity went up when I no longer had to deal with getting dressed for work and commuting to the office. I found my girls to be a much more rewarding distraction than long meetings and chatty co-workers.

A colleague of mine had a very different experience. After six months of working from home, she said she missed the office team environment and had begun to resent her kids' interruptions during the day. Finding it increasingly difficult to separate work from home and family, she returned to the office and she and her family were happier for it. Make a list of pros and cons relative to working from home before you decide, and be brutally honest with yourself. The goal is to be a happy "Mompreneur," and it may take a few adjustments to get it right.

Author Bio

Heidi Drake owns and operates the Write Way, LLC. She worked as a lead writer and editor in the corporate world for over ten years before making the transition to independent contracting. She resides in Oregon.

Experiment With Your Schedule

I began with a rigid schedule: I started at 7:00 a.m. sharp and didn't stop until my projects for the day were done. This ended abruptly when Elise came along. "Shhh... Mommy's working" means nothing to an infant! As she became more mobile and verbal, the interruptions increased as well. Then we added sister Maya to the mix, and I found myself finishing my work at night after everyone had gone to sleep. One of Maya's first words was "zombie" and I'm sure she was describing her mother.

When I stopped compartmentalizing work and family and house responsibilities into scheduled time periods, I was able to create a day that consists of shorter periods of time spent working intermixed with trips to the park, errands, reading books, housework, and eating meals with the girls. By giving them my undivided attention for a while every couple of hours, they are less apt to beg for it when I need to concentrate. I also get breaks I would deny myself if left to my own devices, which turned out to be an unexpected and healthy change.

Keep The Kids Occupied While You Work

Training my girls to nap at the same time proved to be worth the effort, as it provides me with two- to three-hour stretches for work after lunch. I also put Elise in pre-school three days a week, as much for her own socialization as my need for quiet time. For the times the kids are at home and awake, I set up a small desk in my office with paper and art supplies so they can "work" along with me. They love showing me their "articles," and it keeps them in my sight and out of trouble. I do allow them to watch some children's television as well, especially in the mornings when I do high priority work. They watch a little *Sesame Street* or *Dora the Explorer*, and then we go outside or do something physical for a while.

Organize Your Office To Suit Your Needs And Tastes

I started with an office adjoining our living room, close to the kitchen, and in the heart of things. It kept me close to the girls' play area and near the fridge containing frequently-requested beverages and snacks. I could also close the French doors when I needed to concentrate.

At our next house, the office was in a large bonus room upstairs, and we set up the kids' toys and books in that room as well. What I hadn't anticipated was their growing talent for creating massive "toy explosions," which often took over my desk, and the increase in noise level once Maya started talking, too. I found myself constantly running up and down the stairs to meet various demands, which was a great fitness program but not conducive to getting work done.

My next office space was designed to be similar to my first, with French doors separating the girls' and my areas and a "No toys on Mom's desk" rule in place. As my budget has allowed, I have added shelving, file cabinets, and desk organizers, as well as photos and art, to create a workspace I can truly call my own.

Find Small Ways To Keep Work And Home Life Separate

It can be hard to separate work from household responsibilities when you're simultaneously on the phone with a client, dispensing milk and crackers, and starting the next load of laundry—I know this personally. I use the computer in my office for work only, and I use the laptop downstairs for surfing the Internet or paying bills. This is also helpful for the girls, who know that when I'm busy in my office, I'm not to be disturbed for minor things, but when I'm using my laptop, it's okay to interrupt. I also don't answer the home phone while I'm working or answer the work phone after business hours.

I return non-urgent calls later in the day.

The key is to find what works for *you*. Experiment and don't be afraid to toss out old ideas and habits. It is possible to be more productive when you have the freedom to do things your own way, and you just might find time for a soak in the hot tub with the kids after lunch.

How to Avoid the 5 "Laws of Defeat" of Business Leadership

1.) Opportunity Knocking—Do Not Disturb

"Opportunity myopia," notes Dr. Steven Feinberg, happens when narrow thinking rules behavior. "Leaders get so focused on established goals, they often miss opportunities because they don't understand the strategic context in which they can see a way to win." Feinberg cites Sears as a classic example. Sears passed on the opportunity to purchase the Home Depot chain because of their own financial problems, without seeing the value of the proposal to acquire Home Depot.

2.) Perceptual Bias—We Think We Are Thinking, But Are We?

"One of the easiest mistakes leaders make is confusing perception with reality; they don't see what they don't want to see," says Feinberg. "Stepping back, removing oneself to see a true picture of your decision making is difficult to do. In my work, I make leaders aware of perceptual biases and errors that cloud clear, accurate judgment."

3.) Competing Against Yourself—At Cross Purposes

"Businesses shoot themselves in the foot by competing against themselves, and they are rarely aware of it," adds Feinberg. "Some examples include: pushing for growth while pushing for cost savings; promoting innovation but punishing mistakes; giving mandates to people in your organization, but not giving them adequate decision-making authority to carry it out."

4.) Stuck in Your Persistence—Making Sticky Problems Stickier

"The adage: 'If at first you don't succeed, try, try again' isn't always good business," notes Feinberg. "We can get stuck in our own persistence, whether repeated interpersonal conflicts or pushing projects we believe in, even though they are not working after multiple attempts. The road to hell is paved with mishandled interactions. Recurrent problems leave clues—the repeated attempted solutions that don't work. Changing the game, by first stopping the game is a good initial move."

5.) Reactive Tendency—Playing to Avoid Losing

"When a leader is outcome-oriented, the emphasis is on achieving the outcome; you play to win rather than complaining or blaming circumstances," says Feinberg. "Reactive mishandling of situations almost always guarantees lower outcomes. What I call 'Advantage-Makers' are those rare leaders who win more often because they know how to consistently transform challenging situations into the best possible outcomes," notes Feinberg. "They see opportunities where others see problems, influence outcomes where others are stuck, and create advantages where others are challenged. Move forward when others are stuck."

Home Business Magazine

Deadlines and Diapers and Dinner

Author's Comments ———————

I earned my Bachelor's degree in journalism from the University of Oregon. To
my dismay, I found entry level magazine
writers' positions to be low-paying and
tough to get, and I didn't have the experience and confidence I needed to strike out
as a freelancer. After stints as a salon receptionist and a travel agent, I did commercial writing for 13 years, allowing me
to work at home with my young children.

Bored with the writing I was doing, I
resurrected the dream of writing magazine
articles and signed up for Long Ridge
Writers Group's *Breaking Into Print* course.
My instructor told me, "Write what you
know and live." At the time I was juggling
kids and a home office and I noticed a
trend in my community toward moms
working from home at least part time.

After researching *The Best of the Magazine Markets for Writers*, I knew advice for
such "Mompreneurs" would be perfect for
Home Business Magazine. My instructor
agreed and was instrumental in helping
me develop the article and write the query
letter that got the editor's attention and
my first piece published!

When you write about what you know
and love, research is easier (and more fun!)
and your confidence in your subject will
shine through. In my query letter I touched
on my tenure as a commercial writer to
show experience, but it was the fact that I
was living the article I proposed that made
me an "expert" and someone with a
unique slant on the subject.

—Heidi Drake

Artist, Scientist, Technician, Historian Dudley Giberson

by John Walters

Imagine a first-class musician who is also a first-class composer. Now make him a path breaking inventor and instrument builder, whose creations are used by a majority of serious performers. And for good measure, let's say he's a renowned historian who has made significant discoveries about early music.

It's doubtful that such a musician exists. But in the realm of artisan glass, he does. His name is Dudley Giberson. From his studio in Warner, he has had a far-reaching impact on his chosen medium.

"I'd say there are a dozen key figures in the studio glass movement," says fellow glass artist Richard Remsen of Rockport, Maine. "Dudley is in that group."

Giberson has been a glass artist for 40 years. He began as a glassblower, but then he abandoned the blowpipe and pioneered new techniques in glass art. His patented inventions—kilns, burners, annealers—are standard equipment in most glass studios. His book, *A Glassblower's Companion*, is one of the foremost texts on glass art and technology;

Author Bio

John Walters is a freelance writer; his articles have appeared in numerous magazines and newspapers. He is a former host and anchor at New Hampshire Public Radio.

the Glass Art Society Newsletter says it "should be on every hot shop's bookshelf." ("Hot shop" is the insider's term for a glass studio, with its super-hot ovens and burners.) And in recent years, he has rediscovered some of the methods of ancient glassmakers from long before the invention of the blowpipe in the first century A.D.

At first glance, Giberson seems more like a retired factory worker than an artist. He's dressed in a sweatshirt and old blue jeans; his white hair sticks out around the edges of a "Glass Art Society" ball cap. His conversation is a bit reserved, his tone deliberate and understated. Once in a while, a tongue-in-cheek remark is delivered with the faintest hint of a smile.

Calling him a "factory worker" isn't as far from the truth as you might think. In many ways, a glass studio is a factory: full of heat, chemicals, high technology and industrial processes. Giberson is an artist, but he's also a metalworker and woodworker. He knows how to build and run a foundry, and he has a deep knowledge of engineering and materials science. Although he is old enough to be a retired factory worker—he turned 65 in December— he is as active as he has ever been.

Exploring a Studio—and a Life

Along a dirt road on the outskirts of Warner, a handmade sign hangs from a tree: "Joppa Glassworks," Giberson's studio since 1967.

He lives in a 225-year-old house that's, frankly, not much to look at. He bought the place because it was cheap. Cheap enough for a budding artist on a shoestring budget, with no desire to find a job. "I've never had a regular paycheck from anywhere," he says. He shares the home with his partner and professional collaborator Carolyn Rordam, a glass artist and art teacher at Merrimack High School.

He'd rather figure out a way to do a new thing than do the same thing over and over again.

A few years after he bought the house, he built a studio out back—a two-story structure with plenty of room inside and little trace of exterior adornment. Both buildings reflect his personality: fiercely independent, absolutely focused on the things that interest him, unwilling to bother with much else.

The studio contains all the usual hot-shop gear, but there's a crucial difference. It was all built by Giberson himself—a testament to his skills as an inventor, engineer and technician. Those skills came to the fore in 1968, when he invented a new kind of burner head. "I was using my first furnace. I had a metal burner in there. And you know the glass furnaces heat up to about 2,500 degrees sometimes, and metal melts around 2,350. These burners started disintegrating and making a mess! I came up with a ceramic burner that is not totally impervious to heat, but you can't really melt it."

The ceramic burner is one of many Giberson inventions widely used in glass studios. In fact, it could be argued that Giberson's gear has provided the foundation of the studio art movement. It's practical, it stands up to the extreme conditions of glass-making, and it's designed by an artist to serve the needs of an artist.

His inventions have provided a steady source of income that gives him the freedom to follow his own path. In a way, that's a loss to the art world: in recent years, Giberson has focused on historical research and produced very little art.

It might seem odd that a great artist would turn away from his art and dedicate himself to exploring techniques that became outmoded nearly 2,000 years ago. But to him, the ancient times were literally a Golden Age. "Over time, glass has had such a wide range of value," he explains. "In ancient times, it was worth its weight in gold. Today, it's hardly worth anything; we throw it away." Through his research, he is connecting to his artistic forefathers and a time when glass was purely a creative medium, not an industrial product.

Beyond that, it's clear that Giberson is motivated, above all else, by the thrill of discovery. He'd rather figure out a way to do a new thing than do the same thing over and over again.

Canes and Beads

Behind the main studio is a small room that bears witness to Giberson's independence and high standards. "We batch all our own glass from scratch," he says matter-of-factly. From his tone, you wouldn't realize how unusual this is. Most artists buy glass from suppliers. Making it on site is time consuming, costly, precision work—but you do get exactly the kind of glass you want.

An adjacent room contains glass rods, or "canes," in a huge variety of colors. "Over the years, we've made these different colors. Draw it off into cane and you can store it." Understatement again. The canemaking process involves taking a glob of molten glass and, in a matter of seconds (before it becomes a solid again), stretching it to a length of several feet while maintaining its shape and integrity. To an outsider, it looks almost impossible; for Giberson, it's routine.

In the past, he used the technique to make glass beads, which may be his best-known product in the marketplace. In the late 1970s, he'd become dissatisfied with the creative possibilities of standard glassblowing. That's when the historical research began; as he says, "From 1979 until now, I've tried to stay on the other side of the invention of the blowpipe." While trying to discover how ancient artisans did their work, he developed what he calls the drawn-tube method: he taught himself to draw out a long tube of multicolored glass. Then, having produced a huge quantity of glass tubes, he came up with the idea of cutting them into beads.

At the time, handmade glass beads were virtually unknown. And that was a problem: "Every craft show had blown glass in it, but they had rigorous standards: no strung beads!" A hint of a smile plays across his face. "They were assuming that somebody else was making the beads and you were just stringing them. When we finally got the shows to change their rules, I was able to go to Rhinebeck (New York), which was a major craft fair, the big one at the time. And the first show, we just sold out. We had hundreds and hundreds of pieces, and we literally sold out!"

Today, glass beads are a staple of art and craft shows. They are so popular, in fact, that he stopped making them "because the competition got quite stout." And, of course, because Giberson is always looking for a new challenge.

Upward and Onward

After touring the main floor of the studio, we head upstairs. In front is a woodshop; the back room is set up for photography. There are dozens of small boxes in this room. Giberson opens a few of them, revealing the artistic fruits of his research into ancient glass: small glass bowls no more than a few inches across, multicolored, intricately de-

signed. Some were made by him, some by Rordam. They are subtle but breathtaking. Each bowl includes several distinct design elements that are impossible to do with modern glassblowing techniques.

There's one big problem: the process is financially impractical. "It's so time consuming," he says. "It takes me several weeks to finish some of these pieces. If I asked two or three thousand dollars for it, people would think I'm crazy. And that would be just a pittance for the time I put into it."

To find out why, take a look at "Dudley Giberson's Core Vessel Video," a self-produced documentary about his rediscovery of ancient glassmaking. He starts by hand grinding chunks of glass into fine granules, known as "frit." Then he makes a core vessel from a custom mixture of clay, silica, sawdust

Conventional glassblowing is a lot like jazz . . .

and dung, fired in a plaster cast. The core vessel provides the surface on which the bowl is constructed by painstakingly applying small amounts of frit and water until the right thickness is achieved.

Then the fritted core is fired for several hours in an 1,100-degree oven—much cooler than the temperature required for modern glassmaking.

The initial firing produces the interior surface of a glass bowl. Then you add more frit and premade design elements to the outside, and continue the melting process over what Giberson calls a "volcano"—a cone-shaped oven with an opening at the top. This allows precise placement of the vessel to get just the right amount of heat.

Conventional glassblowing is a lot like jazz: planning and preparation, leading to a burst of controlled improvisation. The ancient methods allow for an entirely different approach: Giberson's bowls are constructed layer by layer, piece by piece, in a way that modern techniques don't allow. But the ancient methods take much more time and effort.

The core vessel and bowl are placed overnight in an annealer, where the cooling process is slow and controlled. Then the core vessel has to be removed from the inside of the finished bowl, bit by bit; the slow heat has turned the vessel into a fragile substance that crumbles into dust. But, even so, it must be done with great care to prevent any damage to the bowl itself.

Giberson doesn't know where this ancient research will take him. Honestly, he doesn't seem to care. He's planning to write a book about his ancient glass discoveries, and perhaps someday, as with his drawn-bead technique, they could open the door to new kinds of glass art. If so, he'll probably do it for a while and then move on to the next big challenge, the next unanswered question.

Kearsarge Magazine

Author's Comments

If a writer's toughest sale is the first one, then I bypassed that obstacle. I became a freelance writer after many years in radio. My name was known in media circles, so it wasn't hard to approach editors.

But then I had to prove myself by delivering good stories on time and within the assigned length. If you can do that, editors will welcome your ideas. That was the case with this story.

This was a tough article to write. Giberson is a multifaceted person with a deep technical knowledge of his craft; I had to simplify things without distorting or omitting key aspects.

I recorded our interview and took photographs. The photos were purely for my own use; they helped me recall descriptive details. Later, I transcribed the interview and read through the notes. Then I fashioned an outline and fleshed it in. If I get the outline right, I don't have to do any wholesale rewriting. It's mostly a matter of refining and (if necessary) cutting the word count.

To me, the most important part of the article is the opening: It needs to pull the reader in. Sometimes it's descriptive, sometimes it tells a key moment or catchy anecdote. In this case, I began with a brief summary. Giberson is so broadly accomplished, I thought this was the best way to make the reader want to know more.

—John Walters

Tapping for Maple's Sweet Gold

by Jessica Stone

In early spring, as the maple trees start their new growth spurts, the sap within them that remained frozen for months begins to thaw. This is what sugar makers wait for all year long. It's the beginning of the maple harvest season, when sugar houses across New England and Canada are busy tapping maple trees of their sap—a clear, slightly sweet liquid that is boiled down to a sweet syrup. The details of when, where and by whom the first maple was tapped are debatable. But one thing is certain: Maple syrup has become one of America's culinary treasures—and a cultural celebration for the select few regions worldwide where sugar making takes place.

The Early Sugaring Process

Before maple syrup came maple sugar, which did not spoil when stored. Journals kept by early explorers reveal that by the time the Pilgrims landed in Plymouth Rock in 1620, Native American Indians had been sugaring—tapping maple trees and cooking the sap over an open fire until it became syrup and eventually a nonperishable sugar—for more than a decade. In fact, the Sugar Moon is linked to the month of March in the Native American calendar when many tribes celebrated the first sugar with a spirited festival that included a Maple Dance intended to set the pace for a bountiful season.

As Janet Eagleson, co-author of *The Maple Syrup Book* (Boston Mills Press, 2006) explains, "The medicine man would often mix a small amount of last year's harvest with the first harvest of the year to extend the blessing and good luck of the season. It was a fantastic party that involved everyone in the tribe, and the better the party, the better the maple season." Today, major maple syrup-producing regions continue the tradition with events like Quebec's annual sugaring-off festival at Sucrerie de la Montagne.

New England explorers recorded three kinds of maple sugar produced by Native Americans: grain sugar, similar to today's brown sugar; cake sugar, which could be poured into wooden molds for easy storing and shaving throughout the year; and wax sugar, made by coating snow with extra-thick syrup. Maple sugar soon became a regular stand-in for the expensive cane sugar from the West Indies and turned into a valuable trading commodity. One early champion of locally produced sugar was Thomas Jefferson, who transplanted young sugar maple from Vermont —the second largest maple-syrup producer worldwide—to his plantation in Monticello, Va. Unfortunately, the southern climate was

Author Bio

Jessica Stone graduated from New York University with a master's in journalism in 1999. She juggles freelance advertising, copywriting, and journalism. She specializes in writing about food and has contributed to the *New York Times*, *The Guardian*, and *The Times of London*, among others. She has lived in London since January 2004.

unsuitable for sap production, and Jefferson was left with thriving trees but no syrup.

A Serendipitous Discovery

According to Native American folklore, the discovery of maple syrup as its own delicacy, and not just another step in the sugar-making process, was a serendipitous one.

Legend has it that Chief Woksis, the great Iroquois hunter, tipped his axe into the trunk of a maple one late winter evening before going to bed. He removed his weapon the next morning and took it with him on a long hunt. The days turned warmer while he was away, and the tree's sap dripped into a container the hunter had left behind. His industrious wife happened upon it, assumed it was frozen water and set about boiling meat with it. As her recipe bubbled away over the fire, the sweetness of the sap deepened, and when Woksis returned, he devoured the dish.

Still, boiling sap down to crystallized sugar was a more valuable commodity to early Americans than turning it into syrup.

Tapping Success

As winter thawed into spring, Native American families—and later New England settlers—would set up sugar camps among the maple trees. There they would slash notches into the trunks and collect the sap in clay or bark vessels, boiling the water away by dropping heated rocks into the containers.

With experience comes experimentation, and the settlers started to look for ways to industrialize the production of their coveted maple syrup. A drill and spile, which is a spout used to draw off sap, replaced the axe, while copper and iron kettles were put to work over open fires. Early spiles were fashioned out of hollowed-out softwood twigs and inserted into the drilled hole in maple trees. Sap spilled out into bark containers placed below. It was then boiled down before being transferred into a succession of smaller and smaller vessels.

When the syrup sufficiently thickened, it was stirred to speed up the formation of sugar crystals and then, finally, poured into molds. It was an assembly-line process, albeit a slow one, and the variety of tasks involved served to bring pioneer families together. As the adults worked the bubbling pots—each one filled with syrup at a different stage of the thickening process—their children, still bundled from the cold, watched excitedly as a newly drilled tree cried its first sweet tears.

Making the Grade

There are four grades of maple syrup according to color and flavor: Grade A Light Amber, Grade A Medium Amber, Grade A Dark Amber and Grade B, which is the darkest of all. The deeper the color, the stronger the flavor. Like wine, the characteristics of the local soil are reflected in its resulting syrup, so you must taste to find your favorite. Vermont and Ontario produce the sweetest syrups. Grade B is the rarest and also the best for cooking since it can hold its own among other flavors in a dish. Try it simmered in baked beans, or as part of a marinade for meat or fish, like Chief Woksis' wife did. Lighter syrups are best poured over ice cream, fresh-cut fruit and, of course, a lofty stack of pancakes.

Metal Power

Through the next century, maple-sugar production became more controlled, cleaner and complex. As metal spouts were introduced, sugar makers substituted metal buckets and shallow, flat-bottomed pans for the early wooden models. The flat pans were suspended in an arch above the fire, and tents were also built over the pans to create sheltered "sugar houses."

By the late 1800s, makers used a purpose-built device called an "evaporator." (A patent wasn't registered until 1884.) Designed by a

Vermont sugar maker, it consisted of a flat pan built with separate channels and compartments that would allow fresh sap to flow in one end while finished syrup could be drawn out the other. Ridges at the bottom of the pan further increased the surface area for heating, greatly accelerating the boiling of sap into syrup. Maple sugar production had never been so efficient.

Then something unexpected happened. Officials removed the import tax on cane sugar, and the new kid on the block knocked maple sugar out of popularity. This wasn't a problem for the New England sugar makers, who cunningly capitalized on the trend by rebranding their business into syrup. The old sugar molds gave way to bottles and cans filled with the signature amber liquid, and sweet success hasn't stopped flowing since.

Reverse-osmosis reduction, steam-and-oil powered evaporation, vacuum systems and computerization are some of the technological advances that have sped up the production of maple syrup, but the basic evaporator design hasn't changed much since the late 1900s. Still, just as the original model was conceived in Vermont, syrup researchers and makers there are at the forefront of maple-syrup production, constantly striving for more efficient, cost-effective ways to produce their precious commodity. Recent innovations include smaller spouts and replaceable "spout insertions," allowing syrup makers to start each season with a brand new spout, thus reducing the chances of outside bacterial contamination. These sustainable initiatives, aside from affording syrup makers the possibility of higher yields, also result in less damage to maples during the tapping process.

Learning to Tap

It's easy to see why Chief Woksis' wife thought the pot at the base of that old tree was full of water: Maple sap drips clear, is only about 2 to 3 percent sugar and is only slightly sweet on the tongue. Maple sap usually has a higher sugar content in springtime that at any other time of the year, which means it takes less time and energy to turn it into precious syrup.

But trying to tap at the right time of year didn't—and still doesn't—guarantee success. If you're thinking about tapping your own trees, you need to grow the right kind (13 native maple species grow in North America) in the right environment, factors found together only in parts of Canada, New England and the upper Midwest. You also need patience. You'll need about 10 gallons of sap to create just one quart of syrup. When trees grow to about a foot in diameter, they are ready to be tapped. Sugar maples take between 40 to 60 years to reach this stage, and most trees can take only one or two tappings per season.

At a basic level, tapping maple trees requires a drill bit, a tapper, such as a battery-powered drill or gasoline-powered tapper, spouts or spiles, a small mallet and a clean bucket. Making your own maple syrup can be rewarding, and many commercial producers hold open houses during springtime so you can learn the tricks of the trade.

The production of sap is a marvelous manifestation of the relationship between earth and air, and it helps to understand what's going on in your maples before you take a tapper to trunk. During late summer and fall when temperatures start to drop, maple trees enter a period of declined growth and begin to store the excess starches throughout the sapwood. As soon as the wood warms to 40 F, the stored starch turns into sugars and infuses the sap.

As Brian Stowe, sugaring operations manager at the Proctor Maple Research Center at the University of Vermont explains, "It's up to the whim of the weather." During a warm day, the tree thaws out, and the sap starts flowing. Then, as the evening turns cooler and the tree begins to freeze, the

Sautauthig

Besides its unparalleled flavor, maple syrup is a source of minerals including calcium, potassium and iron, and it contains fewer calories than sugar. There are many ways to show off maple's marvels in the kitchen.

During Colonial times, Native Americans enjoyed a simple dish similar to porridge that they called Sautauthig (pronounced saw-taw-teeg). The settlers adopted the recipe and embellished it with milk, butter and sugar. One colonist even found it worth writing home about: "...this is to be boyled or stued with a gentle fire, till it be tender, of a fitt consistence, as of Rice so boyled, into which Milke, or butter be put either with sugar or without it, it is food very pleasant."

Feel free to add your own special touches to the following updated recipe.

Maple, Corn & Blueberry Porridge

¾ cup water
¾ cup milk
¼ cup quick-cooking grits or cornmeal
A good pat of butter
¼ teaspoon salt
A pinch of nutmeg
2 tablespoons maple syrup
1 cup fresh blueberries

In a heavy-bottomed saucepan, heat water and milk over a medium flame until bubbles form around edge of the pan. Meanwhile, combine the cornmeal or grits with the salt and nutmeg in a separate bowl. Slowly add the dry ingredients, mix well and stir in the butter until melted. Reduce heat to low and cover, cooking until thickened (about five minutes). Gently fold in the maple syrup and berries. (Serves four.)

dissolved gases in the tree create a negative pressure that allows it to draw water from the soil. Sugar concentration in the sap can vary day to day, hour by hour. Tapping the tree decreases the pressure inside it and frees the sap. While the incision may technically be a wound, it is one that does no damage if the maples are healthy and if we, in turn, continue to cherish, celebrate and respect the trees as the Native Americans did.

American Spirit

Author's Comments

This article began as a freelance assignment. I knew and had worked with the managing editor of *American Spirit* magazine in New York. Knowing how much I love and miss American comfort food—namely pancakes with lots of maple syrup—she commissioned me to write this piece. Since I have constant cravings for real maple syrup, there were no challenges in crafting this article. It was a fairly straightforward piece requiring only one draft.

I always divide an assignment—especially a longer one such as this—into sections. It's easier to look at a piece as individual fragments rather than trying to tackle it as a whole. Think chapters rather than total word count.

Journalism school never taught me how to sell a piece, and it's the one thing that probably discourages new writers the most. And, unless you want to write on spec, you'll need to show editors clips. Instead, I started a blog: www.ripelondon.com. Once I had enough posts, I began to target editors until one finally agreed to take me on. Today, it's especially important for writers to have an online presence. The pressure to post also keeps you sharp.

—Jessica Stone

My So-Called Genius

by Laura Fraser

I learned the word *precocious* long before other kids in my age. By the time I was five or six, I had heard it often—I was always younger than everyone around me and ahead of my peers. Being defined by a long, difficult adjective made me special; it made me, in some essential way, who I am.

I read early and voraciously, squirreling away splendiferously big words to spring on adults whenever I needed attention, which was often. I thrived on being called "smart" and "cute." A psychologist said I had an IQ of 165, a number I thought was as immutable as the color of my eyes. I whizzed through school, skipping grades, racking up awards and honors. By 15 I was writing a column for my hometown newspaper. All the way back in third grade, my teacher told me I would become a great writer—at an early age, of course—and that's just what I figured would happen.

All those early predictions, my dazzling promise? They haven't quite panned out. Despite having published hundreds of magazine articles and two nonfiction books, at 47 I'm no longer an up-and-comer. Peers I was ahead of early in my career have caught up or passed me by: starting their own companies,

writing more books, buying vacation homes, embarking on lucrative second careers. Legions of people younger than I am are much more accomplished, and I'm mightily annoyed whenever one of them publishes a best-seller or wins a Pulitzer Prize. Day by day I seem to be losing my smarts, and we won't talk about my cutes.

All of us in our forties and beyond need to come to a reckoning of what we wanted to be and who we actually are; that's one definition of maturity. Grown-ups can accept that they aren't international opera stars of Nobel Prize-winners in medicine. Rather than live in disappointment, they appreciate the reality of who they've become (perhaps it's manager and not CEO) and acknowledge their skills, accomplishments and lessons learned.

But for those of us whose precociousness forecast an early and spectacular success— and I'm hardly alone in this—our midlife

My age, I figured, was a lot like my weight . . .

accomplishments are much more difficult to reconcile. No matter what we've achieved (one of my books even became a best-seller), many of us feel a nagging sense of failure. I can't say this for sure, but I'd bet it was a formerly precocious person who coined the term *midlife crisis*.

The first glimmer that my future might not be so brilliant came in college. When I entered Wesleyan early, at 17, I was shocked

Author Bio

Laura Fraser has been a freelance writer for 25 years. She has published two books, *An Italian Affair* (Pantheon) and *Losing It* (Dutton). She is a contributing writer at *MORE* magazine.

to find I was no longer head of the class but in the middle of the heap—there were hordes of smarty-pants out there. Still, I edited the school paper and after graduation threw myself into a freelance writing career with such fervor that one editor dubbed me the little engine that could. But over the years my engine chugged slower and slower. Like my fellow ex whiz kids, I entered the stage that I've begun to call post-cociousness. The tried-and-true remedies are drinking heavily, griping at the world for never giving us our due and criticizing more successful people for all their defects. Me, I preferred denial.

In midlife I pretended that I hadn't flowered yet because I was still so young. I dated as if I were in my twenties, put crazy streaks in my hair and avoided most of the trappings of serious adulthood: marriage, a house, children, financial security and a reasonable retirement plan.

George Eliot didn't publish her first novel until she was 40, so given today's life expectancy, that meant I had at least until I turned 53 to write a great one, right? My age, I figured, was a lot like my weight: As long as I exercised and carried it well, no one would ever guess how high the number really was. But on my last birthday—the one that put me in my late forties—I admitted to myself: I am no longer young and precocious.

Where does that leave me? In good, formerly gifted, company. Early aptitude doesn't necessarily predict adult accomplishment; in fact, the opposite may be truer. Author Malcolm Gladwell, in his speech "American Obsession with Precociousness," pointed out that few childhood musical prodigies ever become successful. That's because there's a huge difference between talent and the application of talent. No matter how easily you pick up an instrument, you still have to practice more than your peers to get to Carnegie Hall. (And yes, Gladwell—darn him—is two years younger than I am.)

If everyone tells you when you're 10 that you'll become a great novelist, you just sit back and dream about your book jackets. Not only don't precocious kids think they have to work hard, but deep down, they believe true effort entails too much of a risk. If your entire identity is wrapped up in the magnificent things you're destined to achieve—as a great writer, musician, scientist, politician, chef—the thought that you might produce something mediocre can be devastating. Better, it seems, to hold on to the idea that you could be great than to risk being merely good, or to fail altogether.

In midlife I finally realized how this kind of thinking was getting in my way. People who read my books and articles would congratulate me on my success, but I felt like a fraud. I dismissed my actual achievements because they paled against my supposedly spectacular promise. By then not only wasn't I writing great books, I wasn't working on any new books at all. I needed help.

"Perfectionists always lose . . ."

I turned to Martha Borst, an organizational consultant and coach, and the author of *Your Survival Strategies Are Killing You*. Borst broke down some of the ways my fear of failure plays out: I procrastinate, losing control of my time. I look for approval from others—my agent, my editors, the UPS man—instead of believing in my own judgments and ideas. Most pernicious of all, the impossible standards I internalized as a precocious kid made me a perfectionist. "Perfectionists always lose," she told me. Letting go of being extraordinary was the only chance I had of achieving anything even decent. As Borst explained to me, if you strive for excellence, rather than perfection, you can take more chances. If you make mistakes—say, your novel isn't working—you can learn from them and try again: You rewrite the thing.

Her advice echoed what a psychologist told me several years ago when I was stuck writing my first book—which, of course, had to be great. "You can write a good book, can't you?" she asked. "The bookstores are filled with good books." That advice helped me get to work on what turned out to be a very good, if not great, book.

One day I was working away, writing, when I had a revelation: I'm good at what I do, but I'm never going to fulfill my early, spectacular promise. Instead of depressing me, that sudden insight had me jumping around the room. Time's up! I thought. I've already failed, which means I can stop believing I was born sprinkled with fairy dust and that I just need to keep waiting around for the magic to happen.

Age has been the greatest gift: It has allowed me to finally throw away ridiculous expectations, take some risks, use my talent and appreciate the skills I've worked hard to develop over the years. I'm grateful I was born with certain gifts, but now at midlife I can catch up on others I've missed acquiring along the way: concentration, acceptance, persistence and flexibility. Maybe by letting go of my precociousness, I can accomplish some surprising things in the next phase of my life.

Who knows? I might even be the first among my peers to become a late bloomer.

More

Author's Comments

I frequently write personal essays. This piece came out of a simple observation I made about myself, which is that being precocious was always a part of my identity, but at 45 I'm all of a sudden older than a lot of people who are more accomplished than I am. I usually write with an outline, but often with personal essays I think of a starting point, an epiphany, and an ending and then fill in the rest.

The piece went through a couple of revisions. In the first draft, I spent more time talking about being a precocious kid, when the readers of *More*, who are over 40, were more interested in what it feels like *now*, not then.

I wrote the piece for *More* because I'm a contributing editor there, meaning I write for them frequently, and because it's a subject that appeals to the magazine's demographic, which is women over 40.

My advice for writers who are submitting work for publication is to concentrate on WRITING, not SELLING. Write the best essay you can. It should be well-organized, concise, shorter than you think it should be, and full of muscular verbs and descriptive nouns.

Go read William Zinsser's classic *On Writing Well* for great advice.

—Laura Fraser

I Have a Bunch of Coins. . .

by Harry L. Rinker

I am not a coin expert. Having stated this, I know enough about coins to be dangerous. What follows illustrates this.

When doing "walk through" appraisals, I frequently encounter large collections of coins, both American and foreign. The vast majority, well over 80 percent, are saved from pocket change (i.e., coins that have been circulated).

These coins are often stored loose—in an old wallet or coin purse, in plastic bags, or a box—and found in a desk or dresser drawer. In addition, I receive over a dozen coin questions addressed to "Rinker on Collectibles" annually. The following four letters are typical:

"I do not collect coins, except to spend, but my father did some novice collecting. He collected the 'popular coins' of the 1950s and 1960s—Indian head pennies, wheat pennies, silver Kennedy halves, walking liberty halves, silver dimes and quarters, and some proof sets. I'm looking for someone I can trust . . ." —J. R., e-mail question

"I have a bunch of older coins, mostly pennies, some dimes, some foreign. I read on eBay that some coins are certified. What does this mean?"—K. B., e-mail question

"I have two silver pennies from 1943.

Author Bio

Harry L. Rinker is a national antiques and collectibles expert who has authored, co-authored, or edited more than 25 titles. He hosts a nationally syndicated call-in radio show, "Whatcha Got?"

They are magnetic and in fair to poor condition. What is their value and how do I get them appraised?"—S. G., e-mail question

"I know nothing about coins, but found some in my brother-in-law's things. He must have thought they were worth something. I have nickels as far back as 1940, 1776–1976 quarters, 1966 quarters, and a 1970 Susan B. Anthony dollar. Many seem to have a letter beside the date . . . I would like to sell them without getting ripped off."—S. L., e-mail question

Whenever I am asked about how to handle groups of coins, I offer this universal advice.

First, I remind the owners that at the very minimum, the **United States coinage is worth face value** (i.e., a penny is worth a penny, a nickel is worth five cents, a dime is worth ten cents, etc.). The coinage may not buy what it once did, but it still can buy something.

The same is not necessarily true of foreign coins. Some countries have changed their currency and provided only a limited window of opportunity to exchange the old coinage for newly issued coins. The Euro coins are a modern day example. On February 28, 2002, all the old coinage from countries switching to the Euro was no longer legal tender. Collector value was the only option remaining for the older coinage.

Second, I explain that the amount of time the owner is going to invest in sorting, researching, grading, and selling the coins is going to far exceed the value he is likely to receive from selling the coins. **Be prepared**,

I warn, **to work for less than minimum wage.** Much to my surprise, my blunt, honest assessment usually falls on deaf ears. The owner is lured into proceeding by the faint hope of discovering hidden treasure, the coin(s) whose sale will put him on easy street or, at the very least, pay for that much needed vacation.

Third, recognizing that my previous advice is likely to be ignored, I advise the owner to **sort the coins by country.** All coin reference books list coins by country. Put aside those coins whose country of origin cannot easily be determined. Fortunately, most coin reference books offer pictorial guides. The country of most "unknown" coins can be discovered by flipping through these books and finding a picture of the coin in question.

Fourth, once the country sort is complete, start with the **United States coins. Divide them into four basic groups:** (1) coins having no precious metal melt value (e.g., pennies and nickels), (2) coins made from silver, (3) silverless or clad coins, and (4) gold coins. The Coinage Act of 1965 eliminated the silver from the dime and quarter and reduced the half dollar's silver content to 40 percent. The first silverless half dollar and Eisenhower dollar coins appeared in 1971. Thus, all dimes, quarters, and half dollars minted prior to 1965 and silver dollars minted prior to 1935 have melt value since their silver content is 90 percent. In today's market, coin dealers and others buying for melt pay nine to ten times face. A pre-1965 dime is worth a minimum of ninety cents to one dollar. Obviously, the current price of gold impacts the value of all gold coins.

I strongly suspect you do not track the value of scrap metals. However, if you did, you would find that the secondary market for used copper is quite high at the moment. Hence, your old copper pennies have melt value. Once again, the key date is 1981. In 1981, Congress changed the composition of pennies from 95 percent copper and 5 percent zinc alloy to 97.5 percent zinc alloy and 2.5 percent copper. The coins look the same, but the new coins are 19 percent lighter.

Fifth, coins are graded on a scale of one to 65, with one the poorest and sixty-five the highest grade. Some sophisticated grading services have increased the scale to 70. For modern coins (i.e., 20th- and 21st-century coins), investment grade is uncirculated coins grading MS-60 and higher. The highest grade assigned to a circulated coin is AU-58.

Although there are exceptions to every generalization, a good rule is that if a pile of coins was saved from pocket change, face and melt value are far more realistic values than collector value.

Sixth, the next step for the persistent is to **obtain a coin price guide and begin researching the coins.** Use either David C. Harper's *U.S. Coin Digest: The Complete Guide to Current Market Values* (Krause Publications), Thomas E. Hudgeons, Jr.'s *The Official Blackbook Price Guide to U.S. Coins* (House of Collectibles), or R. S. Yoeman's *Red Book: A Guide to United States Coins* (Whitman Publishing). All are available at your local bookstore or public library. KP/Krause Publications (www.krausebooks.com) is the leading U.S. publisher of price guides for foreign coins. Check out the titles by Colin R. Bruce II, George Cuhaj, and Tomas Michael.

When using any of these guides, keep the following in mind. First, all the prices are retail—what you would pay if you wanted to buy the coin from a dealer, not what you would get if you wanted to sell it. Second, read the material in the front of the book and study the grading charts. Once you feel you have properly graded a coin, lower the grade by at least two steps. While grading is as much subjective as objective, amateurs and novices always tend to over-grade. There is no need to have 20th- and 21st-century pocket change coins graded. Third, unless the coin is worth $50 or more, chances are you are not going to be able to sell it to a dealer for much more than a dime to twenty cents on the dollar. This is why you must always keep a coin's melt value in the back of your mind.

How accurate are coin price guides? The Internet is filled with sites claiming coin guides are self-serving vehicles for coin dealers who are trying to prop the market. I remain neutral. All price guide prices need to be field tested.

Seventh, when researching foreign coins, again **keep in mind the precious versus non-precious metal issue.** Silver and gold foreign coins also have melt value, albeit the metal content may not equal that of the United States.

Finally, why are you doing all this work? As I stated earlier, chance are strong that you are spending an inordinate amount of time and the end result is that you are far more frustrated now than when you started.

As a result, **my best recommendation for dealing with a pile of pocket change is threefold.** First, give it to your grandchildren and let them have the joy of researching the coinage. Hopefully, one or more of them will turn into a coin collector. Second, spend all the post-1964 American coinage on yourself. You deserve it. Third, take the pile of coins to a reputable coin auction. Let the auctioneer sort them and offer them for sale. Admittedly, the bulk of the buyers will be dealers, meaning that the auctioneer will sell 90 percent or more of them at wholesale value. If you are lucky, he will find a few coins with collector appeal. The good news is that the auctioneer has done the sorting and all the work, and you have turned a headache into money in your pocket.

Collector's News

Author's Comments

"Rinker on Collectibles," now in its twenty-second year, is a self-syndicated weekly antiques and collectibles column. The format of the column alternates, with a question-and-answer column one week followed by a text column, often opinionated, the next. There have been two book compilations of "Rinker on Collectibles" columns, including the most recent title, *How To Think Like A Collector* (Emmis Books).

Occasionally I receive generic questions about a collecting category, e.g., coins, rather than a specific object, e.g., an 1898 twenty dollar gold piece. Since the question-and-answer columns are object focused, I stockpile the generic questions. I review the questions every two to three years and select a category about which to write.

It takes two to three months for a column to work its way through the periodicals, and a column often remains posted on an Internet website for a year or longer. As a result, the information must be accurate and evergreen. It is also critical to evaluate the credibility of cited sources.

I do not use an outline. I keep a list of column ideas, ideally three months or more. I continuously churn them over until I see the final column I want to write in my mind.

When I finish writing a column, I do one edit. It is then forwarded to a proofreader for a final check and formatting for distribution.

My columns vary in length rather than adhere to a specific word count. I do not recommend this approach. I get away with it because I give my editors *carte blanche* to edit, cut, reorganize, or do whatever they wish to my columns.

—Harry L. Rinker

Kitchen Knives

by Ken Haedrich

Next to hands, knives are the most important tools a cook can own. All the gadgets in the world can't do what a good knife, in competent hands, can do. Unfortunately, a lot of cooks just aren't comfortable or satisfied with kitchen knives, an unease that holds them back when it comes to learning how to use knives, or makes them dependent on food processors and other cutting gadgets. I'm not against food processors; I realize they can be a godsend in certain cases. But they should never become a substitute for a knife.

Someone gave me my first good chef's knife as a Christmas present. When I say it was good, what I really mean is it looked good. It had a long, shiny blade, a strong black handle, and an impressive French name.

Before long I realized that my knife and I had some serious differences. For one thing, the handle was too small for my hands, so I couldn't grip it with much authority. Even if I had been able to, the blade was so narrow that my knuckles crashed into the chopping board when I minced things. And the entire unit was too light.

I used this knife for years. Had I known more about knives, I would have moved on to something better much sooner than I did. Instead, I ignorantly blamed myself for lacking proper knife skills.

Having learned about knives the hard way, I can help you select a good knife and get started using it right. By way of example, I'll concentrate on the chef's knife, the one most cooks use, or should use, for the lion's share of cutting jobs, but I'll also introduce a basic selection of other knives you may want to have.

Knife Anatomy

Learning the language and structure of knives will make you a better shopper. I'm going to concentrate on chef's knives in the following discussion of knife parts, but most of the terminology and rules apply to any good knife.

Let's begin with the *bolster*, the thickened part of the blade leading into the handle. Besides adding weight to the knife (weight is important in an impact tool like the chef's knife, when you sometimes need the added power for chopping), the bolster is the balance point. On a well-made chef's knife you should actually be able to balance the bolster across an outstretched forefinger without the knife toppling off.

The lower section of the bolster—which protects your fingers from sliding up under the cutting edge—should be blunted, so the finger nearest to it doesn't rub against a sharp edge. German-made knives seem to have the most substantial bolsters.

The part of the blade facing up as you cut is called, simply, the *back*. On better chef's knives, the back will be fairly wide and flat, giving you a safe place to put your knife-free

Author Bio

Ken Haedrich is the author of a dozen cookbooks, as well as numerous articles that have appeared in *Food and Wine*, *Cooking Light*, *Bon Appetit*, and more.

hand when you need extra thrust or stability for rapid mincing. Later I'll mention some other knives whose uses require them to have thin or flexible blades, so don't judge all knives by their backs.

Rounding the point of the blade, we come to the *cutting edge*, which includes the *heel* and *tip,* the latter referring to the point and first several inches of the blade. This is the thinnest part of the chef's knife and the only part of the blade where there's usually any flexibility. It is also the weakest part of the blade, the area most likely to be damaged if you use your knife as an ice pick or can opener.

Because the tip of a chef's knife is so thin, it is essentially a cutting tool within a cutting tool. It is the part of the knife to use for shaving off thin slices of mushrooms or scallions or for making preliminary cuts in onions. It's also what you use to start to slice a ripe tomato, piercing the skin with the point so you don't press down and shower your kitchen with seeds and juice.

Stay away from handles that have a polished, slick feel to them.

Besides being a cutter, the tip is your knife's *rocker*, where most of the blade's taper is. The rocker is the part of the blade that stays in contact with your chopping board when you mince something, the fingers of your free hand resting on the back or holding the food on the chopping board. Just as the tip of the blade is the best place for easy cuts, the *heel* or opposite end of the blade is best for heavy jobs. The more resistance you're likely to encounter (as in chicken joints and rutabagas) the closer you should work to the heel.

From the heel, the blade extends back through the bolster into the handle. This extension is the *tang* and as a rule of thumb (I'll mention an exception later), the fuller the tang, the better the knife. A full tang is the same size as the handle itself and completely visible around the entire edge of the handle. A full tang, properly sandwiched between the handle pieces, makes for a rigid and durable knife.

There are other types of tangs as well. There's three-quarter, half, and something called rattail, referring to progressively smaller sections of tang enclosed within the handle. I own a three-quarter tang knife on which the tang is completely enclosed in a polypropylene handle. It's a top-quality tool and in seven years has shown no signs of loosening. Still, I think a full tang is the way to go.

Standard blade sizes of chef's knives are 8 inches, 10 inches, 12 inches, and 14 inches. Home cooks prefer the first two sizes. I personally like a 10-inch blade. The larger blades are more for the production chopping that goes on in restaurants. I recently walked through a kitchen where they turn out about 2,000 meals a night. Off in one corner I noticed a young cook, a 14-inch chef's knife in each hand, thwacking away like crazy on a mountain of parsley.

Handles come in various types of hardwoods and plastics. Wood looks pretty, but it isn't necessarily the best material for knife handles. It's sad but true that kitchen knives often end up in dishwashers, or soaking in dishwater. After repeated soakings, a wooden handle's rivets may loosen and the handle could fall apart.

For that reason, many of the top knife manufacturers—like Wuesthof Trident, whose knives I own and find exceptional— have switched to high-impact plastic handles. At Wuesthof Trident they start with handle pieces that are larger than the tang and then heat shrink them to the metal to get an extremely tight bond. This handle, they say, will never delaminate, a claim they back up with a lifetime guarantee. Stay away from handles that have a polished, slick feel to them. Knives like that are easy to lose control of when your hand is moist.

On any knife, make sure the handle is evenly finished and the rivets are flush to the handle. Protrusions will eventually cause sore spots on your hand. By the same token, avoid knife handles with complicated contours, such as little grooves where certain fingers are supposed to take up residence. Hands rarely fit the way the designer intended them to and those cute little grooves aren't so cute when your grip slips from them at the wrong time. In handles, simple is beautiful.

Knife Shopping

The first obstacle to overcome is fear of sharp blades. Respect them, but don't fear them. For example, the chef's knife, being the biggest knife in most home kitchens, is intimidating because of its size. But don't let it scare you; learn to appreciate it for what it is. Take a good look at a well-built chef's knife. It's really a beautiful tool: The sleek, glistening blade, honed to a razor-sharp edge, rises from its fine tip, through the hefty bolster, and on into the gentle contours of the handle. You can actually feel those qualities in a good knife, whether it is a sturdy chopping tool or a fine little blade of nearly surgical precision.

The next step is to get the knife into your hand. You wouldn't buy a pair of shoes without first trying them on, and it would be foolish to buy a knife without at least taking it out of the display case. A good knife salesman will be happy to let you do this, and it wouldn't hurt to ask if you could test drive the knife through an onion or two right in the store. Shop in a cutlery store if possible. A cutlery specialist is likely to be more cooperative and knowledgeable about knives than a department store clerk. You may spend more in the specialty store, but it will probably be worth it.

A good knife should fit your hand comfortably. This is the reason I don't recommend buying kitchen knives for anybody other than yourself. The same can be said for purchasing them through the mail or even buying a matched set of knives, based on how one feels. Just because Brand X's chef's knife fits you like a glove, that's no guarantee you'll ever warm up to their paring knife.

Pay special attention to the blade. What type of steel is it? Until recently, you were limited to two choices: carbon steel or stainless steel. Carbon steel blades take an edge nicely, but they corrode easily and react to acid foods, tainting their color and flavor. Plain stainless, on the other hand, won't corrode or react to food, but because it's so hard it is virtually impossible to sharpen.

The recent introduction of high-carbon stainless steel, a wonderful alloy that incorporates the best qualities of both metals into one, solves the problem of having to choose between two evils. High-carbon stainless steel takes an edge nicely, holds it for a reasonable amount of time (a month or so under normal kitchen use with regular steeling), and won't pit or rust. This is the metal you want in a practical kitchen knife.

Specialty Kitchen Knives

Although the chef's knife is your best all-purpose kitchen knife, there are a handful of other knives more suited to specialized cutting jobs. The same guidelines apply to these knives. Look for the signs of quality: full-tang construction, high-carbon stainless steel blades, and smooth, sturdy handles.

Paring knife—Paring knives have become the disposable razors of the kitchen. You can find them in grocery stores for under $3. And you get what you pay for: weak blades attached to cheap handles. Because they're cheap they tend to be treated carelessly and have short lives. It's better to invest in one good knife that will last a lifetime. Because a paring knife is mainly a peeling tool, not an impact tool, it has a small bolster.

Utility knife—A utility knife is not quite as small as a parer but not as big as a chef's knife. It isn't all that necessary if you own both chef's knife and parer. But it can be a good all-purpose knife for someone with small hands or a young cook just starting out.

Bread knife—This long, serrated knife is indispensable if you bake your own bread. The best serrated knives have good-sized teeth to cut cleanly into soft bread without hacking or squishing it. Most serrated knives are hollow ground, making the edge thinner than on other blades. Because serrated knives cannot be sharpened, an all-stainless blade is acceptable. I like at least a 10-inch blade.

Slicing knife—Sometimes called a carving knife, a slicing knife has a long, straight blade with little taper. These blades range from relatively thin and narrow, for slicing through cold, firm meats, to rather broad and thick, better suited to hot, soft-textured meats. There's another category of slicers known as ham slicers, which, like many other serrated knives, are hollow ground to give them added bite.

Boning knife—I use boning knives to filet fish and for boning roasts and poultry. Boning is generally done before you buy your meats, but if you do this at home you should have two boning knives: one with a rigid blade, for large roasts, and another with a flexible blade, for fish and poultry. Because they are so light and flexible, and are designed for delicate work rather than for strength, high-quality boning knives often do not have full tangs.

Country Journal

Author's Comments

I wrote the piece on knives because they are so basic to cooking, yet most people have poor ones, don't keep them sharp, and don't feel comfortable using them; I thought I could help. Much revision between first version and final? Yes, always. I think the willingness to fine-tune your copy separates the men from the boys. Good editors can spot a polished piece in a few seconds, and they appreciate the effort.

Country Journal was the first place I sent that particular idea, but I know I could have sold it to any number of magazines.

—Ken Haedrich

A Sweet and Gentle Land

by Polly Bannister

"**M**uch of the beauty of the Island is due to the vivid colour contrasts—the rich red of the winding roads, the brilliant emerald of the uplands and meadows, the glowing sapphire of the encircling sea."

—Lucy Maud Montgomery, author of *Anne of Green Gables*

Our first sight of the "glowing sapphire of the encircling sea" was as we crossed Confederation Bridge on a summer's afternoon. We had driven to Prince Edward Island—12 hours from our southern New Hampshire home—for this, the endless ocean. Here, in the smallest of Canada's four Atlantic provinces, 1,100 miles of coastline create some of the greatest beaches in the world. Some have red sand and sandstone cliffs, others white sand with gentle dunes. None is crowded.

We had come for these beaches, but within a few hours of driving in a landscape of gentle hills, rich farmland, and brilliant green fields, we realized there would be more than just sea and sand to keep us here.

On an island known for its quiet, we arrived on the noisiest day of the year: July 1—Canada Day. Province House seemed an appropriate first stop. This stately historic building is the birthplace of Canada. Here the important Charlottetown Conference of 1864 was held, which led to the confederation of the provinces of Canada. Like America on its Independence Day, Canada celebrates its birthday with fireworks. That night, colorful bursts of light exploded over Charlottetown's harbor, plummeting into a vast dark ocean.

Charlottetown is small enough for a visitor to feel at home, yet full of things to do. Perfect for strolling, shopping, and sightseeing is a boardwalk that begins at Founders' Hall (where you can learn about the country's history, sign up for a guided tour of Charlottetown's historic district, and buy books, CDs, and souvenirs) and continues seaside to Confederation Landing Park, a green space perfect for picnicking. Fine restaurants and theater abound.

During our island stay, we took in two shows at the Confederation Centre of the Arts, an island gem. Here you'll find the absolute best in Canadian visual and performing arts. The perennial classic, of course, was *Anne of Green Gables—The Musical*. The poignant story of orphan Anne Shirley, who finds her dream of happiness and a real home, was three hours of pure pleasure.

Cavendish is where Lucy Maud

Author Bio

Polly Bannister is a Senior Editor at Yankee Publishing, Inc. In her 20-year career with Yankee Publishing, she has acted as Director of Special Interest Publications, Managing Editor of the *Yankee Magazine Travel Guide to New England*, and Senior Travel Editor. She has contributed to Yankee's sister publication, *The Old Farmer's Almanac*, and has edited two cookbooks and four travel books.

Montgomery, author of *Anne of Green Gables*, lived and wrote the book that makes Prince Edward Island so alluring to its readers. On PEI, the phenomenon of Anne goes beyond tourism to remind us that people and place are inextricably linked. It is easy to appreciate how the romance of the book's characters and the bucolic landscape are entwined. Green Gables (the home of relatives of Montgomery) served as inspiration for the setting of the novel and is the single most popular attraction on the island. Children scurry among tree-lined paths while parents poke into the tidy rooms of the green-shuttered farmhouse.

A short walk from Green Gables is the site of the home where the author was raised by her maternal grandparents, Alexander and Lucy Macneill. When Montgomery was 21 months old, her mother died here, and though the original farmstead no longer stands, the grounds and gardens are cared for by descendants. David Macneill runs a charming bookstore-museum and recommends other reading by Montgomery. At this quieter site, the gentility of the pastoral life that has so captured Anne's readers is palpable.

We found our own home away from home at Shaw's Hotel. It is Canada's oldest continuously operating family-owned inn (1860) and a national historic site. The location—a peninsula on the north shore, overlooking Brackley Beach—is superb. Right on the cusp of Prince Edward Island National Park, Shaw's is a skip away from miles of beach, away from the fray of Anne's Land, and centrally located for day-tripping. Guests stay in the main hotel or cottages, which were designed by Pam and Robbie Shaw, whose eye for simple style is as finely tuned as their skills at innkeeping. At sunset, we sat on our cottage porch. A fox played in tall grasses swaying in the evening breeze. Beyond, the bay glistened.

The Shaws have been told by generations of visitors to "never change a thing." In more than 26 years of running the family operation, Robbie has merged the best of old and new, with hospitality and privacy remaining paramount. Like everyone we met on PEI, Robbie and Pam love the land, take good care of it (witness the islandwide recycling initiative), and find pleasure in sharing its natural beauty. The experience at Shaw's echoes that of the entire island: Take it down a notch.

What could be nicer than coming home to find mussels on the menu?

One morning we headed southeast to Murray River for a sail with Marine Adventures Seal Watching. Within 10 minutes downriver, Captain Tom Clark cut the engine. "Look over there," he said, pointing to the dark, round head of a harbor seal. We made our way to the Murray Islands, home to scores of bird species and other wildlife. Here hundreds of cormorants nested in trees. The big black birds silhouetted against what appeared to be a stand of dying trees made an eerie sight. Hundreds of seagulls nested in the island's grass. Through binoculars we watched a fluffy seagull hatchling wobble toward the shore, where at least 30 seals, grey and harbor, had hoisted themselves onto the beach. Captain Tom spotted several great blue herons and remarked that he regularly sees eagles here, too. Cormorants, herons, and eagles are not the only ones to see the island from the air. We met Mark Coffin, the only certified seaplane operator in the Maritimes, at Peake's Wharf in Charlottetown. We flew up the Hillsborough River and over Tracadie Bay. Below, the patchwork of red earth, green potato fields, meadows strewn with pink and purple lupine, and vast stretches of white sand was a visual feast.

Over the bay, Mark pointed to hundreds of neat rows—mussels maturing in mesh sleeves ("socks") attached to long lines submerged in the sparkling water. The protected coves of PEI are ideal for mussel farming, which exploded here in the 1980s. The island accounts for 80 percent of North American mussel production.

What could be nicer than coming home to find mussels on the menu? The food at Shaw's is wonderful, and the appetizer—mussels steamed with white wine and garlic—was no exception. The flavor of the island is much like its local bounty of mussels, lobsters, and oysters. Authentic, tangy, and rich, the lush landscape of Prince Edward Island will leave you wanting more.

Tip to Tip: 10 Island Highlights

1. Make Your Heart Sing. Seventy percent of the island's residents are descendants of Scottish and Irish settlers, and their heritage is celebrated with a summer-long Celtic Festival featuring piping, drumming, fiddling, step dancing, and singing. Plus, you can find Celtic music nearly every night of the season at local concerts called ceilidhs. (Be sure to pick up a copy of The Buzz, the essential source for arts and entertainment.) 877-224-7473, 902-436-5377. collegeofpiping.com

2. Whitest Sands. Drive the causeway with St. Mary's Bay on one side and the ocean on the other to Panmure Island Provincial Park, where you can climb to the top of PEI's oldest wooden lighthouse. Rte. 347, north of Gaspereaux. gov.pe.ca/visitorsguide

3. Rail to Trail. An abandoned railway has a new life as the Confederation Trail, a walking and cycling path that links villages, woodlands, farms, rivers, and the sea across the entire island. gov.pe.ca/visitorsguide

4. Lobster Suppers. Traditional family-style lobster suppers in church halls, cultural centers, and restaurants are alive and well. Start with New Glasgow Lobster Suppers, which calls itself "the original." Rte. 258, New Glasgow. 902-964-2870. peilobster-suppers.com

5. Flying High. The Inn at the Pier offers the only parasailing on the island. Owner Dale Larkin's skill at letting fliers leave from and land on the boat is almost as admirable as the view of the gentle dunes and beautiful New London Bay. The surprise: how absolutely silent it is when you're hanging in the air at 900 feet. 9796 Cavendish Rd., Stanley Bridge. 877-886-7437, 902-886-3126. innatthepier.com

6. All You Need Is Here. The Dunes crafts center boasts broad expanses of glass, water gardens, and fine galleries full of painting and sculpture, jewelry, and furniture. This might be the initial draw, but inside, yummy aromas will lead you to the café. Begin with mussels in a coconut-curry-cilantro sauce and move on to Nova Scotia cod baked with tomatoes, fresh dill, and feta cheese—all served on Dunes handmade pottery. Rte. 9, Brackley Beach. 902-672-2586. dunesgallery.com

7. Let the Light Shine In. Weird and wonderful, The Bottle Houses are like something out of Alice in Wonderland. On a sunny day, walk through these three buildings made of 25,000 bottles and you'll swear you've just entered a kaleidoscope. 6891 Rte. 11, Cap-Egmont. 902-854-2987, 902-854-2254 (off-season). bottlehouses.com

8. Say Cheese. Don't leave the island without taking home the Cheeselady's Gouda. Martina ter Beek makes fine Gouda by hand with milk from the family's Holsteins. Sample the flavors: dill, onion, garlic,

(cont.)

Tip to Tip: 10 Island Highlights, cont.

peppercorn, and many more. Hit the right days and you can watch cheese making. Rte. 223, Winsloe North. 902-368-1506.

9. Snuggle Up. The blankets produced at MacAusland's Woollen Mills are unrivaled. Warm and soft, they are woven here (and you can watch) from high quality wool that'll last forever. Yarn is available, too. Rte. 2, Bloomfield. 902-859-3005. peisland.com/wool

10. Park It! Between the national park and more than 25 provincial parks, you'll find dunes, forests, wildlife, camping, swimming, archeology, historic sites, and more. gov.pe.ca/visitorsguide

When You Go

Prince Edward Island Tourism. For a complete vacation planner, order a free 2006 Visitors Guide. 888-734-7529. gov.pe.ca/visitorsguide.com

Province House National Historic Site of Canada, cor. Great George and Richmond Sts., Charlottetown. Open mid-June to Labour Day (Canada). 902-566-7626. pc.gc.ca

Founders' Hall—Canada's Birthplace Pavilion, 6 Prince St., Charlottetown. Open mid-May to mid-Oct. daily. 902-368-1864. foundershall.ca

Confederation Centre of the Arts, 145 Richmond St., Charlottetown. 800-565-0278, 902-566-1267 (box office). confederationcentre.com

Green Gables Heritage Place and Prince Edward Island National Park of Canada, Rte. 6, Cavendish. Green Gables

open May–Oct. daily, Nov. and Mar.–Apr. Wed. 902-963-7874. Park open year-round, with full services available late June–late Aug. 902-672-6350. pc.gc.ca

Site of Lucy Maud Montgomery's Cavendish Home, Rte. 6, Cavendish. Open mid-May to mid-Oct. daily. 902-963-2231. peisland.com/lmm

Shaw's Hotel, 99 Apple Tree Rd., Brackley Beach. Rates: $80-$340. Entrées: $18-$24. (Prices in Canadian dollars.) 902-672-2022. shawshotel.ca

Marine Adventures Seal Watching, 9457 Main St., Murray River. 800-496-2494, 902-962-2494. sealwatching.com

Tartan Air. Departures from Peake's Wharf (Charlottetown), Murray River, Montague, and Brudenell. 902-962-2122. tartanair.com

Yankee Magazine

Author's Comments ━━━━━━

"A Sweet and Gentle Land" highlights the beauty and distinctive characteristics of Prince Edward Island. The story, which appeared in *Yankee Magazine*'s annual travel issue, does what any good travel feature does; it covers the information a visitor needs: dining, lodging, attractions, shopping, essentials on getting to and from the destination and so forth. We call this "GO-SEE-DO," but there are other elements in this story that elevate it from straight service to an evocative read. For example, I took advantage of a literary thread to enhance the writing by using quotes and descriptions from *Anne of Green Gables*, a book that made the island famous worldwide.

In fact, the genesis of this magazine story is that our family enjoyed these books and the movie so much that we wanted to visit the landscape that served as inspiration to author Lucy Maud Montgomery. Though *Yankee* is a regional magazine devoted to New England, we occasionally go beyond our borders.

Although we do not determine editorial content based on advertising, we do use advertising demographics as a yardstick for what might interest readers. Since we consistently run advertising for the Atlantic provinces, my editor and I surmised PEI would be a good fit for our readers.

I researched the piece for about two weeks. My main source for preliminary research was the director of Tourism PEI, with whom I spoke extensively to map out our itinerary. My family and I stayed on the island for a week. Each day we took day trips and I filled a notebook with interviews.

As important as these interviews were, I have learned from years of travel writing that visual and visceral impressions are actually more important. For each adventure, I was sure to take time out to sit quietly and record my sensory impressions. These descriptions are what allow a reader to really get into a story—". . . we watched a fluffy seagull hatchling wobble toward the shore where at least 30 seals, grey and harbor, had hoisted themselves onto the beach."

One challenge encountered in this article (and in any travel piece) is how critical the writer should or should not be. Because this story was not a review, I wanted to stay with the positive aspects of PEI. However, when we visited the *Anne of Green Gables* attractions, we were surprised at how tacky much of "Anne's Land" was. I wanted to avoid being negative about the arcade/carnival atmosphere, and I had to dig deeper to find authenticity.

Through conversing with a few docents (you cannot be shy in journalism), I discovered the real essence of Lucy Maud Montgomery's idyllic story, not at Green Gables, but a short walk away at the site of the home (the original farmstead no longer stands) where the author was raised by her maternal grandparents.

In travel writing it is hard to start with much more than a rough outline (itinerary) because the destination must be experienced. If you are fortunate and insightful, a story may unfold in an organic way. The key for me is to review my notes each evening and allow my senses to distill what I want to keep and shed the rest.

My process is to prioritize themes (*Anne of Green Gables* and how the landscape is entwined with the characters, both from the book and present time). With travel stories I set the themes on a timeline, and capture the sensory description for each event—this serves as my outline. Experiences that don't fit the narrative often can go in a sidebar, as I did in "Tip to Tip: 10 Island Highlights."

"A Sweet and Gentle Land" took me a full week to write and I probably revised each paragraph at least three times. An invaluable tip that I learned from one of my colleagues, Mel Allen, the finest editor I know, is to read your story aloud. I ALWAYS do this, paragraph by paragraph, over and over, reading to myself. One's

Author's Comments (cont.) ─────

ear can pick up cadence and rhythm that allows the writer to shorten a sentence or find the perfect word.

The single most important thing for writers to do when they are submitting their work is to familiarize themselves with the publication. If you are sending a query letter, make sure the writing represents your best style. Tell the editor why you are the best person for this story. For example, if you want to write a profile of a baseball player, let the editor know you played in the minor leagues or coached ball—why you are an expert on the subject. If you are sending a completed manuscript, the cover letter has to be finely tuned to make the editor want to read your submission.

—Polly Bannister

How to Be a Great Mom

by Julie Tilsner

7 Qualities you need for your preschooler

RESOLVE

We've all heard about the terrible twos. But nobody talks about the tantrum-throwing threes or the ferocious fours. So lots of parents are surprised when their preschooler hurls himself on the floor, screaming, after not getting a coloring book at the supermarket. Preschoolers, like toddlers, can fall apart when they're tired, hungry, or overwhelmed. We assume that because they have stronger language and reasoning skills, they'll have better control over themselves. But sometimes, they have a *harder* time settling down (bedtime, for example) because they think they're missing out . . . on something. Fortunately, kids this age place great importance on figures of authority: teachers, doctors, and you. Use this to your advantage to set clear, firm rules, says Errika Lynch, a preschool teacher and mom of two in Groton, Massachusetts. Like any tough leader, you can't get too mired down in details. That means no negotiation over bedtime. Being steadfast and concise is key, so they know what's expected.

Author Bio

Julie Tilsner is the author of several books, including *Planet Parenthood: The Funny, Helpful, Absolutely Essential Survivor's Guide*. She regularly contributes to *Parenting* and *American Baby* magazines.

A SENSE OF FANTASY

Actors have nothing on preschoolers—or their moms. On any given day, your child will be a baby elephant, a monster alien, or a fairy ballerina. And you get to play along. "Imagination is critical for their development," says Claire Lerner, director of parenting resources at Zero to Three, a Washington, DC–based children's advocacy group. Preschoolers stretch their language skills as they describe complex story plots for you to follow. They hone their logic ("This happened, so this happened, and then this . . .") and develop social skills playing imaginatively with their peers—describing how to build the fort, for example, and cooperating to make it happen. "Your role is to become a facilitator," says Lerner. "Be careful not to take over their story. The more they do, the better." Offer her ideas, like "Oh, no, there's an alligator! What are we going to do now?" Playing dress-up? Encourage her to make props out of ordinary stuff around the house (a bowl can make a very nice crown). Just remember you're the supporting actor in this play. Let her direct for now.

FORETHOUGHT

When he's 2 or so, your formerly voracious eater may become so picky you'll worry he's malnourished (who can live off PB&J alone?). Experts say you're dealing with a power struggle and a plea for independence, both playing out at the dinner table. Suddenly, kids realize they can exert total, maddening control by refusing to eat what's in front of them. So you need to think ahead in the kitchen—but that doesn't mean making multiple meals or giving in to their demands. It does mean having a few good choices for everyone, and leaving it at that. "Children will not willingly starve themselves," says Nori Hudson, a nutrition consultant based in Berkeley, California.

If your child's not getting the entire nutritional food pyramid every day, don't worry. He'll likely have all his nutritional needs met over the course of a week. So watch what he eats and plan accordingly: If he goes for peas one day, offer him cheese or yogurt the next. Another tactic is to get your preschooler involved before dinnertime. Ask him to help

> *Act like an English monarch, with a blasé, "I am not amused" face.*

you mix the mac and cheese so he feels like he's in control. Or at the market, let him pick out a fruit that he finds interesting-looking. "It's never too early to let kids experience a variety of textures, tastes, and colors," says Hudson. "Eventually they'll grow out of the pickiness."

STOICISM

One of the hardest things to do as a parent is to let your child walk alone into the scary world of jungle gyms and new people. But preschool beckons, even for just a few hours a day. "I've hugged more crying parents than I have children on the first day of school," says Allyssa Lamb, a veteran preschool teacher in Berkeley. To quell your queasiness, make sure you feel good about the person you're leaving your child with, and focus on what your child will gain from school. It gives her rules for every task, which kids this age thrive on. It makes her feel proud and independent that she can eat her own snack and throw away her own garbage. It enables her

to be away from you for a while, trust her own decisions, and, hey, have some fun.

Preschool can also accomplish a lot of the stuff you're still working on, like ridding your child of her pacifier or lovey. "I couldn't get my daughter to stop using her Binky, put her shoes on by herself, or sleep by herself," says Tressy Pelonis, a mom of 2½-year-old Allison, in Long Beach, California. "Since she started preschool, she's like a different kid!" If your child has a hard time adjusting to her new routine, comfort her but don't indulge her fears by letting her stay home or lingering at drop-off. Keep a stiff upper lip and remind her that she's a big kid. Remember, you can cry on your spouse's shoulder when she's not around.

NONCHALANCE

Preschoolers know the power of words. From repeating "poop" in between uncontrollable fits of laughter to uttering the most chilling words in the English language—"I hate you"—your 3-year-old is beginning to understand that certain language elicits dramatic reactions. That's why it's important not to overreact to potty humor or take hurtful proclamations personally. "It's another form of testing, to see how far they can go," says Lynch. Now that kids have moved on from diapers and think about potty issues more, they sense that these topics are taboo. And taboo=hysterical. The best way to deal? Act like an English monarch, with a blasé, "I am not amused" face. The more you react—positively or negatively—the more you reinforce the behavior. Explain that while he can engage in a little bit of toilet humor at home, it's not okay at preschool, a friend's house, or anywhere else in public. Or divert him with a nice clean joke ("What did five say to six? Seven ate nine!").

When it comes to mean words, use the same approach. Kristy Hill's 3-year-old told her to leave the room because he didn't like her. The Keller, Texas, mom says it was hard not to feel upset, but she managed to keep calm and said, "Oh, that's sad because I love you very much." Overreacting will only let

. . . crack your knuckles, stretch your calves, and get ready to hop, button, and more.

your child know that this a good way to get your attention. As with potty humor, non-chalance is key—but you do need to make it clear (later, when he's calmer) that language intended only to hurt people is never okay.

DEXTERITY

During preschool, kids' motor skills and hand-eye coordination really take off: Witness the one-foot hop and the buttoning of shirts. Your child learns by trying these things out—repeatedly—and it helps immeasurably to be able to see someone as skilled as yourself doing them, too. So crack your knuckles, stretch your calves, and get ready to hop, button, and more.

A slightly less tiring way to help your child's development is with crafts. Playing with clay or stringing beads is a great way to build up the small muscles in his hands and hone his hand-eye coordination. You can also ask him to do housework with you. He can stir cake mix, plant flowers, or sort laundry by color—he'll be improving his coordination and having fun. When my son Jack was 3, I gave him a little squirt bottle filled with water and he would "clean" stuff around the house. "This age group lives to help, because they get attention and the praise makes them feel good," says Lynch. "They feel like they've accomplished something, like they're grown-ups."

EMPATHY

It's not all about rules and schedules with preschoolers. As much as your child thrives on knowing what to expect, she's also just a little kid. It's hard growing up: There's potty training, a big-kid bed, maybe a new sibling. *You* try three (or more!) major life changes in one year. That's why it's important to show your child you feel her pain, too. It could mean a hug and a new do when she flips over her hair being braided "all wrong." Or it might mean just understanding that it's tiring to spend a long day at preschool, remembering the rules, getting along with other kids, and generally keeping herself together. Help her decompress with a snack and a chat, and don't rush into chores or errands. Your empathy will not only keep the both of you calmer, it's also a quality well worth modeling. And if you'd be proud to see your child mimic the things you do, then you can definitely call yourself a great mom.

Parenting

Author's Comments

This piece was assigned by my editor at *Parenting*, whom I've worked with in the past. In reporting it, I sent a query out to my "mom's list," a 100-plus name email list I use to get anecdotes and stories from moms around the country for use in my articles.

I generally think up a "lede" (opening paragraph), and go from there, using choice anecdotes to wrap the "service" (advice) around. For *Parenting*, the editors want stories and advice from real moms more than "experts." The article went through probably one rendition (editors will tell me they want more of this or less of that), and was edited for length.

I would strongly advise new writers to hook an editor with a strong story idea, submit a polished piece quickly, then build a relationship with that editor.

In my 20-year career as a magazine writer, I've found that building relationships is the best way to assure yourself lots of assignments. Editors want to work with writers they like—writers they know they can depend on to give them strong copy on deadline. When you can give this to them, they'll use you over and over.

Editors who move to new publications will usually take their writers with them. It's hard to break in at first, but persistence and lots of good ideas will pay off (some spark in your writing doesn't hurt either!).

—Julie Tilsner

The Ugly Wedding Present

by Sasha Aslanian

When it was time to open our wedding presents, my husband tore in with a gusto that astonished me. He was also the one who had gone wild with the scanner gun at the department store where we registered, while I sank into an existential crisis over the crass commercialism of the wedding gift transaction. Our guests had been more than generous and my husband unwrapped box after box of grown-up treasures. Then he hit an odd one.

"Huh." He shot me a nervous smile. Out-of-state friends of his parents, people important during his childhood, had made a daring departure from the registry.

My husband looked quizzically at the 9-inch-tall figurine of a bridal couple. They were delicately carved out of light stone and preternaturally skinny—picture bride and groom corpses. Their faces were distorted, like they had started to melt together, leaving him a weak chin and her a sunken cheekbone.

He nervously turned it over. Is this for real? A joke? Regifted? Or did they find it beautiful and choose it just for us? Its sentimental depiction of marriage hardly fit our Generation X questioning of, and finally relenting to, the institution after 12 years of dating. I was very relieved it came from his side. A sticker on the bottom identified it as a Valentino from Italy, but it felt like bad faith to eBay a wedding gift. So we kept it.

A few days later I walked into the house and stopped short. The statuette posed alone on the window ledge. Exiled from our house, but held inside by the screen, the ivory couple would perch half-in, half-out of the house all four seasons. Though facing the maelstrom of family life around our dining-room table, they would see nothing, their eyes closed, his arm encircling her, gently touching her wrist. The rapture of newlyweds. They have made it seven years and so have we.

No one has ever asked us about this object, or its more unusual placement, perhaps wondering the same questions we once did: Is this for real? Or a joke? Twice a year, as we install the storm windows, I take the couple out. Laugh. And put them back. There is grit in the part of his hair now, and in the flowered texture of her dress.

This year our 5-year-old daughter saw me holding the figurine and begged, "I want it on my desk."

"But why?" I asked.

She answered, "Because it reminds me of you two."

Perhaps our gift-givers had seen something we hadn't.

Modern Bride

Author Bio

Sasha Aslanian is a documentary producer for American Radio Works. She lives in Minneapolis.

The Ugly Wedding Present

Author's Comments ──────────

"The Ugly Wedding Present" snapped into focus when the ending anecdote happened—my kid turned my earlier thinking upside down. *Voilà*, a story arc. Then, like stringing beads, I searched my memory and strung together the scenes that led up to it: my meltdown while registering for gifts, our surprise when unwrapping this one, the silly diorama in the windowsill.

I emailed the essay to an editor at *Modern Bride* who had been encouraging to me in the past, and she took it with very few revisions. She said she liked the tone and the writing and that it went in an unexpected direction. I was lucky that she just happened to be planning the first-ever essay section.

Write conversationally, use short sentences, and give the audience a picture. Study the publication to get a sense of what works and ideally, you'll chance upon an editor who's open to new voices and likes your sensibility.

—Sasha Aslanian

Plant-Based Tableware Redefines the Word Disposable

by Marc Schoder

You can get taco salad in a tortilla chip bowl. Willy Wonka had his three-course-meal chewing gum. And now you can get take-out with forks, plates and cups that are edible—well, at least compostable.

A number of companies are changing the definition of disposable tableware. The new word is greenware. There are cups made from cornstarch, forks from potatoes and plates from yucca. They're microwavable, will hold hot liquids and can be given to animals as feed or tossed on a compost pile when you're done with them.

Not only do these products conserve valuable landfill space, their manufacturing process has a considerably smaller environmental impact. The carbon emissions for a take-out clamshell container made from sugar cane residues are 30 percent less than producing one from petroleum. And, of course, there are no toxic byproducts as there are with plastics.

Prices vary, but in general, greenware is comparable to its plastic counterparts.

"Our products are 33 percent more efficient to make than petroleum-based products and 50 percent more efficient than paper," says Aseem Das, founder of World Centric, a Palo Alto, California-based nonprofit that sells greenware. Polystyrene may remain the cheapest to manufacture, but it has great long-term environmental costs. Greenware's sustainability gives it an added value and costs are certain to come down as more manufacturers discover its environmental and economic advantages.

Eating a fork made from a potato isn't recommended, but it's possible. Or you could simply toss it into the garbage and it will degrade at the landfill within 90 days. Better yet, throw it on your compost pile or take it to your community's composting bin—if you're lucky enough to have one where you live. Immersed in water they will generally disintegrate in a week.

The city of San Francisco recently banned the use of foam-to-go containers.

Products labeled biodegradable need moisture, heat and microorganisms to degrade. Greenware is compostable, which means it biodegrades when exposed to oxygen. But that doesn't mean the products have short shelf lives. The products offered by UK-based Vegware will last up to two years if kept in their original packaging and in a dry

Author Bio

Marc Schoder is a freelance reporter and writer whose work has appeared in several newspapers and various Internet publications.

Plant-Based Tableware Redefines the Word Disposable

environment. If you're using them to store food in the freezer, they'll hold up for three months.

For almost all greenware products, heat can be an issue, but only in relation to plastic or polystyrene. Vegware's cassava fiber plates can withstand the heat of a microwave, but it's suggested cooking time be limited to two to three minutes. Cups made from cornstarch can handle liquid as hot as 190 degrees Fahrenheit and their thermal properties eliminate the need for a hand-protecting heat sleeve.

"Have your lunch from a Styrofoam container and see how it tastes after an hour," says World Centric's Sean Kvengedal. But taste isn't the only personal benefit. Studies have shown dangerous styrene molecules can migrate from polystyrene containers to food. The effect is even greater with hot foods.

The greenware industry is getting another boost. The city of San Francisco recently banned the use of foam-to-go containers and other cities are following that lead. But as word of its benefits spreads, it won't take a law to get people to start using it.

Five

Author's Comments

At the time I wrote this piece, I was back in school after being in the workforce for five years. Its publication gave me the encouragement I needed to start hunting out local magazines that were looking for freelance writers.

One of the biggest challenges I had with this story was writing it in a more conversational, informal style. I was trained as a journalist, and was always told to ask questions and practice the five w's (who, what, where, when, and why). This particular story was revised four times. I talked with the editor about what direction I should go in, which allowed me to tailor the piece specifically to the magazine's readership.

The best advice I can pass on to new writers is to never stop reading. It will help strengthen your vocabulary and make you a better writer.

—Marc Schoder

284 Nonfiction

Completely Lovestruck

by Majid Mohiuddin

"That's it. You're engaged." My father laughed and gripped my shoulder in a gentle hug. "Your mother and I have been waiting for someone like Rasha for a long time. You couldn't be luckier."

Our families had just spent a July afternoon in light, polite conversation in the western suburbs of Chicago. Rasha's family had prepared a sumptuous lunch and had invited her grandaunt and grandmother, and my parents and sister. We took chai and cake after, in the drawing room. Rasha sat across from me in traditional Pakistani dress—a pink *salwar kameez*—gazing shyly at her feet. I squirmed in my sofa seat, choked by my tie. Eyes fell upon me, appraising me, while everyone sipped away.

I stood in her driveway later, shaking my head. What happened to getting down on bended knee? To eating the same spaghetti noodle from each end, à la *Lady and the Tramp*? Then again, this had been my choice. Falling in and out of love is so hard, I wanted to do the first part only once. So I decided on my culture's traditional route, which brings to mind the words *arranged marriage*.

I got out of the dating game before it began: in seventh grade. I grew up in America

Author Bio

Majid Mohiuddin is a physician and lives in Texas. He and Rasha married in Chicago in a two-day ceremony with 700 guests in attendance.

with the Muslim rules of no premarital sex or dating. There's no holding hands, let alone kissing. Some Indian teenagers pay lip service to these cultural or religious norms and sneak out behind their parents' backs, but I consciously chose to remain chaste in body and spirit in the search for "true love." From the high-school prom to potential hookups in college, my attitude was "Thanks, but no thanks." I was waiting for something more: the real thing.

It sounds rough, but it wasn't. My search for a wife had started a long time ago, without me. My mother had consulted the "Auntie Network" and sent out an all-points bulletin for the ideal girl. Here's how it works: Parents spread the word to a wide group of friends and family spanning nearly every major city in the United States. Prospective candidates are pretty well screened by the recommendations of other family members who have watched these kids grow up in their communities. Based on a tip, interested families may meet up in a home or at a mutual wedding and give the kids an opportunity to talk. A guy and girl may go out for a casual cup of coffee. The rules are relaxing a bit, but the meet-up is never an all-out date (such as dinner and a movie), but more a chance to talk while in a safe, public space (like a walk in Central Park or at a lecture series). E-mail addresses and phone numbers may be exchanged.

Thanks to the Auntie Network, I wasn't limited to someone I happened to meet on the Boston subway. "The One" could have been growing up in San Francisco or Arkansas. This took a tremendous amount of pressure off me: I felt more like a prince holding a glass slipper, with the whole kingdom on the lookout for me.

My own Cinderella came to me by accident. My mother was visiting Chicago and dropped off my cousin at her apartment. Her roommate, Rasha, opened the door and in-

I couldn't tell you if she liked her orange juice with or without pulp.

vited my mother in for some tea. My mother was smitten with Rasha's poise, maturity and innocence.

"You have to meet this girl," she insisted. "She's a medical student with an English major."

The onus was now on me. I dropped Rasha on AOL instant message, and when my fickle Internet connection went down the second time, I gave her my cell phone number. She called that night, and we began to talk, of all things, about the moon and its tides. (Pathetic, I know, but I was nervous.) I didn't tell my parents because I didn't want them to get too excited. Rasha kept it a secret, too. Early on, I had asked my cousin to send me a photo of Rasha; she was supercute in a wedding group shot with a button nose and large innocent eyes. Now I was ready to fly out and meet her.

I went to her family's home on a Sunday evening. After an hour of mild interrogation from her parents (when would I be done with my residency?), I finally got a chance to sit with her in the family room. Her younger brother sat nearby playing Nintendo, a distracted "chaperone." In an hour, we had talked about religion and *Calvin and Hobbes*, Cold Stone Creamery and humanitarian aid to Third World nations. Her nose twitched when she got excited. Need I say more?

After six months of numerous phone conversations, frequently laughing and whispering

together until 3:00 a.m., our relationship had become serious. We met again in person, this time with our families present. We had strong feelings for each other, but neither of us was prepared for our parents to jump the gun and decide that day that we'd be getting married.

Rasha's father pulled her aside in the kitchen to tell her. I was outside when I learned. Our conversation next was awkward, given that "our" moment had involved everyone but us. I knew my fiancée very, very well, and yet I hadn't a clue about certain aspects of her life. I knew she had a sarcastic sense of humor. She could quote Conan O'Brien and Shakespeare. Without a doubt, she would make an excellent wife, mother and physician. But having never spent time with her in a grocery store, I couldn't tell you if she liked her orange juice with or without pulp. Or if she had a penchant for high heels and would run an hour late to every dinner party. But we saw eye to eye on religion, on emphasizing education and community service, on giving to charity, and taking care of our parents in their old age. Oh, and dark chocolate.

I wanted to give Rasha an engagement ring, but not in front of others. It was hard for me to visit Chicago often, even harder to get a free moment alone with her, so not until one month before the wedding did I find a chance to do it, sneaking the ring upstairs to her in her house.

Recently I asked my fiancée how she felt about our courtship. Rasha's response was to paraphrase a poem by the Nobel laureate Rabindranath Tagore: "Whenever I hear old chronicles of love . . . [we] shared in the same shy sweetness of meeting . . . [an] old [story of] love but in shapes that renew and renew forever."

In short, ours is an old love story in a new form.

Modern Bride

Author's Comments

From the outset, the image of Disney's *Lady and the Tramp* sharing a spaghetti noodle and inadvertently kissing stuck in my head. It reminded me of the samosas at teatime, the ice cream shop we went to chaperoned, the orange juice at the supermarket. I do not write linearly; I often write islands of thoughts or catchy phrases that eventually connect by isthmuses (in this case) chronologically.

Once a rough essay formed, I lopped off the boring beginning and started at the crux of the matter: I had just gotten engaged. This begged the question: How? And so the story ensued. I had a small fear of anticlimax with this beginning, but it seemed to pull the reader into the story early. At the end, I provided closure to show that the marriage was working out.

For revisions, I usually read my writing aloud so I can catch dissonance or poor transitions. Also, I have a tendency to write winding, complex sentences, so I pare them down.

I won the NJ Governor's Award for Arts and Literature in high school and was a Rose Writing Fellow at Brown University. I wrote poetry in medical school and published a book of traditional Islamic ghazals in English called *An Audience of One*. I've published a few short stories and essays since—"Completely Lovestruck" was a self-reflection piece I was encouraged to share.

I was dissatisfied with the portrayal of an impersonal arranged marriage in Mira Nair's *Monsoon Wedding*, but on the other hand, I was not a believer of the *Sex in the City*, new-person-of-the-week tryout solution to the marital conundrum. Being a romantic at heart but a pragmatist by trade, I'm a modern American with old-fashioned values who wished to put a realistic but positive spin on the story.

—Majid Mohiuddin

Under India's Spell

by Steven Slon

Midway through what will become a seven-hour drive to cover roughly 150 miles, I am asking myself a simple question: *What have I done?* I am white-knuckled with fear.

The two-lane road, the route from Agra (where my wife and I just visited the Taj Mahal) to Jaipur, is a fantastic, chaotic mess. It's clogged with rickshaws, bicycles, horse carts, ox carts, homemade vehicles of all kinds, tractors, buses, trucks, and, oh yes, cars and jeeps like the one we're riding in.

Our driver repeatedly crosses to the opposite lane to pass slow-moving vehicles. But then, he just . . . keeps driving on the wrong side of the road. Oncoming motorcycles and small cars, which seem to know their place in the universe, skitter off to the shoulder, where there's just enough space for them. But when a bus or a truck comes towards us, the rules change. At the last possible instant, our driver honks loudly, brakes hard, and squeaks us back into our proper lane behind a creeping tractor.

"You need good brakes, good eyes, and a horn to drive in India," he says meaningfully, turning all the way around. I nod, unable to muster a reply.

By my watch, we suffer approximately

one near head-on collision per minute. But some part of me must have wanted this.

* * *

Before you travel to India, someone will ask you about the poverty.

It's everywhere. It's devastating. And there is an odd casualness about it—the very wealthy living in a fabulous high-rise alongside the very poor in a pitiful hovel. Why isn't there more anger, more bitterness? Expat Indian friends say it's a mistake to try to judge this culture by First-World standards.

One day, at a stoplight, a girl of about 12 presses her face to the window of our car, cupping her hands and signifying hunger by mimicking eating gestures. I hesitate for a moment, since we'd been told not to hand out money. As I start to reach for some coins, the light changes, and we lurch away.

After this we start carrying a box of nutritious food bars and hand these out to beggars. In India a gift of food is gratefully received.

But months later, I still see that little girl's face.

* * *

Before you travel to India someone will ask you about the crowds. It's not the crowds that are disconcerting, but the lack of personal space. The few cubic feet of air that Westerners surround themselves with simply does not exist here. One evening in Mumbai,

Author Bio

Steven Slon is a former editor of *AARP The Magazine.*

I venture out for a walk near the Gateway of India, a giant stone arch, built on the waterfront. Even at night the streets around it are jammed with vendors, beggars, hustlers, and tourists. I just want to walk, but I'm incapacitated by the Western habit of feeling obliged to respond to a greeting.

A man approaches, with an offer for a guided tour of Elephanta Island, a popular tourist destination across the harbor. I make the mistake of saying no thank you. Where do I want to go? He can arrange anything. I try ignoring him for a while, but it's too late for that. He follows at my side like a lifelong companion. Finally, I put on my most

Travel is everything unknown, everything out of rhythm.

earnest American tone, look him in the eye, and say, "Listen, I just want to take a walk. Alone!" This finally seems to register. After one more entreaty to come to his family's clothing store where, he promises, I can have the most fantastic suit custom tailored at a most fantastic price, he gives up.

Moments later an elderly man in a robe comes toward me holding something in his hand. I swerve to avoid him, deliberately avoiding eye contact.

"Holy man!" he says irritably. (Religious wanderers give offerings of sweets to strangers in exchange for alms.) Now, he is offended that I had presumed him a common beggar.

I keep walking, shoulder to shoulder with the crowd. After a while, I begin to relax. Slowly I am getting what I wanted, which is to cease to be "other." I take a deep breath.

* * *

Before you travel to India, someone will ask you about spirituality. It is a constant

presence, like magic in the air. The Hindu deities, in particular, seem very real, like well-connected uncles or aunts you can ask favors of. At one of the oldest Hindu temples in Mumbai, we watch a long, snaking line of joyous families waiting patiently for hours to

When I drop my guard, well, that's when the magic happens.

make an offering to Mumba Devi, the city's patron goddess. The soft, happy murmuring of the crowd is punctuated by the loud clanging of a brass bell (to waken the goddess, our guide tells us) as each of the supplicants enters the temple. But the magic isn't only in religion; odd and exotic sights appear all the time: a woman in a brilliant orange skirt and veil, walking slowly down a country road balancing a huge bowl on her head; a painted elephant on a busy city street; a bored snake charmer with his dutiful snake rising and bobbing to the blaring of his pipe.

* * *

Before you travel to India, someone will ask you why on earth you would go to such a place. The answer is itself a question: Why travel at all?

Home is where the stuff is. It's where, without realizing it, I had settled into rhythms and routines, from working to eating to TV time.

Travel is everything unknown, everything out of rhythm. (It's the total reliance on the kindness of strangers.)

But travel is exhilarating for the very same reasons. Freed of routines, I am forced to give up the illusion of control. When I drop my guard, well, that's when the magic happens.

Late one afternoon near the southern

town of Kumarakom, we are approached by an ancient man with an equally ancient canoe. He offers in sign language to take us out to explore the region's famous canals. Along the canal is a bird sanctuary where he points out egrets, herons, migratory Siberian cranes, and huge, sleeping fruit bats, looking like coconuts hanging from tree branches. As the sun begins to set, we signal to our boatman that it is time to return. He shakes his head no and says something that sounds like "Bots." Since we're paying by the hour, we are suddenly uncomfortable. Is he trying to cheat us? But moments later, just as the last glimmer of light is wrung out of the sky, the air is suddenly filled with thousands of the awakened bats, each with a wingspan of three feet or more. They're coming right at us, like the flying monkeys in *The Wizard of Oz*. We duck. We point foolishly upward. "Bats!" we say. The boatman grins. I look at my wife. Something wondrous passes between us. We can't stop laughing.

AARP The Magazine

Harry London Chocolate Hall of Fame

by Robert Fuller Davis

As we exited the Ohio Turnpike onto Interstate 77, we felt the tug of chocolate. We had picked up a brochure that described the Harry London Chocolate Hall of Fame in North Canton, and we knew we had to go there.

Gabriela met us at the front desk with a tray of chocolate Buckeyes. "Help yourself," she said, "These are seconds and we can't sell them. Eat what you want and fill your pockets."

Joining a group of like-minded chocolate lovers, we watched a short movie about the history of chocolate and the history of the Harry London Candy company.

Aztecs and Mayans discovered cacao 4,000 years ago and made a potent drink from the nuts. Christopher Columbus took cacao to Spain in 1502 and by 1528 it became a beverage reserved for royalty. It was accepted as currency by all nations and was considered the ultimate gift for grand occasions.

In the 17th century, chocolate houses sprang up all over London and became gathering places for people of leisure. Physicians prescribed chocolate as a cure for physical complaints, and many people still consider it to be the best prescription for almost every illness.

Cacao trees bear their first pods at five years of age. They are grown around the world in a band of latitude 20 degrees north and south of the equator. Farmers plant banana trees next to the cacao to provide shade. The most valuable beans are grown along the Ivory and Gold coasts of western Africa. Those are the beans that Harry London uses.

The darkest chocolate has the most cocoa butter.

Harvested seeds are split open and dried in the sun, then shipped to buyers. Chocolatiers roast the beans according to proprietary formulas to bring out their aroma and taste. They are then ground and heated. Cocoa butter surfaces during the heating process and is skimmed off and used as an additive to make the various types of finished chocolate.

The darkest chocolate has the most cocoa butter. The various gradients from dark to milk to white are determined by changing the proportions of milk, sugar and butter.

The next stage is "conching," a kneading process that gives the chocolate a smooth texture and allows delicate flavors to come through. The proper Harry London consistency requires 72 hours of conching.

The product is then ready to be poured into molds, decorated and eaten.

After we learned the basics of chocolate

Author Bio

Robert Fuller Davis has published over 200 articles in the *San Luis Obispo Tribune*, *SLO Journal*, *Sierra Heritage*, *CC Motorcycle Newsmagazine*, and *Journal Plus*.

making, Gabriela led us through the Harry London Hall of Fame.

Harry was a steelworker descended from a long line of candy makers. He made chocolate candy as a hobby in his house in Canton to give to friends at Christmas. People began asking if they could buy more, and his father, Gilbert, persuaded him to quit his day job and make candy full time.

Harry bought a second house next door to his residence and made candy in both basements. As Gabriela told us, "Chocolate is a gentle thing, very sensitive and frail," so Harry could not make candy in cold or hot weather, which Ohio has in abundance. He eventually came up with the idea of excavating a tunnel between the basements and producing chocolate underground.

In 1953 one of the houses burned down and Harry moved his factory to Main Street in North Canton. His wife, Iola, decorated the specialty candies, such as 25-pound Easter eggs and 50-pound Santas. A few years later, he built the current factory, which is now stretching its seams because of the growing popularity of the various specialty lines of confections.

Meltaway mints, London's signature candy, was first served in the White House by President Reagan, and Harry London Pretzel Joys are Oprah Winfrey's favorite cookies. Gabriela said that Oprah's friends introduced her to the treat. Since she was always on a diet, they sent her Pretzel Joys and Cookie Joys and Krispi Joys "to help her break up the monotony of dieting. That's what friends are for, to make your life interesting."

Drop mocha melts into your coffee and they add flavor and texture.

London's also makes Kisses and pays Hershey to use the name—but is not allowed to use the shape and makes funnel Kisses—4-ounce, 7-ounce and 4-pound.

The most recent exhibit in the Hall of Fame is a framed shadow box from Steve Smith, the American astronaut who visited the candy factory with his family. The flag and patch in the display flew into outer space and next time he goes, he promised Gabriela he will take London mints with him.

Gabriela asked us to put our cameras away ("The ladies don't want their pictures taken wearing hair nets." In fact, every employee wears a hair net and bearded employees wear beard nets—they come in three sizes.) and led us into the factory, advising us to "take a deep breath as you go in."

We saw five tanks of chocolate, each holding 80,000 pounds, or 10,000 gallons, enough to fill a swimming pool. Think about that.

Each tank makes 7,680,000 pieces of candy, and the Harry London factory goes through a tank a day. This is where the conching takes place, at a temperature between 104-120 degrees. This is closely monitored because chocolate absorbs scents. A single small patch of burnt chocolate will spoil a whole tank. (In addition, employees are asked to refrain from wearing perfume or scented deodorant to work for fear of contamination.)

No one is allowed to eat the product inside the factory.

In the gourmet kitchen section, fudge, caramel and flavored fillings are heated in copper kettles, then poured onto tables to cool before they are cut into individual pieces. Cold water runs beneath the tables to cool the fillings and a conveyor takes them into a chocolate shower and thence into a machine that wraps 72–100 pieces per minute.

Most of the work is done by machinery, which makes it look simple. One exception is the sorting line, called the Lucy and Ethel line, where workers inspect and pull out damaged pieces. No one is allowed to eat the product inside the factory for sanitation reasons, but trays of rejects are placed in the employee break rooms and they can eat as much as they want when they're not working.

London makes several specialty candies for clients, such as Disney, using copyrighted molds and packaging. Banks and doctors can have business cards made of chocolate. Gabriela said that she is encouraging her dentist to sign up for this.

The last step of the tour was into the gift store, where Gabriela invited us to sample a tray of Harry London rejects and reminded us that chocolate isn't just candy, it's a lifestyle.

INFORMATION: Harry London Candies is located off Exit 113 from Interstate 77 in North Canton, Ohio, a few miles from the Professional Football Hall of Fame. Tours are given Mon-Fri from 10-3. Reservations are required. For additional tour information and reservations, contact the Tour Department at (800) 321-0444 ext. 119 or tours@harrylondon.com. For full disclosure of Harry London delicacies, see the website at http://www.harrylondon.com.

Journal Plus, The Magazine of the Central Coast

Author's Comments

My wife and I found information about the Harry London Candy company at an Ohio truck stop, where we pulled over to use the bathroom. When my wife read "Chocolate Hall of Fame," she had to go there.

I carry a recording device, either a voice recorder or a notebook and pen, to record what I see, hear, feel, smell. I write everything down—recording things as you go makes shaping the ideas into an article easier.

After writing the story, I go over it again and again to look for holes. If I need more information I use Google. The article must flow easily from one thought to the next—I don't want to surprise the reader by jumping about. The hard part is cutting out the surplus. Good writing comes from good editing; less is more.

Find a publication that carries the kind of story that you are writing and tailor your story to the audience. Practice. The more you write, the better you get. If you find a topic interesting, so will other people.

I write for my friends. I want to share experiences and make them feel as if they are there with me. For this article, the best compliment from a reader was, "I could smell the chocolate."

—Robert Fuller Davis

Where the Creek Turkey Tracks: Wild Land and Language

by Tim Homan

In the mid-to-late 1970s, when I began exploring the mountain trails of North Georgia, written directions to trailheads were often short, cryptic, and inaccurate. In general, directions, trailhead signage, and parking areas were all primitive by today's standards. Back then, a trail was often more difficult to find than to follow. In part, those problems led to my decision to write a guide that would include easily understood and accurate directions to the trailheads.

To that end, I began hiking all of the official forest paths for the first edition of *The Hiking Trails of North Georgia*. But I had to find them first. Again and again, throughout 1979 and 1980, I had trouble following what directions there were, most of them written from memory and guesswork rather than from actual road signs and odometer readings. And when I couldn't find a trailhead after a few tries, I would often stop to ask directions from the people who lived along the paved roads leading to the dirt-gravel Forest Service roads, or in the pockets of private property bordering the Chattahoochee National Forest. I quickly learned three things

about the highlanders who gave me directions: they were friendly and willing to help; they, especially the old-timers, could often recall the contours of the land for miles around with an uncanny accuracy that comes only from long and intimate familiarity; and they frequently included colorful and inventive language in their descriptions.

In Georgia's share of the Southern Appalachians the people—whether in country stores or in their front yards—generally invited the stimulus of conversation, even from an outlander asking directions. They stopped loading Coke machines; they shut off their lawnmowers; they motioned me up to their porches. They often shot the breeze about the weather or something else innocuous and unlikely to cause disagreement either before or after the business of directions.

One lady, after providing the best directions she could, asked me—a bearded stranger—if I wanted to see her garden. After a five-minute tour of her pole beans and squash, eggplants, okra, and sweet corn, she gave me a ripe cantaloupe to eat on the trail. Several other times when I asked directions from folks who were working in their gardens, they offered me some tomatoes to take home before I left. Once, after I had given up hitchhiking and was walking fast down a darkening dirt road toward my vehicle, an elderly farmer stood up on his porch and quickly appraised me—a sweat-stained

Author Bio

Tim Homan has written five Southern Appalachian hiking guides and is currently at work on a sixth. He lives in Georgia with his wife, Page.

stranger carrying a daypack and stout hiking stick—before calling out in a strong voice, "Young man, you look hot and tired, would you care for some ice-cold lemonade?" Thirty minutes and one pitcher later, he drove me the rest of the way to my truck.

Sometimes, the old men would weave a running narrative . . .

Not one person was ever rude, mean, or even dismissive. But, in the interest of honesty, I never stopped at a trashy home with a pit bulldog tied up outside either. I never came face to face with author Bill Bryson's Cyclops, that malignant "Deliverance" stereotype he exploits as arrogant humor and presumed superiority to willing urban readers, especially northerners. In fact, whether on dirt road or remote trail, I remained as safe from human harm as an angel inside the eye of a hurricane.

Since their surroundings have never been sequences of city blocks, street signs, and stoplights, it was only natural that the directions provided by the hill folks included the common features of the mountains: hollows, branches, creeks, bottoms, knobs, ridges, slopes, and the like. Sometimes, the old men would weave a running narrative, braiding personal and natural history into the directions. Or maybe it was the other way around. Maybe they just wove the directions into their stories.

The best one I ever wrote in my notebook went like this:

You take this road here past a hollow full of pole-timber poplar on your right; I remember when there were big trees down in there, but that hollow's been cut twice since then. Turn left onto the first road past the rainbow-crowned oak (he made a shallow arching motion

with his hand) in Crowder's field, then drop down and cross Corbin Creek—it's named after my great-grandfather on my mama's side. There's a deep swimming hole just upstream from the bridge, and there's good-sized native trout in there too. I've caught many a supper there. After you cross the bridge, follow the rise onto the west slope of Chestnut Lead. Way down the first hollow is my folks' old homeplace; it's government land now, nothing left but an old stacked rock chimney and the corner stones. I killed my first bear, a big male, down in there when I was fourteen years old in 1919. I had to round up my father and older brother to help me drag that big rascal out of the woods. I remember when the chestnuts up on the lead first started dying of the fungus blight in the '40s. That disease was a damnation; the forest and the wildlife haven't been the same since.

"What's your name? Do I know any of your kinfolk?"

After you drop down to the toe of the mountain, turn toward the sunrise onto the very next road you come to. It's a Forest Service road, got a Forest Service number, but we call it Miller Gap Road. Take that road uphill a good piece to Miller Gap; it's probably a good three or four miles. Miller's the second gap you come to. The first is Calf Stomp Gap; it's not on any map that I know of; the folks hereabouts call it that because the Miller family once had a corral up there for summer-range cattle. The track runs off into the woods to the right of the road in the gap; there's a pull-off big enough for a couple of cars there. Back in the depression, when I was about your age, I used to hunt squirrel and turkey along the hogback where you're going to walk. What's your name? Do I know any of your kinfolk?

At first, I listened through the mist of my smugness toward grammatically backward ways. But the cumulative evidence of the linguistic richness of mountain speech soon wrenched my preconceptions out of their pigeon holes. I found I greatly enjoyed talking to the mountain people, the grayer the better. Some of the old-timers were masters at language: first-rate storytellers with impeccable timing and razor wit. They sprinkled their anecdotes with novel country sayings and language I liked, language straight from the "hill'n holler" land. They were the first to tell me how

> *. . . streams "so clear you could count the spines on a trout's fin while looking at its shadow."*

to walk through "roughs"—mountain land ribbed with narrow spurs and furrowed with hollows "so steep that, going down, you'll want hobnails in the seat of your pants"—and about woollyheads, laurel hells, laurel slicks, or just plain slicks and hells—their words for extensive heath entanglements, mostly rhododendron and mountain laurel.

Occasionally, when I was camping for four or five days at a stretch, I sought out men with long memories to ask directions I didn't need, a conversation starter that primed the pump for my questions about the Appalachian forests before chestnut blight and industrial logging. The men recalled huge trees, recognizable as individuals from a distance, that served as landmarks, living waypoints during travels without compass or GPS. They remembered chestnuts 8

and even 10 feet in diameter at the base, eastern trees mythologically large by today's diminished standards. They reminisced about the richness of north-facing coves, where "the land smiled at its own magic show" of spring wildflowers quilting winter's brown thatch with bright and welcome color, of high, overarching fountains of great green trees, of cold, clean streams "so clear you could count the spines on a trout's fin while looking at its shadow."

I heard the land and its lost glories in their voices as the old men wistfully described the virgin forests felled in their youth or early manhood. They told me of white pines towering, pagodalike, above the hardwoods on the slopes; six-hundred-year-old hemlocks standing dark and silent watch over the streams, shading them summer and winter; stands of massive yellow poplar in the coves, their gray columns rising straight as a carpenter's chalkline; wide-crowned white oaks, 4 to 6 feet in diameter, dominating the canopy in the flats; chestnuts whitening the ridgetop woods with their spring blooms, and showering the forest floor with their fall mast every year without fail—a benevolent manna from above.

Some of the people I asked directions from—again, especially the graybeards—utilized two systems of distance measurement. They sometimes even combined the two in the same few sentences. One set was the standard system based upon miles; the other employed nonstandard units much more vague and antiquated than accurate or systematic. I wrote down these country terms and, since I was recording mileages anyway, often noted how far a "piece" or a "fer piece" turned out to be. Based upon the folks I talked to—an admittedly small and much older than average sample—I compiled five alternative measures of Appalachian distance. The smallest component was tater chunk, as in "you're real close, it's just another tater chunk down the road." Following tater chunk in progression were yonder, hoot and a holler, a piece, and a fer piece.

This system was based upon old culture, subtleties of hand gestures and head nods, and assumed familiarity with the mountains. At first, nonstandard mountain directions were problematic for me—a man raised on yards and miles in the right-angle, farm-grid country of central Illinois. But the more I listened and watched and measured, the more I began to have an intuitive feel for the variable distance of a piece. Although these classifications were nowhere close to systematic— ten tater chunks did not equal a hoot and a holler—there were rules and intricacies that helped the terms become both more flexible and accurate than you might expect. The first rule was that only tater chunks and hoot and a holler had plurals: two tater chunks down the road, a couple of hoots and a holler (never a hoot and a couple of hollers). I never heard anyone say two yonders, three pieces, or four fer pieces. It just wasn't done.

A measured mile is just a mile whether you walk it, drive it, or make arm gestures and head nods while you're talking about it. But a piece and a fer piece expand and contract with the situation; they have fluid parameters, low and high ranges, an easy piece or a good piece. A walked piece is shorter than a driven one. After

> *"The hemlock you're looking for is to the right where the creek turkey tracks."*

you learn the nuances of gesture and voice, the low and high ranges of a piece accompanied with the correct sequence of natural features are about all you need to find your way. Before long, you can drive the correct distance— whether it is a piece or 2.6 miles—to the right ridgeline and find the trailhead on the first pass. And when you get there, you think,

"Yeah, the man was dead on, it was about a hoot and a holler downhill from the gap."

During those two years, I did much of my hiking on weekdays, so most of the people who gave me directions were farmers, second-shift workers, retirees, or store clerks and their customers. Most of the folks I found outside on tractors, porches, or in gardens were over 50 years old, many over 70. The majority of people gave me directions in approximate miles, which were often wildly inaccurate. But the others, the old hands who had learned the land's language through the soles of their shoes, the ones whose mental maps were fluent narratives of well-known natural features, often used informal measures lingering from before hurry came to the mountains.

These men didn't know the measure of the roads in miles. They knew distances measured from memory and a hard won but proud sense of place. Before motorized transport came to the hills and hollows, a mile afoot, or on horseback or wagon, was much more the sense and feel and rhythm of a mile than the codified distance. Miles become systematic when and where they are easily measured. Back when many of my informants were growing up, one person's mile was different than another's. And since unmeasured miles are arbitrary, there really wasn't much difference between "a piece" accompanied with a natural-feature narrative and roughly estimated mileage. In fact, directions with guesstimated mileage and no accompanying natural features were often the worst.

During my last month of hiking for the book, I asked a slender fisherman if he knew the general location of a lunker hemlock a backpacking buddy had described as "humongous." Knee-deep in water rushing over rounded rocks, he squared up to me and said, "I know exactly where that tree is; I've been walking past it for fifty years. The hemlock you're looking for is to the right where the creek turkey tracks." That was all he said, but it was better than a National Geographic map. I was walking upstream and had seen many of the three-toed turkey tracks on past rambles, so I knew what to look for. After a little more than a mile I came to the obvious spot, the place where three narrow runs braided around two flood-wracked islands before flowing back toward each other with the precise splay of a turkey track. The mountaineer's eight-word directions—to the right where the creek turkey tracks—proved to be both creative and accurate. The massive old-growth hemlock, a totem of the primeval past, loomed just upslope to the right.

Before measuring the magnificent conifer's girth at DBH—diameter at breast height, 4 feet up from the forest floor—I sat down and tried to write the directions with as much economy and creativity and coupling to the land as the man had just tossed off the top of his head without hem or haw. I couldn't come close.

I had long known that the landscape in and around my hometown—a Midwestern rustbelt city rimmed with newer suburbs and flat, fertile fields of corn—was geographically boring, botanically impoverished, and tame beyond redemption. Native prairie plants took refuge in cemeteries, the tag ends of an

. . . culture still blends gently into the landscape.

ecosystem protected from the living by the dead. Wildness worth the word had long been lopped from the land, neutered; the country round about could no longer muster a single howl or caterwaul to animate the night. The last of the wildlife was leashed to hedgerows and river bottoms. All was safe for cows and corn. The old land had slipped from memory. The new land punched a clock, worked summer shifts without rest.

I had never given any thought to the relationship between wild land and language, the living connections between nature and culture. I had never thought about what happens when an ecosystem-wide mosaic of wetlands, forests, and prairies is converted to the monoculture of corn and the geography of the market place. About what happens to the possibilities of language when buffalo standing shoulder deep in tall-grass prairie are converted to geometrically precise row crops in square-cornered fields and a few unwanted weeds. About what happens when the land's former language is interred to the dark indoor existence of museums and herbariums, of old books and maps—to become ghost words of loss and lament.

I realized as never before that my homeland's language of itself, of its native life and landforms, was pinched and impoverished compared to the robust language of the Southern Highlands, where despite multiple abuses, the mountains have maintained their essential character. Here, especially in the large tracts of publicly owned land, culture still blends gently into the landscape. Here, the many words of life and landscape are still linked to the region's complex topography and bewildering diversity. In the Southern Blue Ridge, almost all of the physical features labeled on the old topo maps have survived in recognizable form, and for the most part, the plant and animal portions of their names still cling to the land. There are still buckeyes leafing out first in Big Buckeye Coves, still three kinds of leaves on the sassafras atop the Sassafras Knobs, still black bears flipping rocks to find provender along the Bearden Ridges. And in the ancient Appalachians, away from roads and power lines, an honest wildness, obdurate as bedrock, still clings to the land, offering beauty and challenge to the prepared and punishment to the foolish.

While most of the older mountain people could use and understand both of the distance systems in the late 1970s, I still know and really understand only one system. I grew up smug and sure that feet and Fahrenheit were unassailably standard. But now, now that I'm gaining tenure as a geezer myself, my cultural security blanket is being ripped asunder in a steady tug of war. I am increasingly told by the rest of the world—and my own government and young friends on occasion—that my feet and pounds and miles are antiquated, backwards and nonstandard.

I haven't stopped to ask directions in the north Georgia mountains for 20 years, and I suspect much of the old, colorful language, archaic and laughably nonstandard to most, has been homogenized from the hills. But the next time I ask, I hope I can still find someone who can read the land's language, not someone who thinks a gap is a clothing store and who will tell me to travel four or five kilometers before turning left at the resort where all the roofs are red.

Appalachian Heritage

Author's Comments

My initial desire to write began in my early 20s, when I became infatuated with the written word and the Southern Appalachians at the same time. I thought writing might enable me to remain in the mountains, hiking and camping for months at a time—an embarrassingly flimsy notion, all pipe dream, no reality.

My first freelance newspaper piece paid ten dollars and a roll of black-and-white film. The editor cut the best descriptions to fit the article between advertisements. Having learned that piece work didn't pay, not even for gas money, I began writing hiking guides as a plausible excuse for spending several years' worth of days tramping the trails of Highland Dixie.

The biggest challenge I encountered while crafting this essay was the usual one—foaming at the pen, taking side trails down interesting tangents, wasting time and effort. I wrote at least four drafts by hand before my wife typed the manuscript. Then I revised on the computer until I was reasonably satisfied. I offered it to my wife and a couple of friends for their comments. More revisions, then finally off to *Appalachian Heritage*.

I did not utilize an outline, but I did jot down objectives, themes, and ideas—a rough outline without order or alphabet. I selected *Appalachian Heritage* because it had published my previous essay, and because I knew "Turkey Tracks" meshed with its "hill'n holler" niche.

My advice to writers who are submitting their work for the first time is short and stern: Don't even think about sending in your work until it is well written and accurate. I have read far too many articles that were laughably inaccurate, a discredit for both the publication and the author. When you think your effort is almost ready, give it to a few critical friends. If three people think a paragraph should be deleted, or a bit of humor doesn't work, chances are they are right. However, if one person urges a dramatic shift in subject or emphasis, listen but hold your ground and go with your gut.

Getting published is business: call, email, go to the library, wrestle problems to the ground. Talk to potential editors. If what you are offering is not right for them, ask for names and numbers of other editors or publishers who might be interested in your material. If you are rejected, ask for a critique. Is it the quality of the writing or the subject matter?

My best advice is not my own. More than 35 years ago an elderly publisher told me, "Ideas are a dime a dozen. Doing the work—the research, the writing, the marketing—that's everything."

—Tim Homan

Be Sensitive When Moving the Elderly

by Robert B. Mills

Every person tends to collect treasures throughout the years. These articles can be knick knacks, bric-a-brac, trinkets, plaques, pictures, rocks and a whole host of other objects acquired and/or given to us since childhood. At some time in our lives a relative or close friend will ask our help in packing their belongings for a move to a smaller location. There is a strong possibility that the person we'll be helping will be elderly—and the move will be from a longtime home to a retirement facility.

When helping someone pack and move, elderly or not, a certain degree of tact is required. There is no need to question someone else's quantity and quality of accumulated artifacts. Plan to be a good helper and not a criticizer. Compassion and understanding are necessary when handling a person's lifetime collection of belongings. The trauma of moving at an elderly age to a new and foreign location is severe enough, and there is no reason to compound that situation.

Recently I helped my 92-year-old step mother-in-law move from the home she had occupied for thirty-nine years to a retirement apartment less than half the size of her house. I have moved myself so many times that it appeared that this would be just a routine "pack it up and move it out" procedure. Was I ever mistaken! I discovered in a short time that each item to be packed had its own little history and place in her life. Her mental faculties are extremely good for her age. In a short time I discovered things about her that I had not known before. Then it dawned on me there was a good chance that someday I would be doing the same with my personal collections. After some reflection I have categorized several areas to keep in mind when given the chance to help move a loved one.

1. Do not rush elderly loved ones.

Time is important. Plan on using twice as much time to pack for elderly people. They are generally slow in everything they do. They need time to sort out their plans and make decisions. Patience and understanding are very important qualities to be practiced while packing. Keep in mind that you will likely have this same experience someday.

Stay with them in the conclusion-making process, but allow them to make the final judgment. Going too fast will only bewilder them and cause additional stress. Expect changes at any time and be willing to alter the direction of your thinking during the moving process.

2. Treat their belongings with dignity and respect.

Elderly parents moving into a retirement or nursing home will have to determine which

Author Bio

Robert B. Mills, former editor of a management association newsletter, has written many articles on construction projects for the Spokane, Washington, affiliate of Habitat for Humanity. He has just completed his first novel.

personal items they wish to take and which to discard. Many of these items have a special history in their lives. They will want to share this information with you, and it's a great time to learn more about their lives. Be patient and listen to their explanations even though you may have heard them before.

It may be necessary to hold each item before them and ask for a decision. Even though the personal belonging is cracked, dirty, or missing pieces it could still hold value in your loved one's mind. They may ask you for an opinion of what to do with it. Be prepared to give a tactful and honest answer, considering the importance of an object. Always maintain the mental image of your feelings if someone else was going through your personal possessions.

3. Choice of words.

Avoid the use of negative words such as "clutter" or "junk" while packing. Be sensitive as to the ultimate resting place of personal items. Coupled with the "take with you" phrase, an expression of "someone else might like this," or "let's give this to the Salvation Army" could be used to help the parent decide on the ultimate end of a particular object. Since many of these "things" still have some sentimental value, avoid using expressions like, "let's just throw it away" to avoid hurt feelings.

When helping an elderly relative move from a home of many memories be positive about the new location. Refer to it as "your new home" rather than using "apartment or place." Some seniors have difficulty accepting the fact that they can't do all the things they used to do. Cooking is one of these tasks and sorting kitchenware can be done on the basis of a reminder that food preparation will be done by someone else and only tools and utensils for light cooking need be kept.

4. Let your loved ones reminisce.

As each article reaches the point of being wrapped in packing material, be inquisitive about the origin of those objects that interest you. Letting your parent or loved one refresh their memories about these things helps in the determination process.

5. How to handle the gift offer.

Sometimes you will be offered something as a personal gift. This is a delicate situation, and in most cases you should accept. Avoid argument and accept the object. If the object has value, make an offer to purchase it.

6. Sibling arguments.

There are times that parents promise a certain object to a sibling after it has been promised to a different sibling. It's best if you can compromise these situations before moving day. Avoid negotiations in the presence of the elderly person.

7. Handling trauma.

In all situations, refrain from arguing with the elderly parent. The trauma for them at this time can be severe, and there is no reason to exacerbate feelings within the family unit. Later, after the move has been completed and the situation has calmed down, more rational solutions can be developed that will satisfy all.

Conclusion

In our own lives it is important to review from time to time those items we have accumulated throughout the years. Decisions then can be made regarding the distribution of these objects. When it comes time for us to make these decisions, recollection of the ancient proverb, "Do unto others as you would have them do unto you," will greatly add to the peace of mind for all involved in the moving process.

The Family Digest

Author's Comments

I have dreamed of writing most of my life. This dream was never satisfied in the numerous term papers written for college classes, or various other papers written in conjunction with job requirements, so in early 2005 I enrolled in the Long Ridge Writers Group course, *Breaking Into Print*.

This particular article was written for assignment seven or eight of the Long Ridge course. My wife and I had just helped her stepmother move from her house of over 20 years to a retirement home. Her stepmother was 92 at the time, which added more consideration to the task. I analyzed all the personal considerations needed to complete this task.

The article went through three drafts before submission to my instructor. As part of the assignment I selected a magazine from *The Best of the Magazine Markets for Writers* to submit my article for publication. To my delight it was accepted and published in *The Family Digest*, which has some 150,000 subscribers.

I have found that perseverance is extremely important, not only in writing, but in submission of articles for publication. Enter every contest there is, if you can, and always be on the lookout for new ideas.

—Robert B. Mills

In the Clutch: Better Shifting for Sport-Touring Riders

by Mark Tuttle Jr.

One of the more revealing ways to find out how well a rider shifts gears and manages the clutch on a motorcycle is to ride as their passenger. With no handlebar in front with which to brace yourself, any lack of shifting smoothness or clutch dexterity on the rider's part (not to mention skilled throttle application) will have you lurching about like a Weeble with arms and legs. More importantly, clutch slipping and mangled shifts are hard on your bike's clutch and transmission, and simply aren't cool besides.

The most common shifting mistake is made during downshifts, when the rider fails to raise the engine rpm to where it will be when the clutch is re-engaged. If you don't "blip" the throttle—a quick, small twist of it with the clutch disengaged—while downshifting, during engagement the clutch will have to overcome the engine's inertia at idle or thereabouts to raise engine rpm and match your road speed to the lower gear. At best this creates a sudden lurch in your ride and wears the clutch—at worst the abrupt change in engine speed can momentarily lock the rear wheel. Practice with some methodical down-

shifts and gradual throttle application until you can match engine to road speed with a quick, smooth downshift and a short blip of the throttle.

Blipping also serves to momentarily release the pressure on the transmission gear "dogs"—the teeth on the sides of the sliding gears that engage with the slots in the free-wheeling gears—allowing the dogs and slots to disengage more easily, the first half of a smooth shift. This works both up- and downshifting. Blip the throttle "off" when upshifting, and "on" when downshifting. The second half of a good shift is to be quick about it—lazy shifts can grind the dogs against the rotating slots. Make your shifts certain, quick and clean, and they will be quieter and smoother. You can help things along if necessary by preloading the shift lever with your toe.

Practice until you can start out cleanly without slipping the clutch.

For good clutch work, remember the words I always tell beginning riders—the clutch lever is your friend. Most riders who have trouble using it were never taught about the mysterious band between complete engagement and disengagement called the "friction zone." It extends from the point in the clutch lever travel when the clutch begins to

Author Bio

Mark Tuttle Jr. has been the Editor of *Rider Magazine* since 1989, and on staff at the publication since 1984.

engage, to the point when it's fully engaged. There should be a little free play or initial travel in the lever after the friction zone to ensure that the clutch engages fully.

Coordinating the use of the friction zone and throttle application is key to starting out smoothly and making clean shifts, and like anything else mastering this takes practice. You can do so at a stop with the engine running and the bike in first gear, clutch disengaged (lever pulled in). Slowly let the clutch lever out until the bike begins to move—that's the start of the friction zone and the point at which you would normally begin to apply throttle—but then pull it back in, out, etc., till you're seesawing back and forth a foot or two but your feet remain in place on the ground.

Eventually the force and feel of the clutch engaging and disengaging will become familiar, and you can move on to adding throttle at the beginning of the friction zone. Practice until you can start out cleanly without slipping the clutch. Mastering the friction zone is also crucial for "fanning" the clutch well, a technique in which you partially disengage and engage it to maintain your momentum at a speed lower than the stall speed in first gear (in a U-turn, for example). Dirt riders must learn how to fan to survive, but some street riders aren't even aware of the technique.

Master the friction zone, learn how to fan and shift cleanly and we'll keep the Weebles on eBay where they belong.

Rider Magazine

Author's Comments ——————

As a kid I dreamed of working at a motorcycle magazine, so I studied English, journalism, and motorcycle mechanics in college. I started at *Rider* wrenching in the shop, but most staffers got their jobs after becoming regular freelance editorial contributors.

To be able to shift gears well on a motorcycle requires skill, practice, and knowledge about how motorcycle transmissions work. Done poorly it can cause the bike and rider(s) to jerk back and forth, perhaps even bashing their helmets together annoyingly with every shift.

As with any technical explanation, the primary challenge in conveying the techniques in the article is knowing the subject well. We have short word counts for the stories in *Rider*, so I also needed to get the message across in as few words as possible.

I don't use the typical draft and revision process, unless you consider the unfinished piece in the computer a draft and the improvement made at 8 P.M. a revision. Basically I just keep writing and rewriting until it's finished, clear, and the proper length.

My advice to those submitting for the first time is to query to see if the publication needs the story, and ask for a word length and any other basic requirements the publication has. Then stick to them—they have guidelines for a reason.

Good luck!

—Mark Tuttle Jr.

Let There Be Sleep

by Barbara Stahura

As you gulp your latte while driving to work, grateful for the caffeine because, once again, you didn't get enough sleep last night, ask yourself what the tragedies on this list have in common: the runaground Exxon Valdez gushing oil into Prince William Sound; the chemical leak in Bhopal, India, that killed thousands; the space shuttle Challenger disintegrating in the blue sky; and the radioactive horror of Chernobyl. According to published reports, official inquiries determined that all of these disasters occurred, at least in part, because someone involved was sleepy.

If that doesn't grab your flagging attention, maybe some numbers will. For starters, some studies have estimated the total cost of treating sleep disorders at close to 16 billion dollars per year. The 100,000 vehicle accidents each year that, according to the National Transportation Safety Board, are the consequence of drowsy driving, result in approximately 48 billion dollars per year in damage. How about the 150 billion dollars American businesses lose each year due to fatigue-related mishaps and lost productivity? On a more personal level, consider your teenager who stays up until all hours sending text messages to friends or surfing MySpace.com so that you have to drag him out of bed every morning and nag him about his once excellent grades. Might insufficient sleep have something to do with that?

Sleep disorders are one of the most prevalent health concerns in the United States.

We are indeed a sleep-deprived nation: As many as 70 million Americans are afflicted by chronic sleep disorders, according to a study released earlier this year by the Institute of Medicine, an arm of the National Academy of Sciences, and upward of 30 million of those poor souls suffer specifically from chronic insomnia.

Sleep disorders are one of the most prevalent health concerns in the United States and probably throughout the industrialized world, according to psychologist Rubin Naiman, a sleep and dream medicine specialist at Doctor Andrew Weil's Program for Integrative Medicine in Tucson, Arizona, and author of the book *Healing Night: The Science and Spirit of Sleeping, Dreaming, and Awakening.* Suffering from ongoing sleep deprivation, we live, as Naiman describes it, in a state of "chronically dazed waking consciousness."

We can blame, to some extent, Thomas

Author Bio

Barbara Stahura began writing professionally in 1987 and made the leap into full-time freelancing in 1994. Her articles, interviews, and essays have appeared in numerous publications and websites. She is also the author of *What I Thought I Knew* (Wyatt-MacKenzie Publishing), a collection of personal essays. Her website is www.barbarastahura.com.

Edison for the onset of our lack of Zs. While humans once followed ancient, evolutionary sleep patterns that sent them to bed shortly after dark and kept them there until dawn ten or twelve hours later, the widespread use of electric light at night has allowed us to undercut our biological imperative for adequate rest. Naiman characterizes light at night as "counterfeit energy" because it gives us a phony boost, masking fatigue or sleepiness. Sugar and caffeine, he says, also are counterfeit energies, as are unconscious thought and behavior patterns that spike adrenaline. "We're a culture that's very attracted to hyperbole and drama and excessive excitement," Naiman says. "I think we're unconsciously drawn to these because they compensate for our chronic lack of healthy rest."

"We overvalue productivity and devalue sleep."

Beyond that, our twenty-four hours a day, seven days a week, industrialized, technology-soaked culture—the outgrowth of ubiquitous electricity—has made production king and normal rest a sign of sloth. "We overvalue productivity and devalue sleep. It's not OK to have downtime, according to the cultural ethos," explains Philip Eichling, a doctor and director of the Executive Health Program at Canyon Ranch in Tucson. He's only half joking when he says culturewide sleep deprivation is "all the fault of cable TV." And then he adds, in all seriousness, "Some cartoons are on when no one of the age to watch them should be awake."

Naiman believes there also may be a deeper, psychological reason behind our tendency to be so sleep-leery. We're afraid of darkness, he explains—"not darkness per se, but the darkness within us, the shadow. When we allow ourselves to have a relationship with the literal darkness, it invites us inward, and we can confront our own shadows. But rarely do we do that anymore. I think our dismissal of night and darkness is symptomatic of our dismissal of the shadow."

Amazingly, the physiological reasons for sleep are still unknown, according to Michael Breus, a clinical psychologist and author of *Good Night: The Sleep Doctor's 4-Week Program to Better Sleep and Better Health*. Sleep science has produced many theories about why sleep happens—restoring the body, integrating memories, allowing neurocognitive structures to rest and reboot—but "studies prove that all of these are right and all of these are wrong," he says.

We do know that consistently adequate shut-eye is necessary for optimal functioning. For most adults that means around eight hours every night, even though more and more Americans report getting less than six. Adequate sleep is as necessary for good health as are diet and exercise, says Breus. Without it, we are at greater risk for maladies, such as obesity, hypertension, stroke, depression, and cancer. Some researchers even claim that sleep is the best determinant of longevity, more important than diet, exercise, or heredity.

Americans often seem willing to give up sleep in order to do something else because "many of them never thought [sleep] was important to begin with," Breus says. At the same time, millions of people are desperate for a good night's rest. In its 2005 "Sleep in America" poll, the National Sleep Foundation discovered that seventy-five percent of those surveyed reported experiencing, at least a few nights a week, one or more symptoms of a clinical sleep disorder, while fifty-four percent reported a symptom of insomnia.

Lack of adequate slumber, whether for a night or over a long period of time, creates sleep debt. This is "the burden we carry when we haven't gotten as much sleep as our brains need," explains Mary Carskadon, a professor of psychiatry and human behavior at Brown University and director of the Chronobiology and Sleep Research Laboratory at Bradley Hospital in Rhode Island. At this point, "it's still a puzzle" as to how the brain knows it hasn't had enough sleep, she says. "What's the bean counter in the brain that tells us? Is it biochemical or molecular changes, or something in the neurotransmitters?"

While the consequences of long-term sleep debt have not yet been thoroughly researched, after a few days or weeks of poor sleep, Carskadon says, "there can be short-term irritability and depression. There's growing evidence that cognitive skills decline. The speed at which we process information slows down, and vigilance—being able to attend to your environment—is hampered, too. This plays out in activities like driving—the biggest side of the picture is the risk of falling asleep and creating some tragic outcomes."

Avoiding sleep debt is even more important for teens than for adults, according to Carskadon, who specializes in studying teen sleep patterns and advocates later starting times for high school. This can be difficult,

. . . they are taught to go to bed only when they are ready to fall asleep.

since teens' internal sleep clocks tend to shift toward later hours, keeping them awake far into the night, even though they must still get up early for school. "Learning is the main task of the teen years," she says. "New circuits are being built in the brain then, and we don't know how much brain development is compromised by lack of sleep."

With the introduction of new sleeping pills, such as Lunesta, Ambien, and Rozerem,

the debate about the efficacy and safety of pharmacological remedies for sleep disorders has reawakened. A growing number of medical professionals advocate cognitive behavior therapy, or CBT, instead of medication as a remedy for primary insomnia, or sleeplessness uncomplicated by any other factor, such as pain, apnea, or restless leg syndrome. A recent Norwegian study, reported in the *Journal of the American Medical Association*, indicates that CBT works better to help long-term insomniacs sleep well more often.

In effect, while sleep medications are a crutch, CBT teaches people how to sleep, says Susan Zafarlotfi, a sleep disorder specialist at Hackensack University Medical Center in New Jersey. "CBT will reset the cognition of a person regarding sleep," she explains. "It will change their beliefs about why they can't fall asleep, and it will get their sleep in tune with the circadian rhythm," the daily biological rhythmic cycle.

In many cases, preconceived notions about sleep affect the ability to sleep. For example, people often wake up in the middle of the night, which actually may be a normal sleep pattern, but apprehension about falling back to sleep can keep them awake. Then, by worrying every night about waking up too early, they create a bad habit that prevents good sleep.

With CBT, says Zafarlotfi, patients are taught a variety of techniques that help them sleep better. For instance, they are taught to go to bed only when they are ready to fall asleep, not just because it's a certain time. This prevents the agitation generated by the fear of being unable to fall asleep. They also must learn to get up at the same time every day. So, in the beginning of their CBT, even if they are not tired enough to head for bed until 1 a.m., they must still arise at their normal time. At first, they might be sleepier than ever during the day; eventually, however, they grow tired earlier in the evening and can then sleep longer.

Sleeping pills can be used to good effect, Zafarlotfi says, but only "in a very restricted format" and when used temporarily in conjunction with CBT. Eichling, who uses both approaches in his sleep counseling, believes such medicines can be "absolutely appropriate during times of stress or when traveling."

CBT doesn't work for people with a clinical sleep disorder, such as obstructive sleep apnea, in which the airway closes off, breathing stops for a short time, and the brain must rouse from sleep in order to start breathing again. Other methods are necessary for cases in which a physical problem disrupts or prevents sleep, and these problems can be diagnosed and treated at a sleep lab.

In the final analysis, though, the best sleep medicine might be "night and darkness, and learning to be receptive to, invite, and allow them into our lives," says Naiman. "I think we need to find new ways of honoring night, and, of course, that means we need to be less productive at night."

Science & Spirit

Author's Comments

I wrote "Let There Be Sleep" after reading an intriguing book on the importance of sleep and dreaming. Knowing other people would be interested, I contacted *Science & Spirit*, which had published my work before.

I interviewed the author of the book, as well as other sleep experts I located through him and by using Google—an excellent way to find reputable research. The only challenge I faced was whittling the huge amount of available information to a manageable size.

It's impossible to pinpoint the number of revisions or drafts because I edit as I go, but there were many changes along the way. I cannot think in outlines and so don't use them. Fortunately, my writing seems to arise organically out of my research and interviews, and elements usually fall into place.

For new writers, my advice is to read, read, read lots of good writing of all kinds and then to write, write, write. Find a trusted, honest person or two who know good writing to edit your work and advise you. Then write some more and persevere.

—Barbara Stahura

On the Record: Collecting Oral Histories

by Elizabeth Kelley Kerstens, CG, CGL

Ask two people to tell you about the same event or the same person and you'll get two different stories. The facts may remain the same—Grandpa was six-foot two-inches and born during a snowstorm —but the perspective will be unique to the storyteller.

As the family historian, you probably want to remember each of these individual nuances. And you can, via an oral history.

Why Oral History?

We've all heard family stories. But there's a difference between jotting down your take on a family story and hearing that same story from a person who was there, or even from a person who is a generation closer to the event. When you sit down to record the words directly from the source, you capture that speaker's view, and you create an oral history.

Oral histories are planned, recorded interviews designed to save every word spoken by an interviewee. For the family historian, oral histories result in lasting first-person records—tapes, documents, or both—of people detailing their life experiences.

There are two basic ways to conduct oral history interviews: directed and non-directed. In a directed interview, an interviewer asks questions, based on previous background research, that specifically relate to the individual being interviewed. In a non-directed interview, a prepared list of questions is asked of a number of people—useful, for example, when soliciting responses from a group of people who were all involved in the same event.

Planning an Oral History Project

The first item to consider when planning an oral history is the scope of the project. Who will be interviewed? What do you want to learn? Will you question Grandpa about his entire life or just about specific events?

If you plan to conduct the interview yourself, you should be aware that you may hear stories that you're not comfortable hearing and that the interviewee may not be comfortable sharing with you. In these situations, an outsider might be better suited to conduct the interview.

Next, decide how many interviews you will conduct. While you may have plenty of stamina, your interviewee may have physical constraints or other commitments that keep him or her from spending too much time with you during an interview. If your interviewee is unable to talk for more than an hour, you may want to schedule a series of interviews over the course of several weeks. However, if an interviewee is located a great distance from you, you may be limited to a single interview.

Author Bio

Elizabeth Kelley Kerstens spent 20 years in the U.S. Marine Corps, where she was trained as a journalist. She is the editor of *Digital Genealogist* and the *National Genealogical Society News Magazine*.

> **Elizabeth:** Tell me about your dad. What do you remember about your dad?
>
> **Walter:** My father was a very good bowler and a good golfer. He had a bowling average, about 195, and even after he had a stroke and lost vision in one eye, he still was a good bowler.
>
> **Elizabeth:** I never knew that.
>
> **Walter:** Hmm?
>
> **Elizabeth:** I never knew that.

> **Walter:** We lived in Cedar Lake at that time. Dad owned an ice cream parlor on the main drag in Cedar Lake. It was the main drag but it was only a block long.
>
> **Elizabeth:** Your dad owned the ice cream parlor?
>
> **Walter:** Yeah, he ran . . . he ran or owned. I'm not sure if he owned it or whether he ran it or what. But I know I used to sneak in there and help myself all the time.

You will need a place to conduct an interview. Because of background noise, an interviewee's residence or the local coffee shop may not be the ideal interview location—background noise can make transcribing an interview difficult. If possible, test the recording equipment you plan to use in the location you plan to conduct the interview beforehand to determine if you need to make adjustments or other arrangements.

Detailed research on an interviewee should be conducted prior to an interview. For the family historian, this may mean going beyond a person's birth and marriage date and place. You'll want to know as much as possible about where the interviewee grew up, what family life was like, what jobs he or she held, and other key events, such as marriage and children. Knowing more about a person can help you develop a strong list of questions and help you focus the interview to meet your goals.

As you conduct your research, jot down open-ended questions you'd like to have answered—avoid questions that can be answered with a simple yes or no. Sometimes it's more effective to prepare a list of key points that you want to cover in the interview and a timeline of the interviewee's life to act as your personal guides.

> **Elizabeth:** I understood that at some point the brothers stopped getting along.
>
> **Walter:** Oh the brothers, I don't think they ever got along. Fred I didn't see too much, he was the oldest one, and Charlie was, well, my dad, later on, when we left Marinette and came back down to Chicago in 1939, my father went to work for Charlie in Drake Petroleum Company and Charlie was an SOB. That's all. He just was out to get all he could get and wasn't giving anything to anybody. I think he was responsible for my father's stroke or heart attack. And . . . but he did give Dad a job when we came down from Marinette.

Audio vs. Video Taping

Should you audiotape or videotape an interview? The choice may not be yours—sometimes a person who is comfortable sitting and talking into a tape recorder will cringe at the thought of being videotaped (if you're uncertain, ask the interviewee). Regardless of whether audio or video is more convenient for you, you'll get the most from an interviewee who is comfortable with the environment.

If you're planning to audiotape an interview, use a good quality audio cassette recorder with an external microphone—you may even want to rent professional recording equipment from a local rental agency. Remember to test the equipment before you start the interview and choose durable, high-quality tapes suited for the job and for long-term storage. Specialty audio and electronics stores can help you choose the products best suited to the task.

If you're videotaping, consider enlisting the help of someone else to operate the camera. Without a camera operator, both interviewer or interviewee can become distracted with the operation of the camera. Mount the video camera on a tripod during an interview and attach lapel microphones to the interviewee and interviewer to get the best results. Be sure to check power supplies and batteries in both the camera and the microphones before you start.

Legal Issues

Copyright issues may become a factor, even if you're just conducting an informal interview with Grandma. Legally, both the interviewer and interviewee share the copyright to an oral history interview (an exception occurs when an interviewer is conducting the interview as a work for hire). While copyright may never come into question, you should still protect yourself from potential copyright infringement by having both the interviewer and interviewee sign release forms at the time of the taping.

Sample interview release forms can be found on the Smithsonian Institution's website, www.folklife.si.edu/resources/pdf/InterviewReleaseForm.pdf. To learn more about potential legal considerations, see John A. Neuenschwander's booklet *Oral History and the Law*, available from the Oral History Association (http://omega.dickinson.edu/organizations/oha/pub_ps.html) or review details about copyright law and the Copyright Act of 1976 (and later revisions) at www.copyright.gov.

Now or Never?

There's no time like the present to get started on an oral history project. Often we procrastinate on projects such as these where the passage of time is not our friend.

Shortly after my husband and I purchased a video camera back in the mid-1990s, we purposely sat with each set of parents and asked them to recall what they could of their childhood and of their parents. While these interviews were not conducted quite the way a proper oral history project would be, it's all we have, as both of our fathers have since died. So even if you can't follow all of my suggestions, be sure to follow this one—get your interviews done now before it's too late.

Conducting the Interview

Before you start the interview, check again for background noises; if practical, turn off or remove telephones. Be sure not to place the microphone too close to a fan or other device that creates a constant noise, however slight. Have all props and artifacts, like photos or souvenirs, readily available.

Start your recording with detailed information including who you are, who is being interviewed, and who else is in the room (assisting or not). Also, specifically state the date and location of the interview and what you intend to cover during the interview. Note that both you and the interviewee will be signing a release form. If you are videotaping the interview, you may want to list all of these facts in large print on a sheet or two of paper and videotape these pages as you would a film slate.

If you're audiotaping the interview,

consider bringing a still camera to the interview to take photos of the interviewee at the time of the interview, and to make photographic copies of artifacts that the interviewee brings to the interview.

Proceed with the interview in a manner that makes the interviewee comfortable. Make eye contact and watch for visual cues indicating fatigue or boredom. Be prepared to roll with the punches—the interviewee is, after all, doing you a favor. Offer breaks when warranted and remember not to overstay your welcome, a particularly important consideration if you're counting on follow-up interviews.

> **Walter:** It was cold around Cedar Lake and we had good winters. And there was a railroad track running between the main street and the lake. I was out belly-flopping on the ice on the lake in my sled, and of course, being a little kid—curious—I stick my tongue on the metal part of the sled and it froze. My tongue freezes to the metal part of the sled, so then I have the problem of getting somewhere where it could heat up and melt my tongue off of there. So I get up and start back toward our fire, we had one pot-belly stove in our house, and I start back toward that and a train came along. And here I am holding this sled and I had to wait for a train to go by so I was really in bad shape. So I finally get, the train goes by, and I go to the house and lay down on the floor in front of the pot-belly stove until it . . . and I had to wait until it melted my tongue off the sled. (Laughter.) Very painful experience.

Post-Interview

After the interview, make at least two backup copies of the recording—one for the interviewee, and one for you. Store the original in a safe place. Use your backup, not the original, to make the written transcription.

The transcript you create is possibly the most usable portion of the interview for both researchers and descendants and therefore requires great care during production. If you are unable to prepare the transcript yourself, consider hiring a professional transcribing service to do the job for you.

If you perform the transcription without transcribing equipment, use the stop and start buttons on your tape recorder rather than the pause button—this can help prevent damage to the tape caused by pausing—and use the backup copy so your original doesn't get damaged. Also to save the tape, try to listen, stop the tape, type, and then start the tape again, all without rewinding.

Once you've completed the transcription, you may choose to edit it for clarity or brevity, but be careful not to lose the voice and character of the interviewee. Remember, these are the exact reasons you chose to create an oral history in the first place.

Lastly, after you've completed all edits, consider putting the written transcript into a more readable format. Digitize images and add them with the help of publishing software. Include scans of pertinent documents. Donate a copy of the tape and the transcript to the interviewee's local historical society (include a copy of the signed release form). And always provide the interviewee with his or her own copy of the interview. After all, you've just contributed a small part to preserving his or her legacy.

> **Walter:** Well, we lived in Marinette for ah, till 1939. We lived in three houses in Marinette. The first one was on Main Street and we had a dog named Nertz, a bulldog named Nertz. I remember that. And the second one was on Marinette Avenue, and the third place we lived in was on Marinette Avenue. And I've got a little house made out of

balsa wood that, I still have that house that I've made out of balsa wood, where you can take the . . . open up the house and see the floor plan and everything.

Elizabeth: Which house was that?

Walter: It was our third house in Marinette.

Elizabeth: Did you make it?

Walter: Yeah, I made it myself.

Elizabeth: I didn't know that.

Walter: Well it's here, still got it.

Cutting Through the Tape of Oral History

Lore? Legend? Tradition? Tall tales? Exactly where does oral history fit into a family's stories?

According to Donald Ritchie, author of *Doing Oral History*, oral histories of family members will probably include every kind of story, even folklore, that an interviewee cares to recall.

Still, the true goal of capturing a structured oral history, says Ritchie, who maintains the oral history project for the U.S. Senate Historical Office, is to help a witness to history—family member or not—candidly recall events that happened decades before and to preserve those memories long-term.

Oral histories should benefit everyone involved: interviewer, interviewee, and future listeners. And a well-done oral history will rarely be confused with staid textbook accounts or snippets of information presented on the nightly news.

"Oral historians record the memory and observation and thoughts of the person they're talking to," says Ritchie, "and get

people to express themselves as fully, candidly, and thoroughly as possible." The result is an off-the-cuff, insider's view of a historical event and a record of an interviewee's personality, charm, and character.

That's good news for the family historian whose interviews of family members keep unearthing tales of unimaginable proportions that may or may not be factual. "Oral historians get a lot of folklore," laughs Ritchie. So, as long as it's understood that these tales, which, while not factual, present personal and family character and tend more towards folklore than fact, there's room for even the most fantastic of stories in recorded family interviews.

Ancestry

Author's Comments

I took a journalism course in high school and got hooked on writing and editing. I then served in the U.S. Marine Corps, where I was trained as a journalist, photojournalist, and editor. Later I received a bachelor's degree in journalism, specializing in photojournalism, from the University of Texas at Austin.

Near the end of my Marine Corps career I started writing for *Ancestry* and found my niche. I discovered that I enjoy writing genealogy how-to articles, especially if I can use some of my own family research as a basis for the article.

This article followed the completion of a graduate course on oral history. I have conducted oral history interviews of family members and of local senior citizens for the museum where I work. The information from the course was fresh in my mind at the time so writing the article was not a problem.

I don't usually do "revisions." Instead, I am constantly rereading my writing as I am crafting an article. Sometimes I use an outline to make sure my thoughts are flowing properly, but many times I just start somewhere and go back and forth to make the article work. Once I feel like I'm finished, I usually send it off to a couple of good friends who are not afraid to tell it to me straight. And, I ask my husband to read the article, although I don't always enjoy that experience. (My ego and feelings do get in the way when my husband gives me feedback, even if the feedback is good and warranted.)

The best advice I can give a new writer is to understand that *everyone* needs to be edited. Ego needs to take a back seat to accuracy, grammar, and readability.

—Elizabeth Kelley Kerstens

Flying into Trouble

by George Monbiot

In *An Inconvenient Truth*, Al Gore produces a graphic of the cities to which he has flown (sometimes by private jet) to talk about climate change. There are dozens of them, all over the world. I am glad that he gave those talks—his contribution to the fight against climate change is equal to that of all other environmental campaigners put together. But I was shocked not so much by his mode of travel as by his total lack of embarrassment—even, perhaps, of awareness—about the contradiction between what he was saying and what he was doing.

In Europe, where the environmental impacts of transport have been subject to furious debate for years, a climate change campaigner would never have exposed himself in this way. Had he flown as much as Gore, he would have felt it necessary to explain that he could not otherwise have been so effective. He would never set foot in a private jet. He might have conducted his talks by video link—and made a point of that in the film.

Jets produce staggering amounts of carbon dioxide and other gases that accelerate global warming. But in North America the impacts of transport—especially flying—are only beginning to nudge the political surface.

Author Bio

George Monbiot is the author of several best-selling books, including *Heat: How to Stop the Planet from Burning*. He posts a blog at www.monbiot.com.

Carbon dioxide emissions per passenger mile from a standard airliner are very similar to those from cars. But you can cover nearly 15,000 miles in one day by plane. The CO_2 produced by planes is augmented by the other greenhouse gases they release, magnifying its effect by 270 percent. This means that flying is one of the most destructive things we can do.

Cars and planes could soon become the primary cause of global warming.

It appears that the only ethical option—and I realize that this will be an even less popular message in North America than it is in Europe—is greatly to reduce the number of flights we take. Because our economy has been built around the rapid mobility of goods and people (the volume of US airfreight grew by 372 percent between 1980 and 2004), this could be our greatest political challenge.

Officially, transport is the world's second-fastest-growing source of CO_2 emissions; between now and 2050, they are expected to double. But these numbers tell only half the story. The fastest-growing source of carbon emissions is the power sector, whose output is expected to quadruple by mid-century. But much of this growth should in fact be attributed to transportation, as it is partly driven by the use of coal and gas to make synthetic liquid fuels used for vehicles. Cars and planes could soon become the primary cause of global warming.

The automobile problem is—in engineering terms—relatively easy to address: All the necessary technologies required to slash emissions from surface transport exist already. But dealing with airplanes is a far more complicated problem. It means confronting not just the political and cultural resistance we meet while trying to clean up emissions from cars but also massive technical barriers.

Lifting a large passenger plane into the air and keeping it there is a feat subject to strict physical constraints, and it requires a massive amount of fossil fuel. The standard jet engine has more or less reached the limits

New fuels are the stuff of fantasy.

of efficiency, and there is no replacement anywhere near production. There has been a great deal of talk about "blended wing bodies": planes in which the passengers sit in swollen wings. In principle they could cut fuel use 30 percent. But this is no more than a concept, whose stability and controllability have not been proven.

New fuels are the stuff of fantasy. Richard Branson, CEO of Virgin, is looking for ways to create biofuel for jets; to this end he has started a new company called Virgin Fuels. But biofuels cause more climate change than they prevent. Forests in South America and Southeast Asia are being cleared to plant oil palm, sugarcane and soya for transport fuel. A study by Wetlands International with the Dutch scientific consultants Delft Hydraulics found that the production of every ton of palm oil results in up to 33 tons of CO_2 emissions, as trees are burned and peat is drained. This means that palm oil causes up to ten times as much global warm-

ing as petroleum. Even if you could put it in planes in large quantities, biofuel would not solve the carbon problem.

A more promising alternative fuel is hydrogen, if made from renewable electricity. Jet engines can run on hydrogen; however, because it is a far less dense fuel than kerosene, the planes would have to be much wider to carry it. This means that they must fly in the stratosphere—otherwise they'd encounter too much drag. Unfortunately, the water vapor produced by burning hydrogen in the stratosphere would cause a climate-changing effect thirteen times greater than that of an ordinary subsonic plane.

As the Intergovernmental Panel on Climate Change discovered, "there would not appear to be any practical alternatives to kerosene-based fuels for commercial jet aircraft for the next several decades."

The obvious replacements for planes are scarcely better. Fast passenger ships appear to be even worse for the environment than jets. One set of calculations I have seen suggests that the Queen Elizabeth II, the luxury liner run by Cunard, produces 9.1 tons of emissions per passenger on a return trip from Britain to New York. This is 7.6 times as much carbon as you produce when traveling by plane.

Nor are ultra-high-speed trains the answer. Though trains traveling at normal speeds have much lower carbon emissions than airplanes, Professor Roger Kemp of

The faster you go, the more energy you need.

Lancaster University shows that energy consumption rises dramatically at speeds above 125 miles per hour. Increasing the speed from 140 to 220 mph almost doubles the amount of fuel burned. If the trains are powered by electricity, and if that electricity is produced by plants burning fossil fuels, they cause more CO_2 emissions than planes. Running trains on renewable electricity is certainly possible, but this faces problems: Trains must run on time, and that means there is little room for "demand management," which means reducing the electricity load in response to fluctuations in supply. In all transport systems, high performance is incompatible with low consumption. The faster you go, the more energy you need.

There is one form of transoceanic transport that might help us reduce emissions, but this will not be a popular proposal. The total climate impact of a zeppelin, blimp or airship is 80 to 90 percent lower than the impact of a jet plane. Though forever associated with the Hindenburg disaster, airships are now quite safe. They have a range of up to 6,000 miles. Their top speed is around 80 mph. This is faster than ships but much slower than jet-liners, which cruise at more than 500 mph. A flight from New York to London by airship would take forty-three hours. They also have trouble landing and taking off in high winds and making headway if the wind is against them. This makes travel times less reliable than those of jets.

Less jet travel will be extremely hard to sell.

If we really have to cross the ocean, and if we are to make the reduction of carbon emissions a top priority, airships might be the best form of transport. Already dirigibles are being developed for lifting superheavy cargo in and out of inaccessible areas.

It seems to me that the only way the number of flights by passenger jet can be significantly and permanently reduced is through a reduction in the capacity of airports. Unfortunately, all over the world, airports are expanding. In Britain, for example, Tony Blair's government has instructed airports to double their capacity to accommodate a projected rise in the number of passengers from 228 million in 2005 to 500 million in 2030.

Reversing this trend is extremely difficult, but it is necessary if we are to have a high chance of preventing runaway climate change. Some sectors—tourism and hotels, for example—will undoubtedly suffer. We would need to get used to vacationing closer to home, or traveling less frequently and for longer. Corporations would have to start making better use of technology, conducting much of their business through video conferences and electronic gatherings. But it is surely not beyond the wit of humankind to maintain a healthy economy without having to load 200 pounds of human being onto an airplane every time something needs to be discussed.

Less jet travel will be extremely hard to sell. It flies in the face of everything we have been encouraged to regard as progress. But climate change appears to demand that progress be redefined. It suggests that the sum of human welfare will now be enhanced not by new economic freedoms but by new restraints.

The Nation

The Art of Camping

by Catherine Newman

Across the dirt floor of our campsite a black beetle is scuttling. It's as big as a small rat, and the kids scream and laugh with terror and delight; they can't take their eyes off of it. And I can't take my eyes off of *them*, off of their legs in particular, which I'm looking at now as if for the first time. They're filthy for one thing—pine needles have stuck on one of Ben's shins to a lump of something that most likely began life as a marshmallow—and they're also bruised and scraped, these legs, as bitten-up as candy apples. They give me a feeling of inexplicable joy. Isn't this what children's legs are supposed to look like in the summertime? My kids have *kid* legs!

I'm not saying that you have to go camping for your children to get legs like that,

should you happen even to want such a thing, but boy does it speed things along, what with the incessant bike riding and wood carrying and creepy-crawlies and falling down hillsides in the dark while you're peeing.

Let me start over. Let me sing the praises of camping to the beautiful tune of wide, starlit skies, the drowsy and flame-flickered children bundled around a campfire while tree frogs chirp, while day unfolds into night, time as magically expanding as a pleated fan. We have camped every summer in the very same site (usually) of the very same campground since Ben, now 8, was 1, and our memories are as thickly layered as a fancy cake: the summer the raccoons stole our marshmallows and pitched them down at us from a treetop; the summer Birdy was just a burping-new bump under my swimsuit; the summer the two babes slept late in the breezy shade of our tent while we two parents sat happily alone with our mugs under the dappled sunshine. "Remember the time . . . ?" we all say to each other a hundred times a day, and so, like a kind of vacation matryoshka doll, the latest trip contains nested inside it all of the

Things I Can't Camp Without

Doormat
Camp chairs
Washing-up bin
Clothesline
Paper towels
Air mattress

For the Kids
Bug box
Field guides
Magnifying glass
Art supplies
Disposable camera

Author Bio

Catherine Newman is a "recovering academic" (literature PhD), who's been publishing in magazines for the past decade—as a contributing editor at *FamilyFun* and *Wondertime* magazines, a regular contributor to *O: The Oprah Magazine*, and a freelance contributor of everything from essays in bestselling anthologies such as *The Bitch in the House* to marketing copy for online golf sweepstakes. She also writes a weekly parenting column, "The Dalai Mama," on wondertime.com, and wrote "Bringing Up Ben and Birdy" on babycenter.com, some of which was collected into the book, *Waiting for Birdy*.

trips that came before.

It's things gone vaguely haywire that the kids reminisce about most fondly: the time something winged and furry—a bat? A flying squirrel?—flapped into Dad's face while he was brushing his teeth; the time Ben put down a hot sparkler and melted our vinyl tablecloth ("There's the scar!"); the time our king-size air mattress deflated all night long with a cartoonish *hisssss* and we awoke on the hard ground, the four of us in a laughing heap; the time we repaired the mattress—or tent or swim ring or hiking boot—with duct tape; the time it rained and rained and Ben ate a lobster roll in footie pajamas because he had no dry clothes left to wear to the clam shack; the time we missed the turnoff and drove in an unwitting circle around the entire campground, Ben exclaiming, "Hey, those people have our exact same watermelon tablecloth!" just as I was exclaiming, "Hey, those people have our exact same beach towels!"

> Cardinal rule of camping: Set up your campsite—put up the tent, make up the beds, unfold the chairs, hang a clothesline—before jumping in the pond or hunting daddy longlegs.

There's never a dull moment camping—even when nothing happens. The time you normally pass through on your way to the real destination of your actual day—this time *becomes* your actual day: getting water, boiling water, brushing teeth, cooking breakfast, washing dishes. You don't camp in spite of the fact that the most ordinary activities become challenging; you camp because of it.

Take the bathroom, for example: It's a buzzing, flapping insectarium, and while both kids are vaguely afraid of the drain in the floor, they're fascinated by the bugs (others feel differently, it seems, since we once

spent five minutes ferrying a dozen daddy longlegs out of a stall so somebody's nail-biting 8-year-old could pee). Every activity occasions curiosity, conversation, and detour; we're always asking each other, "Hey, where were you guys?" and always answering, "Watching a red-tailed hawk near the faucet," or "Examining a slug on the firewood," or "I'm not sure." There is nothing quite as thrilling as ordinary life when it suddenly takes center stage.

It's not that I'm a purist: We eat at a clam shack a lot, drink a lot of nice wine, go to the drive-in movies, and buy wood and bottled water nearby, even when it's a rip-off. We sleep on our cotton sheets with our down comforter from home. But camping is great because it so precisely taps into our kids' passions: dirt and water, bent rules (more sugar, for example, and less hygiene), peeing *en plein air*, and, of course, fire. Last year, while Birdy was still content to cozy up to the fire pit with Eebo, her grubby purple hippo, our son made the inevitable 7-year-old turn toward pyromania: He helped his dad build and light the fire; he held a stick in the coals until it became (oy vey) a "torch"; he tossed crumpled paper into the flames, also bark and pine needles and a torn-up tissue box, to say nothing of the primitive thrill of cooking on a stick—marshmallows and hot dogs, of course, but also the less common plums and string cheese. When you're camping, everything tastes good. (Actually, make that everything except an incinerated plum.)

And let me just add: I am a city kid by birth and by nature, more "double-shot latte, please" than "help me balance this percolator on the fire grate." Years ago, in fact, my husband Michael (then boyfriend) and I backpacked in a Pacific Northwest rainforest where it—surprise!—rained the whole entire time, and I sang him the chorus from that Lemonheads song ("I lied about being the outdoor type") before swearing *never again*. But this—car camping with children and a comfy bed and a bottle of wine—I love completely. We stay in the most beautiful places (the California coast, Cape Cod) for next to nothing, and our initial investment (tent, air mattress, a camp stove) was the equivalent of maybe two nights in a hotel—and now we'll use that gear for years of inexpensive vacations.

Finally, no matter how bitterly I resent packing up the car—"Why are we doing this?" I grouse every single year as we cram the trunk with guitars and pillows, life vests and sandwich bread—it's always worth it. We tumble out into the cathedral-hushed shade of our campsite and inhale the clean air deeply into our lungs, and the kids begin the happy process of dirtying their legs.

High Camp

Campgrounds range from pristine hike-in spots in the wilderness to sites complete with swimming pool, horseshoes, and a family watching *Simpsons* reruns in the RV next door. Our favorites are state parks, which tend to offer the perfect mix of a lovely natural setting and flush toilets. An easy way to reserve a spot is through reserveamerica.com, which lists more than 170,000 campsites and cabins at 3,000 state, federal, and private campgrounds. We reserve six months ahead to get specific dates and sites, but we have also gotten last-minute reservations many times. For details on particular sites (terrain, shade, etc.), call the campground itself, rather than relying on its online map.

Author's Comments

For a piece like this, where I'm writing about a topic I know well, I begin with a huge brainstorming session that might include flipping through photographs and my journal, or talking to my family about the things they like and remember best about camping (I also always take tons of notes every time we go anywhere).

Then, of course, I try to balance those heaps of quirky specifics with more universal ideas (in this case, about parenting and quality time), so that the folks who would sooner throw themselves into a campfire than spend a night in a tent will (ideally) keep reading along out of some kind of philosophical/armchair interest.

But then—and this is a good trick for passing off memoir as a service piece—I stuck a bunch of practical service elements (how to choose a campsite, plan a trip, pack) into the sidebars.

I think it appeals to editors when you've already thought about the sidebars. It feels like you've done some of the work for them.

—Catherine Newman

Wondertime

Even Keel

by Jim Freim

After 25 years of training athletes, I have determined trail runners' number-one mistake (drum roll please)—they simply start out too fast. Drivers have AAA to ensure they safely reach their road-trip destination, and trail runners need even energy expenditure (EEE) to carry them to the finish line. EEE involves running at an even pace or intensity level from start to finish, which leads to faster times, reduced injuries and a more comfortable race experience. EEE is a simple premise for optimal performance; however, it is also one of the hardest for trail runners to grasp.

Bursting with anticipation and energy at the starting line, you are tempted to put the hurt on the competition—now! What was planned to be a 9-minute-per-mile pace, once the race is underway, is more like 8:45. Then suddenly, out of the blue, a monkey jumps on your back. No, make it an elephant. Previously effortless strides become a death march as legs turn to granite. Sensing discomfort and fatigue, your brain sends signals to your body to slow down and mitigate the damage. It's too late to revert to a nine-minute pace, and you slow to a discouraging survival shuffle.

TOP OFF THE TANK

The solution to this potentially disastrous race scenario is EEE. Visualize a tank hanging on the wall. Months of sound training and long runs developed your base strength and fitness, filling the tank with energy. To top it off, you add judicious speed and strength workouts. In the period immediately prior to a big race or trail run, rest and short, easy recovery runs maintain your tank's maximum stored energy level and allow your body to recuperate.

TURN ON THE JUICE

When the big day arrives and you're on the start line, open the tank's spigot to let your carefully stored energy gradually flow out, envisioning yourself moving in smooth, relaxed motion. Resist the temptation to open the spigot too wide by running too hard, which would run the tank dry before the finish. "Hitting the wall" is the term mostly commonly used to describe feelings associated with depleted muscle glycogen stores, blood glucose or muscle damage caused by pushing beyond your fitness level.

However, don't let a conservative starting pace lead you to worry about opening the spigot too little, which is rare. Simply open the spigot just the right amount and you'll naturally find your ideal race pace, or "zone," using up all stored energy by the time you reach the finish line.

To maintain a constant level of exertion, monitor your breathing rate or use the talk test (ensure that you aren't breathing so hard

Author Bio

Jim Freim, a personal trainer and former professor at the University of Oklahoma, is the author of two books about energy.

you can't speak), and aim to maintain a constant balance between comfort and discomfort (see sidebar for more exertion-monitoring techniques). Every five to 15 minutes, take a mental account of your posture, stride count, muscular strength and hydration and fuel intake levels.

Through EEE, your fastest times will feel the easiest. Savor the adrenaline rush of passing runners in the closing miles. At the start of your next race, repeat the EEE oath: Never go out too fast.

MONITOR THE MACHINE

Choose one of these three methods to monitor your exertion level:

1) **Monitor heart rate.** In your first few races err on the conservative side, aiming to keep your heart rate 10 beats per minute below your regular training heart rate. You will have to slow down on uphills to maintain an even rate, but this strategy will leave you plenty of fuel in the tank for the flats and downhills. Once you have a feel for EEE and tracking your heart rate, run the next race at five beats below training level and the next at training level. When you are ready to attempt a personal record, aim for a heart rate five beats above your training heart rate.

2) **Use the Borg Scale.** This system rates perceived exertion (PE) levels to help athletes hit pace targets. Runners assign a number between six (no exertion at all) and 20 (maximum exertion) to the intensity level of physical sensations such as increased heart rate, respiration, breathing rate and muscle fatigue. These numbers, when multiplied by 10, provide an approximate heart rate. For example, 13 on the Borg Scale, when multiplied by 10 equals 130, which means the heart is beating around 130 times per minute.

3) **Train in negative splits.** Divide the race into equal segments (measure in time) with the goal of running the last segment as fast—or faster—than the others. Running loop courses in training is an excellent way to practice this. For example, with a loop that takes 30 minutes to run at your fastest goal pace, design a workout in which you run three loops, the first aiming for 35 minutes, the second 32 minutes, and the third in 30 minutes. Progressively faster splits condition you mentally and physically to start out slower than your actual fitness level so that you can recruit surplus speed and energy when you need it most. Making the last loop the fastest is also an important confidence boost to set you up for race-day success.

Trail Runner

Author's Comments

I have been a personal trainer for almost 30 years. At the end of a particular 10K running event where all the trainees had gone out too fast, I realized that I had never told a trainee, "You went out too slow." That was the original title of my article—"What I've Never Told A Trainee"—but the editor of *Trail Runner* changed it. I add this fact because you must be willing to work with editors. You give to get.

When you're writing in an area of your expertise, the words flow. I am a trail runner myself and have successfully competed in numerous trail runs (including several 100-mile races). I wrote three drafts of this piece before sending it out.

Trail Runner was a natural choice to get my foot in the nonfiction door. I was already known to the magazine because of my athletic background: I'm the former athletic director of the Triathlon Federation of the USA; I won several triathlons after the age of 40 (when body parts start to fall off); and I'm a personal trainer. *Trail Runner* has published several of my articles.

—Jim Freim

Wildlife Volunteering in Thailand

by Erika Wedenoja

The local bus stopped at a gas station in town to let me off. Barely an hour later, I found myself riding an elephant into a local lake for bath time. This was to be a daily task for me as a volunteer at the Elephant Refuge and Education Center in Thailand. The Elephant Center is run by Wildlife Friends of Thailand (WFFT), a nonprofit organization founded and directed by Edwin Wiek. With goals including the rescue and rehabilitation of native animals, the Wildlife Rescue Center was opened in 2001, the Elephant Center in 2003. Both are on the grounds of a temple about 100 miles south of Bangkok, with the beach resorts of Cha-am and Hua Hin nearby. Volunteers and educational visits are welcomed.

Volunteers can choose to work at either the Wildlife Center or the Elephant Center. Preferring to focus on one species, I chose the latter. The four females at the Elephant Center were once begging on city streets or living in unsuitable conditions at elephant camps for tourists. Each elephant has her own *mahout*, or elephant keeper, whom the volunteers assist. As the *mahouts* spoke little English, they taught me enough to communicate with them and the elephants in Thai.

At 6:30 a.m. we collected the large mammals from the surrounding forest, where they foraged overnight, and gave them a breakfast of banana tree trunks or pineapple plants. A couple hours later it was time to clean up and feed again. Four elephants can fill a wheelbarrow full of dung in that amount of time. I soon felt like an elephant mommy.

In the early afternoon, we washed the elephants clean in the lake, taking care as they dunked and rolled playfully. Once they were cooled and cleansed, we rode them back into the forest for the night.

The elephants ate through their food supply every few days and then it was time to visit a nearby farmer's field. The locals were happy to have us haul away remaining plants after the fruit had been picked.

While I settled into a standard daily routine with the elephants, volunteers who chose to work at the Wildlife Center had rotational duties. One day might include draining and scrubbing the ponds for the sun bears, another might be collecting leaves to feed the monkeys as well as keeping their water bottles topped up. Much of the work involved cleaning and food preparation rather than physical contact in order to help the animals live as wildlife, not housepets.

Animals end up at the Wildlife Center for various reasons. Some were exotic pets, dumped when their owners tired of them. Others were confiscated from the illegal wildlife trade. Many animals had been exploited for entertainment, obliged to pose for

Author Bio

Erika Wedenoja graduated with a BA in comparative literature and French. She writes articles for the insurance industry and freelances for other magazines. She lives in Portland, Oregon, when she is not exploring the world.

photos or perform tricks for tourists.

Whenever possible, wildlife is treated by on-site veterinary services and released back into the wild. Gibbon families live on islands in the nearby lake to minimize human contact and prepare them for life in their native rainforest. Even when healthy, many animals must remain at the Wildlife Center as they have been raised in captivity and lack the skills to survive in the wild.

During my stay, we volunteers numbered about a dozen Europeans and North Americans, ranging in age from teens to sixties. We each shared a room and private bath with one other volunteer. While breakfast was a do-it-yourself affair, a buffet of meat and vegetarian Thai dishes was prepared by the staff for lunch and dinner. The main building provided kitchen, dining room, TV, books, and movies. Further evening entertainment was a short walk away, in a 1-street town with a weekly market, small shops, and two Internet cafes.

With one day off per week and moderate work schedules, there was plenty of free time to relax or watch the animals. The macaques (a monkey commonly found in Southeast Asia) never failed to threaten me, showing their teeth or rumps as I walked by. The gibbons woke me with their early morning singing. The young sun bears, claws already several inches long, loved to climb, hanging upside down as they fought playfully. And the elephants, despite an imposing size, were sensitive and affectionate. Nong Bo and Tia wrapped their trunks together in friendship, Kjaewta slapped hers on the ground when upset, Nam Phoun rested hers in her mouth when it got too heavy. Like me, many volunteers found it harder to leave the animals than their fellow volunteers when their stay was done.

For More Info

I signed up through www.ecovolunteer.org for a 1-week minimum stay at the **Elephant Center** (about $410); 3-week minimum for the Wildlife Center is about $696. All meals and lodging are included in the volunteer fee. Current news and additional information is available on the **Wildlife Friends of Thailand** website: **www.wfft.org**. You can also e-mail them at volunteer@wfft.org.

Preparation

Minimum age for volunteers is 18. No special skills are required, other than English speaking ability. Vaccinations against hepatitis A & B, diphtheria, tetanus, and polio are a pre-requisite as a precaution for the animals. Volunteers are needed year-round. While the weather is always hot and humid, the dry and cooler season from mid-November to March is more comfortable.

Transportation

WFFT can arrange a taxi service ahead of time from the airport or your hotel in Bangkok. However, I found it easy to take a taxi to the **Southern Bus terminal** (ask for Sai Tai Mai) in Bangkok and hop on a local bus to Cha-am. Buses leave hourly throughout the day and the ride takes 2-3 hours. A taxi from the airport should cost no more than $10 and the bus ticket is around $3. Call upon arrival in Cha-am and WFFT will send a driver to pick you up. This pick up is free but you will need about $10 for a taxi back to Cha-am when you leave.

Transitions Abroad

Wildlife Volunteering in Thailand

Author's Comments ━━━━━━━

Transitions Abroad is a resource I have used for years to help plan my travels. I researched back issues and found they hadn't covered the elephant project I did in Thailand. Since I was already familiar with the magazine, I knew exactly what type of writing the editors were looking for.

When you are a freelance writer, you want to make it as easy as possible for publishers to print your work. I double-check to ensure that I have followed the writer's guidelines explicitly. I also browse a few issues of the magazine I am writing for so I can use a similar tone in my piece.

My writing process always starts with an old fashioned paper outline. This includes the general format of the article as well as specific points I want to make. I usually type just one main draft, highlighting the areas I think I will want to revise. I tend to be long-winded, so I edit for the appropriate length and then finish up by fact-checking and tweaking some wording.

—Erika Wedenoja

"There's Still a Girl in There"

by Karen Hammond

When my mother-in-law, Helen, began developing Alzheimer's disease, my husband and I agreed she could no longer live alone. In July 1991 we moved her from Massachusetts to live near us. During the eight-hour drive, Helen, then 78, clutched two small possessions in her lap: a tiny ceramic dog with a re-glued tail and a three-legged glass cat, both carefully wrapped in tissue paper.

"Those figurines must be special to you," I said when she even carried them into the restaurant when we stopped for lunch. To my astonishment, she burst into tears. "I got these the first summer we went to the Cape," she said. "The boys each picked one out for me. Now I'll probably never get there again."

Suddenly, I understood. Where I saw meaningless knickknacks, Helen saw her two son's freckled noses pressed against the dime-store window and a family tradition of Cape Cod summers that had lasted more than 50 years. While I had chattered during the drive about how much she would enjoy her new life in her new home, she had been mourning the loss of the life she would never know again.

Author Bio

Karen Hammond writes about women's issues, health, and travel for leading publications including *American Profile*, *Woman's Day*, the *Miami Herald*, and the *Boston Globe*. She lives on the coast of Maine, and is an instructor for Long Ridge Writers Group.

Most adult children of aging parents understand the importance of attending to a parent's physical, medical and financial needs. But we often overlook the emotional and psychological aspects of aging, says geriatric nursing specialist Joyce Ferrario, Ph.D., associate dean of the Decker School of Nursing at Binghamton University in New York. It's hard to grasp what it's like to be at a stage of life we haven't reached yet, and aging isn't a subject seniors talk about with ease. But we need to try to understand what they are experiencing so we can be sensitive to their feelings as we take on ever more responsibility for their care.

What would our parents tell us about aging if they could? Here are 12 things that seniors and those who care for them think it's important for us to understand.

1) "It's hard to admit that I need help."

Adult children are often frustrated when parents who can no longer manage on their own still resist having someone come in to help clean and cook for them. To us, it's the only way to ensure they're being well cared for. But to them, the introduction of hired help may mean something more distasteful. "It reinforces feelings that they are losing their independence," says Dr. Ferrario. Accepting help can also constitute an invasion of privacy and disruption of domestic routine. "Suddenly, the house is being cleaned differently, clothes folded differently and meals cooked differently," says Lenard W. Kaye, D.S.W., director of the Center on Aging at the University of Maine in Orono. "A stranger has intruded and altered long-established behaviors and habits that have given structure to the older person's life."

2) "I need time to adjust to change."

Sylvia Wallace, 88, of Philadelphia, initially resisted letting a housekeeper come in to help her and her husband, Oscar. "It took me a long time to admit I could no longer do everything myself," she says. Oscar, who died two years ago, had just as much trouble accepting that he could no longer drive after suffering a stroke. He never did make peace with not being able to "pick up and go." But he and Sylvia did finally accept having a housekeeper in their home.

At first they complained about the loss of privacy and disruption of routine. But rather than cancel the arrangement, the Wallaces' five children kept quiet and gave their parents time to acclimate. "Some seniors accept help willingly as a means of staying in their homes," says Dr. Kaye. "Others are hesitant at first but slowly adjust as they see that assistance makes their lives easier." Now, especially since her husband died, Sylvia has formed a strong bond with her housekeeper. "I am grateful to her now," she says. "I know I couldn't get along without her. But it's hard not to be able to do the things I've always done."

3) "Don't talk down to me."

Imagine living a long, rich, productive life only to be spoken to and treated condescendingly in old age by someone decades younger. "I like people, and most are wonderful to me," says Anne Fennessy, 93, of New York City. But on occasion people are patronizing. "I'm always amused when I'm out and someone says, 'Just step over here, young lady.' I'm not a young lady. I'm an old lady. And I *like* being an old lady. I hope everyone has a life as full as mine."

4) "I'm not helpless."

Just as offensive to seniors is the assumption many younger adults make that age equals incompetence. "People do tend to dismiss you when you're old," says Betty Lang, 97, a resident of the Hodgdon Green Assisted Living Facility in Damariscotta, Maine. Betty, for example, still manages her own affairs but has trouble hearing recorded prompts when doing business by phone. Her daughter, Deborah Lang, helps her with that. "When I reach a real person, I explain the situation and say, 'I'll put my mother on now,'" says Deborah. "Often, the person will say, 'That's O.K. I'll talk with you.'" No, says Deborah. The person will speak with her mother. "People seem to think if she's 97, she can't know her own name."

5) "My biggest fear is being a burden."

Years of caring for her mother-in-law, Margaret Pritchard, had taught Annette Pritchard of Fayetteville, Georgia, how much pride Margaret took in living independently. But she didn't realize how sensitive Margaret was to the amount of care she still required until Margaret developed a kidney infection. As it came on, Annette spent three days and nights caring for Margaret in the apartment Annette and her husband had built for her in their home. Annette didn't give her caretaking much thought, but Margaret did. When she finally had to be hospitalized, she told a nurse how glad she was that Annette would finally get some rest. "She never said anything to me," says Annette. "But I realized then how much she worried about becoming a burden."

6) "I need to feel useful."

Since Margaret died at age 90 in January 2002, Annette has become a regular volunteer at the senior center they often visited.

There, she says, she sees constant evidence of how important it is to seniors to feel like contributing members of the households in which they live. She tells of one woman, for example, who announces her departure at the end of a day's visit by saying, "I need to go home and start dinner now"—clearly proud that she has this important family responsibility to fulfill. Says Dr. Kaye, "Everyone needs to feel a sense of competency, a sense of not being totally dependent on others."

7) "I still need to live my own life."

Rather than live with adult children and fear becoming a burden, some seniors prefer moving to an assisted living facility. That was Betty Lang's choice. After Betty's husband died in 1997, her daughter, Deborah, and Deborah's husband moved in with Betty in the family home in Nobleboro, Maine. The couple expected the arrangement to be permanent. "But after a year I think Mom was almost bored," says Deborah. "She wanted to be around people her own age and get involved in more activities. She decided to move to Hodgdon Green and told me I should get on with my own life." Says Betty, "It was a good decision. There are people here to talk to, and I don't have to be concerned about interfering with my daughter's plans if I need transportation or want to do something."

8) "I miss all of my old friends."

Sylvia Wallace recalls that when she and her husband celebrated their 63rd wedding anniversary two months before he died, the celebration was bittersweet because, although many family members were present, few of their friends were still alive to share their big day. "I've been very sad to lose so many friends," says Sylvia. "I only have two close friends left—one in Florida and one in

Philadelphia—and we can only keep in touch by phone." With help, she still makes it most Saturdays to the beauty parlor where she has had her hair done weekly for more than 20 years. But the parlor, which caters to women her age, doesn't get much business now, and she worries that it may close.

Most seniors with loving family around them realize how blessed they are. But friendships are also important. When they disappear, seniors can find themselves coping with loneliness even when surrounded by family. When chances to share feelings, problems and memories with old friends dwindle, says Dr. Kaye, "the loss can be a major blow to a senior's sense of completeness and well-being."

9) "I don't feel any different on the inside."

It's impossible for younger, healthier adult children to understand what it's like to experience the physical losses, changes and deterioration that accompany old age—especially for seniors who remain mentally sharp and still feel whole in mind and spirit. As Sylvia Wallace once told her son Marc, "Don't ever forget. No matter how old I am on the outside, there's still a girl in there." Gerontologists call this feeling, shared by many seniors, the phenomenon of the ageless self, says Ron Eskew, Ph.D., an associate professor of psychology at Hilbert College in Hamburg, New York, who specializes in the elderly. "People tend to see themselves as the same continuous person regardless of how old they may be. Often the most serious insults to this ageless self come from health changes that limit physical activity and independence."

10) "Walkers are for old people!"

Esther Prentice, 90, who lives at Hodgdon Green, gets around the facility pretty well using a walker, but she resists using it in other places. "I'm too proud," she admits. "When I go out with the walker people look at me like they feel sorry for me, and I hate that. I've always thought of myself as very self-sufficient." When my fiercely independent mother had to start using a cane at age 90, I mainly saw it as a small price to pay to keep her from falling and breaking a hip. She saw it differently. "I hate it," she griped. "I can't do anything that requires two hands anymore." One day as we were out walking, a young couple jogging toward us stepped off the sidewalk to let us by. "See that?" my mother fumed. "People take one look at this cane and think I'm a creaky old lady!" She laughed at her own indignation a moment later, but she was clearly stung that people saw her as someone who needed special treatment.

11) "It hurts to leave home."

When my husband and I moved his mother to live near us, we didn't really understand how traumatic it was for her to leave the house, friends and neighbors she had enjoyed during her long, rich life. The same was true when my mother realized she could no longer live alone and agreed to move in with us. Although she enjoyed becoming an integral part of our lives and family, she often said that she missed the buzz of her hometown—the comings and goings of neighbors and friends, the life she had known for 92 years and the feeling that she had a special niche in the community. "Moving, even within the same town, can be a real trauma for elderly people," says Dr. Ferrario. "It's a signal that their lives have changed forever."

Even when elders decide on their own to give up their home, there is still the issue of what it signifies. Deborah Wilburn of White Plains, New York, says it took her parents three years to finally decide to sell their home and move to a community for seniors that offered varying levels of care. Although they were still well enough to move into an independent-living apartment, "they saw that move as the beginning of the end," says Deborah. "When they were finally settled in, my mother looked around and said, 'Well this is it. They're going to carry us out of here in a box.'"

12) "My memories are precious."

Grace Dance, 94, who has outlived two husbands and her only child, chose to move into Hodgdon Green on the day it opened. She is grateful to the step-grandson and his family who took her in when she fell ill for a while. "They made me feel welcome, and I still see them all the time," she says. But when the facility opened, "I felt it was time to move and let them have their lives back. This way we all have our independence and they don't have to worry about me."

In the bedroom of her Hodgdon Green apartment, a wall of photographs chronicles Grace's life. There are photos of her as a child model, pictures of special occasions and photos of her son, grandchildren, great-grandchildren and two great-great-grandchildren. Says Grace, "I like to lie in bed and look at my photographs and remember."

Words of Wisdom

The dining room at the Hodgdon Green Assisted Living Facility in Damariscotta, Maine, is a cheerful place, brightened by the residents' artwork and made homey with plants and comfortable chairs and pillows. The residents, currently all female, like to gather there for coffee. When they do, the conversation often turns to what used to be and what they miss most now that they are in their eighth and ninth decades of life.

"I miss my husband every day," **Erma Ames, 82**, says softly. Her friends, all widows, nod understandingly. The death of a

(cont.)

---

beloved spouse, or children before their time, or lifelong friends—those are the most difficult losses. But the inability to drive a car, do community service, cook a holiday meal or pet a fluffy cat who slept each night on the bed—these are losses, too.

Betty Lang, 97, minces no words. "I don't like growing old. Who would? I miss gardening, cooking, walking the dog—all those little things that seem like nothing at the time but make up a full life. You don't realize how important they are until you don't have them." But these are feelings Betty prefers not to dwell on. "I do the crossword puzzle in the local paper every morning," she says. "But it's getting too easy. I prefer a challenge. I recently finished rereading everything I could get my hands on by Virginia Woolf. I play bridge once a week, go to the theater, and I'm out a lot with my daughter."

Eyes twinkling, **Grace Dance, 94**, tells of her great-grandfather, a Methodist minister who lived to 94. "He always said he lived that long because he was so good. I plan to live to one hundred and prove he was wrong about the being good part! And when I hit a hundred, I'm going to celebrate by going to New York City for the first time to be on TV!"

What can we learn from these women about the experience and emotions of aging? Seniors face the challenges of growing old in various ways: some with calm acceptance, others with resignation, others with humor and optimism. Whatever path they choose, most ask only one thing of those who love them: to be allowed to walk that path with dignity.

8 Ways to Show You Understand and Care

The more sensitive we are to what our aging parents are going through, the more we can offer the kind of help they really need. Here's how to do that.

1. Honor emotions. Encourage parents to express their feelings about aging, and listen when they do. "This is a generation that was taught not to wallow in emotions," says Andrea Handel, L.S.W., administrator at Hodgdon Green and other assisted-living facilities. "They soldier on. So if they're willing to talk, it's important to listen."

2. Don't overwhelm. "There's a fine line between offering help and taking over," says Dr. Eskew. When Deborah Lang helps her mom negotiate phone prompts and lets her talk to real people, she is striking the right balance.

3. Make decisions *with* parents. Adult kids don't always know what's best for parents. When choosing a housekeeper, for example, they may care most about years of experience, says Dr. Kaye. "But it may be more important to consider personality and cultural background."

4. Be patient. Barbara Vorel Lambert, of Danvers, Massachusetts, recalls that for months after helping her mother, Edith, move to an assisted-living facility, Edith kept asking to go home. This period was painful for both of them, but it did pass. Gradually Edith adjusted, until during one outing she told Barbara, "I'd like to go home now—to my new house, where all my friends are."

5. Stand firm. Dr. Eskew suggests that if parents refuse to consider needed services, hold a family meeting. "Say, 'We're talking about this as a family because we want you
(cont.)

to have choices.'" Come ready to review options, and don't leave until parents agree to try something.

6. Accept their limits. It's hard to watch a parent's health decline, says Dr. Eskew, but adult kids must try to accept these changes. Phil Bruno, of New York City, recalls struggling to accept the toll Parkinson's Disease took on his dad before he died. "Something would come up that he had always done easily, and I'd say, 'Come on, Pop. You can still do that.' I remember him trying to get up off the couch and looking stunned that he couldn't. It was sad to see him that way. It took me a while to accept that he couldn't do the things he used to do."

7. Respect their desires. "As people get older, their appetite for socializing often changes and they may prefer spending more quiet time at home," says Dr. Eskew. "That doesn't mean they're lonely. Sometimes solitude can be healing." If a parent seems very withdrawn, though, it may be time to consider professional treatment. Even the elderly can benefit from such help.

8. Celebrate a senior's life. Aides at my mother-in-law's nursing home responded positively when I brought in framed photos of her as a child, young wife and mother, and respected librarian. Even when suffering from advanced Alzheimer's, Helen loved to show off her photos and occasionally surprised her caregivers with a poignant memory. Another resident born in the former Soviet Union sometimes twirled down the halls, singing in her native tongue, as the staff played music for her. At such moments it was easy to see her as a beautiful young village girl with flowers in her hair.

Family Circle

Author's Comments

My feisty New England mother hated being condescended to because of her age. I also noticed how often her elderly friends thanked me just for stopping by to chat. Eventually I realized how much we tend to focus on seniors' medical and financial issues and overlook their emotional needs.

I had previously published in *Family Circle* and my editor liked my feature pitch on the emotional issues of aging. Coincidentally, she quoted her elderly mother-in-law's favorite comment, "There's still a girl in there, you know." That struck me as a terrific title. Writers' titles rarely survive the editorial process, but this one did.

Much credit goes to the wonderful women in their 80s and 90s who shared their stories. I also interviewed several experts, a key step in writing any in-depth article.

When people ask how many drafts I go through, my answer is, "As many as it takes." I outline loosely and revise relentlessly.

After this article was published, I received emails and letters from around the country. Knowing that something I wrote touched so many lives made all the work worthwhile. The article's selection as the 2006 Outstanding Service Feature Article of the Year Award from the American Society of Journalists and Authors was a highlight of my professional life.

To break into a major publication, consider querying a short piece for one of the magazine's departments. After you've published a few and proven your professionalism, pitch an essay or a feature article.

The first time you flip open a national magazine and see your own name in print will be a day you'll never forget!

—Karen Hammond

Title Index

Artist, Scientist, Technician, Historian Dudley Giberson, 253-256

The Art of Camping, 318-320

Be Sensitive When Moving the Elderly, 300-302

Blood Lilies, 155-164

A Box Full of Nothing, 149-154

Cellmates, 67-70

Chicken-Necking on the Bay, 215-216

A Christmas Farewell, 190-192

Colonial Cuisine and the Road to Revolution, 241-243

Completely Lovestruck, 285-287

The Conspiracy, 203-205

Deadlines and Diapers and Dinner, 249-252

Even Keel, 321-323

Familiar Stranger, 19-22

Fixing Larx, 122-128

Flying into Trouble, 315-317

The Girl with the Click Click Eyes, 27-35

TheGreatGreenberg's Gift, 179-181

Harry London Chocolate Hall of Fame, 291-293

Home Remedies for the Sick Season, 182-184

The House Spider, 165-168

How to Be a Great Mom, 277-280

How to Make Flan, 59-66

I Have a Bunch of Coins . . ., 264-266

In the Clutch: Better Shifting for Sport-Touring Riders, 303-304

I've Looked Everywhere, 16-18

Killer Shift, 83-85

Kitchen Knives, 267-270

The Knitting Madonna, 129-132

Kursk, 25-26

Lake Superior, Winter Dawn, 187-189

Let There Be Sleep, 305-308

The Lover of Horses, 104-112

Love Spells, 113-118

The Man Who Carved Lincoln, 206-207

Menu, 5-7

Mind the Migraine, 193-195

Mrs. Comfrey Wins, 43-45

My Mom's Song, 185-186

My So-Called Genius, 261-263

My Turn, 23-24

Nights at the Round Table, 229-230

No Place Like Home, 208-209

Old Man on Campus, 235-237

One by One, 57-58

One Life, 86-93

On the Record: Collecting Oral Histories, 309-314

An Out-of-This-World Rescue, 201-202

Patience, 76-82

Paul Newman's House, 36-40

Peggy Hedman Is Driven to Keep Her Charges Safe, 231-234

Petri Parousia, 142-148

Pickles and Salsa, 226-228

Plant a Second Season Salad, 217-219

Plant-Based Tableware Redefines the Word Disposable, 283-284

The Puzzle, 8-11

Road Gamble, 133-141

Rumple What?, 169-175

Sharing Memories, Sharing Lives, 244-246

Snakes Alive!, 210-212

Sneaker Obsession Is Baffling, 213-214

Stargazers, 94-103

The Story of Patent Leather
    Shoes, 71-75

A Sweet and Gentle Land,
    271-276

Tapping for Maple's Sweet
    Gold, 257-260

"There's Still a Girl in
    There," 327-332

The Time Machine, 220-221

Things We Do for Love, 222-
    225

Toast and Jelly, 12-15

Tonics, 51-56

The Tortilla Cycle, 196-197

Total Recall, 247-248

The Tree, 119-121

Trucks, 46-50

Turning Heads, 198-200

The Ugly Wedding Present,
    281-282

Under India's Spell, 288-290

Wants, 41-42

When 'Tis(n't) the Season to
    Ride?, 238-240

Where the Creek Turkey
    Tracks: Wild Land and
    Language, 294-299

Wildlife Volunteering in
    Thailand, 324-326

Author Index

Allen, Rebecca, 196-197

Amadeo, Diana M., 190-192

Anthony, Jennifer, 51-56

Aslanian, Sasha, 281-282

Axelson, Gustave, 187-189

Bannister, Polly, 271-276

Barnett, Barbara A., 113-118

Bauman, Richard, 206-207

Bechtel, Amy, 46-50

Beete, Paulette, 241-243

Bellarosa, James M., 119-121

Booker, Tricia, 231-234

Brown, Kevin, 86-93

Carter, Scott William, 133-141

Cormack, Robert, 71-75

Curcio, Julia, 129-132

Davis, Robert Fuller, 291-293

Drake, Heidi, 249-252

Elder, Aida, 238-240

Fisher, Lou, 5-7, 36-40, 122-128

Franklin, Kris, 8-11, 182-184

Fraser, Laura, 261-263

Freim, Jim, 321-323

Gallagher, Tess, 104-112

Gautier, Amina Lolita, 59-66

Giorgio, Michael, 83-85

Gore, Willma Willis, 67-70

Graeff, Scott, 12-15

Grant, Kristin, 201-202

Gruen, Judy, 193-195

Guidry, Jacqueline, 76-82

Haedrich, Ken, 267-270

Hammond, Karen, 327-332

Havazelet, Ehud, 235-237

Henson, Dean, 210-212

Homan, Tim, 294-299

Hughes, Matthew, 142-148

Hutson, Matthew, 229-230

Kaplan, David Michael, 94-103

Kaufman-Orloff, Karen, 213-214

Kerstens, Elizabeth Kelley, 309-314

Klein, Laurie, 222-225

Kunasek, Kim, 220-221

Marcus, Gary, 247-248

Matthews, Carolyn, 23-24

Mills, Robert B., 300-302

Mohiuddin, Majid, 285-287

Monbiot, George, 315-317

Newman, Catherine, 318-320

Newton, Kurt, 165-168

Paley, Grace, 41-42

Pleasant, Barbara, 217-219

Redmond, Shirley Raye, 208-209

Rinker, Harry L., 264-266

Rodgers, Susan Jackson, 16-18

Rott, Cynthia, 215-216

Sánchez, Arthur, 149-154

Scammell, Ryan, 57-58

Schneider, Cathy, 226-228

Schoder, Marc, 283-284

Silverman, Arlene, 244-246

Slon, Steven, 288-290

Springer, Nancy, 169-175

Stahura, Barbara, 305-308

Stein, Philip, 179-181

Stone, Jessica, 257-260

Stoughton, Barbara A., 185-186

Suarez, Maria Elena, 25-26

Thompson, Kathleen, 203-205

Tilsner, Julie, 277-280

Tuttle Jr., Marc, 303-304

Vardeman, Robert E., 155-164

Walters, John, 253-256

Wedenoja, Erika, 324-326

Windsor, Patricia, 19-22, 27-35, 43-45

Wren, Sharon, 198-200

Magazine Index

AARP The Magazine, 288-290

Aboriginal SF, 122-127

Alligator Juniper, 86-93

American Spirit, 241-243, 257-260

Analog Science Fiction and Fact, 46-50

Ancestry, 309-314

Anotherealm.com, 149-154

Appalachian Heritage, 294-299

Back Home in Kentucky, 210-212

BackHome Magazine, 226-228

Bridge, 5-7

Cat Fancy, 201-202

Chronicle of the Horse, 231-234

Cleo Magazine, 19-22

Collector's News, 264-266

Country Journal, 267-270

Country Woman, 185-186

Crab Orchard Review, 59-66, 76-82

Ellery Queen's Mystery Magazine, 133-141

Enormous Changes at the Last Minute, 41-42

Family Circle, 327-332

Family Circle UK, 43-45

The Family Digest, 300-302

Fantasy & Science Fiction, 142-148, 169-175

The First Line, 51-56

First Love, 27-35

Five, 283-284

Flashquake, 57-58

Georgia Guardian, 203-205

Good Old Days, 179-181

Grit, 217-219

Home Business Magazine, 249-252

Journal Plus, The Magazine of the Central Coast, 206-207, 291-293

Kearsarge, 253-256

Leading Edge, 113-118

Liguorian, 129-132

Mary Engelbreit's Home Companion, 220-221

Minnesota Conservation Volunteer, 187-189

Mirabella, 94-103

Mississippi Review, 36-40

Modern Bride, 281-282, 285-287

More, 261-263

MO: Writings from the River, 67-70

The Nation, 315-317

New York Times Magazine, 235-237, 247-248

Orion, 196-197

Outlook by the Bay, 215-216

Pagosa Springs Sun, 8-11, 182-184

Parenting, 277-280

Passager, 222-225

Pirate Writings, 165-168

The Poughkeepsie Journal, 213-214

Psychology Today, 229-230

Radish, 198-200

Rider Magazine, 303-304

Romantic Homes, 208-209

Rosebud, 71-75

Saturday Evening Post, 244-246

Science & Spirit, 305-308

The SeaHarp Hotel, 155-164

Silent Sports, 238-240

Stitches for Patients, 193-195

StoryQuarterly, 16-18, 25-26

The Storyteller, 119-121

Teachers of Vision, 190-192

Thema, 23-24

Trail Runner, 321-323

Transitions Abroad, 324-326

Truckers News, 12-15

Wondertime, 318-320

Workers Write!, 83-85

Yankee Magazine, 271-276

Zyzzyva, 104-112

Acknowledgments

Grateful acknowledgment is made to the following for permission to reprint previously published material.

"Menu" by Lou Fisher. Originally published in *Bridge,* Spring 2005, and subsequently in *Hunger & Thirst* (City Works Press, 2008). Reprinted by permission of the author.

"The Puzzle" by Kris Franklin, from *Pagosa Springs Sun,* February 12, 1987. Reprinted by permission of the author.

"Toast and Jelly" by Scott Graeff, from *Truckers News,* July 2006. Reprinted by permission of the author.

"I've Looked Everywhere" by Susan Jackson Rodgers, from *StoryQuarterly,* 2007. Reprinted by permission of the author.

"Familiar Stranger" by Patricia Windsor, from *Cleo Magazine.* Reprinted by permission of the author.

"My Turn" by Carolyn Matthews, from *Thema,* June 2008. Reprinted by permission of the author.

"Kursk" by Maria Suarez, from *StoryQuarterly,* 2007. Reprinted by permission of the author.

"The Girl with the Click Click Eyes" by Patricia Windsor. Copyright © 1976, 1989, 2009 by Patricia Windsor. Reprinted by permission of the author.

"Paul Newman's House" by Lou Fisher. Originally published in *Mississippi Review,* Spring 2000, and subsequently in *Bar Stories* (Bottom Dog Press, 2007). Reprinted by permission from *Mississippi Review* Vol. 28, Nos. 1–2, and the author.

"Wants" by Grace Paley. From *Enormous Changes at the Last Minute* by Grace Paley. Copyright © 1971, 1974 by Grace Paley. Reprinted by permission of Farrar, Straus & Giroux, Inc.

"Mrs. Comfrey Wins" by Patricia Windsor. Copyright © 1977, 1989, 2009 by Patricia Windsor. Reprinted by permission of the author.

"Trucks" by Amy Bechtel, from *Analog Science Fiction and Fact,* March 2007. Reprinted by permission of the author.

"Tonics" by Jennifer Anthony, from *The First Line,* Spring 2007. Reprinted by permission of the author.

"One by One" by Ryan Scammell, from *Flashquake,* Winter 2007–2008. Reprinted by permission of the author.

"How to Make Flan" by Amina Lolita Gautier, from *Crab Orchard Review,* Winter/Spring 2006, Vol. 11, No. 1. Reprinted by permission of the author.

"Cellmates" by Willma Willis Gore, from *MO: Writings from the River,* Spring 2007. Reprinted by permission of the author.

"The Story of Patent Leather Shoes" by Robert Cormack, from *Rosebud,* 2006, Issue 37. Reprinted by permission of the author.

"Patience" by Jacqueline Guidry, from *Crab Orchard Review,* Winter/Spring 2006, Vol. 11, No. 1.

Reprinted by permission of the author.

"Killer Shift" by Michael Giorgio, from *Workers Write!,* 2007. Reprinted by permission of the author.

"One Life" by Kevin Brown, from *Alligator Juniper,* 2007. Reprinted by permission of the author.

"Stargazers" by David Michael Kaplan, from *Mirabella.* Reprinted by permission of Brandt & Brandt Literary Agents, Inc. Copyright © 1990 by David Michael Kaplan.

"The Lover of Horses" from *The Lover of Horses and Other Stories* by Tess Gallagher. Copyright © 1982, 1983, 1984, 1985, 1986 by Tess Gallagher. Reprinted by permission of Harper & Row Publishers, Inc. This story originally appeared in *Zyzzyva.*

"Love Spells" by Barbara A. Barnett, from *Leading Edge,* April 2007. Reprinted by permission of the author.

"The Tree" by James Bellarosa, from *The Storyteller,* January/February/March 2007. Reprinted by permission of the author.

"Fixing Larx" by Lou Fisher. Originally published in *Aboriginal SF,* October 1986, and subsequently in *The MacGuffin,* Fall 1993. Reprinted by permission of the author.

"The Knitting Madonna" by Julia Curcio, from *Liguorian,* April 2007. Reprinted by permission of the author.

"Road Gamble" by Scott William Carter. Copyright © 2007 by Scott

William Carter. From *Ellery Queen's Mystery Magazine*, June 2007. Reprinted by permission of the author.

"Petri Parousia" by Matthew Hughes, from *The Magazine of Fantasy & Science Fiction*, February 2008. Reprinted by permission of the author.

"A Box Full of Nothing" by Arthur Sánchez, from *Anotherealm.com*, 2007. Reprinted by permission of the author.

"Blood Lilies" by Robert E. Vardeman, from *The SeaHarp Hotel*, Charles L. Grant, ed. Copyright © 1990. Tor Books. Reprinted by permission of the author.

"The House Spider" by Kurt Newton, from *Pirate Writings*, Spring 1995. Reprinted by permission of the author.

"Rumple What?" by Nancy Springer, from *The Magazine of Fantasy & Science Fiction*, March 2008. Reprinted by permission of the author.

"TheGreatGreenberg's Gift" by Philip Stein, from *Good Old Days*, August 2007, edited by Ken and Janice Tate, published by House of White Birches, 2007. Used by permission of DRG Publishing.

"Home Remedies for the Sick Season" by Kris Franklin, from *Pagosa Springs Sun*, January 7, 1988. Reprinted by permission of the author.

"My Mom's Song" by Barbara A. Stoughton, from *Country Woman*, May 2008. Reprinted by permission of Reiman Media Group.

"Lake Superior, Winter Dawn" by Gustave Axelson. Originally published in *Minnesota Conservation Volunteer*, January/February 2006. Reprinted by permission of the author.

"A Christmas Farewell" by Diana M. Amadeo, from *Teachers of Vision*, Fall 2007. Reprinted by permission of the author.

"Mind the Migraine" by Judy Gruen, from *Stitches for Patients*, January/February 2007. Reprinted by permission of the author.

"The Tortilla Cycle" by Rebecca Allen. Originally published in *Orion*, May/June 2007 (www.orionmagazine.org). Reprinted by permission of the author.

"Turning Heads" by Sharon Wren, from *Radish*, July 2007. Reprinted by permission of the author.

"An Out-of-This-World Rescue" by Kristin Grant, from *Cat Fancy*, May 2008. Reprinted by permission of the author.

"The Conspiracy" by Kathleen Thompson, from *The Georgia Guardian*, February 26, 1993. Reprinted by permission of the author.

"The Man Who Carved Lincoln" by Richard Bauman, from *Journal Plus*, February 2008. Reprinted by permission of the author.

"No Place Like Home" by Shirley Raye Redmond, from *Romantic Homes*, May 2006. Reprinted by permission of the author.

"Snakes Alive!" by Dean Henson, from *Back Home in Kentucky*, July/August 2007. Reprinted by permission of the author.

"Sneaker Obsession Is Baffling" by Karen Kaufman-Orloff, from *Poughkeepsie Journal*, April 10, 2008. Copyright © 2008, *Poughkeepsie Journal*, www.poughkeepsiejournal-com. Reprinted with permission.

"Chicken-Necking on the Bay" by Cynthia Rott, from *Outlook by the Bay*, Summer 2008. Reprinted by permission of the author.

"Plant a Second Season Salad" by Barbara Pleasant, from *Grit*, September/October 2006. Reprinted by permission of the author.

"The Time Machine" by Kim Kunasek. Originally published in *Mary Engelbreit's Home Companion*, April/May 2008. Reprinted by permission of the author.

"Things We Do for Love" by Laurie Klein, from *Passager*, Winter 2007. Reprinted by permission of the author.

"Pickles and Salsa" by Cathy Schneider, from the May/June 2007 issue of *BackHome*, a publication focused on sustainable living; www.backhomemagazine.com; info@backhomemagazine.com. Reprinted by permission of the author.

"Nights at the Round Table" by Matthew Hutson, from *Psychology Today*, January/February 2008. Reprinted by permission of *Psychology Today*.

"Peggy Hedman Is Driven to Keep Her Charges Safe" by Tricia Booker, from *The Chronicle of the Horse*, June 1, 2007. Reprinted by permission of the author.

"Old Man on Campus" by Ehud Havazelet. Copyright © 2008. First appeared in *The New York Times Magazine*, April 6, 2008. Reprinted with permission of the Denise Shannon Literary Agency, Inc. All rights reserved.

"When 'Tis(n't) the Season to Ride?" by Aida Elder, from *Silent Sports*, January 2008. Reprinted by permission of the author.

"Colonial Cuisine and the Road to Revolution" by Paulette Beete. Originally published in *American Spirit*, March/April 2007. Reprinted by permission of the author.

"Sharing Memories, Sharing Lives" by Arlene Silverman, from *The Saturday Evening Post*, January/February 2008. Reprinted by permission of the author.

"Total Recall" by Gary Marcus, from *The New York Times Magazine*, April 13, 2008. Reprinted by permission of the author.

"Deadlines and Diapers and Dinner" by Heidi Drake, from *Home Business Magazine*, October 2008. Reprinted by permission of the author.

"Artist, Scientist, Technician, Historian Dudley Giberson" by John Walters. Originally published in *Kearsarge Magazine,* Spring 2008. Reprinted by permission of the author.

"Tapping for Maple's Sweet Gold" by Jessica Stone, from *American Spirit*, March/April 2007. Reprinted by permission of the author.

"My So-Called Genius" by Laura Fraser. Originally published in *More*, May 2008. Reprinted by permission of the author.

"I Have a Bunch of Coins. . ." by Harry L. Rinker. "Rinker on Collectibles" column #1086. Copyright © 2008 by Rinker Enterprises, Inc. See www.harryrinker.com for more information about the author, his columns, and other activities. Reprinted by permission of the author.

"Kitchen Knives" by Ken Haedrich. Originally published in *Country Journal*, November 1988. Copyright © 1988 by Ken Haedrich. Reprinted by permission of *Cowles Magazine* and the author.

"A Sweet and Gentle Land" by Polly Bannister, from *Yankee Magazine*, April 2006. Reprinted by permission of *Yankee Magazine* and the author.

"How to Be a Great Mom" by Julie Tilsner, from *Parenting*, December/January 2008. Reprinted by permission of the author.

"The Ugly Wedding Present" by Sasha Aslanian. Originally published in *Modern Bride*, August/September 2007. Reprinted by permission of the author.

"Plant-Based Tableware Redefines the Word Disposable" by Marc Schoder, from *Five Magazine*. Reprinted by permission of the author.

"Completely Lovestruck" by Majid Mohiuddin, from *Modern Bride*, August/September 2007. Reprinted by permission of the author.

"Under India's Spell" by Steven Slon, from *AARP The Magazine*, March/April 2008. Reprinted by permission of *AARP The Magazine*.

"Harry London Chocolate Hall of Fame" by Robert Davis, from *Journal Plus*, February 2008. Reprinted by permission of the author.

"Where the Creek Turkey Tracks: Wild Land and Language" by Tim Homan. Originally published in *Appalachian Heritage*, Winter 2007. Reprinted by permission of the author.

"Be Sensitive When Moving the Elderly" by Robert B. Mills, from *The Family Digest*, September/October 2007. Reprinted by permission of the author.

"In the Clutch: Better Shifting for Sport-Touring Riders" by Mark Tuttle Jr., from *Rider Magazine*, September 2006. Reprinted by permission of the author.

"Let There Be Sleep" by Barbara Stahura, from *Science & Spirit*, November/December 2006, pp. 44–47. Reprinted with permission of the Helen Dwight Reid Educational Foundation. Published by Heldref Publications, 1319 Eighteenth St. NW, Washington, DC 20036-1802. Copyright © 2006.

"On the Record: Collecting Oral Histories" by Elizabeth Kelley Kerstens, from *Ancestry Magazine*, January/February 2006. Reprinted with permission of *Ancestry Magazine* and may not be copied or redistributed. For further family history resources, visit www.ancestry.com. Copyright © 2006 The Generations Network, Inc. All rights reserved.

"Flying into Trouble" by George Monbiot, from *The Nation*, May 7, 2007. Reprinted by permission of *The Nation*.

"The Art of Camping" by Catherine Newman, from *Wondertime*, July/August 2008. Copyright © 2008 Disney Enterprises, Inc. Reprinted by permission of *Wondertime* magazine. All rights reserved.

"Even Keel" by Jim Freim, from *Trail Runner*, May 2007. Reprinted by permission of the author.

"Wildlife Volunteering in Thailand" by Erika Wedenoja, from *Transitions Abroad*, January/February 2007. Reprinted by permission of the author.

"There's Still a Girl in There" by Karen Hammond, from *Family Circle*, May 2005. Reprinted by permission of the author.